THE WORLD TODAY SERIES

East, Southeast Asia, and the Western Pacific 2000

33RD EDITION

Steven A. Leibo, Ph.D.

STRYKER–POST PUBLICATIONS

HARPERS FERRY WEST VIRGINIA

NEXT EDITION—AUGUST 2001

Steven A. Leibo . . .

A former Fulbright Scholar, he is Director of the International Studies Program at Russell Sage College, Troy, New York, and lecturer in Asian and world history at the State University of New York (SUNY) in Albany. Receiving his doctorate from Washington State University, he is the author/editor of many books and articles, including *Transferring Technology to China: Prosper Giquel and the Self–strengthening Movement, Journal of the Chinese Civil War, 1864,* and *International Conflict in the 20th Century.* He has taught at many institutions of higher learning, including the University of Cincinnati, Skidmore, Union and Blackburn colleges. Widely experienced with the electronic media, he has served as an international political analyst for television and as a commentator for WAMC public radio. Within the Internet, Professor Leibo is known as the co–founder/ co–editor of H–ASIA, a forum for Asian study professionals that includes over 2300 academics from more than 53 countries. The author travels extensively throughout Asia. In late May of 2001, Leibo is leading a trip to Vietnam. Contact him for details.

First appearing as a book entitled
The Far East and Southwest Pacific 1968,
revised annually and published in succeeding years by

Stryker–Post Publications
P.O. Drawer 1200
Harpers Ferry, WV. 25425
Telephones: 1–800–995–1400 (U.S.A.and Canada)
   Other.: 1–304–535–2593
   Fax: 1–304–535–6513
   www.Strykerpost.com
   VISA–MASTERCARD

Photographs used to illustrate *The World Today Series* come from many sources, a great number from friends who travel worldwide. If you have taken any which you believe would enhance the visual impact and attractiveness of our books, do let us hear from you.

International Standard Book Number: 1–887985–26–3

International Standard Serial Number: 1043–2140

Library of Congress Catalog Number 67–11540

Cover design by Susan Bodde

Chief Bibliographer: Edward Jones

Cartographer: William L. Nelson

Typography by The Clarinda Company
Clarinda, IA 51632

Printed in the United States of America
by United Book Press, Inc.
Baltimore, MD 21207

Table of Contents

Gold dragon on the roof of the Happiness and Long Life Temple at the Chinese Emperor's summer palace

UNIFORMS . . . lifesize clay warriors, 4000 strong, somberly guard Chinese emperor Qin Shihuang Di's tomb near Xian (roughly, She-yan), while Japanese baseball ("Yah-kyu") players thrill their fans in Tokyo.

East, Southeast Asia, and the Western Pacific Today

As the new millennium began East and Southeast Asians had more to feel positive about than they had had for years. Not only had they come through the era of Y2K without significant glitches but more importantly their economies were clearly on the mend after three terribly hard years. Moreover, even Indonesia, which was traumatized by the drama of East Timor's departure from its midst seemed to survive the crisis without experiencing the sort of "snow ball" break up that some had predicted. And it did so while building a more democratic Indonesia than anyone might have hoped for even a few years ago.

And to the north, not only did relations between China and Taiwan weather the arrival to power of the Pro-Independence Democratic Progressives better than anyone might have imagined, there was even talk as this year's volume went to press of a summit between the leaders of North and South Korea! Every day brings news of exciting developments important for understanding the region.

With that reality in mind, for more than thirty years the annual publication of *East, Southeast Asia, and the Western Pacific* allowed readers to keep abreast of developments. Today though with the arrival of the Internet and its plethora of on-line newspapers and other daily news sources, materials never before available have become so at the click of a computer mouse.

It is now extraordinarily easy to "keep up." Unfortunately, the availability of materials on the day-to-day developments of for example, Indonesian politics, is still meaningless without the broader context necessary to understand those daily events. Thus, the goal of *East, Southeast Asia, and the Western Pacific* is to offer the historical, political, social and economic background necessary to follow contemporary events.

And while the book's yearly revisions keep the text far more up-to-date than other surveys, in today's fast moving world even yearly updates are not enough. With that in mind the author maintains a website to help readers keep up with the day to day events that occur between the yearly publications of *East, Southeast Asia and the Western Pacific*. It can be found at

http://www.sage.edu/RSC/programs/globcomm/world/esawp.html

Students and instructors, after reading the text itself, are encouraged to check the Web site for the most recent developments in the various countries covered by the volume.

The Asian Economic Crisis Survived?

The economic slowdown discussed in the last several year's volumes turned into an economic rout during much of 1997 and 1998 when, beginning in Thailand, one country after another, from Malaysia through Indonesia and the Philippines found themselves having to seek the help of the International Monetary Fund to stabilize their currencies. Even more dramatic, given the size of its own economy, South Korea went into a tailspin which saw that nation almost unable to meet even its day-to-day expenses.

What had "caused" the crisis after so many decades of economic success often depended on which "expert" one was listening to. Problems from corruption to foreign currency speculators and mismanaged loans were often cited to explain what had occurred. As is always the case, there were both short-term and long-term reasons for the economic downturn. On the environmental level, the very weather itself had contributed to the crisis as *El Niño* disrupted the region's annual rainfall considerably. This caused not only drought in some areas but a related drop in tourism as the Indonesian fires, which would normally have been doused by the anticipated rains, continued to burn and filled the regional atmosphere with smoke.

On the level of more human-made crises was, of course, the financial collapse that began in Thailand in July of 1997. One important element not usually mentioned was the economic growth of the People's Republic of China (PRC) which contributed greatly to developments. For as the enormous PRC's economic expansion took off, coupled by a devaluation of its own currency in the early 1990s, its neighbors, often producers of similar goods, found themselves unable to compete with Chinese goods. But that was only one factor. The rising wage bills in places like South Korea contributed as well to the crisis. For after a generation of growth South Koreans were living much better. All this of course is good, but it also contributed to a steady weakening of South Korea's ability to market its products abroad.

No doubt the most fundamental issue was that after a full generation of astounding growth the region's economies had begun to slow down. Clearly, it was highly unlikely that any country or region could successfully sustain such high rates of growth over so long a period. A slowdown was thus somewhat inevitable and probably economically healthy.

However, the reality is that local budgets and debts had been accumulated on the assumption of continued and extraordinary growth. So, as growth slowed, far too many found themselves deeply in debt having developed real estate properties that stood empty for lack of tenants. Moreover, the astounding expansion of production facilities had created a glut of products that could not find the required ever increasing numbers of customers needed to continue the expansion. Particularly significant in fueling the crisis was the reality that far too many local businesses, seeking better interest rates and loan agreements, had borrowed significant amounts of money pegged in foreign currencies for relatively short term periods. Given the downturn that proved particularly devastating when pressure from international currency speculators forced Thailand and then others to devalue their currencies, suddenly those same local businesses found themselves unable to pay their international debts. For realistically, regardless of how financially sound a loan might have seemed at one currency exchange rate—when locals suddenly needed to supply far more of their local currency to buy the dollars necessary to pay back the loans—they became unmanageable. The fact that locals, recognizing what was happening, started dumping their own currencies for fear of having unwieldy international loans, only made matters worse.

As the crises developed, more and more of the region's leaders found themselves having to ask for help from the International Monetary Fund (IMF) which, while supplying important monies to help stabilize regional currencies, also required important economic restructuring. The IMF's insistence that these countries take important belt-tightening budgetary decisions naturally added to the fears of social unrest as food prices soared and more and more people found themselves out of work. Understandably, while many in the world community insisted the changes were necessary to re-establish international financial confidence in the region, they were often very unpopular.

Not surprisingly the crisis, and the necessity of going hat-in-hand to the Western-dominated international financial agencies such as the IMF, aroused in some areas an anti-Western backlash not heard in years. And of course within the individual countries the crisis often caused dramatic political changes as leaders from Thailand to South Korea and Indonesia fell and even those surviving authoritarian leaders in places like Malaysia found themselves challenged as they had not been for a generation.

Happily as *East, Southeast Asia, and the Western Pacific 2000* went to press in the late spring of 2000 much of the region was clearly on the mend though some analysts noted pessimistically that many of the structural reforms that were required to fully ensure a healthy economic future would probably not be carried out once the intensity of the crisis faded from memory. And there were other concerns as well to weaken the sense of confidence the new millennium brought. On an economic level much of the region was still having problems recruiting the technical workers the new globalized Internet economy required. And on a political level, relations between the United States and the People's Republic, so critical to a stable East and Southeast Asia, continued to balance precariously between cooperation and belligerence. Nevertheless, for the first time in several years there was real reason to feel optimistic about the entire region.

Many people made the author's task much easier as he attempted to both update the book and to revise it in the four years since the task was undertaken. Most of those who helped can be named, but some, for reasons readers can guess, cannot. The author would like to thank the volume's previous authors, the late Harold Hinton and Patrick M. Mayerchak for their insights which still enrich parts of the work. Moreover, several others have helped the present author make the volume much better than it might otherwise have been. They are, Mary Shinners, Kelly Ryan, Marilyn Levine, Robert Swartout, John Tribble, A. Tom Grunfeld, Robert Drake, Robert Cribb, Malcolm Russell, Susanna Fessler and Paul H. Kratoska.

My wife, Sara Zaidspiner-Leibo, was especially involved at every stage in the editing and proofreading. Her help was of enormous consequence and is as always very much appreciated. Special thanks to Phil Stryker for asking me to take on this exciting project. The author would also like to enthusiastically request that future readers, teachers and students alike, contact him with suggestions on how the book can better serve their needs.

Steven A. Leibo. Leibos@sage.edu
Albany, New York May, 2000

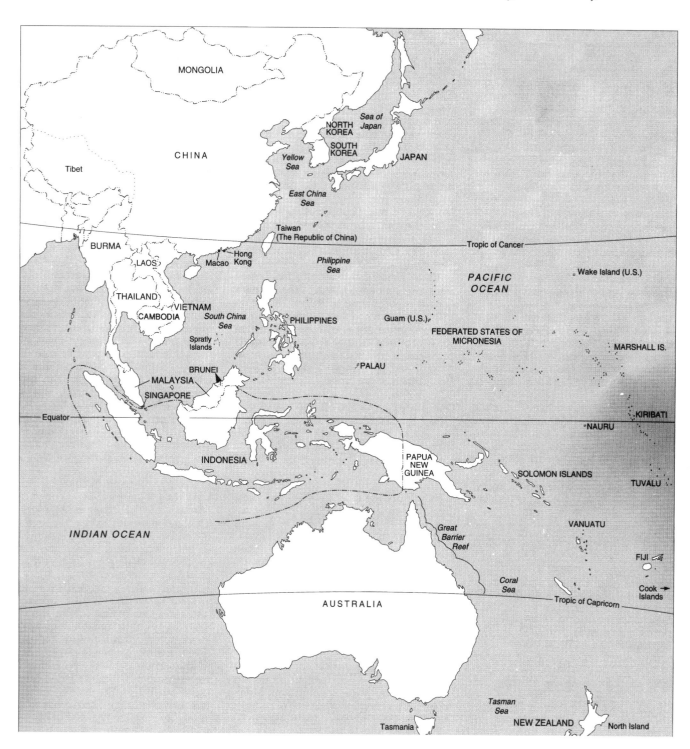

A Diversity of People

The region covered by this volume, *East, Southeast Asia, and the Western Pacific,* covers an enormous range of different ethnic and linguistic groups—from the Mongoloid communities of East Asia and the Caucasian immigrant communities of Australia and New Zealand to the heavily pigmented peoples of Micronesia who most closely resemble the aborigines of Australia. With the exception of a few countries like North Korea, almost every nation in the area includes many different ethnic and linguistic groups. While East Asians, Chinese, Japanese and Korean are largely made up of people from the "Mongolian" racial community, they are sharply divided by their linguistic heritage.

Chinese, for example, is part of a Sino–Tibetan language group which, although it bears a vague similarity in its written appearance, is totally different from the languages spoken in Japan and Korea. Southeast Asia is even more diverse and has at times been called an "anthropologist's delight" in recognition of the extraordinary diversity of ethnic communities found there. Although most nations in Southeast Asia have a "dominant majority" ethnic community almost all of them include both indigenous minority communities like the Montagnards of Vietnam and more recent ethnic communities, often made up of Chinese and South Asians, who immigrated to places other than their origin during the colonial era. The Island communities of the Western Pacific themselves include a wide variety of peoples most notably divided into three groups, Polynesia, Melanesia and Micronesia. More than a thousand different languages are spoken there.

Although not often discussed in the West, many of these countries from East Asia to the Western Pacific, have experienced considerable tensions between the majority and minority communities. In some parts of the region, people of Indian origin are regularly treated as second class citizens and the Chinese in places like Vietnam have had similar experiences. In Burma, the efforts by the Burman majority to dominate the political life of the nation have led to decades of tensions and struggle with non–Burman peoples.

Historical Background

Religious Beliefs

Confucianism

The original Confucianism of early Chinese civilization was more a social philosophy than a religion, perhaps more like the Hellenic thoughts of Aristotle and Plato than the divine musings of the Hebrews across the Mediterranean. In fact, Confucius himself was not particularly interested in issues of the supernatural. For Confucius and his followers, what mattered was the world of humans and how best they could govern themselves.

Originating from a feudal elite society of blood nobility, Confucius nevertheless developed a new theory of nobility based on merit, rather than birth. And how was that merit defined? By a single–minded commitment to nurturing the truly noble of the heart.

The core emphasis was based on the ideas of family and hierarchy with true stability gained from that society in which all understood the appropriate relations between people. And how was that stability to be maintained? By an extraordinary emphasis on the ability of education to elevate the soul of humanity.

Later Confucian thinkers, especially people like Mencius, further emphasized

the necessity of the development of "virtue" specifically through the study of various writings from antiquity known eventually as the Five Classics. Over time, mastery of the material came to be the key to a successful career through the developing Chinese Civil Service Examinations that dominated the selection of elites during the last 1000 years of traditional China's existence. As time went on however, Confucianism was challenged by other more spiritual philosophical and religious traditions—like Daoism and Buddhism, it began to assimilate aspects of their more metaphysical orientation. Thus was born the Neo–Confucianism of later traditional history.

Although it has been generations since millions of Chinese males spent their lives preparing to pass the Confucian civil service exams from whom future bureaucrats were chosen, its influence as a social philosophy remains tremendously strong.

Confucianism, both as a religious and intellectual tradition and as an ongoing theory of social behavior, continues to be very influential throughout most of the region covered by this volume. From China to Korea, from Taiwan to Japan, Confucianism continues to be influential not only among the millions of ethnic Chinese who live in the People's Republic, Singapore and Taiwan, but among those mil-

lions of others who live as Chinese minorities from the Philippines to Malaysia and Indonesia. Moreover, it remains important among many other societies whose people, if not ethnically Chinese, were nevertheless fundamentally influenced by Confucianism even as they developed their own unique cultures. These include not only the Vietnamese and Koreans but other more distant neighbors, like the Japanese, who did not share a common border with China.

Obvious examples of Confucian influence are easy to note. Despite the assaults on Confucianism under Mao Zedong, the Confucian priority given to education and the family remain strong in East Asia. Moreover, the strong sense of the group over the needs of the individual, while perhaps lessening somewhat at the end of the 20th century, still figures prominently as a clear contrast to the Western preoccupation with the individual.

Buddhism

Buddhism remains one of the strongest religious traditions throughout East and Southeast Asia. From Thailand to Vietnam, from Burma to Beijing, Buddhism is present if not in the lives of everyone in the region, then as part of their cultural and architectural heritage. Even within the

People's Republic, which saw so much energy directed against traditions like Buddhism in the 1960s, a revival has been going on. Emerging about the same time that Confucius lived, Buddhism was founded in Nepal by Gautama. (See Russell, *The Middle East and South Asia*). It eventually became an extraordinarily influential tradition through much of Eastern Asia.

Not surprisingly, it often required considerable modification of the originally rather pessimistic Buddhist message to assimilate into the generally optimistic Chinese environment. It actually was, in some ways, a protest against the teachings of Brahmanism, or Hinduism, which was then dominant in India. The Buddha, as Gautama is called, preached the message that beings moved through a series of lives in this world which was largely an experience of pain and suffering. Within Buddhism there is a deep belief that fate can be influenced by human efforts—through the force of "Karma," so that a good person moves upward through successive existence to an ultimate reward. The greatest reward possible, according to this belief, was the attainment of Nirvana—a philosophically complicated con-

cept which essentially postulated that a person who had attained "Nirvana" reached a state of individual nonexistence, often compared to the snuffing out of a flame which as a "practical" matter ended the process of constantly being reborn into a series of burdensome lives.

These teachings, which urged withdrawal from the world for meditation, created monastic communities in the ensuing centuries. The stress on personal and universal religious experience made this much more of a missionary religion than Hinduism and was thus more similar to Islam and Christianity in its core belief in the universality of its message.

The form in which Buddhism migrated to Southeast Asia is known as Hinayana ("the Lesser Vehicle"), Theravada ("the Way of the Teachers") or simply, the Southern School of Buddhism. This school, which is closest to original Buddhism of its early years, had its major home on the island of Sri Lanka (Ceylon) which was converted to Buddhism in the 3rd century B.C.

Hinayana countries in Southeast Asia—Vietnam, Laos, Cambodia, Thailand and Burma—all have large communities of

monks devoted to the daily practice of Buddhism. In recent times, these communities have been influential and increasingly active in national and political affairs. Although the Hinayana Buddhists share the same central beliefs, there is no over arching system of central authority comparable to Vatican Catholicism which attempts to regulate the entire community. Almost every country has its own Buddhist individual sects.

Buddhism also spread north and northeast from India in the first centuries of the Christian era in the form known as Mahayana ("Greater Vehicle"), which entered Tibet, China, Korea and Japan. This form of the religion places less emphasis on good works and monastic withdrawal for contemplation, and greater weight on elaborate scriptures and faith. The canon (authorized texts) was printed in China in the 10th and 11th centuries, using some 130,000 wooden blocks on which characters had been carved. It was widely followed in central Asia until almost eliminated by the growing influence of Islam.

Mahayana Buddhism became widespread in China in the first centuries of the modern era, during a period of consider-

Inside the Liu Rong Buddhist temple (479 A.D.) in Guangzhou, China Photo by Miller B. Spangler

Historical Background

able social disruption associated with the collapse of the Han (206–222 BC) and continued to grow in influence until it reached its height under the Tang Dynasty (618–907). Thereafter, its official influence began to wane, although it continued to be profoundly influential in the lives of ordinary Chinese.

A form of Buddhism developed in Tibet known as Tantrism, which was heavily influenced by a type of Hinduism that engaged in demon worship and varieties of magical practices. It still exists today, particularly in eastern Tibet, but has been largely replaced by another form known as Lamaism, or "The Yellow Sect" to distinguish it from Tantrism. This is a combination of a purer form of Buddhism similar to Mahayana with an elaborate monastic organization common to Hinayana, but actually even more highly formalized. Lamaism, of which the Dalai Lama is the leading figure, spread to Inner and Outer Mongolia in the 16th century.

The teachings of Buddhism have changed over the centuries, and have been modified by many varied external influences. It does not contain a formal universal hierarchy similar to practice in Catholicism and is in general more administratively decentralized in the fashion of traditions such as Protestantism, Judaism, Hinduism and Islam.

Naturalism

Long before the formal development of the major schools of Chinese thought, Confucianism, Taoism and Buddhism, the Chinese had already developed an elaborate intellectual system. It covered ideas of governance (see Mandate of Heaven in the China section) to metaphysical ideas associated with the stability of the entire cosmic order—from the universe to each person's physical body. Chief among those ideas were the concepts of *Yin* and *Yang*, and the entity known as *Qi*.

Yin and *Yang* are often difficult for Westerners to understand because they superficially resemble aspects of the Western idea of duality, of the idea of "good" and "evil." The resemblance though is purely superficial. In the West, this ancient idea, originally derived from the Persian religion of Zoroastrianism, involves a duality of forces in the universe, one evil, one good, that struggle over the fate of the universe and humanity.

Yin and *Yang* are quite different. This Eastern version of duality is one of complementary opposites which both need each other. Some things are associated with *Yin* more than *Yang*, but both are always present and vital for cosmic and personal stability. This distinction may appear minor but in fact it has had dramatic

Buddhist statue, Japan

differences in its impact on how the two societies have viewed the world around them. An understanding of *Yin* and *Yang* are critical to an understanding of things Chinese, from philosophy to medicine. In the same vein, *Qi* is another important aspect of this naturalist world view.

According to Chinese tradition, every living thing possesses a sort of "vital element" that, in the case of humans, is drawn both from our parents and our environment. This *Qi*, which is said to flow through the body is considered absolutely vital to good health. It is the flow of *Qi* that Chinese traditional physicians still attempt to manipulate with techniques like acupuncture and acupressure to heal patients. Thus, an understanding of naturalist thought, issues like *Yin* and *Yang* and *Qi*, from the earliest history of China, remain today a vital part of the tools necessary to understand that enormous civilization which has so influenced most of the rest of East Asia.

Daoism (Taoism)

Daoism (Taoism) is in many ways a complementary parallel to China's long Confucian tradition. Daoism, which was

formalized at about the same time as Confucianism, is often portrayed as a clear contrast to Confucianism's obsession with how human beings in society should behave. Daoism is less social in its orientation and more interested in the individual's relationship with the natural and metaphysical world. A flavor of this tone is captured in the famous Daoist dictum for government that what was really important was keeping people's heads empty and their stomachs full. Overall Daoism is more personal and self–consciously contemplative than the social activism of Confucian practice. Daoism varies enormously from an association with a popular religion of magic and spirits to a very philosophical discussion of the relationship of beings to the universe. On a practical level, the early Daoist's interest in the search for elixirs of life brought to Chinese civilization an acute interest in nature which continues to have a strong influence on contemporary Chinese food and medicine.

Christianity

Although Christian missionaries have been active in Asia for centuries, few people in the region have been influenced by any of its various sects. In China, for example, Christianity was often seen simply as part of Western imperialism and rejected out of hand. Today, although Christianity is a vigorous tradition within the People's Republic, the actual numbers, given China's enormous size, are relatively insignificant. On the other hand, some of the countries covered by *East, Southeast Asia, and the Western Pacific* have been terrifically influenced. The Philippines and Vietnam both developed large Catholic communities during the colonial eras. The Philippines today is almost exclusively Christian with the exception of the southernmost island of Mindanao where Islam remains influential.

Among the East Asian nations, Korea is the most influenced by Christianity due to a curious irony of history. During the nineteenth century Christian missionaries in Korea often sided with the Koreans against the colonizing Japanese thus linking Christianity to the emerging Korean nationalism. Not surprisingly in today's Korea Christianity is a very influential tradition with millions of followers.

The Pacific Islands people are largely committed to the various Christian traditions. Christians are found widely throughout the region among those whose families were originally converted by the earliest Protestant and Catholic missionaries and, more recently, to new denominations ranging from Jehovah's Witnesses in Tahiti–Polynesia, Fiji and New Caledonia and the Solomon Islands, to Mormons in Tonga and Western Samoa. The Anglo communities of New Zealand and Australia, made up as they are largely of immigrant communities from England are, of course, largely Christian as well.

Shinto

Shinto emerged in the earliest period of Japanese history and originally was an animistic religion which gave human form to the various gods that rule the forces of nature. Although indigenous to the Japanese home islands, this religious tradition is in many ways similar to the animistic beliefs found in Southeast Asia, Africa and among many traditional Native American beliefs—in that a strong sense a divinity exists among many natural objects in nature from beautiful trees to waterfalls. Shinto, a tradition that refers to the "Way of the Kami," puts its emphasis on what might be called entities of "awe," the Kami which include myriad objects from ancestors to legendary heroic figures and natural phenomena. Especially important within the tradition is the belief that the Sun Goddess, Amaterasu, sent her descen-

dants to Earth to create the Japanese home islands. It was the association of the Yamato clan line with that tradition that became the basis of its claim to imperial power.

Unlike traditions such as Buddhism and Christianity which developed very elaborate traditions of religious ritual and sacred texts, Shinto tended to be very much more loosely organized and was not surprisingly overshadowed in Japan by the arrival of Buddhism in the 6th century. As Mahayana Buddhism entered the islands, the two beliefs tended to influence each other. Thus, it was possible to profess the ideologies of both without feeling inconsistent.

Buddhism in Japan eventually split into numerous sects, and for several centuries Shinto beliefs were somewhat dormant, although not forgotten. In the late nineteenth and early twentieth century, the Shinto heritage became the state religion; it was reemphasized that the emperor was a descendant of the sun goddess and possessed her divine powers. Although the imperial house had long been respected in traditional Japan, the late nineteenth century development of a cult–like imagery around the imperial house was not a product of Japanese tradition, but rather part of the modernizing effort. It was believed by nineteenth century thinkers that Japan needed a "unifying element" to fully join together the nation. Enhancing the symbolism of the emperor was thought the most appropriate way to do so. Thus, the imperial house was far more celebrat-

ed in the late nineteenth and early 20th century than it had been for centuries. In many ways it is helpful to think of this revival of Shinto as "State Shinto" in contrast to the more decentralized tradition of Japan's earlier history.

This revival corresponded with a rise of militarism in Japan, culminating with World War II. After defeat by the allies, Japan renounced the idea of the "divinity" of the Emperor; Shinto lost its official status. Ironically the supposed "imperial divinity" which Westerners found offensive about the Japanese system was only remarkable when viewed from the outside by Westerners bred in the traditions of monotheism. In the Japanese context the spiritual aspects of the Japanese emperor had operated in a very different context.

Islam

Although most Americans tend to associate Islam with the Arab communities of the Middle East, the reality is that the largest communities of Muslims in the world are found in Asia and among a very wide variety of ethnic groups. Especially large communities of Muslims are found in South Asia (see Russell, *The Middle East and South Asia*) but they are also a very important religious community in East and Southeast Asia as well. From western China to the southern Philippines, from Malaysia to Indonesia (itself the largest Muslim nation in the world) Islam is very important to this region.

A Shinto shrine in Japan

Historical Background

Islam itself, which emerged in the 7th century, is part of the enormously rich Middle Eastern monotheistic religion which had earlier seen the development of Judaism and Christianity. Muhammad, a poor merchant from the Arabian peninsula, developed the religion after experiencing what he called a revelation from the angel Gabriel regarding the Unity of God. As a tradition, Islam is a militantly monotheistic creed that requires giving charity to the poor and a life of regular daily prayer including, if at all possible, a pilgrimage at some point to the holy places at Mecca in today's Saudi Arabia.

Though Islam is a growing movement within the United States, few Americans know much about it and would probably be surprised at how much of its theology it shares with both Christianity and Judaism. The tradition includes the idea of a heaven and resurrection and a system of predestination. Seeing itself as a clear continuation of the line of revelation which had begun with the Patriarch Abraham, Muhammad, revealed himself to be the "final prophet" in a long tradition which extended back through both the traditions of the Old and New Testament. Basically, Muhammad taught that the Judeo–Christian biblical texts are not complete. Thus, the Islamic movement embraced a new document, said to have been dictated by God. That text is known as the Qur'an (Koran). Nevertheless this new sacred document, which makes reference to biblical texts, is distinctly influenced by the Judeo–Christian traditions which had preceded it.

Sometimes stories are derived from the bible texts and modified with startling results. For example, the story of the fall from Eden is also found in the Qu'ran yet in the Islamic version, the female, Eve, is not blamed for the transgression against God! A very thought–provoking modification, especially for those who think Islam can be easily categorized on issues of gender. The text of the Qur'an itself includes 114 chapters which Muslims believe confirms and clarifies the revelation received earlier by the Christians and Jews.

Like many religions, Islam was spread through a complicated series of developments that ranged from militant conquest to merchant activities and mystical religious missionaries. Today it is found widely in parts of Southeast Asia and western China.

The resurgence of militant Islam in the Middle East and northern Africa has had its effect in such Southeast Asian countries as Indonesia and Malaysia. Here, it has taken the form of increased wearing of the traditional dress, stricter dietary rules, and the establishment of Muslim banking operations. Though Islam is more strictly adhered to in Malaysia, religious resurgence in that country or in any other part of Southeast Asia does not approach the fervor which is found today in the Middle East. None of the Muslim states in the region—Brunei, Indonesia, Malaysia or the Philippines (the latter has only a small Muslim minority) has seen the extensive level of Islamic militancy experienced elsewhere. Still, it would be wrong to discount the importance of Islam in Southeast Asia.

Women in Traditional Asia

Although until recently women have lived in few societies that have afforded them even a semblance of equality with men, the women of Asia have often been particularly challenged by the limitations of their own unequal status. Nevertheless, the region covered by *East, Southeast Asia, and the Western Pacific* is large and it is difficult to make generalizations. In some traditional societies and especially hierarchical societies like those dominated by Confucianism, which has had such an important influence throughout much of the region, women are regarded as decidedly inferior to men. As elsewhere, they were commonly less valued both as infants and as adults. Female babies were less likely to be nurtured when young and more frequently experienced infanticide than males. They were raised to serve as a wife for a male chosen by others (if they were lucky). Too often, in times of financial distress, daughters found themselves sold into virtual sexual slavery by their parents.

Nevertheless, the specific nature of their unequal status has varied widely from region to region and from period to period. In China, for example, it appears that Chinese women were more influential early on and that their status deteriorated around the 8th century A.D. By about the 11th the horrendously painful practice of foot binding, that is of forcing the female child's foot into an artificially tiny shape, had emerged, a practice which would cause untold suffering among Chinese

Women suffering foot binding in China

6

women until the 20th century. Elsewhere though, the status and circumstances were quite different. In early Japan, women appear to have been much more important than their latter status suggests and imperial women of the court, individuals like Lady Murasaki, are credited with creating the modern form of the novel, most notably in works like the *Tale of Genji* written around 1000 A.D.

In Southeast Asia, peasant women remained much more important than their peers in either East Asia or South Asia and played an important role in the local economies. Even in places like Vietnam, whose elite were especially influenced by Confucianism, the peasant women's lives remained much less constricted than the elite women of the Confucian aristocracy.

The Impact of the West

One of the most dramatic aspects of modern world history was the enormous movement of colonialism and imperialism which saw the Western nations spread their influence and direct administrative control over a large percentage of the globe. From a period running from approximately 1500 through the early 20th century, the various Western powers, and eventually Japan, gained control over much of the world. Only a few nations remained outside of their control. In Africa the ages–old empire of Abyssinia, today's Ethiopia, managed to resist an Italian effort at conquest in 1896 and in Southeast Asia the kingdom of Siam, today's Thailand, survived albeit hemmed in by english and French colonies on either side.

It was that world of colonial and imperial control that brought the globe into the 20th century, and during much of the 1900s, the era emphasized by *East, Southeast Asia, and the Western Pacific*, deals with the reverse of that process as individual national communities eventually found their way to national freedom from colonial administrations. East and Southeast Asia were not exempt from this global phenomenon and in fact were the original region that had attracted the Europeans in the 15th century at the dawn of the modern colonial age.

The countries of early modern Western Europe, especially Spain, Portugal and the Netherlands, tried to reach East Asia and the Western Pacific in order to acquire the profits from the extraordinarily lucrative spice trade, to gain converts to Christianity and to acquire new territories for their respective governments. Especially significant in those early years were the Iberians, adventurers from Spain and Portugal, who had also led the efforts in the Western Hemisphere.

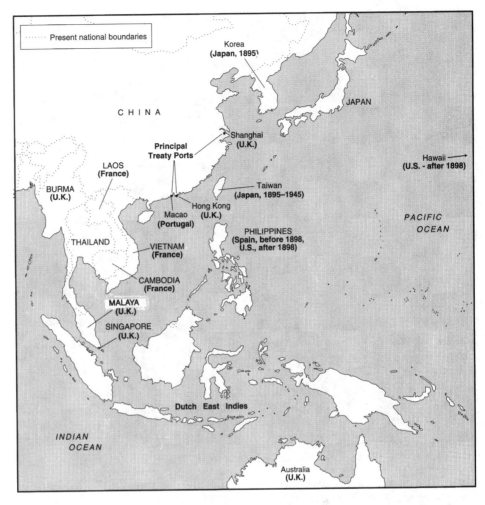

Ferdinand Magellan, a Portuguese in the service of Spain, was the first to lead Europeans to the region. He was killed in the Philippines in 1521. Half a century later Spain, operating from its bases in the New World, began to colonize the Philippines, which it eventually held for three centuries. In the 16th century, Portuguese explorers, traders, and missionaries spread similarly from the Indian Ocean to Southeast Asia and the coast of southern China. They were not strong enough, however, to make much of an impact on the region, and most of their holdings soon fell to the Dutch.

The Dutch East India Company was the strongest European influence in East Asia and the Western Pacific in the 17th century. Its main theater of operations was the Dutch (or Netherlands) East Indies (now Indonesia), the richest in the region in the resources then in most demand in Europe (spices, coffee, etc.). Although the Dutch government eventually took direct control of the East Indies from the Dutch East India Company in the early 19th century, its rule was distinctly paternalistic and did little to develop the islands from either an economic or a political point of view.

The British impact on the region was less than they had in the Indian Ocean and South Asia, where they built up their enormous empire in India, but it was still significant. In Southeast Asia, the British colonial presence began first in Burma. For the British, expanding control was usually a response to growing commercial interests. In Burma, territorial disputes and issues of sovereignty arose in the late eighteenth century. Anglo–Burmese relations deteriorated until 1823, when British forces captured Rangoon. By the end of the 1860's, the British had integrated all of the Burmese provinces into British Burma and into the Indian empire.

By 1826, they had established what was known as the Straits Settlements along the coast of Malaya (today, Malaysia). These settlements consisted of the island of Penang, just off Malaya's north coast, Malacca, formerly a Dutch possession on the central coast, and Singapore at the southern tip of the Malay peninsula. Over the next fifty years their control extended over all of Malaya. They obtained vast quantities of tin from the interior and commerce from the straits settlements. An Anglo–Dutch Treaty of 1824 recognized British dominance along the Malay coast and also acknowledged Dutch interests to

Historical Background

A Chinese Opium "den" in 1898

the south. This resulted in the effective splitting up of the old Malay world. The Dutch eventually established their control over all of Sumatra and Java, and became the colonial masters of the future Indonesia. The British controlled Malaya and Singapore until their independence.

In the 19th century the British East India Company had also become a major commercial force along the South China coast, its main interest being Chinese tea, silk and porcelain. Merchants brought opium, usually bought from the Company in India, to the South China coast and sold it in defiance of an official ban. Machine–made British textiles eventually became a major Chinese import in the 19th century, especially after the British East India Company lost its legal monopoly of its share of the China trade early in the century.

The British government used armed force at intervals to compel China to lower its barriers to expanded foreign trade (including opium imports) and residence (including missionary activity). These pressures eventually culminated in the famous "Opium Wars" of the early nineteenth century and resulted in a series of unequal treaties with the Chinese that saw Westerners establish themselves along the China coast in a series of "treaty ports"

which were outside of formal Chinese control.

Although the United States had been late to enter the competition for empire in the Pacific it eventually became very involved there. By the mid–nineteenth century, the United States had established itself on the American West Coast and begun the effort to extend its influence into the Pacific. The Hawaiian islands came under American control in 1898.

Meanwhile, by the late nineteenth century, a number of educated Filipinos were moved by modern nationalist ideals to declare independence from Spain and cooperate briefly with the United States in expelling the Spanish during the Spanish American War of 1898. Unfortunately for them, after the defeat of Spain, the United States proceeded to take over the Philippines for itself. After crushing a spirited Filipino resistance, the U.S. set up a reasonably efficient colonial regime and did a good deal to prepare the Filipinos for self–government, but like the other colonial powers in the region it did not qualitatively develop the economy, which remained essentially an extractive (mining) and plantation one.

Earlier, the U.S. had, beginning in the mid–19th century, spearheaded the western entry into Japan. In contrast to many other communities in what became the

colonial world, the Japanese, were much better able to control the process, and Japan never became a colony of the West. In effect, in attempting to avoid the fate of so many other Asian peoples, Japan decided to dramatically revolutionize its society. Thus it borrowed from the West (mostly technology and organization) and combined it with the essentials of its own culture. In the process, Japan became a military and imperial power strong enough to defeat China (in 1895) and Russia (in 1905) and itself emerge as a major colonial power with control over the Chinese island of Taiwan and the Korean peninsula.

Certainly not content to be left behind their colonial rivals, Paris was involved in Southeast Asian colonialism. The Treaty of Saigon of 1862 established the French colony of Cochin China in southern Vietnam. The conflict leading to this treaty was in response to several decades of tension as a result of inroads into Vietnamese society by French Catholicism. The French seemed to be as much interested in the spread of their own religion as the potential for economic gain. Especially important, in the minds of the French, was the necessity of keeping up with their English rivals. French control of Cambodia and Laos followed and, with Vietnam, became French Indochina. The Laotians and Cambodians were more favorably disposed toward the French, having been under the authority of both Siam and Vietnam previously. For Vietnam, the period of French domination was culturally much more difficult.

Sandwiched between the British colonies of Burma and Malaya, and the French in Indochina, Siam (now Thailand) was able to survive under its own monarchy without being colonized by any European power. This was partly because the British and French were more interested in penetrating Southwest China from their bases in Southeast Asia than in colonizing Siam and because they both saw the benefit of Siam as a buffer between their respective territories. Siam also benefitted from a highly talented monarchy that earlier saw the need to learn about western institutions and governing methods. When the British did come, the Siamese showed considerable diplomatic skill in meeting the challenge.

An important product of western colonial rule in Southeast Asia was the influx (from about 1850 to 1920) of large numbers of Chinese immigrants, driven by poverty and chaos at home and drawn by the economic opportunities created by colonialism. These "overseas" Chinese have tended to be resented by the indigenous peoples and have never been allowed a share of real political power (except in Singapore, where they are the majority), but their economic activity and influence have been very great.

Major political and military trends of the twentieth century, culminating in Japan's launching of World War II in the Pacific (see Japan), were to sweep away Western colonial rule in Southeast Asia, and make its restoration after the war a practical impossibility. As we shall see, during the post war era, colony after colony emerged out from under Western control though some anti–colonial struggles, like that of Vietnam, were to become particularly bloody as anti–colonialist momentum became entwined with the struggles of the Cold War.

The islands of the Western Pacific were no exception to this process and even as they were among the first communities absorbed into the Western colonial empires, many of them have only recently gained their autonomy. A few, like New Caledonia for example, still remain today as colonies.

Nationalism, Communism and Revolution in Twentieth Century Asia

One of the principal and predictable results of Western influence, which contained the inherent threat of domination because of advanced technology, has been resistance to the idea of external control in Asia. The desire to be independent of such influence is part of the structure of modern Asian nationalism. As long as Western political control over colonial Asia seemed unshakable, there was little basis for the emergence of nationalism. When Japan defeated Russia in 1905, however, the myth that the Western powers were invincible was shattered.

Japan also showed by its example that it was possible, however difficult, for an Asian country to modernize itself along the lines of Western nations. During the brief period that it controlled substantial portions of Southeast Asia, Japan weakened the prestige of the colonial powers to the point where it would be all the more difficult for them to reestablish themselves in the region after the war.

Next to the influence of the West itself and that of Japan's successes, the third great external influence on the emergence of modern Asian nationalism was the example of Soviet Russia. Before 1917 Marxism had almost no following in the area, but many Asian leaders became impressed with the seemingly rapid success of Lenin's Bolsheviks in seizing power within Russia in 1917. Of even greater importance was the loudly declared determination to modernize Russia along socialist lines, and to help the people of the non–Western world to throw off alien influence. The communism of Marx, prescribed for industrial nations of Europe and America, was billed as the medicine which would allegedly cure the ills of the poor, non–Western countries of Asia.

Lenin attracted great attention with his theory that the main obstacle to progress in the non–Western world was Western "imperialism"; he urged that local nationalists, supported by Soviet Russia, could make progress toward expelling this imperialism. This would be, according to him, a preparation for the day when "proletarian" parties, in other words, communist parties, organized along the disciplined and apparently effective line of the *Bolsheviks*, could emerge and seize power. The combination of the concept of *imperialism*, the exploitation of existing nationalism and the triumph in Russia of a communist party has had an enormous influence in Asia as well as elsewhere in the world. These ideas became part of the mental equipment of many, although by no means all, Asian nationalists, whether or not they consider themselves communists. Stated otherwise, many Asian nationalists adopted some communist ideas and techniques without becoming communists—or find it politically useful to act as though they have.

The result is a complex alignment of nationalist and communist elements, in which it is often difficult to see where the nationalistic spirit ends and the communist aims begin. The obvious communists are not hard to identify; Ho Chi Minh was a member of the Communist International, the founder of the Vietnamese Communist Party and yet he was also a committed Vietnamese nationalist. Unlike the situation in Eastern Europe where communists and nationalists were often bitter enemies for most of the 20th century, the dynamics of anti–colonial struggles in much of the world often saw the two groups not only closely aligned but unit-

Historical Background

ed in the personalities of many of the anti–colonial leaders. Sadly, this reality was too often misunderstood by Western leaders and analysts, trained more in the politics of Europe than Asia.

Anti–colonial movements began to assume importance in the colonies of Asia about 1920. The spread of Western education and political ideas, the limited measure of self–government granted by the colonial powers, the influence of Woodrow Wilson's doctrine of self–determination—the idea that every people has the right to choose the form of government under which it will live—and the Bolshevik Revolution in Russia, all played parts in the spread of nationalism.

The Chinese communities living in Asian countries other than their homeland (the "overseas Chinese") were stimulated to nationalist activity by the revolutionary forces then at work within China, but usually preferred a continuation of Western political rule to the possibly oppressive rule of the native majorities where they lived. Non–Chinese nationalists usually resented the Chinese for their hard–earned wealth and economic influence, to the same degree that they also opposed the political control of the Western powers. As a result, their agitation was usually directed against both groups of outsiders.

Prior to World War II, there were no nationalist movements in Southeast Asia able to challenge the well–armed colonial governments. Nationalists were unable to gather sufficient support for the independence cause until the outbreak of the war changed the dynamics of the entire region. As will be seen in the individual national state sections, the combination of the Japanese temporary occupation of the region and the weakening of the colonial powers made a complete reestablishment of the former Western colonial world in East and Southeast Asia simply impossible. Certainly in some areas, like Indonesia and Vietnam the colonial powers attempted to reestablish their power but each in turn was eventually stymied in the face of the worldwide anti–colonial momentum. The age of formal colonies had passed. Only the rise of the Cold War in the late 1940s made this trend somewhat less certain as many nationalist and economic struggles became entwined with the politics of Soviet/American rivalries.

Communist challenges arose in the Philippines, in the form of the *Huk* rebellion in the early 1950's; in Malaya, under the "emergency" declared from 1948 to 1960; and in Indochina and Indonesia. Burma, Thailand and even Singapore also experienced communist activities. In Indonesia, the movement was strongest in Central Java. The Indonesian *Communist Party* met its bloody demise in 1965 when it was destroyed by the Indonesian military under Suharto whose regime continued to maintain stability under an authoritarian government until 1998.

Presently, Vietnam is the only surviving nominally communist regime in Southeast Asia, and that will be increasingly debatable as reforms move ahead. Laos no longer qualifies as a bonafide Marxist state. Laotian politics was for decades a family affair, and with the opening of the country in recent years, economic change will easily overcome the remnants of the past.

It is difficult to find a uniform explanation for the Asian experience with communism. One thing is clear, of the remaining communist states, the People's Republic of China and Vietnam did not begin to expand their GNPs until the decision was made to open up their economies more. And North Korea which has still not seriously done so remains mired in an ever sinking economic state.

Nevertheless, communism was often an essential ingredient in the emerging nationalism of the region. In some cases, it forced colonial and then newly independent governments to address social problems which they might have otherwise ignored. And in contrast to Eastern Europe, communism still remains a vital if certainly evolving force. The tensions of the old Cold War have dimmed in East Asia much slower than they have in Europe.

Post–Colonial Political and Economic Developments

As the new states of East and Southeast Asia began to emerge after the demise of colonialism, hopes were high, especially in the West, that many new economically vibrant democracies would emerge. In fact, many new states began their existence as free countries using models borrowed from the Western liberal democracies which had originally colonized them. Burma, Indonesia, Malaysia, the Philippines and Singapore were all thus born as democracies. Today Singapore and Malaysia survive as single party dominated systems, while the Philippines has only recently managed to reestablish a democratic tradition after a generation of authoritarian rule and Indonesia struggles with its first free democratic election in a generation. Burma to a much greater extent, has lived under clearly authoritarian governments. Thailand has not yet resolved its political future and its military has often been very politically active. Still, democratic rule appears to be growing stronger and stronger. The communist states of course embraced a system of Party domination over both their countries' economies and political life.

In what became known as the East Asian NICs, the East Asian Newly Industrialized Countries, like Taiwan and South Korea, extended periods of strongman government lasted until the late 1980s. In Japan, although the occupation had seen the establishment of a parliamentary government, most of the period has seen the country ruled by a combination of a single party in domination largely led by an especially powerful bureaucracy.

Economically, after the war the hope was of course to see the region recover from the devastation of the war but sadly that was not be to be case. The economies were weakened by both the anti–communist struggles of the era, strife in places like Vietnam and Korea as well as by related struggles like those in the southern islands of the Philippines. That region's natural economic structure was undermined by the continuing turmoil within the PRC as well.

If the immediate post–war years were not very successful in establishing more democratic governments and economically open systems, the region's more recent record is much more promising. As we approach the end of the 20th century, East and Southeast Asia, so recently an area in constant turmoil, has emerged as an extremely dynamic area in the world. The Industrial Revolution that transformed Western Europe a century ago and has now dramatically hit East and Southeast Asia not only radically changed the economic life of its citizens but raised their educational and political aspirations. Not surprisingly, authoritarian regimes have been more and more challenged in their efforts to dominate the political life of their people. From South Korea to Taiwan new leadership has been elected democratically with the support of more politically involved middle classes, the very middle classes required and nurtured by economic changes. How these economic and political changes will ultimately transform the entire region is only just beginning to become clear. What is certain is that the entire region will play a much more significant role in the global arena in the 21st century than it did during the 20th.

Women in Modern East and Southeast Asia

Along with many women of the Western World, the women of the East, Southeast Asia and the Western Pacific have often made enormous strides during the 20th century. In China, although the dominant figure as the century began was a woman, the famous Cixi, the dowager empress, most women labored under both the physical pain of foot binding and the limitations of their educational and career possibilities. Yet within the first quarter century not only was foot binding outlawed and eventually suppressed, but those years saw women in large numbers begin to gain higher education and to take part in political activism as shown in their role in the famous May Fourth Movement.

When the communists came to power in 1949 one of their first moves was to legislate improvements in the lives of women which, if not creating a society of equality, have much improved the lives of millions of Chinese women.

In Japan, the century began with a few women striving to establish their own political and literary activities and more often ending up in trouble with the conservative governments of the time. Nevertheless, Japanese women gained the vote as a result of the changes brought about during the American Occupation of Japan and the end of the century has seen a woman emerge as the head of one of the major Japanese parties, the Japanese Socialist Party.

Throughout the world the development of better contraceptive devices and the growing perception that women need to be educated in order to contribute to the economic lives of their families has also spurred improvements in many areas of East and Southeast Asia. Not surprisingly the women of the more urban classes have gained the most from these changes while poorer women are less likely either to have the finances, access or education necessary to take advantage of the new technologies available for family planning. And in some areas, like the Philippines, where the Catholic Church is influential, there is considerable opposition to birth control.

Politically the single most important element to affect the lives of women of the region was probably the emergence of nationalism as a driving force. In many regions, especially in places like Vietnam, women played important roles in the anti–colonial struggles of the post war era. Moreover, in recent years women activists have been especially involved in encouraging democratic growth in the region. Corazon Aquino emerged triumphant in the struggle that saw the end of the Marcos dictatorship in the Philippines and elsewhere in the region, most notably in Burma, where Aung San Suu Kyi has led the democratic opposition. During 1996 Megawati Sukarnoputri the daughter of the late Indonesian ruler

Sukarno, attempted (unsuccessfully) to challenge the continuing dictatorship of Suharto. By mid-1999 she had become vice-president!

Despite these changes, real improvements in the lives of women have never been even nor routine across the region. In some areas like China where recent economic liberalization has at times given more discretionary power to families and individual factory managers, we have seen the emergence of more traditional values regarding the worth of daughters than was experienced under the height of socialist control. These new freedoms have sometimes actually worked against women's rights. And in some other areas a religious backlash against the secularism of the West has also challenged those gains already made.

Arriving from Hong Kong by train, these high rise buildings are the first evidence of new development seen by visitors at Shenzhen's commercial center, Luohu.

Courtesy: Caltex Petroleum Corporation

11

The People's Republic of China

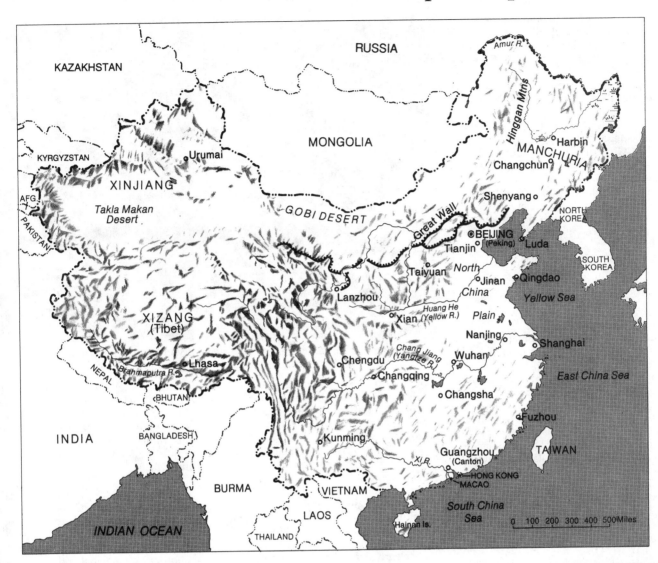

Area: Approximately 3.7 million square miles, including Inner Mongolia and Tibet. (As large as the 50 United States plus another Alaska).

Population: 1,272,694,000 (1999 estimate)

Capital City: Beijing, Pop. 9.9 million, estimated (pronounced Bay-*jing*).

Climate: Dry, cold with bitter winters in the mountainous West and North, temperate in the East, subtropical with rainy monsoons in the South.

Neighboring Countries: Russia (Northeast, sharing a tiny border on the Northwest); Mongolia (North); Kazakhstan, Kyrgyzstan (Northwest); Afghanistan, Pakistan (East); India, Nepal, Bhutan (Southwest); Burma, Laos, Vietnam (South); Taiwan (100 miles off the

Southeast China mainland); Korea (Northeast).

Official Language: Mandarin Chinese, the dialect of the Chinese language spoken in Central and Northern China.

Other Principal Tongues: South and West Chinese dialects, including Cantonese, Hakka, Fukienese and Wu, the Tibetan language. Tribesmen of remote Xinjiang, Inner Mongolia and Manchuria have their own languages and dialects.

Ethnic Background: Chinese, sometimes referred to as *Han* (about 95%). Relatively small minorities of Mongol, Turkic, Tibetan, Thai and of other ancestry live in the remote regions of the interior.

Principal Religions: Confucianism, Taoism, Buddhism, Islam and Christianity, all of which have been intermixed to one degree or another. They have been severely opposed and suppressed by the communist government, but in recent years the anti–religious pressures have lessened and they are enjoying a revival.

Main Exports (to Hong Kong, Japan, U.S., Germany, Australia): Manufactured goods, agricultural products, oil and minerals. Mineral resources have only been partially exploited, but are known to be substantial.

Main Imports (from Japan, U.S., Hong Kong): Grain, chemical fertilizer, steel, machinery, equipment.

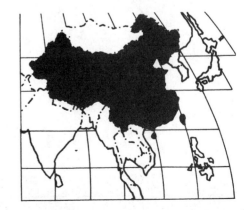

←

Dragon pavement leading to the Gate of Supreme Harmony in Beijing's Forbidden City

Courtesy: Caltex Petroleum Corporation

China

Currency: *Renminbi* (people's currency) expressed in units called *Yuan.*

Former Colonial Status: Some regions were colonized by various Western powers.

National Day: October 1, anniversary of the founding of the People's Republic in 1949.

Chief of State: Jiang Zemin, President (since March 1993).

Head of Government: Zhu Rongji, Premier (since April 1998; pronounced Ju-Rung-gee).

General Secretary, Communist Party: Jiang Zemin (since June 1989).

National Flag: Red, with one large and four small five-pointed stars at upper left.

Per Capita GNP Income: U.S. $750

Taiwan

Area: 13,885 square miles.

Population: 20.5 million (estimated).

Capital City: Taipei (Pop. 2.8 million, estimated).

Climate: Subtropical and humid in the lowlands, with an eleven-month growing season; in the higher elevations of the central mountains the temperatures are cooler.

Neighboring Countries: The Republic of China has been on the island of Taiwan, located 100 miles from the southeast China mainland, since 1949. It is about 300 miles north of the Philippine island of Luzon.

Official Language: Chinese (Mandarin, which is spoken in Central and North China).

Other Principal Tongues: Amoy, a Chinese dialect, is spoken by the majority

A mother and child framed in a decorative wall-window in Hangzhou

Courtesy: Jon Markham Morrow

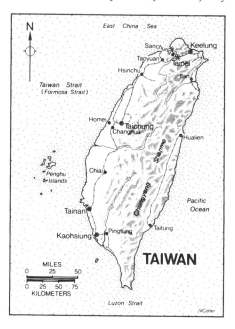

of the population, known as Taiwanese. Tribal aborigines in the mountains speak a number of tongues related to Malay.

Ethnic Background: Chinese, sometimes referred to as *Han.* The highlands are occupied by a small group of Malayo–Polynesian ancestry who resemble the people of Indonesia.

Principal Religions: Confucianism, Taoism, Buddhism. These three, which migrated with the earliest Chinese from the mainland, have not been and are not clearly defined, but are generally intermixed.

Main Exports (to the U.S., Japan, Hong Kong): Textiles, clothing, electrical and electronic equipment, processed foods.

Main Imports (from U.S., Japan, Kuwait): Industrial equipment, automobiles, oil.

Currency: New Taiwan Dollar.

Former Colonial Status: Taiwan was a Japanese colony from 1895 to 1945.

National Day: October 10, anniversary of the Chinese Revolution of 1911.

Chief of State: Chen Shui-bia n, President (since May 2000).

National Flag: A red field with a blue rectangle in the upper left containing a 12–pointed white star.

Per Capita GNP Income: U.S. $13,198.

Note: At the beginning of 1979, the People's Republic of China officially adopted an already–existing system known as *Pinyin* for writing out Chinese names and terms in the Western alphabet. That system is now increasingly used in both the West and even on Taiwan. Thus the capital of China, once known commonly as "Peking" is now more often rendered "Beijing." The Pinyin system is used in the following text except where possible confusion might occur with terms already quite familiar, thus "Daoism," will also be followed by the less correct but more familiar "Taoism."

Occupying a land area larger than that of the 50 United States, China stretches for a distance of 3,400 miles from its Northeastern region adjacent to remote Russian Siberia to the mountainous regions of Tibet bordering on Nepal and India. As for temperature, altitude and roughness of terrain, fertility of the soil, and rainfall, there are two distinct regions. The invisible line that divides the two starts in the distant north at the Amur River and runs southward through the crest of the Great Khingnan Mountains. It follows the contours of the Huang He, or Yellow River, turning northwest and then west to accommodate that part of the river that arches toward Mongolia. Turning again southward, it searches out the upper part of the river, passing through the region around Lanzhou and Chengdu and finally becomes obscure in the hilly southern area of Kunming near the Vietnamese border.

To the south and east of this demarcation "line" lies China proper; to the north and west the area is referred to as "outer" China. The land is relatively fertile south and east of this "line." In the eastern region of central "inner" China there are few hills which break the monotony of the level land. In the south, the land is also fertile, but is more hilly.

In the West, on the left–hand side of the rough demarcation line, the land is a combination of closely crowded mountains with rough surfaces possessing little greenery even in the warmer regions of the lower altitudes. The towering peaks are occasionally interrupted by expanses of flat territory that is also desolate and dry, being surrounded by a natural barrier that withstands the invasion of rain clouds. The mountains in the North on the edge of the "line" give way to the Gobi Desert, filled with shifting earth, harsh rock formations and severe extremes in temperature, all of which combine to exclude more than occasional visits of man and beast. The mountains envelop this desert which extends from Manchuria into southern Mongolia.

These areas of outer China are largely unmapped by Western standards. The thinly scattered people of Tibet, Xinjiang and Manchuria have traditionally relied on herds of animals as their principal resource, although great treasures of mineral wealth may lie buried below the surface of the earth. A short growing season provides the small amount of greenery available. The air is dry in both summer and winter, blowing out of Asiatic Russia (Siberia). The great distance the wind has traveled prior to its arrival in China has taken almost all moisture from the air. The absence of bodies of water in the endless expanses also make the dry winds cold—bitterly so, almost beyond belief, in the winter.

In the spring enough warmth arrives to melt the snow in the lower altitudes of the mountains. This is sufficient to support limited agriculture at the lower edges of the mountains bordering the Gobi Desert of western Manchuria and Mongolia in the area between the mountains and the Takla Makan Desert in Xinjiang and the valleys of Tibet, but only during the brief summer season.

To the south and east of the "line" the land changes into temperate farmland; it is relatively flat and somewhat drier in parts of northern China, notably in the North China Plain. The hillier and more mountainous areas found in southern China have more moisture and warmer temperatures, producing thick growths of forest on the land not under cultivation.

The three main rivers, the Huang He (Yellow), the Yangzi and the Xijiang (West River) have their origins deep within the remote territory west of the mountains, but flow through the more level eastern regions in a sluggish manner. Refreshed by the cool water of melting snow, they are quickly swollen in the spring by rains brought by the southeastern monsoon, and overflow their banks, spreading rich silt over the surrounding land. Rivers overflowing their banks continue to be a major problem. They also are a traditional source of communication and transportation in the region, but this is being replaced by railroads.

The lower valley of the Huang He is temperate and is the area in which the major aspects of Chinese civilization were born. The river itself is unpredictable. It left its old course south of the Shandong peninsula in which it had flowed for more than 800 years, and assumed its present course north of the peninsula in 1853, a shift of more than 500 miles. The immense quantities of silt it carries in its waters gave it the name "Yellow River" and also have built up a river bed over the years which is higher than the surrounding land. When it enters flood stage, the results have been catastrophic.

The growing season increases in the central and eastern region of China which is drained by the Yangzi River; it becomes almost continuous throughout the year in the southeastern area through which the Xijiang (Sikiang) River flows. If the rain-

From the surging waters of the Huang He (Yellow) River . . .

China

... to the parched wastes of the Gobi Desert

AP/World Wide Photos

fall in these regions was uniform from year to year, both would produce great quantities of food to feed the huge number of Chinese. The variations in rain, however, cause periodic loss of crops by either drought or flood. During a prolonged drought, even the violent summer rains are not of much help, since they run quickly into the rivers and flow into the sea rather than watering the land, which then dries out, unless there is further, preferably steady, rainfall.

The island of Taiwan has an elongated oval shape and its entire length is dominated by a chain of mountains rising with regularity to heights of 6,000 to 11,000 feet. These peaks lie close to the eastern side of the island and drop steeply at the coastline into the warm waters of the Pacific. The western slopes descend gently to a fertile plain that occupies almost one–half of the island's surface. The climate varies from tropical to temperate, depending upon altitude. As is true on the Chinese mainland 100 miles across the Taiwan Strait, the summer winds bring abundant rain which supports intense agriculture. The smaller rivers do not cause the catastrophic floods of the three mighty rivers of continental China, so that bountiful harvests of a variety of produce, principally rice, are regularly gathered.

History

The Formative Era

China is the world's oldest continuous civilization in the sense that contemporary Chinese civilization recognizably resembles its earliest origins. Today's Arabic and Islamic Egypt, for example, is far more different from the civilization of the Pharaohs than China is from its early years. Still China is actually of much more recent vintage than the major early civilizations of Southwest Asia and North Africa.

Archeological evidence from north China, where its dryer climate better preserves artifacts, reveals neolithic communities based in several parts of the region dating from around 5000 B.C. These communities cultivated dogs and pigs and, even at that early date, silk worms.

By the period 1800–1000 B.C., the Chinese had begun to develop into a highly stylized, complex pattern. Advanced and very artistic techniques of casting bronze developed. The system of *ideographic* writing was refined and became the method of communicating and recording of ideas. But it did not and it does not now have an alphabet; it consists of a collection of thousands of symbols, each of which represents a word. Somewhat similar to Egyptian hieroglyphics, these characters have evolved far beyond their original graphic origins. Today, merely looking at a character provides few clues to its meaning. For many hundreds of years this system of writing was known only to scribes and intellectuals and has only recently become more widely known among the general population.

Nevertheless, the Chinese, using this tremendously demanding writing system, developed quite early a society more dependant on a wide dispersal of learning than almost any other major civilization. The 20th century has seen many modifications to both the format and structure of the characters to make them more accessible to the average person.

The Early Dynasties

From around 1800 B.C. the Chinese were ruled by kings of the Shang, an apparently feudal and aristocratic dynasty. The Shang rulers were replaced by the Zhou (Chou) dynasty, which formally governed from about 1100 to 800 B.C., after which their power rapidly diminished until it was destroyed centuries later. Although the details of the fall of the Shang need hardly concern us here, what is astonishing is that from that collapse emerged one of the most significant Chinese contributions to political philosophy ever devised, The concept of the "Mandate of Heaven."

In originally justifying their conquest of the Shang, the Zhou leaders explained that the Shang, due to their degeneracy, had forfeited the "Mandate." According to their reasoning, which would dominate Chinese political thought down through the ages, "Heaven" was not viewed as a spiritual place of post–life salvation. It was a conscious entity that insisted that governments on earth must rule for the benefit of the masses. And leaders maintained the right to do so only as long as they continued to behave well toward the people. In a world where too often political power has derived more from the sword or inheritance, this provisional nature of power has been an important idea first developed in ancient China and eventually complementary to many modern democratic theories of government. Some early Chinese thinkers even went so far as to claim that the "Mandate" actually justified the right of the masses to revolt!

The real power of the Zhou dynasty lasted only a few centuries before North China then disintegrated into a number of feudal states led by "princes" who occupied their time and that of their subjects in a variety of wars against each other. The use of iron tools in agriculture during this period produced a high yield from the earth, which, together with irrigation and (after 1,000 A.D.) the widespread cultivation of rice, permitted a correspondingly high rate of population growth. As the people pressed outward, they came into greater conflict with non–Chinese people who inhabited central China around the Yangzi River. The stronger rulers subdued the weaker and smaller states, and the number of feudal princedoms became less, gradually falling under the control of two major states: Qin, which ultimately triumphed in the 3rd century B.C., was in the west central and northwestern part of China and Chu in the central Yangzi valley. Graphically, this period is known as the "Warring States Period."

The Hundred Schools

Though China was divided during the later Zhou period, this diversity of political power proved to be a major benefit for its cultural development. In fact, one of the most interesting features of Chinese civilization is that, given its usual tendency toward centralization and successive government enthusiasm for promoting an orthodoxy of thought, it is most often during periods of relative weakness that Chinese intellectual life most dramatically has flourished.

Several points in modern history, the 1920s and most recently in the era before the clashes at Tiananmen Square in 1989, serve as good examples. The later Zhou was just such an era, a time when in the 5th and 4th centuries B.C. China enjoyed an intellectual blossoming comparable to that of Greece during the same period. Literature and the arts flourished, and the desire for knowledge and social order led to the creation and formalization of the two intellectual systems which originated in China: Confucianism and Taoism, the latter a mystical and contemplative system of belief and magical imagery (see Historical Background).

Confucianism, in contrast, is largely a system of social philosophy, and became a very influential source of satisfaction for the learned Chinese as well as providing a sense of imperial legitimacy and the security arising out of its emphasis on hierarchy and deference to authority, a feature many in East Asia today claim still plays an important role in their recent economic successes.

The First Empires

By 221 B.C. the Qin ruler, who led a highly organized and militarily strong state, conquered his rivals and established control over all of north and central China as well as part of the southern region. For China this was one of the darkest periods in its history. The Qin dynasty unified the empire in more ways than military conquest; the Great Wall of China was constructed laboriously over a period of years to ward off the periodic raids by the nomadic central Asians from the North. Roads and other public works were built and the system of writing and weights were standardized. Obsessed with the needs of state power, the Qin leadership ignored the precepts of Confucianism, even killed many of its adherents, rejecting totally the idea that the state existed to serve the masses.

Not surprisingly the rule of the Qin was extremely oppressive and produced much discontent among the Chinese people. It was soon overthrown by a new dynasty that took the name *Han.*

These new rulers, successfully avoiding the arrogance which had brought down the Qin, eventually governed for almost 400 years (2nd century B.C.–2nd century A.D.) before and after the beginning of the Western Christian era. The people of China today are sometimes referred to as *Han* to differentiate them from the minorities that live in the outer part of what is modern China. In spite of a brief collapse at the halfway point of its reign, the Han Dynasty succeeded in making China into an empire of power, wealth and cultural brilliance comparable to the other great civilization of the same period, the Roman Empire.

Technologically, it was in fact far more advanced than its Roman counterpart on the other side of Eurasia. Its boundaries were pushed well into central Asia, where local leaders were awed by the brilliance of Chinese advances in learning and military prowess. Even if not directly supervised by the Chinese, rulers of the outlying states of Asia were often willing to acknowledge themselves tributary and vassal states of the mighty empire.

When the Han dynasty collapsed, the following four centuries were marked by frequent nomadic invasions from the North which resulted in a series of states in northern China ruled by non–Chinese. A few Chinese, or Han states, did survive in the South, however, under a series of weak dynasties. During this time of

The 1,400 mile long Great Wall of China

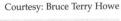

Courtesy: Bruce Terry Howe

China

uncertainty, Mahayana Buddhism, sometimes referred to as northern Buddhism (see Historical Background), spread quickly following its arrival from northern India by way of Central Asia at the beginning of the Christian era.

The Middle Dynasties

China was reunited by the Sui and Tang dynasties after 581 A.D., and under an energetic succession of emperors it once more extended the area of its power far into Central Asia. For the first time in world history, a written examination was developed for civil servants, appointment of whom was based more and more on ability rather than family ties. Ironically, aspects of this movement away from aristocracy and toward a more individually based system of merit had begun earlier under the generally hated Qin dynasty.

Although the officials of the Tang Dynasty were largely Confucian in outlook, it was in this period that Buddhism reached the height of its influence in Chinese civilization. Nevertheless, that influence was not long lasting and the later Tang era saw many cruel persecutions of Buddhists. Though losing its hold on official Chinese thought to Confucianists and Daoists (Taoists), this South Asian belief system would nevertheless remain influential on the popular level into the modern period.

There was a short period of disunity following the decline and fall of the Tang dynasty in the 10th century A.D. The brilliant cultural advances of the ensuing three–century period centered chiefly on the art of painting and the discipline of philosophy. Under the influence of Buddhist theology, official Confucianism was modified by about 1200 into Neo–Confucianism which concerned itself more with abstract philosophy than had the original form of this belief.

The country was ruled by emperors of the Song (Sung) dynasty, and was continually threatened by a succession of powerful non–Chinese states that emerged along the northern border. The end of this era came with defeat by the most powerful northern force, the Mongols, who were able to succeed in their conquest only after a long and bitter campaign. The Song had withstood the Mongols longer than any of the other civilizations of the world into which the conquerors intruded, but ultimately became a part of a vast empire stretching from the Pacific to what is now the Middle East.

The Mongols finally unified all China in 1279 and ruled for a century, taking the name Yuan dynasty. Already disliked by the Chinese in a number of ways, the Mongols had but slight respect for Confucianism and the civil service examinations, factors which led to even greater opposition by the Chinese, particularly the upper classes. The rulers though were religiously tolerant, and permitted small communities of Franciscan missionaries to introduce Christianity into several parts of coastal China.

The Mongols were expelled from China in 1368 in a great upheaval with strong anti–foreign tendencies. This new, ethnically Chinese dynasty, which came to power, the Ming (1368–1644), at first ruled firmly and energetically, creating a powerful empire.

Following the momentum of the outward–looking Yuan Dynasty, the Ming Emperor even sent out huge overseas flotillas toward the west to explore and demonstrate the might of the Chinese Empire. Starting in 1405 the Ming Emperor Yong Le sent out an extraordinary series of naval expeditions which over the years eventually traveled throughout Southeast Asia and parts of India and ranged as far away as Aden in Arabia and Mogadishu in East Africa. The final expedition in 1431 even sent some ships as far as Jedda on the Red Sea! The efforts, whose motives are not exactly clear, certainly had its impact.

The Chinese flotilla intervened in a number of local disputes and worked to further the prestige of the Chinese emperors.

However, they lacked the ongoing significance of the voyages Westerners mounted in the opposite direction several generations later in the 15th century. By the time the Europeans attempted similar voyages, memory of the early Chinese flotillas had been all but forgotten.

Within China, a period of decline began about 1500. Japanese pirates began to increase their activities along the coast. Internal weakness became an increasing problem which was transformed into an even greater liability by the rise in power of the Manchu rulers to the north. In 1644, a combination of domestic rebellion and Manchu might was sufficient to overthrow the Ming dynasty; Within a few decades, the Manchus had subdued all of China.

The Manchus

The new rulers took the name Qing (Ch'ing) dynasty, but are more commonly referred to in the West as the Manchus. Although Chinese culture was by this time static to a degree that made basic changes difficult, under the Manchus the country was once again united and became rapidly powerful. In an effort to consolidate their positions, the Manchus ruled through existing Chinese institutions, including the very formal civil service examination system with its Confucian orientation. For this reason, and others, they were accepted rapidly by their Chinese subjects.

Interestingly, they devised a system whereby major offices and responsibilities were shared by matched sets of Manchu and Chinese officials. After an initial period of wise and successful rule, the Manchus indulged themselves in a period of energetic, but arbitrary and costly, warfare in the late 18th century which undermined the dynasty and coupled with internal corruption and a number of internal revolts combined to make China less able to deal with the challenges the nineteenth century would bring.

Arrival of Westerners

Although Westerners from the Roman era on had periodically visited China, the modern period of Sino–Western relations really begins in the 18th century when Europeans, principally British, started to seek Chinese silk and tea. Unfortunately for these early merchants they had, at first, little to offer, save silver bullion in exchange for the coveted Chinese goods. The Chinese seemed quite disinterested in Western products. In fact, the famous emperor Qian Long even explained to a Western visiting dignitary in 1793 that China had "all

---

The Chinese Exam System

The Chinese examination system, which existed in various forms until the early 20th century, was truly remarkable for a traditional society. Rather than relying on birthright to choose the bulk of their elites, as was so common among the Europeans and even their East Asian neighbors, the Japanese, the Chinese eventually developed a massive system of offering Confucian–based exams to thousands upon thousands of males annually. Those that advanced beyond the first demanding tests went on to even more rigorous exams at the provincial and eventually imperial level. Although few became great officials of the government, the system created an enormous pool of educated people who served the needs of society as local leaders, and for the lucky few, officially within the imperial bureaucracy.

Not surprisingly those who came from educated and reasonably well off households had a major advantage in the competition. Nevertheless, the record of graduates shows that it was a true system of social mobility that allowed many people year after year to rise beyond their families' earlier accomplishments.

Marble sculpture of a Ming soldier at the Imperial Tombs

things" in abundance and was simply not interested in Western goods. Nevertheless, the trade did develop and at the insistence of the Beijing government it was confined to the southern port of Guangzhou known to foreigners as Canton.

For the English though, this "Canton System" although lucrative enough, did cause problems. They were interested in trading further north in China where there might be a better market for their goods and in having direct contact with Chinese officials when various problems, legal and commercial, arose.

None of these things though was possible given the prevailing Chinese disinterest in any Western style foreign relations or commercial exchanges beyond those considered important to maintaining the dignity and universal legitimacy of Chinese imperial claims. For the Chinese, foreign relations as understood in the West did not exist.

The Chinese emperor was considered the "son of heaven" and people interested in having relations with China were expected to take part in the Chinese "Tributary System," largely a symbolic system whereby other communities recognized the supreme symbolic authority of the Emperor. On a technical level, that required a physical prostration before the emperor known as the *kowtow* and an

exchange of various presents. In fact, the presents the Chinese gave away were not uncommonly more valuable than those they received. For the Chinese emperors, it was the symbolism of the relationship that mattered, not the cash transaction. England, the country that some had disparaged as the nation of shopkeepers, had met an empire completely disinterested in commerce. It was a bad match.

But by the late eighteenth and early nineteenth century two developments occurred which led to dramatic changes in China's relations with the Western powers. The British discovered that opium, grown in their possessions in India, could be sold at a handsome profit in China. Over the next decades the amount of opium imported into China by the British grew enormously until by the first quarter of the 19th century the drug was devastating Chinese society, especially in the south.

After first undergoing an internal debate in the late 1830s about how best to deal with the crises, the imperial government decided to force the foreign traders to give up their trade. To that end, an imperial commissioner, Lin Zexu, was sent to Guangzhou in 1839 to attempt to suppress the trade. Although the imperial commissioner managed to confiscate the traders' opium stocks and destroy them, the British government, by then especially committed

to the drug trade, declared war. Over the next generation and during two successive "Opium Wars" one of which culminated in the capture of Beijing itself in 1860, the British, and eventually their French allies, managed to impose a series of "unequal treaties" on the Chinese. Those treaties would dominate Sino-Western relations until the middle of the 20th century.

What had gone wrong for China? For most of world history Chinese technology had far outshone the skills of the Westerners, but by the 18th century, the industrial revolution, especially centered in England, gave the British enormous advantages over the once self–sufficient Chinese empire. That advantage would last for more than the next hundred years with profound implications for our own century.

The Diplomacy of Imperialism

Under the series of "unequal treaties" signed under pressure in the first half of the 19th century, China lost a large part of its sovereignty. The Westerners gained the right to dominate a series of ports, soon known as Treaty Ports along the coast. Hong Kong and Shanghai, are the best known of them. The treaties also gave the foreigners immunity to Chinese law and control over China's tariffs; especially important for later developments was the insistence that foreigners be allowed to preach Christianity in the interior of the country. Moreover, due to the concept of "most favored nation," the rights won by the English and French guns applied to all other foreigners in China including the Americans who had hardly taken part.

Cutting the Melon

The culmination of this era of imperialist greed occurred just as the 19th century was coming to a close. Known as the "Cutting of the Melon," one European power after another began demanding further spheres of influence in China. The British demanded an expansion of their influence in the region east of Shanghai and north of Hong Kong while the French pushed into southern China from their base in Vietnam. To the north the Russians and Germans made their demands while the Japanese insisted on gaining further rights in the Chinese coastal areas opposite Taiwan. In each of these, a particular Western power (with the exception of the United States) was granted sweeping and exclusive economic rights in its area, coupled with a great degree of political influence.

Russian domination was established in Manchuria, but the fertile southern portion of that region went to the Japanese in 1905 after their victory in the Russo—

China

Traditional *Junk* on the China Sea

Japanese War. The Germans established themselves in the province of Shandong (Shantung); the British became the major power in the Yangzi valley region; the Japanese controlled Fujian (Fukien) Province and the French asserted their dominance over Southwest China.

Interestingly for students of modern Chinese history the new demands were often made in the form of forced 99 year leases. Although most of these arrangements have long since been terminated, the lease on the New Territories of Hong Kong continued. Only ninety–nine years later did it run out. Thus the drama of 1997's return of Hong Kong and in 1999 Macau to the People's Republic of China.

That imperialistic high point known as the "Melon Cutting" did not stop at the century's end. Outside what had been China, places like Korea and Okinawa, which had paid tribute to the Manchu emperors, also became colonies or spheres of influence of Britain, France, Russia and Japan. Russian influence became paramount in Outer Mongolia, and penetrated into Xinjiang (Sinkiang) in the 1930's. The British became a powerful influence in Tibet and remained so until 1947.

These losses of territory and authority were dramatic demonstrations of China's basic weakness by the standards of the 20th century Western powers and were an insult to the sense of national pride of the Chinese. The economy of the coastal regions,

traditionally more wealthy than the interior areas, was almost totally dominated by foreign trade and investment.

Although many among the Chinese tended toward an inwardness that made effective response to these pressures difficult, there were other more far sighted individuals within the Chinese leadership. They foresaw crises developing, and began, as early as the 1860s, to adapt to the various Western military techniques needed to maintain the country's sovereignty in that imperialistic age. Led by perceptive individuals at both the imperial and military level, most notably the Manchu Prince Gong, a period known as "Self Strengthening" was begun. He was aided at the provincial level by leaders like Li Hongzhang and Zuo Zongtang. Under this program, during an energetic era dating from the late 1860s through the 1890s, several military arsenals and dockyards were founded and scores of students sent abroad—to America and Europe—to learn Western military and engineering techniques. Sadly, though considerable effort was put out and significant gains made, they were overall too little to stem the flow of China's diminishing strength nor to equal similar but more energetic efforts like those of their neighbors, the Japanese, which were simply far more successful.

As seen below, in the first test of their respective efforts at mastering Western military techniques during the Sino–

Japanese war of 1894, the Chinese accomplishments proved sorely lacking and the country experienced yet another massive humiliation. The significance of these humiliations and the various unequal treaties, cannot be underestimated. It is important to understand that even today many of China's leaders grew up when these special Western and Japanese privileges were still in effect.

The Heavenly Kingdom of Great Peace

Although the long term implications of the Western pressures on China were enormous, the larger issue at the time for the Chinese themselves was the outbreak in 1851 of an enormous rebellion which eventually devastated much of the country over the next fifteen years.

The origins of the Taiping Heavenly Kingdom, as the rebels called themselves, lay in the startling increases in population which had added enormous pressures on the land. Moreover, the Opium Wars themselves had disrupted economic life in southern China. It was in that disrupted environment that arose one of the more curious dramas of world history.

The story began in the early nineteenth century when a frustrated Confucian scholar, who had for years been unable to pass the demanding Confucian civil service exams, decided that he was the younger brother of Jesus Christ and developed a new "trinity" which included "God, the Father", "God, the Son" and in this new theology, himself, the "little brother."

For fifteen years, dating from the original revolt in 1851, China was divided between two governments, the ethnically Manchu, but Confucian–oriented Qing Dynasty, and the unique Chinese Taiping Rebels with their semi–Chinese–semi–Christian orientation. Following ideas found both in the Old Testament and drawn from mythic memories of early China, the Taipings established a theocracy with a communal economic structure. Life was organized, especially at their capital at Nanjing, around a religious military structure which at least on the surface seemed quite puritanical. Women, in sharp contrast to traditional Confucian practice, were far freer. Foot binding was not practiced and the women also took part in battle. But the assault on traditional practice had been too great and by 1864 the Heavenly Kingdom of Great Peace collapsed under pressures from Qing Militia leaders aroused by the struggle to preserve Confucianism (and assisted by Western military soldiers and advisors).

Following the death of the Emperor in 1861, his widow, referred to as the Empress Dowager Cixi, became co–regent during the reign of her son and wielded considerable influence. When he died in 1874 the throne then passed to Cixi's own young nephew and her power continued as before. Probably the most powerful woman in world history, Cixi dominated China, the largest population under a single government in the world, from the early 1860s through 1908. Her influence cannot be underestimated. Ruthless, able and extremely conservative, she embodied the traditions cherished by the Manchu court officials who clung to the security of the past. Nevertheless, under her reign, the first efforts to deal with the Western challenge in the form of the various industrial efforts known as "self–strengthening projects," were begun.

Cixi's power was so great that when she felt threatened by the Emperor Guang Xu's dramatic effort during the summer of 1898 to drastically reorganize the Chinese government and educational system, the better to make it able to withstand imperialistic pressures, she had him arrested. But if the Empress Dowager Cixi had intensely disliked the Emperor's response to the weakening of China, that did not mean that she failed to recognize the peril the dynasty faced. It is probably with that reason in mind that she soon pinned her hopes on yet another approach to the question of saving China. And in that case, one that arose from the popular masses' anger with the disruptions in their lives said to be caused by the foreigners. The results came to be known as the Boxer Rebellion.

At the popular level, there were many anti–foreign and anti–Christian outbreaks of violence in the years following 1870. Both sentiments joined to provide discontent resulting in the famous 1900 Boxer Rebellion a dramatic effort by thousands of Chinese to literally drive the Westerners out of China. In fact, the "Boxers" as the foreigners called them because of their ritualized style of physical and mental exercise, were encouraged by influential members of the Manchu court. For months, especially in north China, the Boxers terrorized Westerners and their Chinese converts.

Eventually, a joint military expedition was sent by the Western powers and crushed the Boxers. American and other foreign troops stormed Beijing in August 1900. Less than fifty years after the 1860 capture of Beijing by the Westerners, it was again under their control!

The Empress Dowager, who had fled the city as a young woman in 1860 was understandably shaken by the defeat and granted her reluctant assent to certain innovations in the imperial government. But it was too late. She died in 1908. The Manchu Qing dynasty had only a few more years to survive.

Trying to Save China

In the years after the 1839–42 Opium War several important officials and thinkers had come forward with theories and projects for reforming the Chinese empire. Some among them, as influential provincial leaders, put into place the various projects of the "Self–Strengthening Movement." More radical reformers later in the century played an important role in the Emperor's dramatic and failed reform effort of 1898, the so called "100 Day Reform." Nevertheless, as China moved into the 20th century its problems worsened and the ability of the imperial Manchu government to respond to the crises became less and less significant. These early reformers were not unified and their disunity prevented them from achieving any real influence on the Manchu court until it was too late.

As the situation deteriorated, the influences of these reformers became increasingly irrelevant, and leadership passed to those calling for more radical actions. It was in that context that a new generation of leaders arose, men not interested in reforming the Manchu Qing Empire but in replacing it with a republic more along the lines of Western models.

The most important of these radicals was Sun Yat–sen, who dedicated himself to the overthrow of the Manchus and to the modernization of China along semi–Western lines. Although he was eventually able to attract a relatively large following, Sun was not very effective in organizing his follow-

ers. Nevertheless due to the drama of Sun having been unsuccessfully kidnaped by Chinese agents in London in 1896, he became very well known in the West and eventually personified, in the minds of many Westerners, the goal of a Chinese republican revolution.

When the Empress Dowager died in 1908, the Manchu court installed the two–year–old Pu–Yi as child emperor. He reigned through regents appointed by the court until 1912. Later he was to serve as the "Emperor" of Manchukuo (Manchuria) when the Japanese attempted in the 1930s to colonize northern China.

The Revolution of 1911

In the fall of 1911, the ability of the Court to maintain the two–hundred and fifty year old Qing dynasty finally failed. A rebellion broke out in the city of Wuhan which, given prevailing frustrations with the Manchu leadership, spread rapidly across the country. One after another, various provinces declared themselves for the revolution. Sun Yat–sen, although at the time visiting the United States, emerged by December as the provisional president of a new Chinese republic. It appeared at first that China was about to take its place among the democracies of the modern world. But that was not to be.

If the forces of the old regime had been unable to maintain themselves, portions of their strength remained potent enough to direct the course of events over the next several years.

American, British, and Japanese troops storming Peking (Beijing), August 1900

China

大清國當今慈禧端佑康頤昭豫莊誠壽恭欽獻崇熙聖母皇太后

The Empress Dowager Cixi

To avoid a civil war, Sun turned over power to Yuan Shikai, a former Qing general who still held considerable loyalty among many government soldiers. There was actually little choice. A civil war between the new revolutionary forces and those of Yuan Shikai would have only weakened China further. The compromise seemed necessary to save what had been already won. But sadly, Yuan was more interested in establishing a new dynasty than serving as a true democratic president, and within a few years China literally collapsed from the stress.

By 1916 China had disintegrated into a score of petty states run by individual military governors, usually referred to as "warlords." They had little governing ability and their rule was almost uniformly oppressive. The legal government of China in Beijing continued to be recognized diplomatically by the foreign powers. In reality, this "government" was an ever–shifting combination of one or more warlords, sometimes under the influence of foreign nations. Communications were extremely poor and there was a thin scattering of modern arms in the outlying regions, making it almost impossible to achieve any genuine national unity.

Sun Yat–sen, the "Father of the Revolution," embittered by his experiences in these developments, established himself in the south and tried in various ways, without success, to overthrow the shadow government at Beijing and to reunite the country. In the following years he devoted himself to the building up the *Guomindang* (Kuomintang)—"National People's Party," or "GMD." But far to the north, an intellectual energy and nationalist momentum was growing that would go far beyond even Dr. Sun's revolutionary plans.

The May Fourth Movements

The May Fourth Movement of the years 1915 to 1921 was a multi–dimensional era which embraced few central themes save a general disregard for China's traditional Confucian culture. On an individual level many of those involved loudly advocated a reorientation of cultural values. The young were told to become more independent, less tied to the more tradition–bound older generation. Confucianism, it was said, simply did not allow China the vitality necessary to withstand the aggressive modern world.

In addition to the trend toward economic modernization in the cities and coastal regions and cultural speculation during the 1920's, there was a marked growth of nationalism among the Chinese, who sought an end to foreign influence in their country. The "central" government was in the hands of a group

under Japanese influence who cooperated with the latter's efforts to have their control over the Chinese province of Shantung formalized by the treaties that ended World War One. An outburst of patriotism, led by students, which became known as the May Fourth Movement, prevented the actual signing of the treaty and sparked an era of intense popular political activity.

On the national level the people of China, particularly the youth, desired the end of imperialism and internal disunity and came to believe that these goals could only be achieved through a major political and social revolution. Some chose the *Guomindang*, while a smaller number joined the infant communist movement.

Communism

The *Chinese Communist Party (CCP)* was founded in 1921 mostly by young Chinese intellectuals. The movement quickly came under the control of the Third International, more familiarly known as the *Comintern* of Russia under its energetic revolutionary leader, Lenin. The picture became even more complicated when the *Comintern* decided to enter into an alliance with Sun Yat–sen's *Guomindang* and ordered the local Chinese communists to do the same. This unstable union was produced by a common, overwhelming desire to expel Western and Japanese influence from China and to eliminate the power of the warlords.

To accomplish these aims, the *Comintern* reorganized and greatly strengthened the *Guomindang* through money and military aid, but it also hoped that communists could gradually acquire control over it by infiltrating top positions, and by putting pressure on the party through communist–dominated labor and peasant unions. Although there was considerable uncertainty about the collaboration of the *Guomindang's* nationalists and the communists, what mattered above all was that their cooperation help unify the country once more. In 1926 that great effort, known as the "Northern Expedition," began. For the next several years, sometimes by fighting, sometimes by negotiation, the nationalists marched north enthusiastically attempting to build a new, stronger and now unified China. The march was to prove ultimately successful, although tensions inherent in the nationalist/communist alliance eventually broke out.

While Sun Yat–sen had been alive, the effort to both unify China and to maintain the coalition of nationalists and communists continued fairly well. But after his death in 1925 he was eventually succeeded by General Chiang Kai–shek, who had become increasingly alarmed at the threat of Soviet domination of China and the more immediate threat of potential communist revolution.

Chiang determined to head off these threats by military force and in 1927 sent his forces into the newly liberated Shanghai to slaughter his communist allies. The alliance between the Chinese nationalists

Dr. Sun Yat–sen addresses a crowd before departing with his troops on the campaign against Beijing

China

and the communists was thus broken. For the moment the nationalists—the *Guomindang* forces, under Chiang—seemed triumphant.

Chiang captured Beijing in 1928, and proclaimed the renewed Republic of China with its new capital at Nanjing, a city which has often served as an alternative capital in Chinese history. Actually the *GMD* controlled only the eastern provinces of China and was faced with tremendous problems: a large army that had to be fed and clothed, floods, famine, and political apathy. After a generation of struggle the *Guomindang* had finally come fully to power. But its ability to attempt a rebirth of China was soon to be severely curtailed when, in 1931, the Japanese began their effort to dominate the country.

The Japanese Invasion

Japanese efforts to establish an East Asian empire for themselves had begun in the late nineteenth century. By the early 1920s, their influence had grown considerably. Korea and Taiwan were already colonies and Japanese influence in Manchuria was considerable. China's weakness during the era of the "Warlords", 1916–1928, had given them even greater leeway to assert themselves. Moreover, the worldwide depression, which struck at the end of the 1920s convinced many Japanese nationalists that Japan's future lay in furthering their hold on northern China. That commitment lead to the Japanese Manchurian army's (see Japan) decision to provoke an incident which would allow them to take over Manchuria.

The Japanese seized it in 1931–32; the territory was renamed Manchukuo and the former Manchu emperor of the Chinese Empire, the youthful Henry Pu-Yi, took the throne as "Emperor of Manchukuo." This interesting character had been tutored in the Western classics by a Britisher after the ouster of the Manchus, who suggested that he take an English name. Having been enthroned as emperor and deposed while still a child, the possibility of once again becoming an emperor must have been exhilarating for the young man. Nevertheless, during his years as emperor over Manchuria, he would prove as powerless under the Japanese control as he had been as a child under the direction of the adults around him in the Chinese imperial court. His story is a fascinating one and it eventually became well known to millions of filmgoers through the movie "The Last Emperor."

To Chiang Kai-shek, the Japanese assault, while dangerous, was still not his most immediate concern. The Generalissimo was more concerned about what he saw as a disease of the "heart," the Chi-

nese communists, who, while weakened by his assault in 1927, had remained a potent force. While Chiang had managed to weaken the city-based Shanghai communists, many others, most notably Mao Zedong in southeastern China, had managed to establish communist strongholds far beyond *GMD* control.

Chiang Kai-shek then made the poorest of choices. He decided to concentrate his energies on dealing with the Chinese communists rather than the Japanese invaders. That decision would eventually put into question whether the *GMD* really had any right to call itself the "Nationalists." His primary opponent, Mao Zedong, himself both a nationalist and committed communist, was often alienated from the leadership of the Chinese communist party; it often saw him as less orthodox in his ideological outlook. But these differences were hardly significant to the *Guomindang* which set out in the early 1930s to destroy the Chinese communist base known as the Jiangxi Soviet.

General Chiang Kai-shek

After long and difficult campaigns—the communist resistance was initially very effective—the communists were forced by overwhelming *Guomindang* military pressures to evacuate their base areas in Central and South China. Eventually , after a long dramatic trek of thousands of miles and extraordinary hardships later known as the "Long March", the temporarily defeated Chinese communists took refuge in the remote and desolate regions of Northwest China. During the march, after a crucial meeting at Zhunyi, Mao Zedong at last emerged as the leader of the Chinese communists, a position he would not relinquish until his death in 1976. While Chiang Kai-shek may have felt some satisfaction with the weakening of the communists, he had more pressing pressures to the north.

World War II

By late 1936 in the midst of yet another effort to completely destroy the Chinese communists, Chiang was kidnaped by his own troops who were angry about his preoccupation with the communists in the midst of the imminent Japanese threat. After a dramatic episode that came close to bringing China to civil war, the *Guomindang* and Chinese communists made yet another alliance. From Mao's perspective and that of many patriotic Chinese, it was absurd for Chinese to fight in the interior while Japan pressed forward in the northeastern part of the country. Moreover, Russia's Stalin had been urging the communists to enter into another alliance with the *Guomindang* in order to resist the invaders. Mao probably saw an opportunity not only to resist the Japanese, but to ultimately overthrow the Nationalists after they had been weakened by the enemy.

The new alliance came none too soon, for Japanese forces invaded eastern China in 1937 and started an assault of extraordinary brutality that at times foreshadowed later Nazi acts in Eastern Europe. The Japanese conquered the prosperous coastal regions of China, depriving the *Guomindang* of its major economic and political bases. Driven into the hills and mountains of southwest China, it became even more conservative and subject to corruption than before. Under Japanese control, cities like Nanjing, the Nationalist's capital, experienced a horror of mass murder and rape that went on for weeks. To the north, Japanese doctors would eventually establish a medical experimentation center that carried out live vivisections on hapless Chinese captives. Though less well known than the Nazi brutalities, they left a legacy of bitterness between China and Japan that still exists.

The expansion of the communists from that time forth was actually at the expense not only of the Japanese but also of the *Guomindang*. Inflation and weakness also sapped the strength of the Nationalists, enabling the Japanese to inflict further heavy defeats on it as late as 1944. Nevertheless, the Japanese were unable to prevent the communists, more skilled in the art of guerrilla warfare than the Nationalists, from infiltrating and setting up base areas within territory that was supposed to be Japanese. Partly in retaliation for this resistance, the Japanese committed more atrocities against the Chinese people in the occupied areas, driving many into sympathy with the communists and thus assisting them to seize political control on an anti-Japanese, more than an anti-*Guomindang*, platform.

The Struggle for Power: Nationalists and Communists

Increasing numbers of Japanese soldiers were withdrawn from China starting in 1943 because of the defeats that were being suffered in the Pacific war. This permitted the communists to expand rapidly, so that by the end of the war they controlled nineteen base areas, in various parts of China, principally in the North and Northwest.

The elimination of Japanese troops from China at the end of the war brought a frantic flurry of political and military activity by both the *Guomindang* and the communists. In the immediate period after the war the U.S. was the major political power in the Pacific area and it attempted to bring about some sort of settlement between these two competing Chinese parties. The talks though, conducted under the encouragement of U.S. General George C. Marshall, special envoy of President Truman, completely broke down in 1946 because neither side had any real desire for an agreement. Each preferred a trial of armed strength. Neither had any interest in sharing China's future with the other.

Unfortunately for the *Guomindang*, the Nationalists, nominally more powerful, were plagued by their inability to deal with China's most serious problems: inflation, corruption and loss of political unity. The military leadership also employed very poor tactics against the communists, especially in the battle over Manchuria, and soon found themselves losing control over the mainland.

By the end of 1949 the *Guomindang* was driven to the island of Taiwan. The Chinese communists under Mao then controlled all of mainland China except for Tibet which

Mao Zedong (Mao Tse-tung) in 1945

had been outside Beijing's control since the collapse of the Qing. They proclaimed the People's Republic of China and reestablished the Chinese capital at Beijing.

The next year the soldiers of the People's Liberation Army invaded Tibet. Although there was some initial resistance, the "roof of the world" was brought under Chinese control again; the Dalai Lama, spiritual leader of the Tibetans, who also was vested with rather wide governing powers, was soon made a figurehead. He eventually fled Tibet in 1959 after an unsuccessful uprising against the Chinese in the eastern part of the region.

The "People's Liberation Army" brought the new regime to power, and it remained important as a defense against possible

enemies, both internal and external. The *Chinese Communist Party* however was the real instrument behind Mao and his regime; its members held and now hold all important public offices. It has proven the only political force since the Manchus that has demonstrated itself able to hold China together. For the first quarter century of the People's Republic's existence, Mao Zedong played an overpowering role. He made himself into a cult–like father figure whom all Chinese, especially the youth, were taught to worship to a degree that would have created envy in the hearts of previous emperors.

Building a New China

The team of Mao, the *Chinese Communist Party (CCP)* and the army, held together quite successfully through the late 1950s and achieved results which were quite impressive considering how devastated the country was after generations of invasion and civil war. The majority of the people regarded the regime as the only hope of escape from the long nightmare of civil and foreign war, chaos and abject poverty, and gave it overwhelming support. Initially following the Soviet model of development, China's new leaders restored the defunct economy and launched an impressive program of heavy industrialization with Russian technical assistance and equipment. After igniting a frequently violent purge against the rural landowning classes, small plots of farmland were distributed to the peasants and then as the years went on collectivized. The lives of women were improved with the passage in 1950 of a new marriage and divorce law that gave women more marital and property rights.

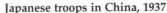

Japanese troops in China, 1937

China

Silk tapestry B. R. Graham

His Holiness The Dalai Lama of Tibet

In short, China progressed from war-inflicted chaos toward a centralized, autocratic and rationally administered state. Traditional Chinese culture and society were forcibly changed in directions desired by the communists with widespread, fundamental and seemingly impossible effects. By 1956 the regime apparently felt confident enough to encourage the masses to voice their opinions on the many changes the *CCP* had brought about. "Let a hundred Flowers Bloom," Mao, the supreme leader, proclaimed though apparently what the *CCP's* leadership heard was not to their liking—by 1957 a cruel repression known as the "Anti–rightist Campaign" had commenced which was to destroy the careers of millions of Chinese intellectuals and others who had been naive enough to actually speak out.

In foreign relations, the Chinese regime initially established a close alliance with the Soviet Union, still led by the aging Stalin. Doing so was not without its difficulties. The Soviet dictator would clearly have preferred a Chinese leadership more servile to Moscow and had even made Mao wait three days in Moscow before receiving him in November of 1949! Nevertheless the tie was formalized into a thirty year treaty of friendship. China also entered into diplomatic relations with all communist countries and with a number of neutral and Western nations. The United States, which had become protector of the Nationalists on Taiwan, refused to recognize Mao's government. With only slight success, the Chinese communists initially tried to promote revolutions elsewhere in Asia, but eventually retreated from this policy somewhat in order to be in a better position to cultivate the friendship of the neutral Asian nations.

The Korean War

Although the Chinese leadership may have wished to concentrate on solidifying their control over China in their first years of power, international developments became impossible to ignore. In June of 1950, the North Koreans, apparently with Soviet support, invaded South Korea with the goal of unifying the entire peninsula under their leadership.

Although the immediate Chinese reaction was somewhat restrained, the American decision to intervene through the United Nations aroused their ire. More to the point, after the American troops successfully drove the North Koreans back across the 38th Parallel demarcation line, they decided to invade North Korea with little thought to the consequences of moving toward the Chinese border. (see Korea section)

From the Chinese perspective, the American troops (the apparent allies of their enemies the Chinese Nationalists) were pushing toward their borders and ignoring Beijing's warning that they would intervene if the Americans continued north. Unfortunately, the American forces *did* continue north and the Chinese, urged on and with the support of the Soviets, committed massive numbers of "volunteers" to stop the Americans and to the aid the besieged North Korean communist government. Whatever possibilities might have existed for a successful relationship between Washington and Beijing was destroyed in the explosion that followed and killed so many Americans, Chinese, and Koreans over the next few years. By July of 1953 an armistice was signed dividing the peninsula between the North Koreans and their communist allies in the north and the South Koreans and their American allies to the south. U.S. forces have remained in South Korea ever since.

The "Great Leap Forward"

By the mid–1950s, the Chinese leadership had at last successfully stabilized the economy and begun the long effort to recover from so many decades of war and civil war. The Soviet model of a command economy with its five year planning models was being used and significant progress was made.

But Mao wanted more; he wanted China to literally leap forward toward a more industrialized and socialized future, not at some distant point in the future but *immediately* with one giant effort of the Chinese people united in the endeavor. By 1958, new and far more ambitious plans were announced for the country. Mao declared that China should catch up with industrialized England within 15 years.

The "Great Leap Forward" as it was known was to have two fundamental aspects, one industrial, one social. Toward the first, enormous industrial goals were announced. Each work unit was, among other things, expected to create "backyard furnaces" to boost iron production. Every industry was expected to dramatically increase its output of goods using an emphasis less on industrial know–how than the cumulative willpower of the energized population.

On the "communitarian/socialist" side Mao's planners herded people into what would become known as "People's Communes," which would dominate almost every aspect of their lives from child care to the use of their labor. Moving far past the Soviet model of state farms and limited private plots, the peasants were now told to live in completely egalitarian communities where there was literally no room for individual family initiative (or privacy). Even such mundane activities as growing a pig and raising it for market were branded "capitalist" and made impossible to carry out.

Most of these programs were terrible failures. Industrial production collapsed. The famous "backyard furnaces" often produced completely useless materials. The harvest revenues plummeted horrendously. Amidst the propagandistic circus of claims and boasts, a very real food disaster developed which turned into an enormous famine. Millions of people died in the following years due to this man-made disaster.

Late in the decade, policy differences and political tensions began to appear between the aging Mao and some of his colleagues who were more pragmatic than he and obviously worried about the suffering brought on by the failures of the Great Leap Forward. Few though were willing to challenge the Great Leader openly. Moreover, problems with their enormous socialist neighbor were as well beginning to develop.

Relations with the Soviets

By the late 1950s, relations with the Soviet Union, the principal source of economic and military aid, were becoming severely strained. The Soviet leader Khrushchev cut off all aid in 1960. Actually a clash between Mao and Nikita Khrushchev was probably inevitable—the former regarded the younger Khrushchev as an upstart and at the same time Khrushchev, blessed with an over abundance of ego, considered Mao a fanatic and an adventurer. China's enthusiasm for considering itself, rather than Moscow, the leader of their world revolutionary movements hardly endeared it to the Soviet Union either.

Soon growing Chinese political pressures on the Soviet Union, calculated to prove the correctness of Mao's brand of communism and the error of the Soviet "deviation," produced serious and fundamental tensions not only between the Soviets and the Chinese, but within the entire communist world. Over these years relations with the Soviets, never close, would continue to deteriorate until by 1956 they seemed in competition for leadership of the communist world.

In the summer of 1958, Mao engaged in another unsuccessful gesture—the shelling of the islands of Quemoy and Matsu, controlled by the Nationalists, close to mainland China in the Taiwan straits. Whatever his original intentions had been, nothing more than an artillery and air–power duel occurred, notwithstanding the alarm of other nations because of the possibility of

a Chinese–U.S. confrontation. The Soviet Union's unwillingness to be supportive during the crises, and later when tensions developed with India, further alienated Beijing's leadership from Moscow.

The Soviet Union was accused of being as great if not greater political enemy than the United States. The task of struggling against the supposed imperialistic designs of the U.S. was in effect assigned to other revolutionary movements in Asia, Africa and Latin America.

The revolutionary zeal of the Chinese, and their tendency to urge radical and nationalistic movements to greater tasks than were possible, with endless quantities of advice and of Mao's "thoughts," coupled with quantities of arms, did not produce the desired results. A number of moderate nationalist and socialist leaders of Asia and Africa became rapidly aware of the not yet serious threat, and took steps to expel Chinese agents. There were especially serious setbacks in Indonesia and in sub–Sahara Africa, which had seemed promising to the Chinese in the years 1963–1965. After the fall in 1964 of Khrushchev, who had handled the revolutionary impatience of the Chinese rather clumsily, his more practical successors offered China a limited agreement, which was spurned by Mao. With this refusal, Mao worsened his relations with some of his critics at home and abroad who wanted a less antagonistic attitude toward Russia.

By the early 1960s, tensions within China's leadership had become more obvious. Mao had withstood the direct criticism of former allies like Peng Dehuai regarding the disasters caused by the Great Leap Forward. But by the early 1960s his influence over events within China was being lost to the more pragmatic bureaucratic leadership of the *Chinese Communist Party,* most notably individuals like Liu Shaoqi and Deng Xiaoping. For the aging leader Mao Zedong, this development was completely unacceptable.

The Great Proletarian Cultural Revolution

By the last half of 1965, Mao became convinced that the time had come to silence his critics within the party. Thus began another mass campaign: the "Great Proletarian Cultural Revolution." His first obstacle, the reluctant municipal boss of Beijing, Peng Zhen, was soon overthrown by a combination of political pressures and military threats. Mao then proceeded to call on the revolutionary young people, organized into "Red Guards" to root out his enemies. Moreover, in his struggle with the leadership of the *Chinese Communist Party,* Mao also had the support of Lin

Biao, the commander of the People's Liberation Army. The youthful Red Guards attacked and terrorized Mao's real and imagined opponents in the universities, in the party structure and anywhere else they were thought to be found.

The victims ranged from party officials to teachers and other professionals in almost all fields from medicine to religion. Almost anyone the young enthusiasts could accuse of being insufficiently Maoist was in danger. The students created their own kangaroo courts to punish their victims and broke into homes looking for anything considered counter-revolutionary. Those found with materials ranging from books by Confucius to Western writings, even possession of materials written by the now purged former leadership of the *Communist Party,* could cause an individual serious problems.

Throughout the country, former officials and others who had held authority previously were beaten and humiliated as they

Harvesting in a *People's Commune*

were marched through the streets wearing banners proclaiming their supposed guilt. The lives of countless millions, were affected by the malicious chaos of the era.

The struggle was as much an assault on the full heritage of Chinese tradition as it was against Mao's enemies. Throughout the country the "Red Guards," aroused as they were against almost any object connected to China's imperial past, destroyed or defaced materials of enormous beauty. Practitioners of traditional arts, from Buddhist monks to magicians and fortune tellers, were hounded from their professions.

Eventually even central power began to break down in many parts of the country as Mao's "Cultural Revolution" went far beyond what even he had envisioned. By early 1967, it was necessary for Mao to urge the army to intervene in order to prevent chaos and yet to keep the Cultural

China

Mao Zedong in 1966   A/World Wide Photos

Revolution moving. The army quickly discovered that these two tasks were inconsistent and increasingly began to emphasize the restoration of order in place of the disorder created by the unruly Red Guards. In 1967, Mao was brought, willingly or unwillingly, to endorse a turn towards a more conservative line. After that time, the impact of the Cultural Revolution on everyday life lessened. During 1968 the army acquired more and more local power, and with Beijing's consent, it forcibly suppressed the Red Guard movement. The young Red Guards were banished to the countryside to "educate" themselves among the peasants.

Though how much they actually "learned" is less certain, what is clear is that a huge percentage of the young people of that era lost their opportunity for higher education and a better life. If many of their older contemporaries, those they had been persecuting, were able, once calm was restored, to resume their former lives, that was not true of many of these youth who were in many ways the real victims of the Cultural Revolution. Not only were they as individuals to lose, but China itself ultimately lost out on the professional skills they would have potentially made available to build a new, more modern China.

The Vietnam Wars

While China itself was going through the chaos of the Cultural Revolution, just to the south one of the longest struggles of the twentieth century, the Vietnam war, was entering an especially critical stage. (See the Vietnam section). For China, despite the eons of tension and ambivalence which separated the Chinese and Vietnamese, there was no question but that Beijing would support North Vietnam in its struggles against the Americans during the

Vietnam War (approximately 1965–1975 for the American stage). But here, unlike in Korea, China did not play a major role.

China sent some arms and personnel to North Vietnam, cooperated for a time in transshipping Soviet weapons by rail to it and sent railway engineering units to help keep the main Vietnamese railway lines open in spite of American bombardment. After the American withdrawal in 1973, China stepped up its flow of arms to Hanoi and in this way contributed significantly to the rapid fall of South Vietnam in the spring of 1975.

But by that time, however, Hanoi had already begun to show signs of abandoning its neutrality in the Sino–Soviet disputes, and was "tilting" toward Moscow. By 1977 Vietnam was involved in a border war with Cambodia, where the pro–Chinese rather than the pro–Vietnamese wing of the Khmer Rouge (the Cambodian communist movement) had come to power in 1975. When China began in 1978 to put pressure on Vietnam in support of Cambodia, Hanoi expelled several hundred thousand "boat people," many of them of Chinese ancestry, and moved still closer to Moscow. At the end of 1978, Vietnam invaded Cambodia and installed a puppet government in Phnom Penh. Accordingly, China then experienced its own Vietnam War for a time by invading Vietnam briefly in February–March 1979 with the announced purpose of teaching Hanoi a lesson.

The lesson though did not take. Vietnamese forces did far better than expected against those of their giant neighbor and relations were tense for decades. And not surprisingly, despite the alliances of the war, centuries of animosity that existed between China and Vietnam were revived.

Tensions have continued for years in the vicinity of their common border, as well as in naval rivalry in the South China Sea. Nevertheless, the collapse of the Soviet Union eventually led to a slight defrosting of relations between China and Vietnam.

A Basic Shift in 1971–2

The military clash along the Sino–Soviet border in early 1969, which turned out badly for the Chinese, eventually led to some astonishing shifts in East Asian politics. Given the reality that China was finding itself "squeezed" between two different antagonists, the jealous Soviets to the north, and the Americans struggling against communism in Vietnam, many in China felt it was time to rethink China's international position. A moderate coalition, led by Premier Zhou Enlai and some of the military, tried to restore a greater degree of domestic stability and more workable foreign relations.

Zhou felt it advisable, after several months of Soviet threats, to enter into negotiations on border problems and related matters, and to downgrade disputes concerning communist theory. Nevertheless, by the end of 1970, it appeared that the negotiations had resulted in a deadlock.

Internal politics also played a role in bringing about the new international alignment when Lin Biao, the long–time leader of the contentious *PLA*, who had supported improved Sino–Soviet relations, conspired against Mao. He was eventually killed in a 1971 abortive plan to flee the country. The way was clear to open relations with the United States, a relationship many in the Chinese leadership hoped would serve as a balance to the potential threats posed by the Soviet Union.

To the surprise of the Americans, China extended in 1971 an invitation to an American ping pong team to visit. This was quickly followed by a visit by Dr. Henry Kissinger in July 1971 and later by President Nixon in 1972. For the Americans, of course, better relations with Beijing offered the possibility of finding a new tool to end their frustrating involvement in Vietnam. Beijing's help did eventually prove significant in developing the treaties which allowed for the United States to withdraw, even though that aid hardly affected the ultimate outcome of the Vietnam war itself. For, despite the hopes of many, by 1975 Vietnam was again united but under the direction of Hanoi.

Nevertheless, American ties to China continued to improve and by 1978 President Carter of the United States formalized diplomatic relations with Beijing. At the same time, the United States terminated its formal diplomatic relations and defense treaty with the *Republic of China* on Taiwan. Other important ties, however, remained intact and the U.S. continued to sell arms to Taiwan and to offer considerable "moral support." Once Beijing and Washington began to improve their relations Taiwan's international position began to deteriorate. In a humiliating move, Nationalist China was expelled from the United Nations and the People's Republic of China became the official representative of China at that organization.

The Emergence of Deng Xiaoping

In the mid 1970s an upsurge of political ferment reflected radical dissatisfaction, especially from the individuals eventually known as the "Gang of Four" which included Madame Mao, Jiang Qing, as its most prominent representative. They were clearly dissatisfied with Premier Zhou Enlai's more moderate policies, desiring another dose of Mao's sloganeering agitation. In spite of this, Zhou, a highly skilled and educated person, though suffering from cancer, remained in power until his death, counterbalancing the influence of the waning Mao, who though physically frail was still perceived as supporting, or at least protecting, the more radical Maoists.

Zhou Enlai was still effectively in charge, though in a hospital, possibly hoping that an early demise on his own part would not give the radicals an opening to resume their initiatives. Whatever his goals, Zhou died in January of 1976 more than ten months before Mao Zedong passed away. The timing appeared to allow Madame Mao and her radical allies their opportunity to come to full power at last.

The death of Zhou Enlai deprived the world of one of its most astute statesmen and placed the future of the moderates in Beijing in jeopardy for a time. Vice Premier Deng Xiaoping, Zhou's main assistant since 1973, had badly antagonized the Maoist radicals and did not remain in office long; he was forced out by April, presumably with Mao's approval. The new premier announced at that time, however, was not formally a radical, but a compromise choice, Hua Guofeng, whose record suggested a closer affinity with the moderates than the radicals.

A major earthquake in July 1976 tightened the political ties between Hua and the army, which handled most of the relief work. Given the trauma and demands required to recover, it was apparent that China needed a breathing spell away from the political bickering of the communist era.

Frail, senile and moribund, Mao died in September 1976. His death removed the main shield of the leading radicals, including his widow, Jiang Qing. They were purged by Hua a month later. The so-called "Gang of Four" soon came to be seen as central symbols of the suffering experienced by so many during the previous decade's Cultural Revolution. After their purge, propaganda against them continued unabated.

Deng Xiaoping, the leader of the more pragmatic communist officials was "rehabilitated" and soon became the most powerful man in the country. Deng's general approach could not be more in contrast to Mao Zedong, his long-time leader. Mao had been committed to an ideological approach to governing that often excluded basic realities, thus making possible movements like the "Great Leap Forward." In dramatic contrast, Deng was more concerned about emphasizing a pragmatic approach to issues, preferably devoid of ideology. And it was with that approach that he set about, in what in hindsight turned out to be an incredibly successful effort, to build a new China.

Building a New China

Under Deng Xiaoping's leadership China underwent an extraordinary series of changes almost unprecedented in Chinese history. Famous for his comment that "it did not matter if a cat were black or white, as long as it caught mice," Deng, while committed to the political power of the *Chinese Communist Party* was first and foremost a pragmatist. Early on he forced the retirement of Premier Hua Guofeng. He ultimately was replaced by Hu Yuobang. Deng then successfully went forward with the trial of the "Gang of Four," thus neutralizing radical opposition, some of which was within the army, making it easier to move against the ideas and policies they and Mao had represented.

The purge of radicals continued in both the party and the bureaucracy during the early 1980s. In 1985, 64 members of the Central Committee "resigned" under pressure from Deng. Zhao Ziyang was named General Secretary of the party in 1987, replacing Hu Yuobang. Eventually, he in turn, after the crises of Tiananmen Square, was replaced by the present president, Jiang Zemin, in 1989.

Deng was also the driving force behind significant agricultural reforms during the 1980s, which led to partial decollectivization. In 1984, control over industry was eased, giving local managers more authority. Prices were set at the local instead of the national level (at least in theory), and food and housing subsidies were reduced for urban dwellers. In 1985, the economy grew by 15%. That astounding leap in GNP would begin a pattern of growth that has continued well into the 1990s.

Unfortunately, inflation and corruption also exploded. Attempts by more conservative forces to reign in the freer economic environment were not successful. Deng also took a more "open" approach toward the outside world. Relations with the U.S. improved after the issue of American arms sales to Taiwan was aired in 1982. A cautious move to improve relations with the Soviet Union was also undertaken.

In 1987, the Thirteenth Party Congress signed off on a policy of moderate political and economic reform. Deng held on to most of his authority. But in 1988, probably as a reaction to rapid uncontrolled growth in the south, a two year suspension of further price reforms was enacted.

1989—Tiananmen Square

The death of Hu Yaobang, once considered the likely successor to Deng, in April 1989, ignited demonstrations by students who had long idolized him as a true reformer. By early May they had turned out by the hundreds of thousands in the larger cities, particularly Beijing, waving banners with statements unheard of in China: "Down with Corruption! . . . Long Live Democracy! . . . Press Freedom!" . . . "Down With Rule By Men, Long Live The Rule Of Law!" A level of student and public activism emerged that had not been seen since the most heady days of the 1919 May Fourth Movement seventy years before.

Tiananmen Square was literally taken over by a huge encampment of protesting students some of whom gained even more support by going on a hunger strike to demonstrate their commitment. Not only students but workers in cities throughout China became involved and their demands ranged from moderate calls for further democratization in China to protests against political and economic corruption. A shaken *Communist Party* leader, Zhao Ziyang, mingled with the student demonstrators and made some vague concessions, but was swept aside by Deng Xiaoping and the more conservative Premier Li Peng.

There were clearly conflicting opinions among the leadership on just how to deal with the protesters. Moreover, the leadership itself appeared divided on larger issues of policy regarding the economy. Should it continue its rapid growth or reign in the increasingly open economy toward a more party–dominated one? Who would win in the leadership struggle thus had clear ramifications for China's entire economic future as well. But the more immediate crisis was in the streets and for the moment, the hardliners both political and economic were in the ascendance. For weeks, during a period of leadership indecision complicated by the visit of the Soviet leader Mikhail Gorbachev, the crisis grew and the humiliation of the government leaders along with it.

Suddenly on June 4th tens of thousands of well–armed troops smashed their way through Beijing to the heart of the city,

President Nixon contemplates the Great Wall, 1972

AP/World Wide Photos

China

Tiananmen Square. The tanks crushed many in their path; estimates of those killed and wounded were in the thousands. There were reports of soldiers firing indiscriminately into the crowds, invading hospitals to yank out life–support systems of the wounded, attacking doctors and engaging in other violent acts. The hardliners had won, at least for the time being.

The massacre in Beijing was followed by a massive nationwide campaign of political repression involving many arrests. This evoked outrage abroad and some limited, largely temporary, sanctions on the part of China's major trading partners, which had little effect on the hardliners dominant in Beijing.

Parallel with this political crackdown, Deng Xiaoping's economic reform program went into reverse. In fact, some have surmised that the economic conservatives among the leadership had used the confrontation for their own ends, to return to a more Soviet style command economy at almost the same time that the Soviet Union was unraveling. Central control over the economy was strengthened, prices were more closely controlled and there was even talk of the "voluntary" recollectivization of agriculture.

Whatever senior leader Deng's commitment to stopping the political challenge and chaos of the streets in 1989 had been, he himself clearly remained convinced that China needed more, not less, economic freedoms. Thus in early 1992, Deng Xiaoping and his supporters prevailed over conservatives to reinvigorate the economic reforms again. The private sector received encouragement and the free market concept was legitimized in the Constitution in 1993. The "open" policy toward the outside world remained in effect, and foreign investment continued to flow in, from the United States as well as from other sources.

In 1990, Beijing tried to improve its international image by taking a moderate public position on the Cambodian and Kuwait crises. It undid much of this, however, by taking advantage of the distraction created by the war in the Persian Gulf to sentence a number of political prisoners accused of involvement in the 1989 demonstrations. That policy of greater international economic involvement, alongside a continuing internal repression of those who would challenge the regime, has continued throughout the 1990s.

Although opposition continued to be sternly repressed, China in the early 1990s experienced one change with important political possibilities. The provinces were gaining in autonomy and authority at the expense of the center. This was especially true of the comparatively prosperous and dynamic provinces along the coast. Nevertheless political discontent in China was prevented from assuming serious proportions partly by the state of the economy, which was doing well in both the private and cooperative sectors although poorly in state–directed enterprises.

The Death of Deng Xiaoping

After years of waiting, the world heard of the news of Deng Xiaoping's death in February 1997. While he had not been influential in decision–making for years, many had waited for word of his death with trepidation. After all, more than once before, the death of a senior leader had set off dramatic developments in the People's Republic. In 1976, both the early death of Zhou Enlai in January and Mao's death in October had set off dramatic changes in the leadership of the country. Indeed, it was only with Mao's death that the forces were released that brought Deng Xiaoping to supreme power. And more recently, the death of the former party Chairman Hu Yaobang, had set off the chain of events that eventually brought on the Tiananmen Crisis of June 1989. But in the first weeks after Deng's death it appeared that nothing of the sort was likely to occur this time around.

Chief among the differences was the very success Deng had brought about. When Deng first emerged in real power in the late 1970s he led a weak China with a military that would soon embarrass itself in the expedition against Vietnam, one which hardly made a dent on the international, political or economic scene. A generation later the China of Deng has been drastically transformed.

In 1978 when Deng's authority began to be significant, Chinese exports to the world were U.S. $9.8 billion, by 1995 they were U.S. $149 billion! Steel production had tripled and urban Chinese lived increasingly in cities that often resembled huge construction sites which were the product of a building boom. More than a decade of double digit growth rates had transformed China. Even the World Bank estimates that the number of people living in poverty had been cut by two thirds!

Thus by the time Deng died an enormous percentage of Chinese felt invested in the new changes. And while there were clear differences between some of the top leaders, the sort of issues that had divided the leadership in 1976 and for a time in 1989 seemed much milder. With even the conservative military making billions from their role in the surging economy there was clearly no turning back from the world that Deng had built. China would be an involved player in the world community. Only the details needed to be worked out. The dramatic and sometimes deadly struggle between the Maoists and the Pragmatists that had characterized aspects of the earlier Mao years seemed to have passed. There was far more general agreement on the new China that Deng had set in motion.

Nevertheless, many in the Western news media, aware of developments which had occurred in the aftermath of the death of other preeminent leaders, had

May 21, 1989: *A People's Liberation Army* convoy is engulfed by demonstrators in Tiananmen Square, Beijing. AP Wide World Photo

spoken of potential dramas after Deng's death, but long time observers generally agreed that the lines of succession seemed to have already been in place.

By Deng's death, Jiang Zemin was already well positioned to establish himself as the new dominant figure. His prominent role during the July 1997 Hong Kong transition and later his leadership at that fall's 15th congress of the Chinese Communist Party only confirmed his power. Especially important was his ability to eliminate his principal rival, Qiao Shi, from power during the personnel changes that occurred during the party congress. Though Jiang might never attain the authority of his predecessors Mao and Deng, he nevertheless has certainly solidified his authority.

Long-time premier Li Peng's term in office came up in early 1998 and the premier, never popular either within China or abroad, departed the premier's office to take up a new position as the head of the National People's Congress. Then as expected, Zhu Rongji, the respected economics expert who has been in charge of the economy in recent years was picked to replace the departing Li Peng.

Both leaders, Jiang and the new premier, Zhu Rongji, are clearly committed to continuing the general lines of reform begun by Deng Xiaoping, but they now face a China much different from that Deng led. China is far more integrated into the world economy. And internally, more centers of authority have emerged to perhaps question the party.

The NPC or National People's Congress is no longer the rubber stamp it once was. Under the leadership of the departed Qiao Shi, it had become more and more effective in occasionally challenging the *Communist Party* and in pushing for an enhancement of the rule of law. In 1995, it successfully opposed changes in the education system and banking reform sponsored by party leaders. The body has also become the locus for increasingly popular expressions of opposition to government policies. Congress members are free to introduce their own legislative bills, and members have even been willing to publicly oppose the government on matters as sensitive as politburo nominations. Public polling in recent years has shown that more and more citizens view the NPC as an important institution they can address their complaints to—certainly a new development in a society so long exclusively dominated by the Chinese *Communist Party* and its powerful leaders. Whether the role of the People's Congress will continue to grow under the leadership of the more conservative Li Peng is less certain.

At the local level it is now more possible for non-party members to hold important positions of influence, something that would have been practically impossible in the past. Even more interesting has been the decision to allow local elections and to even invite former President Jimmy Carter to serve as an election poll watcher. Still, the Chinese *Communist Party* has made it clear it intends to remain in ultimate control. Nevertheless, it has been willing to allow extraordinary freedoms in the social and economic arenas and on the local level even greater political freedoms.

But retaining control does not preclude seeking competence over ideological purity or party cronyism. It looks like China plans to return to some of the roots of its own civilization for help in recruiting qualified personnel. Since 1994, China has moved to return to the time honored system of examinations to recruit candidates for gov-

Deng Xiaoping
(pronounced *Dung Shou–ping*)

ernment jobs. High officials have been quoted as saying that China hopes to abolish the current system of appointment by seniority, personal recommendation or degrees with a more regularized examination for all potential civil servants.

As we move into the twenty-first century the People's Republic is not simply going to proceed on the path Deng laid out a generation ago. Deng Xiaoping was trying to "jump start" an economy that had been artificially wounded by impractical economic leadership. His goal was to reinvigorate that economy through internal reforms and an external opening to the world. But those initial goals were accomplished and his heirs, especially Jiang Zemin, are committed to refining the economic and social message that dominated Deng's years. Given the current weakness of communism as an especially important or unifying message, Jiang has embarked

upon recent efforts to promote what he calls a new spiritual civilization which combines elements of economic growth with both communitarian and nationalist elements. Jiang has even been heard speaking positively of Confucianism, whose memory had become so defamed during the height of the revolutionary era.

But is a greater opening toward democracy on the national level likely? At this point it seems not at all probable. In fact, President Jiang's image of "spiritual civilization" seems to indicate even a lessening of some freedoms. Word has gone out to journalists and others to emphasize support of patriotism and the *Communist Party*. If Beijing is influenced by any outside models at all, it is probably the example set by people like Lee Kuan Yew of Singapore who has been one of the most influential spokesmen for an Asian vision of political and economic governance and a frequent visitor to China.

More than likely the immediate future will be dominated by an economically precarious China led by a Communist Party still unwilling to accept challenges to its leadership. Thus day to day developments will have to be understood in the context of an evolving China that is quite unevenly moving toward a more open future. For example, throughout the last few years the government continued to give mixed signals on its attitude toward reform. On the one hand a new more open attitude evolved for a time which allowed for the publication and discussion of quite radical political ideas. And the government itself experimented with extending the village level elections to the district level. On the other hand those that challenged Beijing—however subtly—felt its wrath. This was demonstrated by the harsh sentences handed down in late 1998 to several dissidents for attempting to organize a new party called the *China Democracy Party*.

Even more dramatically the government moved in 1999 against those who had involved themselves in spiritual activities that seemed beyond official control. Most prominently was the official banning and persecution of members of the Falun Gong, a quasi-religious movement which practices physical and meditative activities and has become enormously popular in recent years. In fact, the movement was so popular that the authorities, nervous about a mass movement able to attract such support and not unmindful of how dangerous such movements had been in earlier eras, set out to brutally suppress Falun Gong. In the months since, thousands of Falun Gong followers have been arrested and many of its leaders given long prison sentences for having played a role, not in an organization that had formally challenged the authority of the state, but apparently for having tak-

China

Deng Xiaoping with the Reagans, Beijing 1984

en part in a movement that might have *potentially* done so!

Still, in the long run there is certainly reason to hope for a more open China. After all, an increasingly educated and sophisticated society has emerged, one where more of the institutions of civil society, of systems of law and divergent leadership are emerging.

Other issues and areas to watch will be developments in Western China, in Tibet and especially in Xinjiang where outbreaks against Chinese rule have resulted in riots and then harsh retribution by Chinese officials. In fact, there is a good chance that developments in Western China could eventually prove far more challenging for Beijing than Tibet has ever been. Additionally, the relatively large labor unrest already apparent is likely to grow as tensions mount over the growth in unemployment associated with reforms of the State Enterprises. Understandably the millions of workers now being laid off by the state-owned enterprises are adding to the potential and reality for social tension.

The Rise of Shanghai

In recent years there have been other important changes at or near the top which may affect the future direction of the country. In September 1994, at the fourth plenum of the Fourteenth Central Committee, Huang Ju became a member of the Politburo, the highest major decision body in the Communist party. He is now the fourth member of the Politburo from Shanghai. The others are Jiang Zemin, Zhu Rongji, (the president and prime minister respectively) and Wu Bangguo.

The four have either served as mayor or party secretary for Shanghai. In addition, several other Politburo members have their roots in Shanghai. Even the new Chinese governor of Hong Kong, Tung Chee Hwa has origins in Shanghai and speaks the local dialect! This suggests that at a

minimum the interests of that region will not be overlooked.

The enormous effort the government has put into building up Pudong, the new economic area just across the river from urban Shanghai, also indicates the central leadership's interest in the city as do the other major projects that have sprung up in recent years. Today, Shanghai is fast returning to its previous position as the preeminent city of the Chinese economy.

Foreign Relations of the People's Republic

In many ways the People's Republic has moved to play a more cooperative role internationally. They made offers to host the Olympics in the year 2000 as well as to serve as the site for the 1995 UN sponsored Fourth World Conference on Women, and a parallel conference of non-governmental organizations (NGO's). Unfortunately, the Olympic bid was ultimately unsuccessful and aroused unneeded tensions during the competition ultimately won by Sydney, Australia. The PRC was able to host the Second United Nation's Conference on Women. The meeting itself though aroused considerable controversy. Some of the advertised facilities were not ready. The NGO meeting was moved and some delegates were prevented by various means from attending.

It is also true however that China has entered a potentially more assertive period in its foreign relations. The PRC's economic progress has created conditions where the country's leaders feel it possible and appropriate for China to assume a higher profile internationally. In effect after more than a century of weakness, Beijing appears ready to assume its former place of significance in the world. Moreover, as mentioned previously, with the weakening of communism, nationalism remains the best means of unifying the Chinese people, something the central government needs to survive. Thus recent events have shown

they are quite willing to play the nationalist "card" to ensure their continuing legitimacy before the Chinese public.

The recent attempt by Japanese extremists to assert their control over the islands known in Chinese as the Diaoyus are a good example of the complexities of nationalism in this new era. Chinese from all walks of life and throughout the Chinese world literally from Hong Kong to Taiwan and the People's Republic were united in anger against these Japanese efforts. From Beijing's perspective, issues with such nationalist sentiment can be helpful as they continue to justify their leadership in the vacuum left by the weakening of communism. And of course, as the Asian economic crisis of the late 1990s impacts China the leadership no longer has the glowing reports of economic success to fall back upon, thus making nationalism an even more attractive unifying force. Similarly Beijing and the larger Chinese community were united in their protests against the attacks which Chinese Indonesians experienced during the unrest of the spring of 1998.

It was also clear recently that in many other ways China's new international connections had produced a more complicated foreign policy. During the winter of 1996–7 it found itself caught between its old ally North Korea and its new friend South Korea in a struggle over a senior North Korean official who had successfully sought asylum in the South's embassy in Beijing. Beijing obviously wanted to find a solution to the dilemma but it wasn't easy. In the end, ties to South Korea proved more influential and the new defector set off indirectly for Seoul.

The economic crisis which enveloped much of the region in the fall of 1997 also gave the People's Republic an opportunity to expand her influence. In contrast to the tensions in recent years over competing island claims, the economic crisis allowed Beijing to show its support for the region both by offering financial help and by making pledges not to undermine the region's recovery by devaluing her own currency. Given the anger some economic restructuring demands of the Western based International Monetary Fund was arousing in the region, the PRC's supportive attitude was no doubt much appreciated.

The fact that China ended the millennium with still reasonably impressive growth rates also helped expand her influence. Over the last few year's economic crises, China, at least compared to some of her neighbors, has often seemed an island of relative economic and political stability.

On a different front, relations with India became much more complicated over the last few years as India's new govern-

President Jiang Zemin

ment not only officially announced its new status as a nuclear power by setting off a series of underground nuclear tests but did so while citing tensions with China as one of the reasons to do so. Not surprisingly that outraged Beijing and played a role in its willingness to work with Washington to try to avoid a nuclear arms race in South Asia.

Within the United Nations China also played an important role as tensions mounted during the spring of 1998 over Iraq's unwillingness to allow continued weapons inspections. The PRC worked closely with other security council members like France and Russia to attempt to resolve the crisis peacefully though these efforts were not always appreciated in Washington. Clearly, China opposed NATO'S violent intervention in Kosovo. On the other hand Beijing was not absolutely against intervention in the internal affairs of other nations. When the United Nations later decided in mid 1999, with the permission of Indonesia, to send a force to East Timor China cooperated by sending a team of Chinese policemen to help.

United States–Chinese Relations

A significant part of China's foreign policy in recent years has centered on resolving issues with the United States. Unfortunately, relations continue to be complicated and often tense. During the early Clinton administration, the United States government's policy was geared toward exacting human rights concessions from China before economic relations could progress. This included holding up most favored nations (MFN) status for China. In May 1994 however, the policy was

modified. Despite his early campaign statements, President Clinton changed his approach to one of "comprehensive engagement" in fact, assuming the same approach to China as the previous Bush Administration.

President Clinton had come to understand that the People's Republic was simply too large and too important economically and diplomatically to withdraw from. Far too many economic and geopolitical issues required Beijing's cooperation. China was critical to dealing with issues ranging from North Korea's nuclear aspirations to progress on nuclear non-proliferation to working within the United Nation's Security Council where China holds a permanent veto.

Still, even as the United States slowly recognized the reality of China's growing strength, many Americans felt compelled to warn of an evolving Sino-American antagonism and to believe that China's growth fundamentally threatened the United States. Not surprisingly, the Chinese side had plenty of critics of the Americans. Especially important was the sense by many in China that the Americans were frequently unwilling to treat them with the respect and equality their size and accomplishments have earned them. The Chinese were also particularly aware that many American groups, from environmentalists and human rights activists to religious fundamentalists and many politicians, had "adopted" China as their "favorite whipping boy." The Chinese were especially unhappy with American efforts to strengthen its security treaty with Japan. It was a move that the Chinese clearly felt was aimed at them. As always there were many willing to over-

simplify issues and to fatalistically predict a new cold war. The reality though was more complicated. As former Secretary of State Henry Kissinger counseled in the days after Deng Xiaoping died, the United States needs to clearly differentiate what in Beijing's future activities represents the natural behavior of a newly powerful great nation and what might more specifically be a threat to the United States. Clearly they are not necessarily the same thing but it requires a more sophisticated view than many are willing to apply to understand the difference.

The U.S./PRC/Taiwan Triangle

From Beijing's perspective, Taiwan remains the single most important issue in Sino-American relations. Offering a constant counter-weight to Taiwan's efforts to officially rejoin the international community, Beijing continues to apply pressure to any country which cooperates with Taiwan's efforts to integrate itself more formally into this world community.

Especially serious in recent years were the tensions which broke out in the spring of 1995. Under pressure from the Republican majority in Congress, the Clinton Administration had agreed to allow President Lee of Taiwan to visit his alma mater, Cornell University, in June 1995. On the surface the visit might appear to have been no more than a personal visit by a former student to his alma mater, but all involved knew it was much more. The visit was a conscious effort by Taiwan's government to continue its quest for international recognition as an entity apart from the People's Republic of China. On both sides of the Taiwan straits it was

Young workers exercising in the Shanghai Petro-Chemical Works

China

understood what granting the visa would imply. Within the Clinton administration, its rejection was strongly encouraged. Nevertheless, Taiwan has long nurtured allies within the American Congress and they vociferously and successfully insisted that Lee be allowed to visit the United States.

From the perspective of Beijing, granting the visa was a clear indication that the United States seemed to have sided with those who encouraged Taiwan's independence. Thus, Lee's visit was viewed as another step toward Washington's abandonment of the "one China policy" which had dated from the Nixon era. From Beijing's perspective, that decision was absolutely unacceptable, and relations between the United States and China entered into one of its most difficult periods.

During 1996, U.S.-China relations continued to be tense especially as Taiwan's first presidential election campaign was going on. In fact, concerned that voters must support a pro-independence party Chinese naval forces even initiated very provocative military maneuvers off the coast of the Republic—actually firing live shells vaguely in the direction of Taiwan's leading port. As the election decision drew near Beijing kept up the threatening stance, clearly hoping to weaken the popularity of those who were calling for Taiwan's independence from the mainland.

Washington responded by sending two carriers into the waters off Taiwan. The election took place with a smashing victory for Taiwan's President Lee who had maneuvered his campaign brilliantly between those on the island emphasizing independence and those who wanted reunification with the mainland. China had not succeeded with its scare tactics. While Washington and Beijing both publicly stated that conflict was not eminent, it remained for them to withdraw from a needless confrontation.

Sadly, tensions over this crucial issue have not lessened at all. During mid 1999 Taiwan President Lee started a firestorm of new tensions by announcing that henceforth discussions between Taiwan and the People's Republic should be carried out as equal "state to state" relations. Hardly the sort of demand Beijing's leaders, who fully anticipate reintegrating Taiwan one day, were happy about! And that was nothing compared to the reaction when, in the spring of 2000 Taiwan elections, the Democratic Progressive candidate, Chen Shuibian, long an advocate of formal Taiwanese independence from China, was quite expectedly elected the new president. Beijing's initial reaction to Chen's election was reasonably cautious but it is safe to assume things could get far more "complicated" over the next few years!

Visits between the leaders of the United States and the People's Republic have of-

ten played an important role defining the relationship between these two international giants. In the fall of 1997 President Jiang made his long awaited official visit to the United States. Although President Jiang was greeted by human rights protesters throughout his trip and various members of the American political elite went out of their way to snub him, the overall tone of the visit was successful. The United States confirmed its commitment to the unity of China and promised to lift some sanctions against the sale of nuclear power equipment.

Perhaps most importantly frank exchanges of views, sometimes quite publicly, were aired that made it clear that each nation's leaders harbored quite different views on an entire range of issues from human rights to Tibet. If the visit did not reflect the warmth of some of the earlier years of the Chinese-American rapprochement, it was still a far more successful encounter than many might have hoped for.

President Jiang's trip was complemented by a visit to China by President Clinton in June of 1998. Clinton's trip was obviously designed to literally force the American media and public into taking another look at developments in the PRC. Leading a population whose only image of China was of the horrors of the Tiananmen Square demonstrations of 1989, the American president set out to show his own people how much more complicated a place China was than the prevailing image of a human rights crushing single party dictatorship. He took part in a very open and publicly broadcast meetings with students, visited local election sites and sat in on Chinese talk radio shows. By the time he left, if few concrete gains had been made, Clinton had helped force American perceptions of China into a broader and more sophisticated understanding of the world's oldest and newest superpower.

Despite these twin visits, and the spring 1999 visit by China's new premier Zhu Rongji, problems have continued. The 1994 decision to again allow high-tech exports to China had become very controversial by 1999 as charges surfaced that sophisticated missile technology had been "accidentally" transferred to the PRC by American companies and claims that the Chinese had gained valuable nuclear technology by spying. These charges, which put the Clinton administration on the defensive, eventually forced a cut back on such nuclear cooperation and destroyed much of the progress made in improving Sino-American relations.

Moreover, the American led military campaign in Yugoslavia also added to tensions in the relationship as the People's Republic sided with those nations who found the NATO bombing campaign

Solitary Beauty Peak (Du Xiu Feng) in Guilin, one of hundreds of such peaks along a 50–mile stretch of the Li Jiang River valley of southern China. Many of these limestone formations have caves with intricate Buddhist carvings Photo by Miller B. Spangler

unacceptable. Concerns over the NATO campaign in Yugoslavia and most probably the accumulated tensions which had developed over the years were dramatically revealed when in May 1999 the United States accidentally bombed the Chinese embassy in Belgrade, Yugoslavia. The resulting explosion of Chinese anger created a new level of tension which may take years to repair. Clearly, the two countries have a lot of work to do to improve their relations and that will be much harder if "hard liners" emerge more prominently on each side.

Tibet

The last years have seen an enormous increase in Western interest in Tibet, the once independent nation that China officially incorporated into the People's Republic during the 1950s. Films from *Seven Years in Tibet* to *Kundun* and the well publicized interest of various celebrities from Richard Gere to Harrison Ford brought Tibet's problems to the American public. And of course, the Dalai Lama, Tibet's exiled leader's many international travels brought the concerns of that troubled nation to the world community as never before.

Sadly, for those interested in understanding the Tibetan situation, discussion of the issue was often marred by the emotionalism that both Tibet's supporters and the representatives of the People's Republic carried into each discussion. All too often it was difficult to find an objective account of Tibetan-Chinese relations.

On the Tibetan side, charges from violations of human rights to genocide were bantered about while the Chinese often vehemently defended their control of Tibet and spoke with pride of their liberation of its people from the previously existing system of serfdom and peasant exploitation. More fundamentally Beijing has usually viewed supporters of the exiled Dalai Lama as enemies seeking to dismember the Chinese homeland. When that support has come from official U.S. sources such as the American Congress Beijing has felt particularly threatened.

As a practical matter, pre-modern Tibet's cultural and ethnic identity existed long outside of the direct control of China's many imperial governments. In fact, until recently Tibet's population did not include Han Chinese. Nevertheless, Tibet has long been under Beijing's either direct or indirect influence. Especially influential in Tibet during the eighteenth century, China saw its role there diminish during the nineteenth century as European imperialism weakened the once proud Chinese Empire and the English, moving north from India, sought to expand their own role in Tibet. Ironically the early years of the 20th century even saw the nation's

leader, an earlier Dalai Lama, flee to China for protection from the aggressive British!

Beijing's long term identification of Tibet as part of China was dramatically demonstrated when, during the first decade of the 20th century, in a burst of uncharacteristic energy, it once again occupied Tibet. Luckily for the Tibetans direct Chinese rule hardly lasted long. As soon as China collapsed a few years later an autonomous Tibetan government reestablished itself although its independence was never internationally recognized.

During the course of the early 20th century the previous Dalai Lama's government directly administered the country but sadly gave in to conservatives who opposed efforts to build a modern Tibetan army for self-defense. Thus when China, reinvigorated by Mao Zedong's communist revolution, occupied Tibet in 1950 there was little the Tibetans could do about it.

Not surprisingly, given that these years were dominated internationally by the tensions of the Cold War, the American C.I.A. was deeply involved in these developments. Seeing the Tibetan issue as a way to weaken Communist China, the Americans not only encouraged the Dalai Lama to flee to India but by 1957 were arming and training Tibetan guerillas to resist Beijing.

Only two years later, in 1959 tensions between the Tibetans, especially those initially from the ethnically Tibetan regions beyond Tibet proper, destroyed the relationship between Tibet and Beijing and provoked a Tibetan revolt which eventually saw the Dalai Lama and thousands of his followers flee to India.

In the years since, Tibet's fate under Chinese control has been tragic indeed. Suffering along with the rest of China during the Cultural Revolution, Tibet saw huge numbers of its cultural monuments destroyed. Her monks were driven from the monasteries and most of these facilities destroyed. It was an assault on Tibet's cultural and religious heritage that it would barely survive.

In the years after Deng Xaioping came to power much was done to rebuild Tibet's monasteries and reestablish its religious and cultural traditions. Today families again dedicate their children's lives to serve in the monasteries and the Tibetan language is widely taught in primary schools throughout the country. For a time, under the relatively liberal communist leaders who dominated in the 1980s, a series of efforts were made to find a compromise between Beijing's identification of Tibet as a part of China and the supporters of the Dalai Lama. But little was accomplished.

Today, if the horrors of the Cultural Revolution have passed, the fate of Tibet still remains deeply in question. For fundamentally, though various Chinese gov-

ernments have tried from time to time to find common ground with the Dalai Lama and his supporters, Beijing is absolutely unwilling to even consider Tibet's demands which have ranged from independence to complete autonomy. Thus while Tibetan cultural and religious life has been allowed to reemerge, any activities that have appeared supportive of the Dalai Lama and the independence movement have been ruthlessly suppressed. Moreover, the Tibetan movement's claims for lands far beyond even those the Dalai Lama had actually once controlled complicate the situation even more.

Sadly, while the Dalai Lama has been extraordinarily successful in building support in the Western world, Beijing appears to have lost interest in seeking a compromise. As a practical matter, Tibet's exiled leader would probably be better off cultivating more friends in Beijing than in Washington D.C. for only there will be found a path likely to offer a compromise that will see Tibetan culture thrive in the 21st century. That of course assumes that Beijing remains interested, as it once was, in finding such a compromise. Official Chinese policy in recent years has allowed large numbers of Chinese to move to Tibet thus swamping the region's original inhabitants while developing those Tibetan community leaders, both secular and religious, who have shown themselves more cooperative and supportive of Beijing.

But things have not always gone smoothly for Beijing either. China's efforts to weaken the influence of the Dalai Lama suffered an enormous setback in 1999 when the 17th Karmapa Lama, the third most important leader in Tibetan Buddhism, fled Tibet complaining that the Chinese authorities had denied him the ability continue his studies. Considering that Beijing had cultivated the young man, who was fourteen when he fled, as an alternative leadership figure for Tibetans, his defection to the home of the Dalai Lama could not have been more embarrassing!

The Human Rights Question

Certainly one of the most difficult issues in the Sino-American relationship is caused by tensions over human rights. Here, as with questions over Tibet, emotions sometimes get in the way of thoughtful analysis of the situation. From the U.S. side, many Americans have been appalled by various reports about the far fewer personal, religious and political freedoms the Chinese enjoy compared to citizens of most Western countries. And of course images remain powerfully charged by memories of Chinese tanks running over peacefully demonstrating students in Tiananmen Square during 1989.

China

Open air market, Shanghai

The many reports Americans hear of forced abortions in the People's Republic, imprisoned democratic activists and the persecution of some religious figures are true enough. But these reports alone often fail to project an accurate image of developments in the People's Republic where the general trend is toward a far more open society than Chinese have experienced in their entire history. Today's China, despite the very real issues Western human rights activists decry, is far more free a place than is generally understood. Millions of people have far more control over their daily lives, worship openly with little interference from the state, have the power to sue the government and to even take part in political elections at the local level.

If a generation ago the Chinese leadership insisted on controlling practically every aspect of people's lives the formula today seems a far more narrow one. The government allows people far more social, religious, political, and intellectual rights as long as they do not challenge the unity of China or the power of the Chinese Communist Party. Thus, for example religion— Catholicism and even Tibetan Buddhism— has been allowed to flourish as long as its followers do not tie themselves to the leadership of outside figures from the Dalai Lama to the Pope. In the same vein the Party is far less intrusive into people's lives and lower level elections are allowed, but it is nevertheless dangerous to question the national leadership itself.

That last point was graphically demonstrated in the fall of 1998 when several democratic activists were given long prison terms for attempting to form a new political party, the Chinese Democracy Party, to challenge the Communist Party. Clearly despite the much greater freedoms available to the Chinese people the government and party is determined to maintain for itself the right to decide how far

and when those freedoms might expand. And given the stresses the recent economic downturn has caused it is not likely the leadership will want to expand political freedoms too greatly in the near future.

Another issue which rose to prominence during the last year was Beijing's increasingly harsh reaction toward religious movements that were perceived to be beyond state control. From the Falun Gong meditative exercise group to Tibetan Buddhism and Catholics who continue to associate with the Vatican, 1999 saw China's leaders increasingly willing to suppress any religious movement they felt capable or *even potentially capable* of challenging their authority.

In short, the Chinese still have far less freedoms than Westerners but far more than many Westerners believe they do. Very real changes, for example, have come in their rights to choose their own employment and even where they wish to live. They are even successfully suing the government and winning in court. In fact, the state is simply less part of the lives of average Chinese. And the real challenge for those outside critics of the PRC will be to respond to the situation in China as it actually exists rather than to the often sensationalist reports in the foreign media.

U.S.–China Economic Relations

The Sino-American economic relationship has taken on a new and potentially burdensome problem in recent years. Although arguments about differing methods of registering trade persist, it is clear that the trade imbalance between the United States and China is now beginning to resemble those between the United States and Japan—thus opening the door to the sort of public confrontations and accusations that have so often strained Japanese-American relations. How serious

that trade imbalance was though depended on whom one consulted. The Chinese estimates of the imbalances were much lower than those the U.S. claimed.

Regardless of the differences in measurement the Clinton administration was committed to basing these newly established economic ties on a more equal footing than had evolved over the years with Japan. Led by the office of the U.S. trade representative, the U.S. and China signed two agreements in recent years, the first providing for the protection of copyrights in China, and the second which further opened up the Chinese market for American business. These agreements came only after Mickey Kantor, the U.S. trade representative at that time, threatened Beijing with a 100% tariff increase on over a billion dollars of Chinese exports to the United States. Unfortunately, the success of the agreements too often relied on success in other areas of the complex relationship. Progress in other areas such as weapons sales and nuclear technology seemed likely to impact positively on the trade imbalance as well if politics does not intervene.

The most important economic issue in Sino-American relations in recent years has been the question of whether the United States would support China's entry into the World Trade Organization. The principal problem has been whether China would be admitted as a developing nation or as an already developed one. The definitional issue was important in that each carried with it different requirements about a country's economic obligations to the rest of the world. The Chinese wanted to be admitted as a developing nation. The West insisted it adhere to the standards set for the developed world. Obviously, China, given its enormous size and diversity represents aspects of both. After years of negotiations real progress was made in late 1999 when the U.S. and China finally signed an agreement on China's bid to enter the WTO. The deal itself obliged China to cut tariffs an average of 23% and offer greater access for U.S. firms. And it is remarkable that it was accomplished given the fact that the talks were going on during the aftermath of the apparently accidental U.S. bombing of the Chinese embassy in Yugoslavia! Naturally, the agreement will still have to be agreed to by the American Congress. And that vote expected in the early summer of 2000 was expected to be a very controversial one within the United States.

Defense Issues for the People's Republic

The military has been enjoying the fruits of economic expansion. One recent estimate was that about one fifth of all domestically produced consumer goods in China were produced in factories owned by the military. All this certainly helped the military's bottom line but in the view of some analysts has threatened to undermine the effectiveness of China's army as knowing about the "bottom line" was becoming more important than knowing about the "front lines." Not surprisingly the lure of huge amounts of money was as well causing a flurry of stories about officers taking advantage of their positions to earn illegal funds. And regardless of whether the entrepreneurial army was hurting its military orientation, their activities were getting in the way of the leadership's desire to remove the government from the economy. Thus as part of Beijing's effort to lessen the importance of the State Owned Enterprises it also recently ordered the military to withdraw from business. Officially at least, the military did so in late 1999 though the People's Liberation Army was allowed to keep control of those industries that directly served its needs.

Still, as a result of this new found wealth, China has purchased billions in military hardware from Russia. China was also able to buy computer equipment from the United States. Not surprisingly China's military growth has begun to worry her neighbors who are concerned about the possibility of military expansionism.

And the recent spending and especially the purchase of former Soviet equipment does add to the overall effectiveness of the Chinese military. Clearly the growing Chinese economy is giving the People's Republic the ability to strengthen its forces, though for the immediate future their effectiveness remains limited. But China does have big goals. As the 20th century passed into history the commander of China's air force announced major plans to build a stronger air force with greater capabilities beyond China proper.

Moreover, Beijing has been willing to assert itself in disputes regarding many islands in the region. These disputes have ranged from the Diaoyu islands in the East China Sea mentioned before to the Spratley islands and Mischief Reef. Over the last year, as in previous years, tensions and minor confrontations have continued between Beijing's forces and those of her neighbors.

Economy

As the Chinese moved into the new millennium there was plenty of reason to feel both apprehension and confidence. On one hand the economies of many of her neighbors had been terribly hurt by the economic meltdown of previous years and were only just beginning to recover— a meltdown which China itself had man-

aged to largely avoid. In fact, despite her neighbor's problems the PRC had managed to maintain a positive growth rate throughout the period. She had also had major advantages over her neighbors during the crisis that had settled into the region in 1997. For example, her own currency was not traded on the world market and the government boasted huge economic reserves—said to be around $150 billion—that most governments in Southeast Asia, fighting to defend their currencies and to meet short term debt commitments, could not even dream of.

On the other hand, though somewhat sheltered from the economic chaos around her over the last few years, China's own economy has also shown similar economic weaknesses. She too had gone overboard in a real estate building boom that was producing office space far faster than tenants were found to fill them. And not only were exports to other Asian countries way down but with Southeast Asia's devalued

currency China's own products were hard pressed to compete internationally.

Investor enthusiasm for China's markets was also falling over the last year. Though China seemed an ocean of economic tranquility compared to some of its neighbors, it too found outside investors, both from the West and within Asia, far less interested or able to invest within the People's Republic.

Moreover, the entire economy continued, as it had for years, to be handicapped by the inefficient state-owned enterprises, the SOEs. Of the hundreds of thousands of SOEs, somewhere between half and two thirds operate at a financial loss and the situation is growing worse. The total cost of propping them up has become enormous. Certainly Chinese leaders have long been aware of the problem but doing something about it has been quite another matter. After all, Beijing's leadership well understands that about 100 million workers or about 70% of the country's

In 1996, China became the largest steel producer in the world.

China

The Great Wall of China, still one of the world's major tourist attractions

industrial workforce is employed in the state sector. Fearing social unrest the government until very recently was very reticent to begin the reorganization and subsequent growth in unemployment that reforming that sector would require.

But with Deng's departure and Jiang Zemin's solidification of power the leadership was finally ready to bite the bullet and begin the transformation of the state enterprises in earnest. At the 1997 fall party congress Jiang announced that a major effort would commence—despite the necessity of perhaps massive layoffs—to reform that lagging part of the economy. The program called for a range of actions from complete shutdowns to mergers and reorganizations to deal with the problem. By the spring of 1998, Beijing, recognizing the dangers of further economic dislocation given the regional economic slowdown and the anticipated problems associated with reforming the state enterprises, had decided to move even more dramatically. It committed itself to further reforms and a massive economic stimulus effort, especially aimed at the agricultural and the housing sector to spur the economy. Well aware of the banking crises that was sweeping much of East and Southeast Asia

the government also moved quickly under the former economic czar and now premier Zhu Rongji to begin reform in that sector as well. As part of the privatization effort and with a goal of stimulating the economy Beijing also ended promises of free housing and required people to buy their own homes. To finance these efforts mortgage credit was made more available.

Perhaps even more dramatically, during the late spring of 1999 the Chinese Parliament decided to officially recognize capitalism as an important part of China's new socialist market economy. And a few months later Beijing announced that henceforth private enterprises would be put on an "equal footing with state-owned enterprises"! These steps were no doubt taken to further encourage the sort of private economic growth the nation's leaders knew the country required to create new employment opportunities.

For Beijing, moving decisively was of fundamental importance. After all, the economy which had boasted double digit growth rates in the previous decade had slowed to 9.7 in 1996 and dipped to an official 7.8 in 1998. And much of that growth was simply a result of government infrastructure spending. The official figures for

1999 (which some have questioned) are still healthy, but lower still at 7.1%—certainly impressive numbers but perhaps not good enough given the demands of China's growing population.

Especially significant as well was the decision by the influential rating agency Standard & Poor's to downgrade China's international financial evaluation. Another obvious example of economic uncertainty is the drop in consumer spending. People are simply too nervous about their future job security to make large purchases, and that is hurting the economy as well.

Given the importance of maintaining enough growth to absorb the unemployment associated with the reform of the SOEs, and the arrival of new workers into the economy, keeping economic growth to a reasonable rate is imperative. All this also highlights one of the most important challenges to the economy and the political leadership, the growing migrant worker population. The private sector is not growing fast enough to meet the demand for jobs. And, as economic growth slows, the situation will worsen. The urban sector's unemployment numbers have been growing significantly in recent years and the situation is likely to worsen before it gets better. Urban areas are also feeling the influx of poor, less educated, rural Chinese. And if the Asian economic meltdown was not traumatic enough, the summer of 1998 saw enormous floods that cost Beijing around $20 billion in losses!

Nevertheless despite the economic challenges, the last year has brought economic planners in the People's Republic reason to feel some optimism as well. The economy had not succumbed to the worse dislocations of many of its neighbors and its leadership seemed committed to making the hard decisions necessary to ensure that economic success continued well into the next century. And China entered the new century well positioned economically. In 1999 she shipped $184 billion in goods around the world—made 2/3 of all the toys sold in America and produced one-third of all the suitcases and handbags made in the world! And real progress was made as well toward the long term goal of entering the World Trade Organization when, as we have seen, it finally reached an agreement with the United States, (not yet ratified as of this writing) on terms for the PRC to enter the WTO.

Culture and Society in China

The twentieth century has seen extraordinary changes in culture and society in China. Ironically, Chinese communities in Hong Kong, the PRC and Taiwan spent much of the late 1900s moving farther apart while during the last decade of the

China

20th century, their societies have started to appear more similar again. Keeping up with these changes is breathtaking for the outside observer; actually living them would be astounding.

In 1900 when our century began, most Chinese were rural peasants living very simple lives as farmers. The fundamental and lasting institutions of family life and farming completely dominated Chinese culture for thousands of years; this was certainly true throughout most of Asia, but these two foundations were developed to a higher level within China. Agriculture combined the careful cultivation of cereal grains, skillful efforts to control water by the construction of levees and irrigation ditches, and the return of all available fertilizer, including human waste, to the soil. This permitted high nutritional content of the harvests, which in turn permitted a rapid rate of population growth. The family was the basic social unit—above it stood the village, governed usually by the heads of the leading families; contact with central government officials was avoided by the elders with varying degrees of success.

The society was dominated by an intellectual elite known as the scholar gentry who were very influential on the local level and supplied most of the personnel for the imperial bureaucracy which ran the empire. The traditional upper class culture was also based on the family and on the group of related families which together formed a clan. Ancestor worship, involving sacrifices to dead forebears, who were not considered to be actually divine, had begun among the upper classes and spread to the lower classes. The wealthy avoided manual labor and regarded literacy and education—especially in the Confucian tradition—ownership of land and public service, as the highest social goals and symbols of status. This upper crust, dominating education, government service and land ownership, was not so exclusive that the lower classes were entirely excluded from it. Unlike India, China never had a caste system as part of its culture, but in reality, it was highly unusual for a person of peasant origin to acquire enough education, wealth or influence to move to the top of the social scale.

In spite of tendencies toward conservatism and anti-foreignism, traditional Chinese culture was probably the richest, and certainly the longest lived and most continuous of the great civilizations, ancient and modern, of the world. It was relatively free from the religious bigotry and intolerance that was evident in much of Western history. In contrast to the principles of decaying despotism of France under the Bourbon kings, China's traditional philosophy and culture greatly impressed

well-educated Jesuit missionaries who came to China in the 17th century.

Through his writings, the French writer and philosopher Voltaire communicated some of the Chinese ideals to the educated of Europe. Sadly, the decline of the traditional Chinese political system in the late 19th and early 20th centuries brought a loss of confidence in many aspects of traditional Chinese cultural values. Education was increasingly altered to conform to Western ideals; literature began to be written in the vernacular, or conversational language, rather than in the old, more difficult and formal literary language.

By early years of the 20th century new groups of elites and workers became significant. On the elite level, new types of soldiers, business people, and intellectuals emerged as well as the formation of a new industrial working class that lived in the Western ports. China was starting its extraordinary century-long transformation.

During the 1920s, the new ideas and values including Marxism were gaining ground among intellectuals. At the level of the uneducated, the solidarity of the family was greatly weakened by the beginnings of economic progress toward industrialization, which created jobs for women, drawing them away from their families to the factories in the cities. The Japanese invasion in 1937 and the ensuing chaos uprooted millions of people and heavily contributed to the further break-

down of the traditional social and cultural order.

In the first generation after the Second World War, society in the several parts of China began to diverge. Both Taiwan and Hong Kong were aligned with the Western capitalist economies and each saw tremendous economic changes in their respective communities over the years. Economic growth was significant and people's lives were dramatically altered by the changing circumstances.

Within the People's Republic in contrast, while economic growth remained the principal goal, Mao Zedong's ideologically driven approach as demonstrated in the Great Leap Forward and the Cultural Revolution, failed to economically raise people's living standards; indeed at times the situation simply deteriorated dramatically. Even a casual visitor to the area in the late 1970s and early 1980s could see a great differences in the life style of these different parts of the Chinese community.

But again, the revolutionary cycle has changed and since the late 1970s under the direction of Deng Xiaoping, the People's Republic has itself chosen to enter and compete in the world market. And it has done so with enormous success. Real gains have been made in people's economic possibilities. Individual citizens can now purchase their own apartments, and professionals like lawyers are free to privately organize themselves to develop

Billboard encouraging family planning

Photo by Miller B. Spangler

计划生育 是我国的一项基本国

PLANNING—A BASIS NATIONAL POLICY OF CHIN

39

China

clients. Chinese now travel abroad far more often then they ever did before.

Although the West hears much about the harsh repression of individual dissidents who have chosen to challenge the state, the reality of a more general improvement in human rights is also true. Unlike in the past, criminal lawyers are now officially allowed to represent their clients rather than the state; and people have successfully sued the government for false arrest and detention.

Chinese Women

Chinese women have been among the biggest winners of the 20th century. Beginning the century with almost no rights or education they were more often than not controlled partly through the painful process of foot binding. Yet by the early years of the century, women's education, even at the college level was much more common and foot binding, long outlawed, less and less practiced. The Communist Revolution of 1949 moved as well to improve their status and the next year laws were passed giving them more rights. At the height of Mao Zedong's influence, the circumstance of women and men did not widely vary. Neither had much personal freedom.

On the other hand it was difficult for those who controlled the factories to dismiss anyone, so at least more economic security was possible. The more recent economic changes though have again altered the circumstances of many women and given the progress made in earlier years of the century have at times seemed to have slowed the momentum toward improving women's rights. For example, given the decision making powers to hire and fire, many employers have made it clear they prefer males as workers to avoid the expenses associated with maternity leave. Industries which have been associated with female labor have been especially hit by cutbacks. This despite the fact that women, in the rural areas, generally get only around 77% of men's wages for the same work. Moreover, in the rural areas, given the incentives for families to take responsibility for growing more on the land and the common migration of men toward city work, agriculture itself is increasingly becoming a female activity.

Thus, since more than 80% of Chinese women still live in rural areas, traditional attitudes toward women still strongly affect their lives. Most importantly it's the still common practice of women to leave their native villages and move to the village of their new husbands thus making their own social position less secure than that of their spouses. And sadly, rising school fees are making it more and more difficult for families to afford to send their daughters (and sons) to school—pressures which often mean keeping the daughters out of school.

Among the urban and more educated classes women have made important strides but they are limited. They constitute around 14% of the communist party's membership but their representation goes drastically down as one looks at the higher ranks of party administration. Though traditional values often prevail with regard to women's roles the new openness has allowed Chinese women far more outlets to reflect on their circumstances. The new social and political openings have allowed for an enormous expansion of media outlets from radio talk shows to magazines which often frankly discuss women's concerns. If issues like sex, domestic violence and individual self-fulfillment were hardly discussed at all a generation ago, today they are often a common part of the public culture.

Women have as well been especially impacted by the efforts to control the population. With a burgeoning population of more than one billion people, China has been pursuing since 1979 an energetic program to reduce population growth to zero or below. A very real system of "carrot and stick" has been employed under the title of the "One Child Policy" though that has never been an absolute goal for the entire country. Stringent regulations have been promulgated which include stiff taxation, occasionally forced abortions and criminal penalties upon couples who exceed the established limit of one child, while significant financial and other incentives have been offered to those who cooperate. Not surprisingly there have been abuses. Local officials have forced pregnant women to abort. The program has been relatively successful according to the government, but this is impossible to verify.

Moreover, though the government has often had to allow rural families to try for second children when the first born were girls, the pressure to reduce the population especially affects females. On one hand, as in other parts of Asia, fetuses, once determined to be female by modern technologies like ultra-sound, are more likely to be aborted. And when such drastic choices are not taken it is also common for rural families to simply not register their newly born daughters, a decision that can have drastic effects on the young women later when their lack of legal existence will hurt their chances for education and health benefits.

Here again, China is following the path common elsewhere in Asia, where the number of boys sharply exceeds the number of girls. For China, official reports suggest there are 95 women for every one hundred males. By contrast, in the United States there are ten more women or 105 women per every one hundred males. Clearly these "missing " Chinese females may merely be unreported but it is clear as well that in China, as with many other Asian countries, the traditional preference for boys still determines the numbers of female fetuses which will be carried to term and eventually raised.

The "one child policy" is very controversial both inside and outside China; yet no one would argue against the importance of China maintaining a stable rather than constantly rising population. But the burden of adhering to the population control measures more often affects women than men. They are of course the principal targets for efforts to monitor fertility and are most responsible for pressuring people to adhere as well.

In short, Chinese women have experienced extraordinary changes during the 20th century though those changes have been most obvious in more urban areas and especially in large coastal cities like Shanghai and of course on Taiwan and in Hong Kong. Yet however much these women's lives have been enriched by the changes, most Chinese women remain in the huge Chinese interior, much less affected by the changes brought on by the late 20th century.

The Internet

Like so much of the rest of the world Chinese society ended the 20th century grappling with the meaning of the emergence of the personal computer and the networking of much of the globe through the Internet. Even in the People's Republic, which initially lagged behind in computer use, sales are booming as parents buy P.C.s hoping to give their children an edge in the future job market. And the government itself has committed the country to a major Internet presence as it moves into the new millennium. And the Internet use which included no more than 100,000 people in 1996 has grown enormously. The government, while well aware of the importance of the Internet to its goal of building a modern economically sophisticated nation, is also aware of how easily the Internet can bring in unwanted outside influences and undermine the Communist party's power. For example, when mainland Chinese students used the Internet to create their own organizations dedicated to protesting Japanese occupation of controversial islands, the leadership became uncomfortable and closed down the student networks. More recently 1998 saw the first arrest of a Chinese businessman specifically for the crime of distributing Chinese e-mail addresses to overseas organizations. Clearly the government is afraid of the use of the

Internet as a tool of potential subversion yet equally afraid of losing out on the new economies that are emerging due partly through the Internet.

Clearly the Internet represents both a tool to integrate China further into the world economy and a threat of further Westernization of the sort the government found so threatening in 1989. Don't expect China's "Internet dilemma" to be resolved any time soon.

The Future: The People's Republic

For much of human history China was at the forefront of the human experience in both the arts and sciences but that extraordinary series of accomplishments ground to a halt in the late 18th century as the West, newly invigorated by the Enlightenment and the Industrial Revolution, surged ahead. For almost two hundred years, dramatic internal problems and external pressures ranging from Western imperialists to Japanese invaders kept China from regaining its traditional place at the forefront of the human drama. But things

have now changed. The generation long surge of economic building set off by Deng Xiaoping has helped China pull itself out of the two century long doldrums within which it had fallen. The central reality of our time is that China is back and ready to resume its place of importance. The ramifications of that development are monumental. Sometimes it was simply the sheer size of China's projects that overwhelmed observers as with the famous Three Gorges dam project which has been making real progress. That enormous project, designed to control the waters of China's longest river, is expected to displace more than a million people as it proceeds. China is simply so large that almost anything it does impacts on the world community.

Some have warned about the potential dangers of China's industrialization on the world's environment or food supplies. Others speak of a flood of industrialized goods overwhelming the world's economic system and some even talk of a new "cold" and even possibly "hot" war with China. The only thing that is really certain is that one of the world's great people has found

its way into the modern industrialized world. Adjustments will have to be made.

And an enormous adjustment it will be, not only for the Chinese people but for its leaders as well. For China is not only entering the modern world but transforming itself as it does so. The leadership is committed to making that leap toward the future while maintaining itself in power. The democratic dissident movement fights for and assumes a political transformation as well. And though the democracy movement may not attract large numbers of followers, movements based on spirituality, from the Falun Gong to Catholicism, have attracted large numbers of new followers whose strength has clearly made the country's leadership feel somewhat threatened.

Meanwhile, tensions arising from both dissatisfaction with corrupt officials to labor unrest caused by growing unemployment make stability sometimes questionable. For the immediate future it is probably best to expect an on-going tug-of-war between the government and dissident community over how Chinese society will enter the first decades of the 21st century.

On the way home from school, Beijing.

China

HONG KONG
Special Administrative Region of the PRC
since July 1997

Area: 398 square miles.
Population: 5,952,000 (1999 estimate).
Administrative Capital: Victoria.

The former British Crown Colony of Hong Kong consists of three parts. The first is the island of Victoria (or Hong Kong Island) on the north side of which the city of the same name is located. The second part is the small area known as Kowloon, at the tip of the peninsula jutting from the Chinese mainland toward Victoria. Between Victoria and Kowloon lies one of the world's busiest and most beautiful harbors. The third part is composed of the New Territories, which extend northward from Kowloon to the Chinese border, and also include some islands in the waters around Victoria. Kowloon is connected by rail with the Chinese city of Guangzhou (Canton).

Most of the area of Hong Kong consists of hills and low mountains, but there are enough level lands in the New Territories for large quantities of food to be harvested; Hong Kong is actually dependent for much of its food and water on the mainland of China. The population is almost totally Chinese, many of them having arrived since 1949 in order to find greater safety, freedom and economic opportunity than was allowed on the troubled mainland of China. The climate is subtropical and monsoonal in the summer, but relatively cool in the winter.

Realizing the potential value as a naval base, although not seeing at first the commercial possibilities of Hong Kong, the British annexed it from the Manchus in 1842, after the first Opium War. Under an effective British administration, and sharing in the increase of British trade with and investments in China during the nineteenth and early twentieth centuries, Hong Kong experienced rapid growth as a port. Kowloon was annexed in 1860, after Anglo–French forces again attacked China. The New Territories were added in 1898 in order to provide agricultural land and living space for the growing population but were held on a 99–year lease. It is of course that lease that ran out in the summer of 1997.

Given their large population, Victoria and Kowloon could not survive without the New Territories.

During the damaging Japanese occupation of Hong Kong from 1941–45, and the Communist takeover in China in 1949, Hong Kong's "trade" with the mainland of China was increasingly confined to the import of food, water, and consumer goods.

Nearly forty–five per cent of the mainland's foreign trade passes through Hong Kong. The former colony has excellent port facilities and commercial relations with the rest of Asia. In the 1960's, foreign capital, including that from America and Japan, poured into Hong Kong, building apartments, erecting office buildings and light industrial plants in particular.

Toward Unification with the Mainland

Much of Hong Kong's recent economic success is directly tied to the changing policies of the People's Republic of China. The ideologically driven PRC of Mao Zedong hardly needed Hong Kong's economic strengths, but Deng Xiaoping's arrival to power in the late 1970s brought change. Deng was determined to open China up to the world and to begin the effort in the southernmost parts of China. Under the circumstances, the British colony, with its abundant knowledge of both China and the Western world was in a perfect position to contribute to and take advantage of Beijing's changing economic policies.

Just north of the Hong Kong border, Beijing established special economic zones which would eventually become the earliest engines of China's resurgence in which Hong Kong was able to take part. Hong Kong's economy, which had earlier been less tied to the People's Republic, actually began the first steps, at that point economic, in its reintegration with the mainland. Thus China's economic accomplishments became Hong Kong's as well and the momentum toward 1997 already begun.

Ironically, given some of the tensions which arose in the years before the 1997 hand–over of Hong Kong to the PRC, it was the British who had pushed for treaties to resolve the impending end of the 99–year leases of 1898. In Beijing's perspective, none of the nineteenth century treaties imposed on China by the imperialistic West had any validity, so there was no reason to consider 1997 any different.

But the British wanted the fate of their colony, the last Asian remnant of their once enormous Asian colonial system, resolved, and insisted on negotiations. Happily, during those years the two powers worked well together and the Sino–British Joint Declaration on Hong Kong was signed in 1984. The United Kingdom even agreed somewhat later to coordinate its changes in Hong Kong with the People's Republic. Thus, Britain unilaterally gave up the right to change the Hong Kong political system which for the colony's entire history had meant being ruled undemocratically by a series of governors sent from London.

Within the agreement Beijing promised to leave the existing economic and social systems essentially unchanged for at least fifty years after 1997 as well as to permit a degree of self–government. Although there will be no way to compel Beijing to honor this pledge if it chooses not to do so, most of the population of Hong Kong—who have nowhere else to go—appear to have resigned themselves reluctantly to a future under the Chinese flag. White collar and professional workers however have emigrated in considerable numbers, over 500,000 alone in the last twelve years. The British announcement that many of the more elite Hong Kong families would receive the right to live in the United Kingdom if they so chose was made to help shore up confidence in the aftermath of the Tiananmen Square demonstrations of 1989.

Ironically, during the last years before 1997 both Beijing and London showed an increasing willingness to violate the spirit of the 1984 treaty. Britain on its part, long happy with governing Hong Kong under its own benign colonial dictatorship, moved aggressively, especially under its last colonial governor, to transform Hong Kong into an increasingly democratic political entity, something Beijing had hardly agreed to. Even a bill of rights was introduced by 1991.

With the appointment of former Conservative Party MP, Chris Patten, to the post of Governor of Hong Kong in 1992, the British had apparently decided to take a stronger hand in determining the future of the colony's government prior to their withdrawal in 1997. Even before Governor Patten's appointment, the British had taken some steps to strengthen the democratic process in Hong Kong. In September 1991, elections were held for 18 of the 61 seats on the Legislative Council (Legco). Sixteen of these seats were won by pro–democratic candidates. This election gave a considerable boost to the pro–democracy movement, though it did not make the Chinese on the mainland happy. The first truly free election did not occur until 1995—only two years before the turnover.

Not surprisingly these last minute British changes aroused the anger of the Chinese government. The basic disagreement between the British and the Chinese had to do with the type of government Hong Kong would have. Beijing had in mind an executive–dominated government for Hong Kong, where the legislature plays the role of an adviser. The British in contrast moved to establish a strong, elected legislative assembly and more freedoms than they themselves had ever tolerated.

In December of 1996 Tung Chee Hwa, a shipping company magnate, was elected by the 400 member selection committee to be the first chief executive for Hong Kong after the transition. Almost 6000 people had applied for membership in the committee and a final 400 eventually selected Tung. Tung Chee Hwa to many seemed an especially appropriate choice. His personal background has well prepared him to deal with challenges ahead. A Shanghai–born Chinese who speaks the same dialect as many of China's new leaders, Tung lived for a decade in the United States and has many ties there. He has been involved with the United States Chamber of Commerce, the Hoover Institution and the Council of Foreign Relations.

He is said to count former president Bush among his personal friends. Moreover he had already served as an advisor in the British administration of Hong Kong. That China's leader Jiang Zemin favored him was also known previous to the election.

Following Tung's selection, Rita Fan, a former legislator and advisor for the British colonial administration was chosen to lead the new provisional legislature with which China planned to replace the current Hong Kong legislature.

A Not So Smooth Transition

Throughout early 1997 tensions ran high regarding the upcoming transition. Beijing, following through on its long standing rejection of those political changes Britain had made since the handover agreement, repealed many of the new laws—some made within hours of the changeover.

During the transition there had also been considerable talk about the undemocratic aspects of Tung's election though with little appreciation that he was actually the most democratically elected leader in Hong Kong's history and the first Chinese! If anything, these tensions during the hand over underscored how little the two groups had come to understand each other despite more than a century of interaction.

The last minute British efforts toward democratization clearly complemented Western political and social values though one might ask sarcastically why Britain had waited so long to introduce them. What they did not complement was efforts to make a smooth transition from Hong Kong's earlier status as a colony to its future as part of the People's Republic, which despite Western preferences, continues to be controlled by an authoritarian single-party government.

Hong Kong and China: The First Years

In the months leading up to the handover, commentators varied widely on

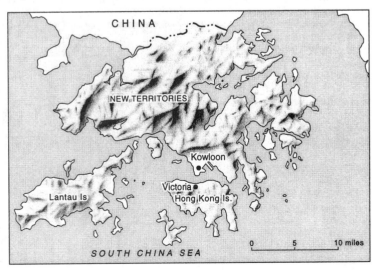

China

Chief Executive Tung Chee-hwa

what would occur next. Some predicted that China would dramatically transform the colony for the worst, stifling its freedoms and dynamic economy. Others insisted with equally great conviction that little would actually change within the former colony and that the doom sayers were raising unnecessary panic. They were both wrong. The first year after the transition turned out to be quite traumatic though for reasons few had predicted.

The principal menace arrived not from Beijing, but from the failing economies of her East and Southeast Asian neighbors. As well known financial institutions faltered and the Hong Kong markets plummeted, Hong Kongers found their life styles and hopes under siege. Throughout 1998 and early 1999 economic news continued to be very discouraging. Hong Kong, following the lead of its Southeast Asian neighbors moved into the worst recession since the early 1970s. Unemployment was up to a fifteen year height and tourism, an important source of revenue way down.

Responding to the crisis the government not only expended considerable resources to defend the strength of the Hong Kong dollar but announced several economic stimulus packages. Ironically, considering all the Western rhetoric about how Hong Kong might be threatened by its reintegration into the People's Republic, Beijing now turned out to be a source of strength. Not only did the PRC's leaders work to defend Hong Kong's economy, they went as far as to threaten international currency speculators against efforts to weaken her currency and even began encouraging more mainland tourism there. Clearly, Beijing was committed to maintaining the health of Hong Kong.

But what of all those fears of Beijing's new power over Hong Kong? The PLA soldiers who had marched into the territories with such fanfare in July 1997 withdrew from public eye and some were even rumored to have been relocated back to the PRC for financial reasons. Perhaps most controversial

were the new pressures upon the educational system regarding the expansion of education in Chinese. From the fall of 1998 the expectation was that Chinese, both the local Cantonese dialect and Mandarin, would become the principal language of instruction. Given the importance of English for international business, this demand was heavily criticized in some quarters.

Particularly significant was the furor raised in early 1999 over a ruling by the Hong Kong Court of Final Appeal that children born of Hong Kong residents had the right to reside in the former colony. Clearly a blessing for many Hong Kong parents of mainland children but one that raised considerable controversy over the local court's right to decide such important immigration issues and fears about a too large influx of new residents to Hong Kong especially as it was struggling with a financial turndown. When, somewhat later, the Chinese National People's Congress, following a request by Tung Chee-hwa, chose to modify the Hong Kong court's decision, concerns were also raised about Beijing's growing power over Hong Kong.

Politically the long anticipated May 1998 elections brought the return to power of many of the former colony's most outspoken democrats. Martin Lee's Democratic Party did especially well in the elections, both in competition for those openly allocated seats and for those reserved for the professional classes. In the end, Hong Kong's democrats emerged with the status of being the single largest party. In the aftermath of the demonstration of popular support, Lee was invited to a meeting with President Clinton of the United States. Still, Hong Kong's government revealed no great commitment to expanding its resident's democratic rights. In fact, in late

1999 new councils were formed at the local levels which were less democratic than their predecessors. Clearly, the SAR's official government, despite the gains made by some democratic activists, remained similar to the relatively open but also authoritarian regimes of countries like Singapore.

As for the Chief Executive himself, Tung Chee-hwa found his own popularity dropping over the last year even as some clearly wished him to be reelected when his term came up again in 2002. And by early 2000 Tung's chances of reelection began to look somewhat better as Hong Kong's economy finally began to show some promise of regaining its economic momentum. Most interestingly, Hong Kong's government signed an agreement in late 1999 to build a Disney Theme park in the former colony.

The Future

Particularly important for Hong Kong's future was the obvious commitment Beijing's leaders felt to the SAR. Though one might have imagined a greater emphasis on Shanghai as the latter continued to grow. Still it became obvious as 1999 ended that despite the PRC's commitment to Shanghai, Hong Kong's vitality continued to hold a very important priority for them.

Overall, Hong Kong enters the millennium with some trepidation. Clearly the fate of the People's Republic, politically and economically, is going to play a major role in her own future. And Hong Kong's moves toward integrating itself into the new Internet based economies were still too new to have a sense of their eventual success. Nevertheless, compared to these "doomsday" warnings of so many in the months before her return to China in 1997 Hong Kong had done very well indeed.

View from the Peak on Hong Kong Island looking towards the North Point

MACAU
Portuguese Dependency until 1999

Senate Square, Macau

Area: 6 square miles
Population: 430,000 (1999)

Until its return to the mainland late last year Macau was Portugal's only remaining overseas territory. Macau, is divided about equally into Macau proper, which has a common land frontier with the Chinese mainland, and two nearby islands. The terrain is mostly flat. The offshore waters are muddy with silt carried by the Pearl River. The climate is subtropical, with a summer monsoon and a relatively cool winter. Except for a small community of Portuguese (officials, soldiers, police, missionaries, businessmen, etc.) and other Europeans, the population is overwhelmingly Chinese.

Portugal acquired Macau in the mid-16th century for use as a base from which to trade with nearby Canton by an agreement with the Ming dynasty of China. It prospered in the 18th century, but during the 19th it was rapidly overshadowed by Hong Kong. From its earlier days of prominence, Macau has retained some beautiful old buildings and something of a Mediterranean flavor. It has a reputation, partly justified, as a center of opium and gold smuggling and assorted vice. Gambling is unquestionably the major feature of the economy, and auto racing

and bullfighting have been introduced as well. Sadly, in recent years, gang warfare has become a particularly violent part of the life of the colony and government attempts to impose order have invited bloody retribution from criminals.

The new government of Portugal after 1974 wanted to return Macau to China, but Beijing would not accept it, because of the disturbing effect such a transfer might have had on Hong Kong. Portugal did agree to allow more internal autonomy to its former colony in 1976 and granted it increased powers in 1990. After the Sino-British agreement was reached on Hong Kong in 1984, negotiations began between Lisbon and Beijing for the reversion of Macau to Chinese control. It was agreed in April 1987 that reversion would take place in December 1999, along lines similar to those already worked out for Hong Kong. Certain concessions were granted to Macau's leaders. For example, it was later agreed that capital punishment, common in the People's Republic, would not be employed in Macau.

In the months leading up to the handover two issues dominated the life of the colony. First the on-going gang violence and the question of who would lead the colony after its return to mainland control.

As in Hong Kong, a special committee of 100 notables was formed to plan for Macau's future leadership and Edmund Ho, the 44 year-old son of well known diplomat and banker, was selected.

In sharp contrast to Hong Kong's reversion to China, Macau's was a much smoother transition with a considerably more cooperative attitude on both sides. Nevertheless, there were some features of the transition that were harder on Macau than Hong Kong. For example, unlike Hong Kong which had already put into place a largely home grown bureaucracy, the departure of the Portuguese saw younger less experienced Macau Chinese taking up the reign of administration.

One important controversy was the mainland's decision during the fall of 1998 to station troops in Macau after the handover. It was a decision that clearly contradicted previous understandings but one that was probably a logical outcome of Beijing's concern about the on-going criminal violence that had plagued the colony in recent years.

Overall, Macau enters the millennium hoping to expand its economic base beyond gambling and to gain more Mainland Chinese resources to help curtail the recent crime spree.

Taiwan: Republic of China

For *BASIC FACTS* on Taiwan: Republic of China, see page 14

Downtown Taipei

Politics in the Republic of China constitutes one of the more clear and encouraging cases of how democratization can take place over time alongside a modern, rapidly developing economy. Even critics of the *Guomindang*, the Nationalist Party which has dominated the political system since the break with the mainland in 1949, would have to acknowledge that substantial progress has been made.

By 1991, most of the holdovers from the National Assembly elected on the mainland in 1948 had retired. Discussion of politically sensitive issues such as whether Taiwan should be independent of the People's Republic was permitted at last by the *Guomindang*. A viable political opposition in the form of the *Democratic Progressive Party* emerged, and free, relatively clean, elections have become part of the political landscape. Disaffected *GMD* members have also left to form the *Chinese New Party*, making for the possibility of a three party system.

Much of the contention among the parties has centered on the independence versus unification issue. The *New Party* was more representative of the old line

GMD which claimed the right to rule over one China. President Lee's *GMD* took a centrist approach, while the *DPP* was openly supportive of an independent Taiwan. *The Chinese New Party* was not able to establish itself nationally.

Further evolution of the political system also came about when steps were recently taken to strengthen the position of the president. Constitutional amendments provided for the direct election of the president and also granted the president the authority to appoint and dismiss high government officials without the consent of the prime minister. The *GMD* dominated legislature also strengthened presidential power over three important agencies. The position of president has become far more than ceremonial.

On March 23, 1996, Taiwan held its first ever presidential election. The incumbent president, Lee Teng–hui, was elected with 54% of the vote. The voters rallied around their serving president who had skillfully raised Taiwan's diplomatic profile by meeting with several ASEAN heads of state, and visiting the United States. Peng Ming–min, the *Democratic Progressive Par-*

ty candidate, came in second with 21% of the vote. Peng is an open supporter of Taiwan's independence.

Beijing, no doubt concerned about the rising popularity of efforts to disassociate Taiwan further from the mainland, made a crude effort to intimidate voters there by staging military maneuvers in the weeks leading up to the election. While Beijing's exact motives are not completely clear the result of their threats was to complement President Lee's efforts to fix his candidacy in the middle of the Taiwan political spectrum. Thus he became the election's big winner while the votes of both those advocating declaring formal independence and those encouraging closer ties to the mainland went down. Beijing ended up with a newly strengthened Taiwanese President with something of a mandate to continue his politics of ambiguity toward the mainland.

Once Lee's new authority was established the government set out to attempt a major administrative reform of the island's governing system. The results of these fundamental changes saw the president's authority grow and power of the

President Chen Shui-bian

provincial-level administration weaken vis-à-vis the central government.

Taiwan's political life has been especially dramatic of late. There had been until quite recently a growing popular support for the opposition Democratic Progressive Party's calls for more formal and official independence from the mainland. But that momentum seemed to be waning over the last year and for a time, the ruling Nationalist Party had reason to celebrate.

The Nationalist's comeback was most evident in the late 1998 electorial defeat of Chen Shui-bian, the DPP mayor of Taipei by Ma Ying-jeou, a member of Taiwan's Nationalist Party. And the victory was not insignificant as Ma got 51% to the incumbent Chen's 46%. Legislatively the GMD/Nationalists did well also. It raised its percentage within the legislature from 52% to 55%.

But all that occurred before the race for the March 2000 presidential election really heated up. To the frustration of President Lee Teng-hui and his Nationalist Party,

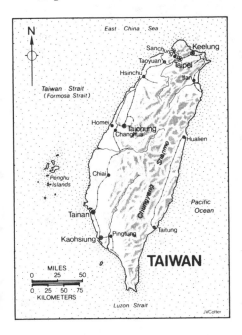

their hopes of a smooth transition from President Lee to another Nationalist Party president were dashed when the former Provincial Governor James Soong declared for the presidency. That development was hardly what President Lee, who had been supporting his own vice president Lien Chan, had hoped for. In fact, James Soong's challenge was particularly galling to some Nationalist Party members because he had once served as their own party's secretary-general before falling out with his former colleagues. By the early spring of 2000 the race had become a three man struggle between Soong, the pro-independence candidate Chen Shui-bian of the DPP and the President Lee's vice-president Lien Chan. For a time James Soong himself became the front runner partly because of an impression that he was best suited to successfully manage Taiwan's complicated relationship with mainland China.

But when the results of the March 18th 2000 presidential election were finally announced they proved to be far more of a watershed than almost any analyst had predicted. Chen Shui-bian, the former mayor of Taipei, and leader of the pro-independence forces, had won election to the presidency! Clearly the split within the ranks of the ruling Nationalists had made Chen's victory possible. More important than the details of the win was the reality that after a half century of rule by the Nationalists, who had moved their government to the island after their defeat on the mainland, the Guomindang no longer held the presidency of the Republic of China—an astounding step forward in Taiwan's effort to build a more modern democratic society.

But while some were celebrating this demonstration of the growing vitality of Taiwanese democracy, many were concerned about how Beijing would respond to the arrival to power on Taiwan of the Democratic Progressive Party which has been so much blunter in its calls for a formal declaration of official independence from China than the Nationalists.

As a practical matter, Chen appears to have won far more on the votes of those who were angry about corruption in Taiwan than any specific support for a confrontation with China, but as *East, Southeast Asia, and the Western Pacific 2000* was going to press it was still not clear how this dramatic new evolution of Taiwanese politics would play out in the international arena.

Taiwan's Foreign Relations

The fundamental goal of Taiwan's foreign policy is to gain international recognition. This is seen as essential to the island's survival as an independent state and has become even more important

each year. Taiwan is drawing economically closer to mainland China because of huge investments flowing in that direction. Thus her leaders know that they will need a counter-balancing political legitimacy capable of preventing the country from being swallowed up. There is no question that Taiwan is an independent entity in economic terms. The question of its official political standing has not yet been settled. Nevertheless Taiwan, with its NIC (Newly Industrialized Country) size economy has long been viewed as an independent actor by much of the global community. But politically things are less certain and Taiwan's efforts to gain further international recognition have regularly met with Beijing's active opposition.

Beijing's influence has continued to insure that Taiwan's president is not able to take part in the annual meetings of the Asia-Pacific Economic forum, APEC. Nor has Taiwan been able to make any real progress on gaining admission to the United Nations. Among the most significant recent disappointments was South Africa's decision in late 1996 to withdraw its recognition and open relations with Beijing. More recently Taiwan lost official recognition from three more nations, Tonga, the Central African Republic and Guinea Bissau. Clearly Beijing has won the most recent rounds in the struggle over Taiwan's official international position.

Unexpectedly the Asian economic crisis which began in 1997 opened up new opportunities for the island to expand its influence throughout Southeast Asia. Taking advantage of its own relatively stronger economic position than its neighbors, Taiwan's government and business community were quick to act as her neighbors' economies went into tailspins. Acting under a program called "Go South" her economic leaders looked for ways to expand Taiwan's economic and thus diplomatic influence in the area. The goal was to strengthen ties to the larger region as an important economic counter-balance to her growing ties to China. The government itself, helped by very healthy financial reserves, made it clear it was willing to help its neighbors through the crisis. It was after all a rare opportunity to expand Taiwan's international position even as Beijing, as usual, sought to lessen it.

On the diplomatic level President Lee had been especially active working to diplomatically distance the island further from China. In fact, he had spent a lot of recent effort publicly emphasizing Taiwan's independence in tones that could only antagonize Beijing further. Lee's campaign even included a warm reception for the visiting Dalai Lama, Tibet's exiled leader.

Interestingly, that visit had a significant impact that had not perhaps been anticipat-

Taiwan: Republic of China

ed. After the visit Beijing added a new demand to those it expected of the Tibetan leader. He was now expected, if he wished to work with Beijing, to officially announce that Taiwan was part of China. Most recently Lee infuriated Beijing by announcing that henceforth relations between the island and the mainland should be carried out in the manner of "State to State" relations. Not quite a declaration of independence but a pronouncement that set off another fire storm of denunciations from Beijing that is as determined as ever to eventually integrate the island into the People's Republic. And of course the new DPP government on Taiwan, however cautiously its newly elected leaders appeared to be acting during the early months of their arrival to power, is not likely to make Beijing any more optimistic about its eventual goals of reintegrating the island into the mainland.

Relations with the United States remained strong over the last year despite irritation in Taiwan over President Clinton's comments on the island during his visit to the People's Republic of China. There during his 1998 visit President Clinton had quite unambiguously stated that the United States did not support moves toward official independence for Taiwan. Obviously aware of how easily the United States could be dragged into a crisis between Taiwan and the People's Republic, the American president clearly wanted to eliminate any ambiguity which might make confrontations more probable in the future. But that hardly calmed Beijing which was also hearing a contrasting and decidedly more pro-Taiwan tone from members of the United States Congress many of whom have been working to strengthen American-Taiwanese military ties.

Taiwan's Economy

As the world saw, Taiwan was hit last fall by a devastating earthquake. The only positive aspect to the earthquake that struck in September of 1999 was that it had little impact on the island's economy. But for Taiwan's citizens, it was a terrible tragedy. Over 2000 people died and a far larger number lost their homes. It was the worst earthquake the country had experienced during the entire 20th century!

Although Taiwan's economy had been slowing down for some time, the economic turmoil of 1997–1998 actually saw the island relatively unaffected by the economic crisis that hit its neighbors so hard. In general, trends continued as before. In 1997, the economy repeated the performance of previous years with growth at about 6.7%. And 1998 ended with a healthy growth rate of around 8%—a figure many of its neighbors facing negative growth rates surely envied.

Nevertheless, Taiwan was not immune to the region's problems. It too had experienced weaknesses in its banking sector and a growing unemployment rate. And Taiwan's leaders have also resorted to governmental infrastructure projects designed to stir economic growth.

While official political relations with the mainland continue to be discussed in at times harsh terms, the economic reality is that Taiwan is growing more and more close to the mainland. Taiwan has invested billions in the mainland and connections between the two grow more and more common. In recent years plans were finally formalized to allow direct shipping between Taiwan's largest port at Kaohsiung to Xiamen and Fuzhou. For the time being the arrangement is only for the ships of foreign nationals and no direct cargo will be carried from the mainland to Taiwan but that day is surely coming. In fact, influential businessmen have been encouraging such direct trade. Last year Acer, the well known Taiwan based computer maker, even opened a production facility in Guangdong province.

But despite these growing economic ties the government has continued to insist that Taiwan's business community take a slow approach to investment on the mainland. Additionally, like so many rapidly developing countries, there is also a problem with infrastructure. Progress though is being made. After more than a decade of work, parts of Taipei's new mass transit system finally began operating recently.

In the long term some economists are also worried about the possibility of an economic weakening due to rising wages, and land costs and the increased costs of dealing with environmental issues. As the economy matures and wages rise, it is understandably harder to maintain competitiveness with the "younger" economies of Southeast Asia. Their forced devaluations during mid 1997 will only make competing with their now cheaper exports even more of a challenge in the future.

The Future: Taiwan

Economically Taiwan has reason to be satisfied. It has come through the last several years of horrible regional economic news in far better shape than most of its neighbors. Still evidence suggests that the population is nevertheless quite unsatisfied with developments. Especially high on the public agenda is mounting anger over a perceived breakdown in law and order. Several well publicized cases of kidnaping and murder were clearly making people feel far less secure.

Taiwan also needs to continue on its quest for international legitimacy if for no better reason than as a counterbalance to her growing economic integration with the mainland. The island's economy is still sound and its politics more and more democratic. If it can protect itself against shock waves coming from the mainland, its future can be bright. The biggest challenge will remain gaining as much political legitimacy as possible in the international community without arousing Beijing too much. Continuing to involve itself internationally is important. Declaring independence would be quite dangerous.

A Chinese painting class

Taipei metro under construction (1997).

Tokyo's shopping district, the Ginza, at night. *Courtesy: Japanese Embassy.*

Japan

Area: 142,726 sq. mi (370,370 sq. km.)

Population: 125,449,703 (est. 1996).

Capital City: Tokyo (Pop. 9.5 million, estimated).

Climate: Subtropically warm in the extreme South, becoming temperate in the North. The high elevations have much lower temperatures than the coastal areas. There is a rainy monsoon from June to October.

Neighboring Countries: The islands of Japan are closest to Russia (North); Korea (West); and mainland China (Southwest).

Official Language: Japanese.

Ethnic Background: Overwhelmingly Japanese—99.4%—and some Koreans. There is a very small community of *Ainu* on Hokkaido Island who are physically very different from the Japanese, possibly descended from the earliest inhabitants of the islands.

Principal Religions: Shinto, the earliest religious tradition, and Buddhism. The latter is especially widespread and split into many old and new sects; Christianity (less than 1%)

Main Export (to U.S., nations of Southeast Asia and Western Europe): Products of heavy industry, including ships and autos, products of lighter industry, including consumer electronics, cameras, and a wide range of other items, i.e., textiles, iron, steel, fish.

Main Imports (from nations of the Middle East and Southeast Asia): Oil, raw industrial materials, foodstuffs.

Currency: Yen.

National Day: December 23 (birthday of the Emperor).

Special Holiday: Sept. 15, "Respect for the Aged Day."

Chief of State: Emperor Akihito.

Head of Government: Yoshiro Mori, Prime Minister (since April 2000).

National Flag: White, with a red disk representing the rising sun in the center.

Per Capita GNP Income: U.S. $40,940.

The island nation of Japan consists of four larger bodies of land, Hokkaido, Honshu, Shikoku and Kyushu and the smaller Ryukyu Islands south of Kyushu. The southern half of Sakhalin and the Kurile Islands to the north, which Japan possessed at the height of its World War II power, were lost to the Soviet Union at the close of the conflict.

Geographically, Japan is part of an immense hump on the earth's surface which extends from Siberia on the Asian continent through Korea and Japan southward, rising above water again in the areas of Taiwan and the Philippines and extending further south Into the eastern portions of Indonesia and Australia. As is true in other portions of the ridge, Japan is geologi-

cally unstable and subject to frequent and sometimes violent earthquakes. Thermal pressures from deep in the earth escape periodically through the many volcanoes which are interspersed among the mountains. Mt. Fuji, its lofty crater surrounded by a mantle of snow, is visible from the streets of Tokyo on a clear day—one of the most beautiful sights in Asia. It has not been active since 1719. All of the mountainous areas, volcanic and non–volcanic, are scenic—the taller peaks on Honshu have justly earned the name "Japanese Alps."

The mountains leave little level space; only about 15% of the total land area is level, and much of the only large plain is occupied by the huge and busy capital of Tokyo. As a result, farms are located in the hilly areas of the islands and are made level by the labors of the farmers, who have

constructed elaborate terraces in order to win more land for their intense cultivation. Japanese farming is actually better called gardening, since the small units of land, an average of 2–1/2 to 5 acres per farm, are tilled with such energy that none of the soil or available growing season is wasted. This tremendous agricultural effort produces almost enough to feed the

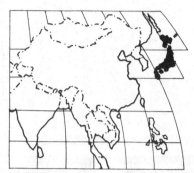

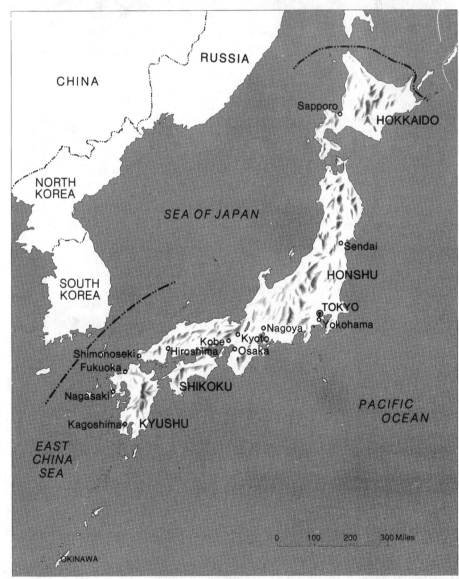

Japan

"Bullet" train streaking commuters home against the majestic background of Mt. Fuji

people, most of whom live in densely packed urban areas.

The climate of the islands is totally dominated by the seasonal winds, or monsoons. Cold winds blowing from the Asian continent invade the land beginning in September each year. All of Hokkaido and some of Honshu lie buried in snow from December to March. In the spring, the winds shift, blowing from the warm equatorial South Pacific; the growing season of Honshu and Hokkaido then commences.

The subtropical island of Kyushu remains warm all year around, permitting two or three harvests of paddy rice each year. Only one crop of dry, or field rice, grows in the much shorter summer of Hokkaido. In the last half of August and in September, the southern monsoon brings typhoons (hurricanes), laden with rainfall and often destruction from the Pacific to the shores of Japan.

Rainfall and weather are also affected by the oceanic water currents which envelop the islands. The warm southern *Kuro shio* dominates the summer months; the arctic *Oya Shio* descends as far south as Tokyo in the winter. Both currents bring a huge number of fish to the off–shore areas on the Pacific side, and an even larger number to the Sea of Japan. Depending almost wholly for animal protein upon this bounty from the sea, the Japanese raise only an insignificant number of livestock on the islands.

History

The earliest known inhabitants of the Japanese islands were probably the Ainu, a people who are physically very different from the Japanese. For much of Japan's history the Ainu people were driven steadily northward by the people arriving from mainland Asia. The Ainu exist today in small reservations on the

An Ainu elder　　　　　Courtesy: Jon Markham Morrow

island of Hokkaido where in recent years they have launched efforts among them to revive their ancient culture. The men have much more body and facial hair than the Japanese. Archeological evidence reveals the existence of a neolithic culture in Japan from about 10,000 B.C. known as *Jo-man*, from the rope patterned ceramics they produced. This community was apparently displaced around 300 B.C. with the arrival of other people from mainland Asia who introduced a rice–growing culture known as *Yayoi.*

The people who eventually formed the community we know as "Japanese" had themselves come primarily from the mainland of northeast Asia, by way of Korea, and are of the same linguistic ancestry as the Koreans. They were mainly of Mongolian stock whose ancestors had lived a nomadic existence on the continent of Central and Northeast Asia. This ethnic group became the predominant one, but there were also other elements from the South China coast and the Southwest Pacific.

All of these elements gradually blended into a people possessing very similar physical characteristics, considering the large size of the present population. In the first centuries A.D., the Japanese lived mainly around the Inland Sea, a body of water almost completely enclosed by three of the four large islands. They were organized into many warring clans and had no writing system with which to express their language, which is derived from dialects originally spoken in what is now Manchuria, Mongolia and Siberian Russia.

Japanese tradition tells of the creation of the islands by the sun goddess whose descendants founded the Yamato clan which eventually emerged as the Japanese imperial family. Actually, there is considerable evidence to suggest that the real origins of the imperial elite are to be found, not in Japan itself, but in Korea. In fact, some authors, going beyond the more vague references to "continental influences" have argued succinctly that the original Japanese ruling family was founded by the early southern Korean kingdom of Paekche. Whatever the specific ties to Korea, it is certain that the evolution of Japan was fundamentally altered by its leadership's decision to immerse itself in the culture of the continent in the 6th century A.D.

Encounter with China

The Japanese were greatly impressed by the tales told of Tang (618–907 A.D.)—China's power, wealth, prestige and culture. They quickly set about importing many aspects of Chinese civilization. Religiously, Buddhism was at its height and it was through that medium that a range of cultural, linguistic and political elements of Chinese civilization entered Japan. On a political level, the Yamato clan was interested in borrowing the Chinese imperial system since it offered the possibility of greatly enhancing their power far above the influence the clan had long held.

In an attempt to imitate the Tang dynasty, the Japanese imperial court built a capital at Nara, near the waters of the Inland Sea on the island of Honshu; they worked to establish a centralized governing system along Chinese imperial models. For a time the influence of China was enormous. The Chinese language was adopted as the official writing system and played a role similar to that of Latin in the medieval west. Later Kyoto emerged as the new imperial capital in the late 8th century and became the home of a brilliant culture. Histories were produced to "prove" the divinity and supremacy of the Yamato imperial clan. The 7th century B.C. was selected as the time that the sun goddess was said to have given the blessing of creation to Japan and established the reign of her descendants on the islands.

Imperial Court Life

Within court life at Kyoto, the arts flourished, especially a particularly distinctive literature which many believe to have

been the world's first formal novels. The physical form of the novels, produced by women of the imperial court, was influential as well. Interestingly, although literary production was considered a fundamental talent for both men and women of the imperial court, the men largely wrote in the adopted language of Chinese. Women, who in contrast, wrote using a system of modified characters known as

Kana to represent the sounds of Japanese, went on to write these profoundly influential works.

The best known of them, the *Tale of Genji,* a thousand page work about the romances of Prince Genji of the imperial court, is a sophisticated novel which deals with an extraordinary range of human emotions and sentiment. It is a far more personal and introspective work than the romances that had preceded it either in Japan or elsewhere. Written by Murasaki Shikibu during the early 11th century, the work ultimately became the model of refined behavior for educated Japanese, a literary influence that could only be compared to that of Shakespeare in the West.

As time passed and Imperial Tang China itself faded, the more direct links to China were severed. After the tenth century no more formal missions were sent to the Chinese court. By then the Japanese aristocracy was ready to build their own syntheses from both earlier Japanese traditions and the more recent borrowing from the court. If however, many aspects of the period of tutelage continued to in-

fluence Japan over the centuries, the Yamato imperial family's efforts to establish themselves as Chinese–style emperors failed.

The creation of a true central government was not possible because many clans, particularly those in central and northern Japan, were strong and independent—preoccupied with battling the Ainu people and each other. These clans did not

Japan

Shogun in Court attire

attempt to overthrow the imperial court, however. They contented themselves with largely ignoring it. Moreover many had ties to powerful court factions which gave them additional autonomy.

Although the more martial, semi–independent clans outside the capital admired and imitated the cultural achievements of imperial Kyoto, they were primarily interested in the military power. The Taira, one of the two most powerful military clans, defeated the other, the Minamoto, in 1160 and then temporarily seized control of Kyoto. Shortly afterward, the Taira were in turn defeated by the Minamoto, whose leader Yoritomo was appointed as the first *Shogun*, or Generalissimo, of Japan by the emperor. Thus was founded the *Kamakura Shogunate* which remained in power for 150 years and an entirely new system of ruling.

The Shoguns

With the emergence of the Minamoto family and the Kamakura *shogunate* they founded, Japan moved into a new phase of its development, one that would last in various forms until the 19th century. Although it varied over the centuries, it usually operated as a generally feudal society dominated by successive shogunal families best thought of as military dictators. For the next seven hundred years real

power usually existed in a somewhat precarious balance between regional lords and various shogunal families that emerged from time to time.

The imperial court remained largely irrelevant to the real issues of power. In fact, not until the nineteenth century, and then more in symbol than reality, would power appear to gravitate once again around the imperial court. For the feudal era even that appearance of power was gone.

Japan's feudal era has often been compared to feudalism in Western Europe, and indeed there were many similarities. Although Japan's feudal experience developed later than that in Europe it too was characterized by the dominating presence of an aristocratic military elite loyal to various regional lords or *daimyo* as they were known in Japan. In both regions, feudalism reflected the decentralized nature of power and a system that was built upon the labors of peasant farmers. Nevertheless, there were clear differences as well. The ties between the military elite, *samurai*, and the *daimyo* tended to be more personal and based on kinship than that of the more contractual minded Europeans who developed elaborate contracts to cement feudal relationships. And, of course, Western Europe never developed the institution of the *shogunate* which eventually became a sort of "halfway stage" between feudal society and the centralized governments of a modern country.

The Kamakura *shogunate* was soon faced with the external threat of the powerful empire established by the Mongol emperor Khubilai Khan in China in the 13th century. Two attempted Mongol invasions were defeated by a combination of Japanese military resistance and timely, violent typhoons. Interestingly, the Japanese perception that they had been saved by the intervention of divine winds, i.e. *Kamikazi*, was an inspiration under far different circumstances many centuries later as young Japanese suicide bombers attempted once again to save their country from invasion during the last days of the Second World War.

In the centuries after the 14th A.D., the fall of the Kamakura *shogunate* led to other weaker powers moving into the breach to establish their own dominance for a time. More importantly, the powerful regional lords known as *daimyo* came to dominate the life of the islands. These feudal lords were supported by highly trained and loyal *samurai*, who followed a warrior's creed of honor and loyalty known as *Bushido*. It was the bloody struggles among these regional leaders that made the late 16th century an exceptionally violent time in Japanese history.

The Tokugawa System: 1603–1868

Japan disintegrated into a state of feudal warfare in the 16th century resembling that of the Wars of the Roses in England. Commercial interests continued, however, to promote trade and build roads. Warfare was gradually brought under control in the later part of the century by two persons—Oda Nobunaga and his brilliant general, Toyotomi Hideyoshi, who succeeded Nobunaga as dictator when his overlord was killed by a dissident general. After two unsuccessful attempts to invade China (see Korea section), Hideyoshi was assassinated. Though things were a bit unsettled for a time, Japan was about to enter into one of its most stable eras, the *shogunate* of the Tokugawa.

In 1603 Tokugawa Ieyasu, a feudal lord from the region around present day Tokyo, then named Edo, emerged triumphant and established a new *shogunate* which lasted until the nineteenth century. The Tokugawa developed a complicated system which can be described as a sort of "centralized feudalism." On one hand the Tokugawa retained very considerable power, yet the regional lords, the *daimyo*, controlled their own domains. To retain power, the Tokugawa insisted that the lords maintain a residence and the permanent presence of themselves or family members at Edo. In short, the Tokugawa maintained control through a formal hostage system.

For generations thereafter, anyone on Japan's main thoroughfare was treated to the vision of aristocratic lords and their *samurai* entourages regularly traveling through the countryside to and from Edo. There is a curious irony to this system, sometimes known as the "alternative attendance" system. The Tokugawa *Shogunate* had been powerful enough to impose it on the many feudal lords of Japan, yet weak enough to need such a system to maintain control. Moreover, the system, designed to freeze the political and social structure of Japan under the Tokugawa, ironically had the unexpected effect of vastly improving the resources of the despised merchant class which served this enormous and peripatetic nobility.

The Arrival of the West

It was in the 16th century that the western ships, Spanish and Portuguese, began to arrive in Japanese waters and the various Catholic missionaries, from the aristocratic Jesuits to the more populist Franciscans, began to build commercial and religious ties to the islands. The Jesuits converted a large number of people, particularly in the island of Kyushu and its largest city, Nagasaki. Their position was enhanced by the conversion of a leading feudal lord of the island, which led many vassals and followers into the arms of the Church. Firearms and other Western methods of violence were introduced and eagerly adopted by the Japanese.

Spanish Franciscans, who arrived in 1593, began a period of even greater efforts toward conversion of the Japanese and also complicated the situation by periodic bickering with the Jesuits. If the missionaries were at first well received, the tensions among the Westerners and the Japanese' knowledge of their role in colonizing the Philippines, soon combined to arouse Japanese suspicions. Hideyoshi, who was in domination by the 1580s, became convinced that Christianity was nothing but a veil concealing a future European invasion and embarked on a course of persecution of priests and their converts. Later, also concerned that the Westerners could threaten their own power, the Tokugawa authorities moved not only to persecute Christians but to close the entire country to the outside.

For the next two hundred years the only Westerners allowed into the country were those on a yearly Dutch ship permitted to trade at Nagasaki. Ironically, Japan under the Tokugawa chose to isolate itself just as the West was beginning to dramatically emerge.

During this period of isolation, the clans, each ruled by a powerful *daimyo*, built ornate castles around which towns

Commodore Perry's fleet in Tokyo Bay

arose. Agriculture prospered, sporadically interrupted by revolts of the peasants, who lived in abject poverty. Trade flourished and the population increased. A merchant class emerged which quickly acquired a great deal of influence over the *daimyo* and the martial *samurai* by making loans to them. There was much intellectual activity, which was conservative, to the extent that it advocated that the imperial clan, which had survived over the centuries, be restored to full power and replace the "usurping" *shogunate*.

Over the next centuries sporadic attempts by the Western powers to "open" Japan to foreign trade were largely unsuccessful until the mid nineteenth century when the Russians, British and U.S. developed more serious plans to penetrate the islands. For the United States, which was to take the lead in Japan's departure from isolation, the effort was a logical extension of its generation-long thrust toward the Pacific and beyond. In 1846 San Francisco had been taken and an eye clearly directed to the possibilities of commerce beyond. Though Japan itself was of less interest than the riches of China, it was seen as a stepping stone to the Asian continent. Ironically, if the Americans who wanted to open the islands knew very little about Japan, many in Japan itself were quite knowledgeable about the outside world— they had had access to Western materials smuggled into Japan during the periodic visits of the Dutch ships at Nagasaki.

The Opening of Japan

The uncertainty among the Japanese when Commodore Perry of the United States sailed his fleet into Tokyo Bay in 1853–1854 is understandable. They had a good understanding of the military power the Westerners had demonstrated against China in the Opium War a decade earlier and knew they did not have the weapons to match the West. On the other hand, the policy of exclusion, now more than two centuries old, had become the accepted custom. No mere request by the arriving American flotilla could easily change that. The situation was even more complicated by the continuing antagonism of the southwestern domains of Satsuma and Choshu and the growing imperial sentiment which itself undermined the authority of the Tokugawa *Shogunate*.

Uncertain how to respond to Commodore Perry's demands, the *shogun's* government took the unprecedented step of asking the several hundred *daimyo* for their advice. Even though the answers received were not unanimous, they did demonstrate a generally anti–foreign tone. Nevertheless, the *shogun's* government, facing the potential military power of the Americans, signed the foreign treaties anyway thus even further alienating them from many of the feudal lords over whom they had so long dominated. Commodore Perry was therefore able to get the treaty desired by the U.S., and other powers

Japan

soon had their own agreements. All of these were patterned after the "unequal treaties" that were then being imposed on the waning Manchu dynasty of China.

The opponents of the Tokugawa, especially the powerful clans of the Southwest, accused the government of weakness and continued an anti–foreign campaign under the slogan "Honor the Emperor—Expel the Barbarians." But their enthusiasm for driving the Westerners out proved militarily impossible. Western naval bombardments at Kagoshima in 1863 and Shimonoseki in 1864 convinced them of the folly of their demands. Eventually they did an about–face, becoming eager advocates of learning as much as possible from the West in order to be better equipped to resist its influence and power.

The immediate problem though was frustration with the Western pressures. The Shogunal court found itself caught between the Western demands and the aroused *samurai* class. After a series of confrontations, the two–hundred and fifty year old Tokugawa *shogunate* collapsed in the face of a coalition of forces which included the southern domains of Satsuma and Choshu in alliance with the Kyoto–based imperial court. This truly revolutionary development known perhaps inappropriately as the "*Meiji Restoration*," due to the reemergence of the imperial court as a player, was to be the central turning point in modern Japanese history.

The Meiji Restoration

The *Meiji Restoration* was ostensibly the restoration of the Japanese emperor to power by the southern regions of the islands. What really occurred though was the arrival to power of an oligarchy of extraordinary young mid–level *samurai* mostly from the Southwest who were fundamentally committed to modernizing Japan in the face of the Western challenge. The leadership set up a strong central administration and governed in a style that nevertheless made some concessions to the concerns of those *samurai* elite left outside of the new constellation of power. Their fundamental goal was to build a "rich country and strong military" and to have Japan enter the Western family of nations as a full partner rather than, as was the case so often elsewhere, yet another victim of Western colonization.

Determined to make a dramatic break with the past, the new leaders issued a series of goals known as the "Charter Oath" which outlined their hope of reforming the social structure of Japan and to learn as much as possible from the outside world. The period of feudal isolation was clearly at an end. These new *Meiji* leaders wiped out the old clan system of authori-

Entrance of a Shinto temple at Nagasaki, c. 1880

ty and at the same time modernized land tenure. The landowning peasants were heavily taxed, however, yielding greater funds for modernization. Modern communications were established and new machinery was imported to manufacture textiles and other goods. An entirely new system of banking and other modern industrial techniques were imported and many "foreign experts" were temporarily engaged to help in the transformation.

A modern education system, eventually geared to the production of literate and obedient subjects of the Emperor, was cre-

ated. An effective army and navy and a modern legal system also emerged within a short time, eventually permitting the Japanese to renegotiate the "unequal treaties," but the leadership avoided foreign military adventures at first. On a political level, the *Meiji* oligarchies continued to dominate, though by the 1880s they found themselves pressed by a "popular rights" movement led by wealthier members of the peasant class and former members of the *samurai* elite. Eventually, after studying Western governmental systems, the leadership adopted a modified version of the imperial German parliamentary system.

A *Diet*, or parliament, was created under a constitution of 1889 that proclaimed the emperor as the supreme ruler. Nevertheless, behind the scenes the governing oligarchy continued to rule. The period of indiscriminately adopting foreign institutions and techniques diminished and practically ended by 1890. After that, although the interest in Western science and technology continued unabated, more emphasis was now placed on traditional Japanese institutions and customs. The emperor became the object of still greater glorification, even though he possessed little more than nominal power. This veneration interestingly was less a product of traditional Shinto imperial myths than Japan's search for modernity. The oligarchies who created the new governing system felt that the nation needed some sort of unifying principle to support its modernization and the ancient system of the imperial dynasty seemed to suit their purposes.

Economically, a small group of *zaibatsu* (large family–owned holding companies) arose which dominated the beginnings of industry in Japan in a manner reminiscent of Carnegie, Harriman and Morgan in the United States, but there was abundant room for small business as well. This balance between central control and local initiative, coupled with the rapid urbanization of Japan, its fairly low rate of population growth and the fact that the people demanded little in personal comforts, permitted a rate of modernization unparalleled in history.

By the end of the *Meiji* period (1868–1912), Japan had largely achieved its goal of modernization, a feat not duplicated by any other traditional nation in the world in such a brief period, or indeed anywhere on such a tremendous scale. Nevertheless, despite the changes in the material circumstances of Japan, many martial feudal values from the Tokugawa era would continue to be influential for generations.

The Rise of the Japanese Empire

The international arena that Japan had chosen to enter during the late nineteenth century was an aggressive one of imperialism. After centuries of colonization, the imperial urge had continued to grow at an even faster pace. Africa and Southeast Asia were being carved up by the Europeans, and the Americans were beginning to turn an eye toward the Hawaiian islands and eventually the Philippines. In central Asia, the Russians and English were competing for influence and China, the giant of traditional East Asia, was

struggling to maintain even a modicum of influence. Within Japan many would argue that they too had to take their place among the imperial powers and begin to assert themselves abroad.

For many, the first goal was obvious, the Korean peninsula. In fact, as early as the 1870s some in government had forcibly argued for a move against the then closed "hermit kingdom" of Korea. That early effort had not been carried out but by the 1890s the Japanese were aggressively competing with China for influence on the peninsula. By 1894 a full scale war had broken out. The Japanese army and navy seized control of Taiwan and conquered Korea, which was annexed in 1910. In its war with China, Japan fought alone, without the support of any of the major Western powers and aroused the antagonism of the Russians who had their own interests in the area. Working with other European powers, they forced the Japanese to give up at the bargaining table much of what they had won on the continent itself.

This lesson left a lasting impression on Japanese leaders. In their minds, the "Western imperialists" had their own set of rules; outsiders, like the Japanese, were not part of their "club" and were not permitted the same freedom of action as other world powers. Nevertheless, in 1903, the Japanese concluded an alliance with Britain that lasted until the 1920's. The ensuing period saw a tremendous growth in Japanese military and political power at the expense of its neighbors, in part a result of its strengthened position as a member of a Western alliance.

The Japanese, of course, did not conquer territory from the Chinese alone. By the turn of the century the dramatic episode known as the "Cutting of the Melon," had begun which saw the Western powers grabbing even more power for themselves throughout China. The Russians' actions particularly aroused Japanese anger. The two were competing for influence in northeast Asia. The Russians had established a "sphere of influence" in Manchuria dating from 1898. By 1904 The

The late Emperor Hirohito at his coronation, 1926

Japan

Japanese felt ready to challenge them and launched a victorious land and sea campaign (the Russo–Japanese War) and thereby established themselves as the leading power in East Asia—in fact, one of the world's major powers.

A decade later Japan did not waste the opportunity offered by the vulnerability of Germany during World War I. It quickly declared war and seized its holdings in Shandong Province in China, as well as several small island groups in the Pacific. At the same time, it shipped considerable quantities of munitions to the Allied Powers, including Russia, its former enemy. At the end of the war, and after the Bolshevik Revolution of 1917, Japan sent a large military force to occupy eastern Siberia to see if the region could be added to the growing Japanese empire. Internal and external pressures though forced them from Siberia and also from Shandong by 1922.

The newly installed *Orchid Emperor of Manchukuo* reviews Japanese troops at Dairen in 1934

Taisho Democracy

The post–World War I period in Japan was one of transition. The original *Meiji* Constitution of 1889 had not worked quite as anticipated. The cooperation of the parliamentary parties had become more necessary than expected for the smooth operation of government and they had thus gained in power. Party leaders such as Hara Kei emerged in power as prime ministers and Japan entered an era where more experimentation was carried out in democratic decision making. The voting lists were enlarged to include the whole of the adult male population. The political parties became more influential than ever before. By the 1920s two political parties rotated in power and a system of formal parliamentary government seemed to be at hand.

Nevertheless, the parliamentary leaders found much of the real power needed to run the country still denied them. The military and bureaucracy remained extraordinarily influential and the aging oligarchic leadership still powerful. Internationally these parliamentary governments were more inclined toward negotiation and signed a treaty limiting the growth of the navy much to the irritation of the Japanese right wing.

But the speed of modernization in Japan left unsolved some problems and created many others. The rural population remained isolated from urban progress, while continuing to pay for it by increased taxes, rents and difficult conditions in the countryside in the 1920's, all of which created much discontent. Moreover, Japan had changed greatly since their days of isolation. The country's economy was far more integrated into the international order than ever before. Thus, not surprising-

ly, the onset of the great depression hit the country very hard and the rural peasants especially so. The cause of the peasants was championed by ambitious army officers, partly in sincerity but also for political reasons. The officers, who were often of rural origin, found allies among some civilian nationalists. They adopted the position that rural poverty had two basic causes: poor government by the political parties and economic practices by the large combines. They criticized the political parties, who were more influential during the 1920's than at any previous time.

The *zaibatsus,* also came under fire for their devotion to the goal of high profits. The military and civilian nationalists also blamed injurious and "insulting" tariffs and discriminatory trade policies of some foreign nations for the adverse conditions of the peasants. The answer to Japan's dilemma was, in their eyes, usually further expansion into the mainland which was seen as a "new frontier" which could be developed for Japan's benefit and receive its excess population.

This line of argument had a broad base of appeal, and the rightists strengthened their position by taking forceful action in the form of assassinations and coups. The extreme right wing did not succeed, but it was able to force the parliamentary parties from power.

Toward War With China

From the early 1930s, though the extremists failed to gain power, Japan was again controlled by conservative leaders often drawn from the military. All political parties were abolished in 1940. Within China, Japan took advantage of the conflict between the nationalist forces of Chiang Kai–shek and the Chinese communists. Increasing pressures, both diplomatic and military, were brought to bear

in order to give Japan great influence over China. The Japanese army seized Manchuria in 1931–1932, soon after the local authorities had threatened Japan's interests by accepting the authority of Chiang Kai–shek's government.

Renaming the area Manchukuo, the Japanese military established the youthful Henry Pu–Yi, the "last emperor" of the Manchu dynasty, as its puppet emperor. Frequent military clashes with China led to an invasion of eastern China in 1937, in the course of which a multitude of atrocities were committed by the invading soldiers. The best known of these came to be known as the "Rape of Nanjing" for the reign of terror the Japanese soldiers inflicted on that city's hapless residents. With that development World War II had begun in Asia. Within two years it would be expanded by Hitler's invasion of Poland.

Merciless bombing of the mainland cities alienated the Chinese completely and enabled both Chiang and Mao to rally support for their separate struggles against the Japanese. Eventually an uneasy truce emerged between the two Chinese leaders because of the Japanese threat. Nevertheless the Japanese forces remained in occupation of the major cities of eastern China. These Japanese efforts at expansion led to increasing criticism and pressure from the outside world, including the United States. Unfortunately for the Chinese, only the Russians initially offered any significant official help.

Eventually though, in an effort to limit the capability of the Japanese war machine, the U.S. gradually cut down shipments of oil and scrap steel. This reduced shipment of strategic materials caused the Japanese to look for sources elsewhere, particularly to iron in the Philippines and oil in Indonesia. By the 1940s the successful German victories provided an example of the rewards of aggression and weakened those Western colonial powers the Japanese were soon also to challenge. Fortunately for the rest of the world, cooperation between Nazi Germany and Japan was always very unsteady even though they and Italy formed an alliance in 1940. All three, but most of all the European "Axis" powers, had the habit of making bargains with other nations without consulting or informing their allies.

World War II in the Pacific

In late 1941, Japan decided to force the issue with the Americans. They demanded an unfreezing of its assets in the United States, a measure which had been undertaken in response to the July 1941 Japanese invasion of Indochina. Washington refused to continue oil and scrap steel shipments, and in addition, encouraged the Dutch in Indonesia to withhold their oil unless the Japanese agreed to a political settlement, which would have involved an end to aggression and withdrawal from China. The Japanese had no interest in such a dramatic retreat. The Americans were unwilling to compromise with a nation many felt would not dare attack. The die was cast for an even greater extension of the developing world war.

Believing that the U.S. would oppose any Japanese seizure of the resources of Southeast Asia, the Japanese decided to destroy the U.S. Pacific Fleet stationed at Pearl Harbor in Hawaii. On December 7, 1941 Japanese airplanes without warning almost completely wiped out the U.S. battleship fleet stationed at Pearl Harbor. The imperial forces of Japan then quickly attacked the many Western colonies in Southeast Asia. Initially, their superior might in the Pacific was impressive enough to cause fear of an imminent naval attack on California. While that threat never materialized, it did arouse enough popular sentiment on the American west coast to round up the region's Japanese–American population, regardless of their U.S. citizenship, and relocate them to prison camps over the next several months.

The Japanese army met its greatest resistance in the Philippines, where the people cooperated with the U.S. defense force led by General Douglas MacArthur. But ultimately the islands fell. Apart from unwise attempts to gain still further territories from Australia and India, the Japanese military settled down to occupy and exploit their newly won empire. The only land resistance during this period was sporadic and weak, from Chiang Kai–shek's forces, which were contained in southwest China, and from Mao Zedong's troops in the northwest.

Although many Japanese convinced themselves that they were on a great mission to free Asia from Western colonialism, their own brutality against the local peoples very quickly alienated these communities and created an anti–Japanese sentiment in parts of the region that continues to this day. In the later years of the war, active resistance to the Japanese formed in most Southeast Asian lands they had conquered.

As the war economy of the United States came into full production, the Japanese suffered increasing defeats in naval and air battles with the U.S. Australia initially served as the main base for the Allied campaign; it and New Zealand also contributed fighting units to the war. Island after island fell to American Marines and Allied Army units. U.S. aircraft and warships, principally submarines, cut the Japanese islands off from Japanese Southeast Asian and the Southwestern Pacific conquests by sinking tremendous amounts of shipping and by defeating the Japanese navy. By 1944 General Tojo, who had led Japan to war with the U.S., was deposed as premier and disappeared from the circle of military officers who were in control. Important persons in the imperial court and the government saw that the war was lost and believed that peace should be negotiated as soon as possible in order to save the Emperor and avoid a communist revolution. The military however insisted on continuing the losing battle; the Emperor might have overruled them but chose to remain silent fearing that a move on his part might create an even more destructive civil war. The stage was set for the Americans to force a surrender without invading the Japanese home islands.

The Atomic Bombs

On August 6, 1945, the sky above Hiroshima was lit by the fiery destructiveness of the first atomic bomb used in the history of the world. The Japanese were already hard pressed by the Allied troops, who were being reinforced by soldiers that arrived in the area after the fall of Germany earlier in the year. On August 8, the Soviet Union declared war on Japan. It had agreed to do this the preceding February in exchange for postwar control of Outer Mongolia, and territories like southern Sakhalin Island and the Kurile Islands. A second atomic bomb was dropped on Nagasaki on August 9; the next day the war and peace factions went to the Emperor and submitted the choice of war or surrender.

The Emperor, in an act of great moral courage, chose surrender. The final terms of capitulation were agreed to by August

14, 1945, and the formal agreement was signed aboard the U.S.S. Missouri in Tokyo Bay on September 2, 1945. The islands had been terribly battered and exhausted by the war. National morale was almost completely crushed; some army leaders and high government officials chose *seppuku*, a formal suicide which eliminated the necessity of facing their conquerors or the people they had led.

The American decision to use the atomic bombs has continued to arouse heated controversy more than a half century after their use. Some have argued that Japan was already defeated—that the bomb was used more to intimidate the Soviets than to end the Pacific War. Considerable documentation exists to suggest the usual combination of mixed motives on the part of the American leadership. Nevertheless, regardless of the decision–making process then going on in Japan, which American leaders were not privy to, many believed then and now, however correctly or not, that the use of the bombs would eliminate facing a bloody invasion of the Japanese home islands with an accompanying loss of lives which was incalculable. Whether the war could have been ended without resort to either atomic weapons or an invasion we will never know.

Japan's Foreign Minister Shigimitsu signs the documents of surrender aboard the *U.S.S. Missouri*, while General MacArthur broadcasts the ceremonies

Japan

Their Imperial Majesties Emperor Akihito with Empress Michiko

The Postwar Occupation

The American occupation of Japan after World War II was initially an ambitious attempt to remake Japan's political, economic, and educational institutions in a way that would prevent the future reemergence of militarism. In reality, the occupation can be divided into two distinct periods, the period of the transformation of a defeated enemy and the period, after the commencement of the Cold War, of working to revive their former foe and transform it into a loyal ally in the struggle against communism. During that early phase, the Supreme Commander of Allied Powers (SCAP), MacArthur's headquarters, rewrote the Japanese constitution, began to break up the powerful *zaibatsu* business conglomerates, and completely revamped the Japanese educational system.

In many respects, some of the reforms forced on Japan in the war's aftermath were more liberal than many comparable U.S. policies. Most importantly, the circumstances of the rural Japanese were vastly improved as the occupation forces moved to lessen tenancy and help establish the peasantry as a land–owning class.

Moreover, the right wing of both the military and civilian sectors were purged with the goal of rebuilding Japanese governance on a new more peaceful basis. The pre–war parliamentary system, which had been largely suppressed during the 1930s, was revived and this time its authority was more clearly established and codified. Unions were encouraged as never before as the Americans sought to rebuild Japan largely in its own image. Women were granted the vote during this restructuring as well.

The American efforts were as much the product of ignorance, however, as they were of a concerted effort to remake Japanese society in America's image. And as the Cold War developed by the late 1940s many American reforms were abruptly curtailed as the U.S. hastily sought to firmly anchor Japan as an anticommunist bastion in the Far East. Union activities, earlier encouraged, were now often suppressed in the name of the supreme struggle with communism.

The war in nearby Korea also had a profound impact on the course of the occupation. The socialists, who naturally supported some of the liberal reforms proposed by the Americans, were now eyed with suspicion and many were purged from government positions by SCAP authorities. Japanese moderates were genuinely frightened by prospects of political unrest and they feared a communist takeover right on their Korean doorstep. Discredited conservative politicians, removed from office due to their support of Japan's war effort, were rehabilitated as anti–communist allies. The war had a number of other effects as well. While the Japanese adhered to the constitutional prohibition against maintaining armed forces, under U.S. pressure a national armed constabulary was formed. Heavily armed, these "police" effectively replaced U.S. occupation troops, freeing them for combat on the Korean peninsula. Japan's devastated industries were slowly revived by the Korean war boom, providing supplies and equipment for the U.S. war effort. Almost overnight, the nature of the U.S. occupation and U.S.–Japanese relations had changed dramatically.

A peace treaty was signed with the United States and some other Western and Asian nations in 1951, but the communist bloc refrained from concluding formal peace accords. Under the U.S. treaty, Japan regained its independence, but lost all of its empire outside the home islands. Further reparations were left to be determined between Japan and each individual country concerned. A security treaty was signed with the U.S. under which America was to maintain military bases in Japan and to administer Okinawa in the Ryukyu Islands, where the U.S. had established its largest military base in the western Pacific. This treaty was renewed in 1960, but was modified at that time by the inclusion of certain concessions to Japan. It was renewed a second time in 1970. The island was finally returned to Japanese jurisdiction on May 15, 1972.

The Structure of Postwar Politics

The new constitution introduced in 1947 under the occupation had established a constitutional monarchy and a parliamentary system resembling those of Britain. It also provided (in the famous Article Nine) that Japan forever relinquished the right to make war and or even to maintain armed forces. This article, which on the surface would appear to ban even self–defense, has been gradually loosened over the years. Japan created an armed constabulary in the early 1950's, which, after being armed with heavy weapons, aircraft, and tanks, expanded into the Japan Self Defense Force. Japan's deepening commitment to the U.S. alliance and growing global importance have today expanded the role of self–defense to include responsibility for shipping lanes out to a 1,000–mile radius from the Japanese islands; Japan's navy (Maritime Self Defense Forces) is one of the largest in Asia.

The constitution failed to mention, and in this way repudiated, any divine attributes or political power on the part of the emperor. In spite of this, or perhaps because of it, Emperor Hirohito remained a generally respected symbol of the nation. In 1986 he celebrated his 85th birthday and also the sixtieth anniversary of his accession to the throne—one of the longest reigns in modern history. He adjusted remarkably well to the tremendous changes in Japan since World War II—essentially from a military–dominated authoritarian state to a parliamentary democracy. He was kept informed of political developments by the prime minister.

After one of the longest reigns in history, and after a lengthy illness, Emperor Hirohito died on January 7, 1989. He was succeeded by his modern–minded son Crown Prince Akihito (sometimes referred to as the Rising Son), who took the

Japan

title *Heisei* (Achieving Peace) for his reign. This transition evoked a great deal of soul searching in Japan about the responsibility for World War II in the Pacific and about Hirohito's role in that war. The fairest verdict seems to be that Hirohito had not favored Japanese aggression but had felt bound as a constitutional monarch (although theoretically divine) to accept the advice of his officials. At the end of the war, he certainly showed great moral courage in dealing first with his own militarists and then with the American Occupation authorities. New information available after his death suggests that the Emperor had feared an earlier intervention on his part might well have provoked a civil war within Japan.

Ironically, the parliamentary parties that had represented the official left wing of Japanese politics in the pre–war era became in the post war years, after the militant ultra–nationalists were purged, to represent a conservative front of big–business, pro–American politicians. Merging in 1955 into the *Liberal Democratic Party*, the domination of the *LDP* was so great that the opposition parties had no realistic chance to come to power. In fact, real politics revolved within the *LDP* where the party's many factional leaders competed for power within the party and thus over the Japanese government itself. They continued to dominate the political scene until the 1980s when their power began to weaken. Nevertheless, though the *LDP's* influence was enormous in the decades after the war, even its power was dramatically limited due to the extraordinary control of the entrenched Japanese bureaucracy.

Suburban Washington, D.C.? No, suburban Tokyo!   Courtesy: Alfred Magleby

Seaweed, widely used in cooking, is gathered off the rocky coast.
Courtesy: Marilynn and Mark Swenson

Moreover, Japan, like so many other countries, has been dominated by "money politics." Politicians have very heavy expenses, since they are expected to make presents to many of their constituents and to make outright gifts of money to their supporters. The funds for these transactions come mostly from business, in one form or another. For this reason, the political clout of the enormously wealthy business community has increased greatly over the years.

During the post–war era much of the wind was taken out of the opposition's sails by the remarkable growth of the Japanese economy which began in the 1960's. Premier Hayato Ikeda (1960–4) avoided

the controversial behavior of his predecessor Kishi, cultivated a "low posture" in politics and launched a program to double the gross national product by the end of the decade, a goal that was more than achieved.

His successor, Eisaku Sato (1964–1972), was more "high posture" and created considerable controversy, mainly by staying in office for the unusually long period of eight years and by being perceived, especially in Beijing, as being too pro–U.S. and too pro–Taiwan. In 1965 Sato announced his determination to regain jurisdiction over Okinawa, and after prolonged negotiations with the U.S., the island, as well as the rest of the Ryukyus, reverted to Japan in 1972. Sato also cooperated with the U.S. to a degree during the first several years of the Vietnam war, from which Japanese firms made large profits by selling supplies and equipment to the U.S. for use, as they had during the Korean War.

Japan's special relationship with the United States did not save it from the geo–political dramas of the early 1970s. Long supporters of the pro–Taiwan stance of the United States, the Japanese were shocked when the White House, without any advance warning, set out to improve relations with the People's Republic of China. Although Prime Minister Sato hesitated, his successor moved quickly to establish relations with Beijing.

Kakuei Tanaka, a farmer's son and popular politician was elected president of the ruling *Liberal Democratic Party* in 1972, thus assuring him the prime ministership. He then paid a successful visit to Beijing and established diplomatic relations with the People's Republic of China. But in 1973 a series of political and economic setbacks badly eroded the Tanaka govern-

Japan

Former Emperor Hirohito addresses the opening of the Diet.

Courtesy: Japanese Embassy

ment's popularity. Inflation, pollution and ever–present corruption continued to be major issues.

Japan's international vulnerability due to its limited national resources was especially demonstrated in late 1973 when there was a temporary Arab oil embargo against Japan arising from the Middle East war. The *LDP* government had long supported American policies in the Middle East that had usually meant a generally pro–Israeli position. But Japan was importing 80% of its oil from the Middle East. The price of oil quadrupled. Recognizing the situation, the government made statements critical of Israel and began to woo the Arab states, in particular, by promising them $3 billion in aid. Moreover, it set about, as the United States was doing as well, to attempt to create a strategic oil reserve which, it was hoped, would make Japan less vulnerable in the future.

This crisis reduced Japan's economic growth in 1974 roughly to zero and further weakened the Tanaka government. In order to recover, the ruling *LDP* spent large sums of money received from business contributions in an effort to influence elections in mid–1974 for the upper house of the Diet, the House of Councillors. The party emerged with only half the seats they had previously held and suffered a further setback when business contributions began to decline. Several leading figures resigned from the cabinet, and the feeling grew that if Tanaka stayed in office until his term expired in 1975, he would bring disaster to his party in the next elections to the lower house of the Diet, The Watergate affair in the United States and President Nixon's resignation

in 1974 had heightened the attention of the Japanese public on the behavior of their own leaders. The final blow fell in October–November 1974, when a series of press articles exposed Tanaka's personal wealth and the questionable means by which it had been obtained.

Feeling that it might be facing its last chance to save itself from losing power, the Liberal Democratic Party dispensed with the usual jockeying for the premiership and chose the moderate Takeo Miki as its standard bearer. The latter published a list of his personal assets—an unprecedented step in Japan. Nevertheless, in the years after the Tanaka scandal was exposed concern over corruption in Japanese politics and specifically within the LDP would continue to grow.

And worse news was to come. In early 1976 it was revealed in the United States that over the previous twenty years the Lockheed Aircraft Corporation had paid about $21 million in bribes to various Japanese officials and politicians to promote the sales of various types of military aircraft.

Over the next years the long term political domination of the LDP continued more and more in question and a series of relatively nondescript leaders led the country until late 1982 when the able and energetic Yasuhiro Nakasone, emerged as Japan's new prime minister.

Nakasone was a controversial figure, partly because of his desire for a larger defense budget and partly due to his close connection with former Premier Tanaka—in fact, the two were sometimes referred to collectively as "Tanakasone." Nevertheless, the *LDP* did well in the elections to the House of Councillors in mid-

1983. In spite of its successes, the party continued to have a major burden—Tanaka remained in the Diet (even though he had nominally resigned from it) and controlled the largest faction of the party. Worse yet, he was convicted and sentenced to four years in prison, although he never went to jail.

Without opposition, Nakasone was re-elected to a second term as president of the party and, therefore, prime minister in late 1984. However, he faced continuing and serious problems. He was still dependent on the support of the disgraced Tanaka. Further, it was only after considerable delay and great effort that he was able to push Japan's defense budget to a level above 1% of the gross national product. He did not however take effective steps to reduce the huge trade and payments imbalance in Japan's favor as requested by the United States. The prime minister also faced a rising level of political activity by opposition parties, especially the *Socialists* under their new, moderate leader, Masashi Ishibashi.

Prime Minister Nakasone maintained a high profile abroad as well as at home. He visited the United States in January 1983 and Southeast Asia the following May. President Reagan returned the visit in November. Nakasone threw his considerable prestige and popularity in 1985 behind an appeal to Japanese business and the Japanese public to import and buy more foreign (especially American) goods, so as to reduce Japan's huge payments surplus. This appeal had little effect, except to worry the Japanese about their economic relations with the United States and the possibility of American protectionism.

Japan

Early in 1986, Nakasone decided to call an election for the lower house of the Diet for July, to coincide with the regular election of one half of the upper house every three years. He apparently wanted a third two-year term as President of the *Liberal Democratic Party* and as Prime Minister. The issue he selected to campaign on was the denationalization of the efficient, but unprofitable, Japanese National Railways, a very controversial move. In reality he appeared to be trying to distract public attention from a potentially even more controversial issue, certain legislation, including an Official Secrets Act, that he was trying to get through the Diet so that the United States would consider the Japanese government able to maintain security on sensitive information and thus eligible to take part in the lucrative American effort to develop the "Star Wars" defense initiative.

In the 1986 elections, helped by the premier's good image, the *LDP* won 309 seats in the lower house, more than ever before. Its main gains were in the cities and at the expense of the *Japan Socialist Party*, which dropped to 87 seats in the lower house. In an effort to make a fresh start, the *JSP* then elected a woman, Takako Doi, as its chairwoman, an unprecedented step for a major Japanese political party.

Despite Nakasone's accomplishments his premiership did not always go smoothly. His efforts to reform the tax laws and to privatize institutions like the Japanese railroads aroused opposition. And he also damaged his prestige with some remarks he made in 1986 to the effect that Japan's relatively homogeneous population gave it a marked advantage over the U.S. and its more multi-ethnic society.

Thus, in spite of the July 1986 electoral victory, Nakasone's political career was weakening and by 1987 he resigned in favor of Noboru Takeshita a low profile politician who had just taken over the leadership of former Premier Tanaka's sizable faction in the Diet. With Nakasone's departure went the last relatively strong LDP leader Japan would see for many years.

The End of *LDP* Domination?

With the advent of the Takeshita government in 1987, Japanese politics began to change. The years of domination and corruption charges had clearly taken their toll on the *LDP*. No longer were they the masters of Japanese politics, and an era of instability, of revolving door prime ministers and governments, began that would continue until the mid 1990s. In fact, there were eight prime ministers in the period from October 1987 to July 1998, with the longest term in office being just over two years! And despite the weakening of the

LDP it can be argued that many of the fundamentals of Japanese politics during this revolving door period differed little from what came before. That is, factionalism, corruption, the dominance of big business and money politics still pervaded the system.

While the Japanese political spectrum had been dominated by an essentially conservative majority, factions built around prominent and powerful individuals within the *LDP* were common. Thus, the *LDP* could not be thought of as an extremely homogeneous party. As described below, these factions eventually broke to form new independent parties.

The country's electoral system also has contributed to the instability. Until the changes in the electoral law in 1994, Diet members were elected entirely from multi-member districts. The presence of factions and more political parties guaranteed a large number of candidates and that candidates from the same party would have to compete against each other. Essentially, under this system, the way to get elected was to buy votes. Since each voter had only one vote, there was a fixed number of votes to be divided up. It is obvious, therefore, what a significant infusion of campaign spending could do. A new structure of voting patterns would not emerge until after the 1994 reforms were implemented in the elections of late 1996.

Among the many crises which affected Japanese politics in those years was the controversy that swirled around the Recruit Cosmos Company. The roots of the scandal began as early as 1984, when a rising but outsider firm, the Recruit Cosmos Company, began to try to buy influence by making interest free loans to politicians and senior bureaucrats which allowed them to purchase the company's stock. Two years later, when the stock was publicly available, huge profits were earned. Later though, when one of Japan's most influential newspapers, the *Asahi Shimbun,* exposed the transaction large numbers of Japan's most influential people, some 160 individuals, found themselves caught in the scandal. It would help tarnish the reputation of Japan's political establishment that it has yet to recover from.

CONTEMPORARY GOVERNMENT

Japan is a constitutional monarchy, with the constitution dating to May 3, 1947. Administratively, the country is divided into 47 prefectures. It has universal suffrage at age 20. The legal system is modeled after European civil law with some English and American influence. The Supreme Court has the power of judicial review over legislative acts.

Tokyo's expressways curve and divide as they crisscross the city.

Courtesy: Japanese Embassy

Japan

The Emperor is the ceremonial head of state. The Prime Minister heads the government and has the power to appoint the cabinet. The legislature, or *Diet,* is bicameral, consisting of the upper House of Councillors and a lower House of Representatives. New electoral laws took effect on January 1, 1995, but were not tested until the fall of 1996. The reforms left untouched the upper House of Councillors which is less significant in the legislative process. Under the new system, the lower house consists of 500 members. Of these, 300 are elected from single member districts. The remaining 200 are chosen through a system of proportional representation.

Parties with at least five Diet seats and which received at least 2% of the vote in the last national election receive government funding. Candidates can receive funds from their party, may accept a corporate contribution up to $5,000, and must report contributions over $500. The original bill banned corporate contributions, but the *Liberal Democratic Party* changed this. The reforms on campaign spending resemble those implemented in the U.S. in the 1970s. If the American experience is any example, then it may be assumed that big business will still find a way to use its money.

For a time, the results of the October 1996 elections suggested that Japan's recent era of revolving door governments might finally be over. As expected the new rules weakened the ability of the small parties to compete. Moreover tensions within the opposition, especially the *New Frontier Party*, eventually allowed the *LDP* to regain for the first time in four years, a majority in the powerful lower house of parliament. To some observers these developments suggested that the several years of instability which had followed the end of the *LDP* 's longtime dominance might be over.

Leading the LDP's comeback was Ryutaro Hashimoto, the reelected Prime Minister, who initially seemed posed to be a far more long-lasting leader than his weak predecessors. He first became prime minister in mid-January 1996. This was the fourth change in government since the July 1993 elections, and it had temporarily returned the *LDP* to control of the premiership. It then fell to Hashimoto to build on that temporary return to power.

Hashimoto was admired for his strong stand against former American Trade Representative Mickey Kantor in discussions over automobile imports and other issues. The new Prime Minister also handled well the difficult negotiations over the American bases in Okinawa. In the end he built an agreement that seemed to satisfy at least some of the demands of each side.

Through mid 1997 Hashimoto, who seemed particularly popular with the public, was well positioned to attempt major reforms of the economy. And there was plenty of reason to push for reform given Japan's poor economic performance during the 1990s.

For much of Japan's modern history, despite the domination of the *LDP*, the real governors of Japan were the prestigious bureaucrats that controlled the major government ministries. But recent trends within the *LDP* and in the population at large suggested that the reign of the bureaucrats was at long last about to be challenged.

Moreover, while much of Japan's post war politics were driven by the successful economy, those more certain years seem to be fading into the past. Meanwhile there has developed a strong conviction that over-regulation has not only added impediments to the economy but made day to day life for Japanese citizens harder as they struggle with extraordinarily high prices on consumer goods.

Especially interesting is that recent calls for profound reform of the country's system of regulation have been coming not from foreigners, as is common, but also from the Japanese themselves. In fact they have often appeared increasingly interested in making whatever changes are necessary to revive the economy after so many years of weakness.

But missteps weakened Hashimoto and slowed the progress of reform considerably. Especially embarrassing was his early decision to appoint a known bribe taker to a cabinet position responsible for rooting out corruption! Though the decision was reversed the slide in Hashimoto's popular support had begun.

But the core of Hashimoto's problems was the reality that Japan's economy kept sliding from stagnation to genuine recession and by the elections of July 1998 the voters were ready to make their dissatisfaction known. In an especially high voter turnout the LDP's vote totals went down as those of their opponents in the newly reorganized Democratic Party, the LDP's largest rival, went up. Anti LDP sentiment was so strong that even the votes of the Communist Party went up.

Hashimoto resigned the next day and after an internal struggle within the LDP, Keizo Obuchi, leader of the largest LDP faction emerged the party's new leader and Japan's new Prime Minister. Seen as a relatively bland individual, Obuchi presented himself as a leader committed to regaining Japan's economic momentum. Thus recent years have seen the Japanese people presented with a dizzying array of different plans for recovery from tax cuts and new spending programs to govern-

ment payroll cutbacks. Fortunately, for Obuchi, as Japan moved into the new century her economy was finally showing clear signs of recovering economically. And Obuchi himself was strengthening his position by enlarging his government by building a new coalition that included important segments of the political opposition including the leaders of the Liberal Party and the New Komeito Party with its ties to significant parts of the Buddhist community. But Obuchi's personal luck ran out during the winter of 2000 when the newly installed prime minister suffered a massive stroke and became unable to carry out his responsibilities. In his stead, Yoshiro Mori was chosen to succeed him.

New Stresses

The last several years have not gone well in Japan. The political and economic weakening has been complemented by other even more disturbing events and trends. The country experienced a "reality check" of sorts when its long assumption of being well prepared for earthquakes was severely challenged by the government's often poor performance in responding to the Kobe Earthquake of January 1995. The quake measured 7.2 on the scale and the death toll eventually climbed over 5,000, with 26,000 injured and 300,000 left homeless. Offers for assistance poured into the country which in some cases the government was very slow in accepting. But that was not the only trauma of recent years.

In mid-1995 Japanese prosecutors secured the indictment of cult leader Shoko Ashara, for masterminding the poison gas attack which killed 12 people on the Tokyo subway earlier in the year. Since the incident, numerous cult officials and members have been detained and there have been fears of additional gas attacks. One observer referred to the matter as Japan's spring of terror. *Aum Shinrikyo,* the cult which had masterminded the gas attack, has now been shown to have had far more ambitious projects in mind. Investigations have revealed efforts to obtain samples of the deadly Ebola virus in Africa, the employment of nuclear engineers in Russia and an apparent effort to mine uranium in Australia. How much more terrifying their effort might have become for Japan and the world is only just now being assessed.

By late century the sense that Japan was somehow free from the social ills that beset much of the rest of the world was crumbling. During a 1996 holiday party in the Japanese embassy in Lima, Peruvian leftists broke in and took hundreds of guests hostage. That the rebels had singled out Japan, whose ties with Peru had grown since President Fujimori came to power in Peru was something quite new for the Japanese.

For so many years such international incidents had been the problem of other nations, not Japan. One writer, commenting on the full range of Japan's recent experiences even went so far as to write an article about Japan finally becoming an "ordinary" country.

Perhaps the most obvious example of Japan becoming an "ordinary" country has been the significant increase in the number of Japanese firms that have found themselves taken over by huge foreign multi-nationals. That more and more Japanese now find their ultimate employers to be foreigners is certainly something new for Japan but quite familiar elsewhere.

Foreign and Defense Policy

Several issues have dominated Japanese foreign and defense policy recently. Especially significant in the last year were questions about relations with the Korean peninsula. While ties to South Korea were helped by the visit of newly elected Kim Dae Jung to Japan and Prime Minister Obuchi's willingness to show further Japanese regret about the Japanese Occupation of Korea, relations with North Korea became more complicated. On August 31, 1998, North Korea quite unexpectedly fired what appeared to be a three stage missile over Japanese territory. While there was some uncertainty whether it was an example of missile launch or an effort to put a satellite in space—what was obvious was that North Korea had demonstrated an ability to hit urban Japan with missiles. Especially upsetting for the Japanese was that they had needed to depend on the Americans for technical information on the launch. Stunned Japanese officials talked of jointly building a new missile defense system with the Americans even as they continued, somewhat reluctantly and hesitantly, to cooperate with Pyongyang on other matters.

Another important issue of recent years has been the revision of the guidelines for the Japanese-American Security Pact which dated from 1960. Those revisions have aroused considerable controversy within Japan and abroad. Though somewhat ambiguous the new guidelines suggested that Japan was willing to send military personnel abroad during times of crises in the region. Clearly this represented a more ambitious Japanese military stance than recent generations have known and one that aroused considerable anger in some quarters. The People's Republic saw the new guidelines as a threat to itself and within Japan many argued over whether

the revised guidelines were even constitutional given the country's post war prohibition against military activities.

As always the trade imbalance has also been a constant irritant in Japanese-American Relations. Over the last decade Japan has consistently had a sizeable trade surplus with the United States.

In an earlier attempt to address this problem the U.S. Congress passed the Omnibus Trade and Competitiveness bill in 1988. The Special 301 section of that bill provided a powerful weapon in the form of heavy tariffs on U.S. imports from countries deemed to be engaging in unfair trading practices. Special 301 was used with limited successes by both Presidents Bush and Reagan. The Bush Administration also introduced the Structural Impediments Initiative (SII) to be used with Special 301. SII talks were aimed at eliminating the fundamental economic differences between the two countries that resulted in large trade deficits. These areas included the high Japanese savings rate and low level of support for public infrastructure, high land prices, and other Japanese business practices deemed unfair by the Americans.

In a somewhat curious irony from the usual American association with free trade the Clinton Administration early on opted for an aggressive "managed trade" approach which insisted on establishing set targets. In 1994 and early 1995, the major issue was access to the Japanese market for American autos and auto parts. In May of that year the talks collapsed. The Clinton Administration responded with a plan to place a 100% tariff on the major Japanese luxury cars. Though the Japanese did not accept the U.S. concept of managed trade

Prime Minister Yoshiro Mori

On June 9, 1993 Japan's attention was riveted on a solemn but joyous event. Concern for political scandals and economic troubles were set aside. For this was the day on which the son of Emperor Akihito, Prince Naruhito, was to marry American educated career woman Masako Owada. The ancient ceremony was watched by millions of Japanese throughout the country on high definition TV (HDTV). The ceremony, which takes the better part of a day, involves several costume changes and rituals performed in different locations. The Prince's parents did not attend the ceremony but received an official report from the Prince at the end of the day informing them of the marriage. For weeks prior to the wedding, the newspapers and television carried stories about the princess to be, complete with interviews of friends she hadn't even seen in a decade or more.

But the excitement regarding the wedding of the crown prince in 1993 was embarrassingly complemented by published reports in Japanese newspapers during 1999 of the crown princess' possible pregnancy—a public treatment of the Japanese family more typical of media behavior toward the British Royal family than anything the public had been previously treated to in Japan.

enough progress was eventually made to lower the level of rhetoric.

There were times during recent years when the Japanese-American economic relationship seemed particularly tense. This was especially so during late October 1997 when for a time it looked like a dispute over American shipping rights in Japanese harbors would disrupt the entire trading relationship. Happily, after a considerable amount of economic brinkmanship the crisis was resolved.

Still some newer developments are likely to improve trade relations. The long term weakening of their economy has added to the Japanese consumer's interest in less expensive goods and the drop in land prices have combined to allow the introduction of more American style superstores and even for the planning of U.S. style malls. Changes in regulations regarding such investments have also facilitated this development. It seems likely as well that more international marketing over the Internet is going to transform international trade in ways we have not yet even begun to imagine.

Throughout the late 1990s the deficits continued to be significant though less

Japan

political because there was a somewhat greater awareness within the United States that the imbalance had more to do with the weakening economy in Japan than to any particular trade barriers. Though such sympathy hardly impressed American steel workers who charged the Japanese steel industry with dumping cheaper steel on the American market.

Lastly, Japanese-American economic issues were less likely to make waves in the media. China is rapidly becoming the country with which America has its largest trade relationship. Thus, "Japan bashing" may well give way to "China bashing" as the U.S. deficit with that country grows. As the Asian economic crisis unfolded Japanese and American economic planners also clashed over the latter's insistence that Japan take a more active role in attempting to deal with the economic collapse that had enveloped so much of the region. In fact, though Japan was quite involved in contributing to the various financial packages prepared for its neighbors, the United States kept insisting through 1998 that Tokyo needed to take an even more active role in helping both the region and its own domestic economy to recover from the downturn. The advice was not always appreciated in Tokyo.

Another important foreign policy issue was the controversy over the renewal of the American bases in Okinawa, which harkened back to the era of American occupation of the islands after the war. For years resentments have grown in Japan over the presence of these bases. These sentiments are especially strong in Okinawa where the bulk of the American bases are located. Several factors have added to the tensions, some tied to a more general evolution of the international arena and others linked directly to events in Okinawa. The Cold War has been over for more than a decade and the Japanese public is no longer as supportive of the American presence. Within Okinawa, American insensitivity and domination of some of the island's best lands have added to the problem. The American establishment of an artillery range which once fired over a public road was only one of the most egregious examples. But the rape in 1995 of a young Japanese girl by soldiers from one of the American bases dramatically increased the anger of the Okinawans.

Until recently Okinawa itself had been led by Governor Masahide Ota who had been particularly anxious to expel the Americans from Okinawa, but the elections of November 1998 brought a more pragmatic conservative Keiichi Inamine, a businessman who has argued for a more gradual approach to the problem and one that recognized that the Ame-

ricans did pump a considerable amount of money into the local economy. Clearly tensions will continue, but the era of frequent confrontations seems for the moment over.

Japan's relationship with China was also in the spotlight recently. Japanese ultra-nationalists made more efforts to stake claims on the disputed East China Sea Daiyous Islands, known to the Japanese as the Senkaku Islands, during the summer of 1996. Not surprisingly, Chinese from all walks of life, from Hong Kong to Taiwan and the People's Republic were angered. Unfortunately the Japanese government's rather casual attitude about the affair only helped reinforce some of the remaining fears of Japan. Happily, the government of the People's Republic seemed more concerned than Tokyo that the situation not become too explosive. But if these issues did not get out of hand, Tokyo's willingness to play a greater role in what some called a "contain China" policy hardly endeared them to Beijing.

Nor did the November 1998 visit of President Jiang of the People's Republic make much progress in improving relations despite hopes in some quarters. Aware of the apology Japan had offered Korea a few months earlier China's leader made it clear he expected something similar regarding the brutal Japanese invasion

of China earlier in the century. Unfortunately, the Japanese government, apparently under pressure from its own conservatives refused to offer a formal written apology.

Beyond Asia and the Pacific, Japan has continued to expand its international role, assuming more of the posture expected of a major power. This was most evident in the country's participation in UN sponsored missions. Japan recently sent forces to Rwanda to perform a human relief operation. Japan's Air Defense forces also served in Kenya ferrying supplies to the Rwanda operation. Japan is also a major aid giving country. Japan continues to work toward gaining a permanent seat in the United Nation's Security Council.

CULTURE AND SOCIETY

Before the arrival of Chinese influence, Japanese culture was, compared to its giant neighbor, rather unsophisticated; it was centered around the Shinto belief in spirits existing everywhere in nature. With the adoption of so many aspects of Chinese civilization Shinto was somewhat overwhelmed by the growth of Buddhism. In the modern era though Shinto experienced a revival of sorts with the Meiji Government's decision to use it as a feature of its enhancement of the role of

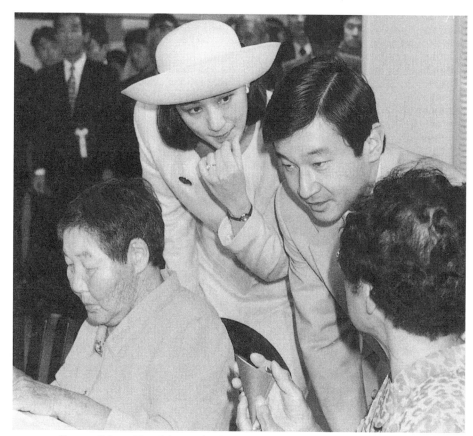

Crown Prince Naruhito and Princess Masako visit a nursing home.

Japan

the emperor. After the Second World War, that "State Shinto" as it is sometimes called, was again de-emphasized. Today both Shinto and Buddhism are somewhat eclectically interwoven in Japanese society. Today it is acceptable for a Japanese to marry in a Shinto shrine and to venerate his ancestors at the Buddhist Temple. And the Christmas season has become an important time for socializing.

Traditional Japanese society itself has experienced an extraordinary transformation over the years since the Meiji Restoration. Japan had begun the nineteenth century as a society that saw itself largely divided hierarchically into classes of samurai, peasants, artisans and merchants with the samurai the uniquely dominant elite. By the late twentieth century Japan had become a much more homogeneous society more divided by intellectual and professional accomplishment than family background.

Since the Japanese were the first non-western country to industrialize along Western models they faced earliest a dilemma that communities around the world continue to deal with—how to modernize one's society without simply becoming "Western." After considerable struggle they did manage to find a comfortable balance. Today, the older cultural patterns are not dead—in fact they are often creatively blended with modernity.

The increasingly urban life of the Japanese is a distinctive one. The business sections of the city are usually constructed of reinforced concrete. Sadly, the simple, yet attractive wood and paper housing that so charmed earlier visitors to Japan, has given way in recent generations to long rows of concrete apartment blocks. The people who work in the central city during the day go to the suburbs in the evening thus the morning and evening commuting hours are as frantic as those in the cities of the United States. Very long commutes are the norm and the common pattern is one that Americans who commute by rail into cities like New York could easily identify with.

Happily for the Japanese their transport systems, particularly rail, are as modern as can be found in the world. The famous and efficient *Bullet trains* run throughout the country. Television, radio and computer games are widely enjoyed and while not yet quite as enamored of the Internet as many Americans, its use is growing very rapidly.

All of the fine arts are widely found in the cities, particularly Tokyo. Traditional European and Western musical works and ballet are heavily attended, as are cultural expressions which are distinctly Japanese such as the Kabuki and Noh theater performances.

Marunouchi, Tokyo's business district

Courtesy: PANA, Japan

On another level, blue-grass and country-western music sung in Japanese has a large following. And today, McDonald's and Kentucky Fried Chicken are the top two restaurant chains in Japan. Underlying this shift to Western food is a far more significant outcome. Rice consumption is down 50% in the last quarter century. Consumption of meat and dairy products is skyrocketing and Japanese young adults are growing taller and bigger.

As we approach the end of the 20th century, the single most important aspect of Japanese society is the reality that it is aging rapidly. Today, more than 14% of the population is over 65. By 2020 more than a quarter will be. How more and more pensioners are going to be supported by fewer and fewer workers will be the challenge Japan and many other developing countries are soon going to have to face. For example, Japan has always attributed part of its economic success to the high savings rates of its citizens. But the days of huge individual savings accounts which could be used to finance industry may soon be over as the rapidly aging Japanese population begins to drain their accounts to support themselves in retirement. Some have suggested that the result could result in as much as an 18% reduction in the Japanese standard of living in upcoming years.

Perhaps even more of a challenge for the relatively isolated and homogeneous Japanese society is the diminishing number of workers available to run its economy. The reality is that the aging of the population and the lowering of the birth rate have combined to created a decline in the number of potential employees so significant that economists have projected that Japan, a country long uncomfortable with outsiders,

will have to allow 600,000 new immigrants a year just to maintain its work force! Whether the Japanese would actually agree to such a change in their society though is quite another matter.

Despite Japan's obvious accomplishments in science and technology there are some unusual elements in its delivery of modern medicine. Until recently Japan adhered to a more traditional definition of life which was defined by the presence of a beating heart regardless of the condition of the patient's brain. This definition has often made it difficult for Japanese medicine to offer its patients some procedures common in the rest of the industrialized world such as heart transplants. That taboo is though beginning to weaken and Japanese practices may soon be more in line with other parts of the world on this important issue. In contrast to the United States, procedures like abortion are not controversial in Japan while the use of the birth control pill has only just become legal for contraceptive purposes (it had previously been available for hormonal regulation).

Japanese Women

On paper Japanese women have rights that American women are still struggling for. More than a decade ago, a Japanese law similar to the American Equal Rights Amendment was passed. As in the United States, the issue of sexual harassment has become an important topic in contemporary Japan. Stirred on by a 1998 American court's expensive judgment against Mitsubishi Motor Manufacturing of America, Japanese political leaders strengthened their laws against sexual harassment and sex discrimination.

Japan

The art of Japanese *Sumo* wrestling is a highly stylized, ritualistic and beloved sport in Japan. Here, *Yokozuna* (the former "grand champion") Akebono holds a young boy aloft.

Despite these gains, Japanese women still earn only about 62% of what a man earns and hold far fewer seats in the lower house of representatives. There have of course been gains. A women ran the Japanese Socialist Party early in the last decade and more recently Fusae Ota, a career civil servant was named the first female governor of the Osaka Prefecture.

Studies of Japanese women's lives suggest that they face many challenges when trying to establish themselves as professionals. The general tendency on the part of employers is to assume they will quit their job once they have children and of course society often does pressure them to do so. Thus it is difficult for women to advance as easily as men. Later in life they are more expected to spend time with aged parents than their male counterparts. And for those Japanese women who stay at home the demands of parenting are greater than for most Western women. Japanese men are not expected to take much responsibility in the home and even if they are so inclined, their work schedules rarely allow them enough time to actually do so.

Japan has also finally begun to make progress in dealing with its responsibilities toward the World War Two era "comfort women" it enslaved for sexual purposes during the war. Government sponsored private charities are now funneling funds to its wartime victims though the government's unwillingness to officially confront its treatment of women during the war is still a subject of considerable anger in some parts of Asia.

EDUCATION IN THE U.S. AND JAPAN

On both sides of the Pacific, the growing importance of the United States and Japan to each other has led to comparisons of many aspects of the two countries, especially their economic ties. Another frequent subject of comparison is their respective educational systems.

On the U. S. side, the public school system below the college or university level is highly decentralized thus making it very difficult to generalize about the American system as a whole. Control rests with state and local officials and boards, including popularly elected members. The

system is permissive in many ways, the most obvious being with respect to dress. Academic standards vary widely. There are often serious disciplinary problems (violence, drugs, and pregnancies) especially in the big urban schools.

The comparatively less official pressure in the U.S. toward conformity produces a typical situation in which the general level of achievement has markedly declined compared to other countries such as Japan. However, there are incentives and opportunities at least in the better schools for able students to do original and advanced work. Private (including parochial Catholic) schools charge tuition rather than being tax-supported, and on the average have higher standards than the public schools, although not higher than the best public schools.

At the college level, the situation also varies widely to the point where few generalizations are possible here either beyond the observation that there are both public and private universities and colleges with a wide qualitative gap between the best and the worst. A student usually spends the first two years completing his or her general education, and the last two (or perhaps three) specializing ("majoring") in some particular subject or field. At the graduate and pre-professional levels, there is less variation in the quality of programs offered, and American institutions offering such programs are widely admired abroad and attract large numbers of foreign (including Japanese) students. One of the signs of the creativity that is not only permitted, but encouraged by the American system, is the high proportion of all Nobel Prizes gained by their graduates. Only at the graduate and professional school levels are standardized admissions tests, such as the LSAT and the GRE important.

On the Japanese side, the situation is quite different in spirit and outcome, as well as in form. The system is much more centralized and on a practical level easier to generalize about. At all levels the public schools, and to some extent also the private schools, are under the control of the Ministry of Education in Tokyo.

From the kindergarten level through high schools, Japanese students and their parents are under tremendous competitive pressure, mainly because ultimate career success is assumed to require graduation from some prestigious university (ideally Tokyo University). Below the college level, students generally wear uniforms, and conformity is expected as to hairstyles, behavior and effort. Students who rebel, as some do, are usually severely dealt with and that in a system where corporal punishment administered by teachers is still common. The emphasis in education is on memorization. Individuality and creativity are discouraged and even penalized.

Very competitive entrance examinations for schools are common, even below the college level. Parents and students spend an enormous amount of time and energy on special programs and "cram" schools to improve their chances of admission into the better schools. Not surprisingly there are frequent reports of students committing suicide from the pressures imposed upon them and their families. Fees of $400 a month were not uncommon for after-school training and a week-long cram school program for entrance into middle school could cost as much as $5000!

Although hard to get into, Japanese colleges are not hard to stay in. The instruction generally adds little to what the student has already learned. There is slightly more scope for originality, but not much. The real accomplishment more often than not is admittance and graduation from a particularly prestigious college rather than the material learned. Professional training, except in law and medicine, tends to be received on the job rather than in graduate school. By the "Nobel test," the Japanese system of higher education does not stand up well; relatively few of these prizes have been won by graduates. The growing awareness of the problem has been especially highlighted by reports of Japanese successes in science earned by those who have worked outside of the system in other countries. By comparison, however, U.S. employers seeking technical job applicants and even clerical help in virtually every field find that potential employees often lack basic skills they should have learned in the first eight years of education.

In short, the strengths and weaknesses of the two systems vary dramatically from each other. American society at its best has been able to create a world class system of higher education but has all too often fallen dramatically short at the lower levels while Japan's system has been much more able to supply a uniform level of accomplishment through high school but less so at the university and graduate levels.

ECONOMY

The experience of Japan in the half-century since World War Two has been one of extraordinary sacrifice, impressive accomplishment and more recently of bitter disappointment. World War II brought on the virtual destruction of Japan's physical plant, but not of the human qualities that had built that plant. Among the most important of these were (and are) energy, persistence, a high level of education and basic technical skills, a high rate of saving and a willingness (somewhat declining at present) to accept relatively modest living standards.

The American occupation helped the Japanese economy by not imposing war reparations or other excessive burdens on it. The Korean War gave it a major shot in the arm (as did the Vietnam war in the next decade), in the form of official U.S. "offshore procurement" of supplies. By that time, various American specialists were beginning to advise Japanese industry how it could increase its productivity. And it was not long before Japanese efficiency began to approach the highest world levels.

The Japanese government, after the end of the Occupation in 1952, systematically pursued an Asian capitalist style of "industrial policy" aimed at stimulating Japanese recovery on the basis of "export-led growth." Anti-trust policy in Japan is much less severe than in the U.S., and this made it possible for Japanese industry to "rationalize" itself to a high degree in the mid-1950s. The government, through the Ministry of International Trade and Industry, MITI, was much more involved in economic planning than is common in the United States (at least at the federal level) and more concern was put on retaining workers and markets than shareholder's profits. "Sunset industries" such as textiles, were de-emphasized, although not phased out entirely; industries using "leading edge" technologies were promoted: steel, automobiles, electronics, etc. This "rationalization" process had a spectacularly beneficial effect on Japan's industrial

Morning traffic on Uchibori–dori Avenue

Japan

production and its export position, beginning in the early 1960s. So too did such domestic factors as political stability, social cohesion and a low defense budget, held by treaty to a bit under 1% of the GNP until 1987. External factors such as the relative openness of the vast U.S. market also helped greatly.

These elements were coupled with relatively high tariffs imposed by the Japanese government on imports and a maze of import regulations which were actually barriers, a generally stable international scene and the conscious undervaluing (at least until 1971) of the yen, with its stimulating effect on Japanese exports.

But even from the Japanese point of view there have been some real drawbacks to this process. The cost of living has been kept unnecessarily high due to factors ranging from the undervaluing of the yen and the extensive system of middlemen in the distribution system through barriers to imports, including agricultural products. The Japanese agricultural population (about 12% of the total) is guaranteed high prices and protected from foreign competition for political reasons. Thus, food is very expensive. The retail distribution system is very inefficient; it is divided between chains of large, expensive department stores and a huge number of mom and pop corner stores, also expensive. Housing, public utilities and the like have been the victims of cumulative under-investment, so that the average Japanese lives under conditions considerably less pleasant than the overall wealth of the country (with currently a GNP of well over one trillion U.S. dollars annually)

would suggest. Energy costs, especially for oil (all imported) are necessarily high; Japan is developing a major nuclear power industry (also based on imported raw materials) as a partial solution.

In spite of these problems, Japan is an industrial giant, second only to the United States. It has proved better able than other industrial economies to cope with the rise (since the end of the 1960s) in the cost of imported oil. Its large trading companies have proved very effective in penetrating foreign markets, especially that of the U.S. They cope with import quotas, when imposed by foreign governments, through "up scaling" (keeping the number of exported units within the quotas, but improving their quality and increasing their price, while staying somewhat below the prices of competitive goods produced in the countries of destination).

Japan's regional economic role within Asia had also grown significantly over the past decades. In fact Asia, rather than the United States, had become the principal area of Japanese trade before the drama of 1997's economic meltdown in much of the area. And there were many reasons Japan had become so involved in the region.

Japanese corporations had turned to Southeast Asia to solve some of their own economic problems. Facing a tendency for Japanese workers to demand higher pay and shorter hours, Japanese industry moved much of its production—usually the lower end of the technology spectrum—off-shore, especially to China and Southeast Asia (Thailand in particular). This Japanese investment, coupled with the opening of China under Deng Xi-

aoping had spurred impressive economic growth in much of Southeast Asia. Japan had also become a leading investor in Vietnam, a country that because of the long lasting U.S. economic embargo, was unable to obtain U.S. investment.

Unfortunately, all this meant that Japan has become especially vulnerable to economic losses stemming from the financial problems in countries from Korea to Thailand and Indonesia. While these potential losses were said to dwarf the problems Japan was having within her own economy they hardly helped instill much confidence in an economy that had so recently been the envy of the world.

In short, for much of Japan's recent history, while the individual consumer was often hard pressed to make ends meet, the economy as a whole had done well. But that situation has changed in recent years. Bank failures have grown, the stock market has weakened and the economy has lost the momentum which made it seem invincible only a few years ago. The bubble has burst on land prices and they too have declined dramatically to prices far below what they were only a few years ago. Growth has been very slow in recent years. Low consumer demand has also hurt the economy.

Most of the most significant economic developments within the Japanese economy in recent years has been the growth in foreign control of some of her most important industries. The American Ford Motor Company recently took over a controlling interest in Mazda and last year Britain's Cable and Wireless bought Japan's International Digital Communications. The idea of foreign firms purchasing domestic companies was something quite familiar to citizens of many other countries. But for Japan it was something quite new. Clearly the weak Japanese economy of the previous decade had made these dramatic changes possible. The insular and security oriented Japanese economy seems more and more a relic of the past rather than of the new century.

But these changes have had some positive aspects—if not for Japanese corporations—then for the Japanese public. Japanese consumers have long shouldered the burden of artificially high prices for most of the goods they consumed from rice to electronics. The Japanese model seemed to be one of excellent service coupled with high prices regardless of what people actually wanted. But those days may be passing. The declining price of land coupled with changing consumer attitudes and regulatory changes have made it possible for the larger American style super store and malls to make significant inroads into Japan. These developments

Refrigerator inspection line.

Courtesy: Japanese Embassy

A steel mill.

may not please the Japanese corporations or small businesses but will certainly have a positive impact on consumer satisfaction.

More importantly, as the new century unfolded the Japanese economy, after so many years of recession, was finally showing signs of a healthy recovery. Whether it would be sustained or not was hardly clear as this year's *East, Southeast Asia and the Western Pacific* went to press but there were plenty of positive economic indicators.

THE FUTURE

The face of Japanese politics continued to change in 1999, but not its substance. Changes in the electoral system have had a significant impact on the House of Representatives and appear to have allowed the LDP to resume its effort to lead a coalition government . But if the LDP's problems have lessened, those of Japan as a whole are still very significant. Today's LDP leads not an insular economic giant, as it did in an earlier era, but an aging industrial nation

with greater international responsibilities and enemies abroad than Japan has been used to in the post war era.

The most important issue for the immediate future will be how well the Japanese face the economic challenges of the upcoming years. Clearly, the future will require important and original thinking. The Japanese will have to successfully face the challenges brought on by the aging of their population and the new economic world of globalization which is transforming the entire planet.

Korea

Sketch of a street scene in Seoul about 1880

The Republic of Korea (South Korea)

Area: 38,452 sq. mi. (98,919 sq.km., somewhat larger than Indiana).

Population: 45,717,000 (1997 estimate).

Capital City: Seoul (Pop. 9 million estimated).

Climate: Temperate, with a short winter, hot and humid in the summer with a rainy monsoon from July to September.

Neighboring Countries: North Korea (North); Japan (East).

Official Language: Korean.

Other Principal Tongues: Japanese, spoken by many older Koreans; English, spoken by many of the educated Koreans.

Ethnic Background: Korean, related to Manchurian and Mongol.

Principal Religions: Buddhism, Confucianism, Christianity.

Main Exports (to U.S. and Japan): Textiles and clothing, electrical machinery, footwear, steel, ships, fish, automobiles and electronics.

Main Imports (from Japan and U.S.): Machinery, oil, transport equipment, chemicals, grains.

Currency: Won.

Former Colonial Status: Korea was a tributary state of the Chinese empires for certain periods until 1895; Japanese protectorate (1905–1910); Japanese Dependency (1910–1945); it was occupied by the U.S. from 1945 to 1948.

National Day: August 15, 1948 (Republic Day).

Chief of State: Kim Dae Jung, President (since February 1998)

Prime Minister: Park Tae Joon.

National Flag: White, with a center circle divided equally by an S–curve into blue and red portions; there is a varying combination of 3 solid and 3 broken lines in each corner.

Per Capita GNP Income: U.S. $6,500.

The predominantly mountainous peninsula of Korea is actually an extension of the mountains of southern Manchuria, from which it is separated by the Yalu and Tumen Rivers. The spine of the mountains runs from northeast to southwest, but remains close to the eastern coastline area of Korea—eastern Korea is thus rugged, containing many scenic mountain peaks. The famous Diamond Mountains *(Kimgan–san)* in North Korea are particularly spectacular, reaching their greatest height in the Changpai San at the northern border, where the peaks are snow–covered all year.

From these immense mountains, streams gather to form the Yalu River which empties into the Yellow Sea, and the Tumen River which flows into the Sea of Japan. The steep descent of these rivers provides one of the world's best sources of hydroelectric power, with a great potential that has only begun to be developed. The western coastal regions contain most of the peninsula's level plains, interspersed with frequent rivers—this is the agricultural belt where rice predominates, raised in wet paddies in the South, where two crops are harvested each year, and grown in the North on dry plantations, where only one crop matures at the end of the summer.

Skyline of modern Seoul. The grounds of the Duksoo Palace, built in the 15th century and carefully preserved, are seen in the foreground, surrounded by the bustling city.

The Democratic People's Republic of Korea (North Korea)

Area: 46,814 sq. mi. (121,730 sq. km., somewhat smaller than Mississippi).

Population: 22 million (estimated).

Capital City: Pyongyang (Pop. 1.2 million, estimated).

Climate: Temperate, with a longer and much colder winter than in the South; summer wet season from July to September.

Neighboring Countries: China (North); Russia (Northeast); South Korea (South).

Official Language: Korean.

Other Principal Tongues: Japanese, spoken by many older Koreans; Russian, spoken by many of the educated Koreans.

Ethnic Background: Korean, similar to both Manchurian and Mongolians.

Principal Religion: Buddhism, Confucianism. The government discourages religious activity.

Main Exports (to Russia, China, Japan): Minerals, meat products, fish.

Main Imports (from China, Russia, Japan): Petroleum, machinery, grains.

Currency: Won.

Former Colonial Status: Korea was a tributary state of the Chinese empires for most of its history up to 1895; Japanese protectorate (1905–1910); Japanese Dependency (1910–1945); from 1945 to 1948 it was under Soviet occupation; after 1948 it developed an independent communist regime allied with both the Soviet Union and with China.

National Day: September 8, 1948.

Chief of State: Kim Jung–Il, Head of State.

National Flag: Two blue stripes on the top and bottom separated by two thin white stripes from a broad central field of red which contains at left center a white circle with a 5–pointed red star.

Per Capita Annual Income: About U.S. $200.

Tidal variations along the west coast are extreme; there is sometimes a difference of 30 feet between low and high tide. The offshore islands, numbering about 3,500, are the remnants of the mountain chain, standing with their shoulders above water. The long coastline and the nearness to some of the richest fishing grounds in the world have made the people, especially in the South, skilled fishermen and have led to frequent squabbles with individual Japanese and with Japanese governments, because the people of the over–crowded neighboring islands desperately need the same protein which the Koreans harvest from the sea.

The cooler climate of North Korea resembles that of Manchuria. It is better endowed with minerals, hydroelectric facilities and capacity, and the lower regions of the mountains support thick stands of timber. South Korea has a warmer climate, which supports a greater agricultural production. In December, the temperatures in Pusan may be mild at the same time that frigid blasts of below–zero arctic weather envelop the remote mountains of the North. The Siberian black bear and leopard mingle with fierce wild boars, Manchurian tigers and smaller Korean tigers in the thinly populated northern region. As the warmth increases to the south, the animal life becomes more nearly tropical, dominated by herons, gulls and other birds with colorful plumage.

History

From their appearance and language, the Koreans appear to have similar origins to the Turkic-Manchurian-Mongol people who have inhabited northeastern Asia for more than 4,000 years and migrated to the island of Japan as well as to the Korean peninsula. It appears that people have lived in Korea from long before 10,000 BC, but the more specific origins of the Korean people appear to lie with the arrival of two distinct groups to the peninsula, first a neolithic culture of fishermen and shellfish gatherers who arrived around 3000 B.C. and later, around the 7th century, a community that lived as well by hunting. These early inhabitants of the peninsula were clearly similar to other Altaic, Tungusic tribes that inhabited the regions

Korea

The medieval dance-drama, *Tomi*.

now known as Manchuria and Siberia as is evidenced by comparing their various tools, from ceramics to daggers and mirrors. One particular type of knife associated with women was, in fact, common among peoples from East Asia to North American Indians and Eskimos.

Although the exact chronology is less than clear, it appears that the use of bronze metal technology came into existence somewhere from 1000 B.C. to around 800 B.C. Archeological evidence suggests the presence of many tribal communities of limited size, the most important of which was eventually the state of Old Choson which emerged around the 2nd century based in the northwestern part of the peninsula in the area around the present day North Korean capital of Pyongyang. But Korean society then, as now, was intimately tied to developments within their enormous northern neighbor China and in the first centuries B.C. much of Korea came under Chinese control.

The Chinese Commanderies

By 108 B.C. the Choson capital had fallen to the Chinese armies and their leaders the emperors of the famous Han Dynasty which established several administrative divisions in the northern part of the peninsula. Especially important was the Chinese establishment of a base at Nangyang where an enormously sophisticated soci-

ety largely based on Chinese models would emerge. New artistic and philosophical systems were introduced as well as the Chinese administrative styles. Significant numbers of Chinese colonists arrived as well, and Nangyang would remain important for the next several hundred years. Though the Koreans would strongly resist direct Chinese control and eventually regain their independence, the influence of Chinese cultural norms and the interest they would hold for Koreans would in many ways continue through the modern day. Nevertheless, like the Japanese, the Koreans would reject important aspects of Chinese civilization from the more merit-based Confucian examination system to its historical disdain for the military. Both Korea and Japan, despite their twin enthusiasms for Chinese civilization, would retain their emphasis on an hereditary aristocracy and honored military elite.

The Three Kingdoms

By the first century B.C. three Korean kingdoms would establish themselves; Koguryo in the north, Silla on the southeast part of the peninsula and Paekche in the southwest. In each kingdom a powerful hereditary monarchy evolved that ruled with a centralized system of control. Each of these kingdoms were under strong Chinese cultural influence, including Ma-

hayana (northern) Buddhism, Confucianism and the Chinese written language.

Especially interesting is the fact that there is now considerable evidence to suggest that the original Yamato Japanese state that later developed on the nearby offshore islands may have been an offshoot of the Paekche kingdom.

During the 7th century, the Silla kingdom, initially working with the powerful Tang Dynasty of China, defeated each of its rivals and emerged in domination. Later in the century, Silla's leaders even managed to drive out the Chinese and establish themselves dominant over most of the peninsula.

Over the next years, as Silla's leaders established themselves, the influence of Korea's nobility lessened temporarily and a more centralized Chinese style administrative trend was adopted that even included an exam system similar to what the Chinese were developing themselves. The Chinese language was used as the principal language of communication and even Tang clothing styles were adopted. It was during Silla's domination that the effort was begun to establish a phonetic system for writing Korean which by the 1400s would become today's modern Korean alphabet-like system known as han'gul.

It was also during these years, inspired by the interest of Silla's leadership, that Buddhism became particularly important on the peninsula. A large number of Koreans studied in China itself and the Buddhist establishment grew enormously with the emergence of large numbers of monasteries.

Externally, Silla, although dominant on the peninsula, considered itself part of the Chinese world order. Practically this meant sending tribute missions to the Tang capital and having their representatives perform the *kowtow* to the emperors, which meant to kneel and touch the forehead to the ground in deep respect. But if Silla managed to maintain Korea's independence from China it was less lucky with its own internal enemies, and by the early tenth century they had lost control of the peninsula to a new state which called itself Koryo, from which we derive the modern name for the country.

Korea's years of independence were brutally interrupted by the arrival of the Mongol armies who occupied the peninsula and used it as a launching pad for their two attacks against Japan in the 13th century. At the beginning of the 13th century the Mongol attack forced the Koryo government to withdraw to an island north of modern day Inchon. Within a generation after more devastating attacks the Koryo leadership was forced to submit to Mongol demands which included taking part in what were fated to be the unsuccessful Mongol invasions of Japan. In two attacks late in the century, Mongol warriors, sailing in ships made by the accomplished Korean ship building industry, tried to expand their power to Japan. But as discussed in the Japan section of *East, Southeast Asia, and the Western Pacific*, the attacks failed in the face of adverse weather conditions and Japanese resistance. For Koreans themselves, involvement in the campaigns was a disaster.

Nevertheless even during the era of Mongol control Korean culture survived. Socially the aristocracy continued its influence and, now disdaining Buddhism, embraced a Chinese style neo-Confucianism, a particularly metaphysical form of the historical Chinese system of social relations.

Not surprisingly the overthrow of the Mongol dynasty in China by the new Chinese Ming dynasty had ramifications within Korea which contained supporters of both ruling groups. For Korea itself, the ultimate outcome of these tensions was the capture of the Koryo capital by General Yi Song-gye and the establishment of the longest lasting of Korean dynasties, which lasted from 1392 to 1910 when it was abolished by the Japanese. Formally known as the Choson dynasty it is also known as the Yi dynasty after its founder. Its capital city, Hanyang, is today better known as Seoul.

Yi Korea (1392–1910)

Violent power struggles within the ruling family marked the first years of the dynasty. Still, overall the Yi showed great creativity, wisdom and artistry, advancing in the field of astronomy and perfecting han'gul, an alphabet-like system which by the 20th century would become the common instrument of writing Korean. Although ruled by a local line of rulers, Korea remained a faithful tributary of the Chinese empire and one so devoted to Confucian civilization that it quite vehemently rejected the Buddhist orientation of previous generations. Eventually they were to embrace a neo-Confucian ideology so completely that most scholars believe them to have been far more Confucian than even the Chinese themselves. The government strengthened the Chinese style administrative structure and examination system even more thoroughly than previous Korean regimes though the Chinese emphasis on true social mobility never really took hold. For Koreans, the system of hereditary elites remained more attractive.

Nevertheless, despite their more noble births the Korean aristocracy in these years, like others in East and Southeast Asia, very consciously modeled themselves on China's scholar-gentry ruling class. And of course, as Japan would also do, they created their own distinctively Korean

variation of the Chinese model. In Korea the elites were known as Yangban, a hereditary class whose members were most respected when they combined impressive ancestors, land and office holdings and, above all, devotion to scholarly accomplishments. This Korean version of elite society was to prove remarkably resilient and to survive well into the modern era.

Given the introduction of han'gul as a system for phonetically writing Korean and the educational priorities of the Korean Confucian elite, it is not surprising that these years saw an enormous growth in the production of printing, the first large scale efforts anywhere in the world.

Socially, traditional Korea had differed dramatically from China in its earlier treatment of women. Korean women enjoyed a level of freedom that is said to have amazed visiting Chinese. They were able to inherit and, unlike the more common Chinese practice, a new husband could marry into a woman's family and reside there among his in-laws in contrast to the usual Asian pattern of brides always being the one to relocate.

But as we have seen during the 15th century, Korea's new leader's embraced a neo-Confucianism that was more orthodox than even found in China itself. Sadly for women, this closer embrace of Confucianism did not bode well for Korean women whose status diminished over the centuries.

Technically, Korea was throughout this era far ahead of the West. From its accomplishments with printing to mathematical and instrumentation skills Korean society was far more accomplished than Europeans on the eve of the modern era.

But these accomplishments were dramatically interrupted when, once again, Korea's location between two powerful neighbors put its people at risk. Just as in the 13th century Mongol armies had used Korea to attack Japan, by the late 1500s Koreans once again found themselves condemned by their location when in 1592 the Japanese led by Toyotomi Hideyoshi invaded the peninsula with almost 160,000 soldiers in an ill-fated effort to conquer China.

The Koreans defended themselves with a remarkable flotilla of the world's first armor-plated warships, the famous "Turtle Ships" which effectively destroyed the Japanese fleets. Moreover, with the help of the Ming they were successful in defending the peninsula, but the damage was overwhelming. After a second assault in 1597 when, after Hideyoshi's death, the Japanese finally withdrew, both nations entered an era of increased isolation from their neighbors.

But while life would soon calm in Japan Koreans experienced more trauma. The recovery had hardly begun before Kore-

ans faced yet another trial, the conquest of China by the Manchurians and their own inclusion in this new emerging Sino-Manchurian Empire. From the Korean perspective, the fall of the much admired Chinese Ming empire to the Manchurians was an astounding cultural disaster that left many of them believing that Korea alone remained the last bastion of Confucian civilization. It was a sentiment many Russians had felt a century before when the exalted Christian Byzantine Empire had fallen to the arriving Ottomans. In Eastern Europe many Russians had begun to think of themselves as the new or Third Rome after Constantinople fell, and at the other end of the enormous Eurasian land mass, Koreans observing the collapse of Ming China often felt themselves playing a similar role as the last defenders of true Confucian civilization.

Over the next centuries though Korean pride in its Confucian accomplishments soared, so too did intellectual and court factionalism that would eventually make the nation less prepared to deal with the challenges to come. On the international level Korea became intensely isolationist, as committed to its own inward looking perspective as its much disliked Japanese neighbors. But in contrast to Japan, Koreans did not have a group of scholars, the equivalent of the famous Japanese "Dutch Scholars" who could at least keep the nation somewhat aware of developments in the outer world. Thus when later forced open by the pressures of imperialism, Korea would have fewer resources to fall back upon than Japan.

Over the next centuries occasional Europeans who were shipwrecked on the rough coastline were held captive while Japanese and Chinese who happened upon the Korean shores were expeditiously sent packing. It was a far cry from the Korea of earlier centuries which is said to have been much more open to the world. During these centuries which immediately preceded the arrival of the Westerners the Koreans were content with their many official expeditions to Beijing. Nevertheless even during those activities Korean concerns about the outside world remained profound. While they were able to roam freely within Beijing during their visits, the Chinese envoy's movements were severely restricted in Seoul.

The Dawn of Imperialist Pressures

By the middle of the nineteenth century Western pressures in East Asia had become intense. The Europeans during the two Opium wars forced open China and the Americans had done the same thing in Japan. It was now Korea's turn to feel the pressures of imperialism, but in her case

Korea

it would ultimately be Japanese greed that would determine her fate. But that thrust would be later. Early on it was the Westerners, specifically the French and Americans, who offered the first pressures. Within Korea, as we have seen, the Yi Dynasty like Japan a generation before, was vehemently committed to maintaining its isolation and the first contacts suggested that goal might be possible.

In 1866 the Koreans successfully drove a force of French away from an island near Inchon. A few years later a confrontation broke out between an American commercial vessel, the General Sherman, that ended with the death of all those on the American ship. But unfortunately, these early and successful efforts to resist outside pressures did not last. When the Americans later retaliated against Korea for firing on American ships, the assault resulted in the deaths of more than six hundred Korean soldiers a few years later.

In 1882 the United States became the first Western nation to open treaty relations with the Koreans. It was though with Japan that Korea's external relations were to become particularly complicated and painful.

The Beginning of the Japanese Assault

Koreans had long looked with disdain at their island neighbors. Japan's efforts to remake itself on a Western model in the decades after Perry's arrival only made the Koreans more suspicious, especially after the Japanese began styling their Yamato rulers as emperors as the Chinese did, and to wear Western style clothing. In fact, their initial disdainful reaction to these changes almost provoked an indignant Japanese attack early in the 1870s! For the moment the Japanese decided against an expedition but a generation later Japan's attitude would be quite different. Over the next years, at China's urging, the court signed a series of treaties with the various Western powers. From China's perspective—which saw Korea as part of its own world order, Korean treaties with the Western powers might provide some protection from Japanese demands.

Inside Korea, nationalists and the more educated youth often looked to Japan as a source of inspiration and direction. On the other hand, the elderly conservatives remained attached to the traditional Confucian empire of the Manchus. When an internal power struggle broke out during the 1870s the Japanese decided to intervene and dispatched a flotilla to the peninsula. It was an act not so very different from the American effort in the 1850s. Though this time it was the Japanese who were making the demands rather than being the victims.

The resulting treaty opened several Korean ports to the Japanese and not sur-

prisingly aroused the ire of Korean conservatives and their supporters in China.

In the following decade an intense rivalry between the Chinese and Japanese over their relative influence in Korea was carried out and was paralleled within Korea by different factions who preferred one over the other of their neighbors. Ironically, given later events, the more progressive among the Koreans favored the Japanese having been impressed with that nations' willingness to embrace Western technical skills. More than once tensions and violence between the two groups encouraged the further meddling in Korean affairs by its two powerful neighbors, China and Japan.

Given the intense imperialistic tone of the age a clash was inevitable. The explosion came in 1894. Nevertheless, it was originally internal developments, not international events, that set the stage. Within Korea a new popular movement, the Tonghaks, somewhat like the Chinese Taipings, had arisen. It was a movement that emphasized both traditional values and some elements similar to Catholicism. It was anti-Japanese as well as antagonistic to the Westerners. More immediately it was driven by the distress of many of the peasant class who were hard-pressed by the exploitative demands of the Korean ruling classes. The movement was inspired by a general egalitarianism and elements of traditional Korean spiritualism. The new Japanese economic demands also added to the peasantry's plight and by the early 1890s a full scale revolt had broken out. By the time the movement turned into an uprising it had become a full scale agrarian revolution.

In the ensuing turmoil, the Korean King Kojong called for Chinese help and the Japanese used the occasion to rush their

own troops to the peninsula. With little resistance, the Japanese drove the Chinese forces out of Korea. It was the first stage of what would become Korea's nightmare experience as a Japanese colony.

But the Japanese were not yet able to establish their undisputed control over Korea. The nearby Russians, whose empire bordered on Korea, had also developed considerable interest in the peninsula. But within ten years the Japanese and Russians would also fight over the increasingly prostrate Korean peninsula. After more than a millennium of independence, Korea was once again caught by its own geography between more powerful forces.

Becoming a Japanese Colony

When the short Russo-Japanese War of 1904–1905 resulted in a Japanese victory and the establishment of a Japanese protectorate over Korea, Tokyo was ready to make its move. With no opposition, Japan simply annexed the peninsula in 1910; Korea became the largest dependency of the growing Japanese empire. It was, after all, the age of Imperialism and such exploitative moves were common during these years. In fact, the Japanese had only just finished watching the Americans subdue those Philippine forces who had attempted to resist the American occupation of their land. But sadly for the Koreans, the Japanese occupation was to prove considerably more brutal than what the Americans imposed in their colony.

Japanese rule was harsh and military, devoted to creating investment opportunities for Japanese capital, raising rice to feed Japan and establishing military bases for further expansion on the Asian conti-

The Gateway in the Ancient Walls of Seoul

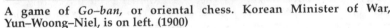

A game of *Go–ban*, or oriental chess. Korean Minister of War, Yun–Woong–Niel, is on left. (1900)

A young Korean and his wife in street dress, Seoul, 1902.

nent. Whether most Koreans agreed or not the long isolated peninsula was being transformed by the changes introduced by the Japanese.

On a purely technical level the Korea which eventually regained its freedom half a century later was the most developed of East and Southeast Asia's former colonies. But those industrial advantages hardly outweighed the humiliations of Japanese harsh control.

Almost from the start a committed Korean resistance movement began which did everything in its power to resist Japanese control. They even managed to assassinate Ito Hirobumi, Japan's revered hero of the Meiji Restoration during his tenure as Japan's highest official in Korea. Not surprisingly the Japanese were outraged and the peninsula's formal annexation occurred soon after.

The best known efforts at resistance occurred in the spring of 1919 when, angered by open Japanese exploitation and inspired by newly learned democratic slogans used in World War I, hundreds of thousands of Koreans, many of whom had been converted to Christianity, staged a massive, peaceful demonstration in favor of independence.

Outraged by the thousands of demonstrators who took part in declaring a Korean Declaration of Independence, Japanese officials brutally suppressed the peaceful demonstrations arresting and killing thousands. For Korea these years were a traumatic time indeed but hardly an era during which they passively accepted Japanese control. Throughout these years Koreans both within Korea and beyond its borders fought against Japan's control and hoped through efforts ranging from guerrilla warfare through international protests to force the Japanese out. But as with most other occupations it is true as well that many Koreans threw in their lot with the Japanese and attempted to advance by serving within the colonial administration.

Relaxing their rule briefly during the 1920s because of adverse Korean and world popular opinion, the Japanese intensified their exploitation when they undertook the conquest of Manchuria and China in the 1930's. In an effort to avoid further unrest, they attempted to absorb the Koreans by forcing them to adopt Japanese names and to speak the language of their conquerors. This had no lasting effect and actually served to

further embitter the Koreans against the Japanese.

As the Pacific War developed in the 1930s the Koreans naturally found themselves caught up again in Japanese ambitions first to conquer China and later the assault on Southeast Asia.

What the Japanese colonial authorities wanted of their Korean subjects was their labor. Millions were sent to Japan to serve as forced laborers during the war. But work in Japan's factories and mines was not the only thing the Japanese demanded of their Korean victims. Along with young women from other parts of Asia thousands of Korean women were forced to serve as prostitutes for the Japanese army. Euphemistically referred to as "Comfort Women," somewhere between one hundred and two hundred thousand Korea women were thus forced into sexual slavery during the war.

It was also during these years that Korea's post war leaders, men like the American-oriented Syngman Rhee and his later communist opponent Kim Il Sung, made their reputations as leading Korean nationalists and prepared the groundwork for their later arrival to power in the months after World War II.

Korea

The Division of Korea

At the close of World War II, when Japan had all but surrendered to U.S. and British forces, the subject of the future of Korea was considered by the leaders of the "Big Three" at the Potsdam Conference in mid-1945. Russia's Stalin reaffirmed his promise that the U.S.S.R. would declare war on Japan, which it had refrained from doing prior to that time, and proposed that it would secure the Korean peninsula from the Japanese armies. It was ultimately decided that Soviet forces would occupy the northern part of Korea and accept the surrender of the Japanese troops in that region, and the U.S. forces would do the same in the southern portion.

The American expectation was that the whole peninsula would come under the supervision of the then infant UN. This decision, made half way around the world from the helpless Koreans, was to be the basis of continued conflict and friction for years, and also was to cost the loss of thousands of lives. It also ultimately was to result in an economically harmful division of the peninsula.

Two days after the first atomic bomb had burst with a terrifying holocaust on the Japanese city of Hiroshima, the U.S.S.R. declared war on Japan. The Japanese accepted the Allied surrender terms on August 14, but during the few intervening days the Soviets had easily occupied North Korea. The boundary between U.S. and Soviet troops was fixed shortly afterward at the 38th parallel by two young colonels in the American army who were given about a half an hour to pick a place on the peninsula to divide the two forces. It was a decision that Koreans themselves would think back on with bitterness from then through today.

In the North, the Russians promptly installed a satellite regime run by Korean communists under the control of the Soviet occupation forces. In the South, U.S. occupation forces, who operated a full military government from 1945 through 1948, followed a shifting policy primarily devoted to economic recovery and to the creation of a democratic government.

There were seemingly unending negotiations between the two powers in 1946–1947 on the formation of a provisional government for the entire peninsula. But events on the ground made most of these discussions irrelevant. The Soviets for their part had chosen to support Kim Il Sung, the well known anti-Japanese fighter, and the United States increasingly settled on supporting the aging Syngman Rhee who by then had lived in the United States for decades. In essence the tensions associated with the Cold War of the late 1940s had already begun within Korea immediately after World War II.

The southern, American-oriented Republic of Korea was soon declared independent and was admitted to the UN. Elections, carried out under the occupation's mandate, confirmed Rhee as the new President and the American occupation officially ended. The Russians reacted by establishing the "Democratic People's Republic of Korea" in the North and withdrew their own occupation forces. Soviet control and support of local communists were sufficient to maintain North Korea within the Soviet bloc with little or no Russian military presence.

Though the two regimes were poles apart on whom they chose to associate with and on economic matters during the developing Cold War, each was led by committed nationalists who were determined to reunite their nations. Over the next two years activists in both parts of the peninsula hoped for some sort of clash which would ultimately reunite the peninsula under one or the other government's leadership.

The Korean War

America on the eve of the Korea war was very involved in developments in the Republic of South Korea. Not only was it contributing more than a hundred million dollars a year to the country but it was influential in practically every aspect of the new state's existence from government through cultural and educational affairs. Clearly the United States wanted the South to be well able to withstand a potential attack from communist North Korea. On the other hand many Americans were more immediately concerned about those South Koreans who were anxious to begin their own effort to unify the peninsula from the south.

President Rhee himself, the American sponsored president, was among those calling for an attack on the north. But despite Rhee's efforts to gain American support to unify the peninsula under his control, it was his northern rival Kim Il Sung and the latter's Soviet allies that made the fateful decision to begin what would become a vicious civil war. In June of 1950, bolstered by a heavy dose of Soviet military aid, North Korean forces invaded South Korea. Their attack, well planned in advance, was very effective and they were barely prevented from overrunning all of South Korea.

Angered by the north's invasion, President Truman, despite earlier U.S. statements to the contrary, viewed the attack as an assault on America's national interests and ordered a military intervention on the side of the South Koreans. Choosing to work within the structures of the newly formed United Nations, President Truman arranged for the UN to condemn the aggressive acts of North Korea and to order military sanctions against the Soviet satellite. Ironically, the representative of the U.S.S.R., who could have employed its veto power, was not there to do so. The U.S.S.R. had been boycotting the council due to controversies surrounding the question of who should hold the China seat, the People's Republic of China or the recently defeated Nationalists on Taiwan.

The Southern counter-attack itself, while nominally carried out by a UN force, was

U.S. Marines in Korea, November 1951

primarily an American military effort. General Douglas MacArthur commanded the UN forces. Demonstrating the same energy and self-will he had shown during most of World War II, MacArthur planned an aggressive campaign to drive the Northern forces out of South Korea.

A combination of mass bombing of the North and a flank attack by an amphibious landing at Inchon, a coastal town near Seoul, succeeded in driving the North Koreans from the territory they had conquered. Then having successfully driven the northern troops from South Korea, MacArthur insisted, and found support among his superiors, for an attack on North Korea and yet another unification drive, this time from the south.

Even as the American forces were moving closer and closer to the Chinese borders, MacArthur, ignoring Beijing's warnings, was certain that the forces of the People's Republic would not intervene. Sure of his judgment, MacArthur ordered his forces toward the Yalu River, the border which divided Korea from China. MacArthur was wrong. China was not prepared to accept foreign and probably hostile troops directly on its borders. Moreover both Moscow and Beijing wanted to save the communist regime in Korea.

Beijing's forces struck with great force, using the same successful tactics they had learned in their battles with the Japanese and Chinese Nationalists during the previous decade.

The Chinese effort to drive U.S. and UN forces out of North Korea succeeded, but ultimately they could not mount a successful invasion of South Korea, though Seoul, the capital, fell once again temporarily into their hands during the early fighting.

General MacArthur, realizing he had been put on the defensive, very publicly advocated a wider war effort, including the bombing of Chinese Manchurian bases. Eventually the famous general's utterances caused a public break between himself and President Truman who had lost faith in his judgment. MacArthur was replaced, but the war itself waged on.

Chinese forces tried to retake Seoul in April and May 1951, but their supply lines had become too long to support the effort. Armistice negotiations began in July 1951, but since neither side had won a clear victory, the talks dragged on for two years, while fighting continued. Each side sought to obtain a defensible position, and gradually the lines of battle hardened with heavy fortifications which would have made a major breakthrough by either side almost impossible.

A crisis over the repatriation of prisoners also prolonged the conflict—the Chi-

90 CHURCH STREET, ROOM 1303
NEW YORK 7, NEW YORK

7 November 1961

Dear Mr. Stryker:

Thank you so much for your cordial letter of November 4th. It was thoughtful of you to write me as you have and I appreciate it.

The Fuller's lived next door to the MacArthur's on Marshall Street in Milwaukee. My father made it his home on retirement from the Army and I visited him there many, many times. Secretary Stimson was a life long friend. I admired him greatly.

Had we gone on beyond the Yalu we would have destroyed Red China and it would no longer be a growing menace to the free world. We could have done so very easily and the whole outlook of mankind would be different today.

With best wishes,

Most sincerely,

DOUGLAS MacARTHUR.

Mr. Philip F. Stryker,
312 Marlborough Street,
Boston 16, Massachusetts.

MacArthur's blunt comment eight years after the Korean War

nese and North Koreans disliked and refused to recognize the proposition that their soldiers—many of whom were former Nationalist soldiers—might not want to return to their homelands. Nevertheless, an armistice was reached on July 27, 1953, a few months after the death of Stalin which had led to a reduction of Soviet support for the war.

American politics also contributed heavily to this armistice. The popular military hero of World War II, General Dwight Eisenhower, was chosen by the Republican Party to oppose President Truman's Democratic successor. Eisenhower's promise during the campaign to use his influence to end the Korean War greatly influenced the American public. Privately, President Eisenhower threat-

ened to use nuclear weapons to settle the dispute. The threat worked.

The eventual armistice was a stalemate of military might—the demarcation is along about the same line as it was prior to the conflict. The real result of the struggle was the loss of several hundred thousand lives and an almost utter devastation of both Koreas. The fighting may have ended but the two parts of Korea then settled in for a generation-long struggle for domination of the peninsula. Over the years that new struggle would take many forms.

The Two Koreas in the Post War Era

Shortly after the armistice, the Soviet Union and China began providing

Korea

Mechanized rice harvesting in Korea. Although Korean rice yields are among the highest in the world, mechanization has become necessary as demand rises with the standard of living, and agricultural workers leave the land for jobs in industry.

substantial economic aid programs to North Korea. As a result, it acquired a broad industrial base and a per capita industrial production which rose to a level higher than that of China. Kim Il Sung, the political leader selected by the Soviets in 1945 to lead North Korea, soon acquired exclusive control over the local communist party at the expense of his rivals.

Eventually the Korean War and subsequent Russian-Chinese ideological disputes over what is "true communism" gave Kim a much wider degree of freedom of action within the communist sphere. For a few years after 1960 Kim tended to favor the Chinese. After 1964 he swung back toward the Russians, then again toward the Chinese for a time, and after 1983, toward Moscow until the Soviet Union collapsed.

In South Korea, despite massive American aid, the postwar economy floundered and the elderly President Rhee grew increasingly senile, autocratic, and unpopular. In 1960 he resigned and left the country after his government faced rebellious student demonstrations which the army made no effort to suppress. There followed a year of political ferment and regrouping under a weak government which ended in 1961 when the army seized control of South Korea.

South Korea Emerges Economically

After an initial period of direct military rule, General Park Chung-hee, the leader of the military junta which had seized power, nominally became a civilian and was elected president. He was reelected in 1967. In 1972, not satisfied with his authority as the elected president of South Korea, Park pushed through legislation which allowed him to become a dictator. With that development, the entire peninsula had fallen under the control of autocratic governments, the communists in the north and Park's supporters. Park justified his actions by citing the need to retain national unity in the south in the face of the northern threat. But if the political situation of the two Koreas was growing more similar, the beginning of their modern economic divergence was also gaining momentum.

The roots of South Korea's modern economic "miracle" are diverse—ranging from both external to internal factors. What is clear is that from an economy that saw the average per capita income in 1963 at around $100, it was by 1990 over $5000. And as the century reached its termination some Korean laborers were earning salaries comparable to Americans in the Midwest.

Obviously such an economic transformation was caused by myriad developments, but for Korea certain key factors can be noted. Especially important among the external factors were ties with both the Americans and the Japanese.

The United States, since the decision to intervene during the Korean War, had been committed to a stable South Korea and had helped create the conditions there necessary to such stability. By the 1960s, the Korean willingness to align themselves with the internationally unpopular American effort in Vietnam was especially helpful and lucrative. In fact, some of the most important South Korean construction firms profited greatly from the projects they carried out in South Vietnam during the war. Their role, in some ways, resembled that of the Japanese during the similar American involvement in Korea during the earlier Korean War. Moreover, the ties forged in this way to the Japanese themselves also helped.

Though the memories of the Japanese occupation remained bitter, the reality was that the Koreans, and especially many in the elite, were well positioned to take advantage of the economic growth then going on in Japan. These Korean leaders including General Park himself were fluent in Japanese and quite willing

Korea

General Park Chung–hee

to gain the advantages of close economic ties to Japan. That strategy worked quite well as Japan invested enormously in South Korea. For example, Mitsubishi owned about 10% of the South Korean company Hyundai and supplied many of the most important parts.

These advantages would not have been realized if the Park government had not chosen to move his committed and inexpensive labor force into the world export market, an economic decision already well trodden by Japan itself. President Park's economic policy and the advantages of the international environment, especially after the early 1960s, was a major success. One has only to look at the modern industrial skyline that Seoul has become and to recognize the very real improvement in living standards today to understand how much was accomplished in those years on the economic front. But on the political level Park's leadership was much less successful.

President Park's increasing personal power aroused considerable opposition, especially from the intellectuals, students, and the powerful Christian churches. This opposition was cruelly suppressed on the grounds that it gave aid and comfort to North Korea at a time when American protection of South Korea was becoming increasingly unreliable. Kim Dae Jung, later president, though then an influential opposition leader who had received a large minority of the popular vote for the presidency in 1971, was himself kidnaped in Japan by the South Korean Central Intelligence Agency in 1973 and brought home. The next year President Park's wife was fatally shot in mid-1974 in what was officially described as an attempt on the life of the president himself. Since the as-

sassin had some Japanese connections, the government launched a dispute with Japan, but there were reasons to believe that this quarrel, as well as tensions in North Korea-South Korea relations which existed in 1974, were at least partly efforts by the Park government to distract attention from its domestic difficulties.

Despite his easy victory in a rigged referendum held in February 1975, Park's heavy-handedness might have cost him crucial American support. For a time after Jimmy Carter became president it even looked like the U.S. might withdraw its forces.

The fall of Indochina to communism in 1975 left South Korea the only non-communist nation on the East Asian mainland and intensified the sense of danger felt in the country. This was exploited by President Park to increase his rigid control through repressive measures.

Nevertheless, The ruling *Democratic Republican Party* came closer to defeat in a 1978 election when it won only 68 seats in the National Assembly to 61 for the opposition *New Democratic Party*. In reaction President Park reorganized his cabinet and released a number of political prisoners, including the *New Democratic Party's* leader, Kim Dae Jung.

President Park's Death

President Park was assassinated by the head of the South Korean Central Intelligence Agency in October 1979 during an argument over internal disturbances within the country. After an interlude of confusion, the army under General Chun Doo Hwan seized power in December 1979. In mid-1980 it proclaimed martial law and viciously crushed a revolt in the southwestern city of Kwangju. The Kwangju Massacre, as it was to become known, was one of the most violent incidents in recent South Korean history and has continued to affect the course of South Korean politics ever since. Chun then became Acting President and began to install a new government. Martial law was finally lifted at the beginning of 1981.

Chun then launched a policy of "national reconciliation" under which thousands of people imprisoned or barred from public life were pardoned.

Despite the repressive measures used by the government to control South Korea, the surging economic figures during the 1980s nevertheless helped maintain a reasonable level of satisfaction among the population. Seoul's international prestige was helped as well when it was chosen to serve as the site of the 1988 Olympic Games.

In many ways the assassinated President's emphasis on economic growth al-

lowed the Republic of South Korea to surpass its northern rival without a military confrontation. South Korea was increasingly able to demonstrate by virtue of its accomplishments that its own economic system was stronger.

A Weakened Dictatorship

By the mid 1980s President Chun faced serious political problems. There were mounting student demonstrations against the government, and the leading opposition politician, Kim Dae Jung, had returned from exile in the U.S. Although Kim was placed under house arrest, a new political party with which he was affiliated, the *New Korea Democratic Party*, did unexpectedly well in National Assembly elections held shortly after his return, winning 50 out of 276 seats.

The events of February 1986 in the Philippines also had a considerable impact on South Korea, not only because Marcos, the dictator, lost power, but because the U.S. had withdrawn support from him in spite of its large strategic interest in the country. If the United States, reacting to popular Philippine democratic pressures, could turn its back on a long-time ally like Marcos, then it might just as easily do so in South Korea as well. The military generals who dominated South Korea thus decided it was time to move toward opening the system before they were forced to do so.

An intensified dialogue ensued between the government and the legal opposition centering on the *New Korea Democratic Party (NKDP)*. A deadlock soon developed, however. It related to the na-

General Chun Doo Hwan

Korea

ture of a new constitution. The government and the ruling party, the *Democratic Justice Party (DJP)*, wanted a cabinet (parliamentary) system, with the real power vested in the premier who would presumably be a *DJP* member; the opposition insisted on a directly (rather than indirectly, as at that time) elected president as the effective head of the government. The opposition however was hampered by disunity within the leadership of the *NKDP*.

Other elements of the opposition, including Christian clergy, lay believers, and activist students, demonstrated from time to time against the government. The demonstrators, although fairly numerous, were generally outnumbered by the huge numbers of police that the government deployed to cope with them.

South Korea's huge ally, the U.S., clearly favored compromise between the government and the opposition, and a further democratization of the political system. The activist elements of the opposition tended to view the U.S. as the main supporter of the hated South Korean "establishment," which they regarded as a military and police dictatorship. Many also blamed the United States for the continuing division of their country caused by the tensions of the Cold War.

Toward A More Democratic Korea

In the summer of 1987, as Chun's *DJP* was preparing to hand over the reins of power to his designated successor, fellow former general and *DJP* politician Roh Tae Woo, a public outcry began. Recognizing he faced a potential disaster, Roh called for an end to press censorship and free

elections! Clearly Roh was counting on a loyal (but minority) *DJP* rural political base and hoped he could count on a divided opposition to salvage victory. His assumption that he could still win the election given the splits in the opposition proved correct.

The first direct presidential elections in more than 16 years were held in South Korea in December 1987. The candidate of the ruling *DJP* was Roh Tae Woo. The two top opposition leaders, Kim Young Sam and Kim Dae Jung, were unwilling to cooperate, and the result was predictable: the winner was Roh Tae Woo with 39.9% of the vote, while the two Kims split the majority opposition vote 27.5% and 26.5%.

Amid anti-government protests, Roh Tae Woo was sworn in as president in February 1988. For the moment Roh, the former general, had prevailed, but the momentum toward a much more open system had nevertheless begun. Korea would never be the same.

In an election for the National Assembly held in April of 1988, the ruling *Democratic Justice Party* won only 125 of the 299 seats. Flexing its new power the opposition then held hearings on various abuses of power during the tenure of former President Chun Doo Hwan, and especially on the Kwangju Massacre of May 1980. Chun himself refused to testify, and President Roh refused to compel him to do so. Chun did make a public apology, turned over his assets to the state, and retired to the countryside. Dissatisfied, a number of opposition politicians and radicals continued to demand that he be put on trial. That demand, though, was to wait until more progress was made in the democra-

tization of the country. Nevertheless, early in 1989, approximately fifty people, including two brothers of Chun, were arrested on charges of corrupt practices under his administration.

President Roh himself had a better image than his predecessor, but the opposition in the National Assembly hoped to pass a vote of no confidence in his administration and compel his resignation as well.

The several years leading up to the 1993 presidential election was an important transitional period. Many did not trust the ruling party or President Roh Tae Woo. It was believed that he might seek extra-legal means of holding onto power. The new constitution was untested and the opposition was, for the most part, weak. There was also concern that the United States might significantly downsize its commitment to the republic. In spite of these concerns, 1993 did mark the beginning of a new, more democratic era for the country.

An Emerging Democracy

The election of 1993 finally brought to power Kim Young Sam, a long time democratic reformer who along with Kim Dae Jung had been especially involved in trying to bring about democratic reform. His election represented the arrival to the presidency of the first civilian elected leader in a generation, though members of the former ruling elite were still very influential.

Upon coming to power, the new president, who was initially quite popular, put forward very specific goals including the achievement of civilian control over the military, a more caring government, and an anti-corruption program.

By 1994 President Kim had initiated reforms to improve the political process. In a bi-partisan move, the National Assembly passed bills dealing with campaign spending, election procedures and local government. Government subsidies for political parties and candidates were increased. The overall limit on campaign spending was lowered (how much a candidate could spend on his/her own campaign). The legislation did not place a limit on how much a *party* could spend on a candidate. Overall, these changes made it easier for the opposition to compete on even footing with the ruling party. The legislature was also given increased authority over the budget and actions of the *National Security Planning Agency (NSPA)*.

President Kim Young Sam also succeeded in obtaining the agreement of all top military officials not to interfere in the political process. Charges of corruption were brought against top military figures and

The Olympic Highway in Seoul along the Han River.

Korea

several were relieved of their positions, including the army chief of staff. The new government also moved to dismantle the *National Security Planning Agency.* A further significant move involved the release of almost 40,000 criminals and political prisoners. Helmeted riot police withdrew from the streets and the number of student demonstrations decreased. Anti-corruption measures were initiated against a number of high ranking government officials. After some thirty years of military participation in the political process, it is remarkable that the new president had as much success as he did.

South Korea had changed a great deal since President Park had ruled with an iron hand! President Kim was even named the winner of the Martin Luther King Prize for his contribution to building democracy and human rights in South Korea.

To the astonishment of many who had watched the long-time domination of South Korea by the military, President Kim even put on trial his two predecessors, Chun and Roh, for their roles in both the coup that brought them to power and the subsequent 1980 Kwangju Massacre. The trials ultimately concluded with former President Chun sentenced to death and President Roh to life imprisonment (lessened on appeal to life sentence and 17 years respectively.) If President Kim had thought the trials would work to his advantage, he guessed wrong. The investigations also uncovered the depth of corruption inherent in the South Korean

General Roh Tae Woo

political system which eventually spilled over on to Kim's own administration and even his own son

Economic Corruption Scandals

A flow of corruption revelations then swept over the political landscape in a tidal wave that has not ended. Former President Roh Tae Woo admitted receiving over $600 million in contributions from businesses during his term in office. Roh's admissions came after two of his associates, one of whom managed a secret fund, revealed its existence.

It then became apparent that in return for the huge payments, large corporations such as Hyundai, Samsung, Daewoo, and Lucky Goldstar received large government contracts.

Another revelation was that Kim Dae Jung, an unsuccessful candidate for the presidency in 1992 had received over $2.5 million from Roh for his campaign.

The corruption charges though were not exclusively the problems of the former Presidents Chun and Roh or even of President Kim's long time democratic rival Kim Dae Jung. Early 1997 saw charges of collusion between President Kim's closest advisors and even his son with the Hanbo Group industrial group.

The President was struggling, as his last year in office began, to find a way out of the growing scandal with his own reputation intact.

But the corruption scandals which were rocking South Korea by mid 1997 were not the only thing that weakened President Kim's prestige. Well aware that South Korea's soaring economy of the 1980s had stalled, the President became convinced that new economic laws needed to be implemented to give South Korean businesses more flexibility over their work forces. That in itself might have been an understandable conclusion but when President Kim's supporters called an early morning meeting of the Korean Parliament on December 26, 1996 and passed legislation allowing businesses to lay off workers or adjust their hours more easily he aroused a huge civil disobedience movement. For weeks, in late December and January of 1997–98 the world watched as South Korea's democratically elected president was challenged by thousands of workers for reducing their economic security and acting undemocratically.

Eventually, President Kim, his earlier insistence on standing firm not withstanding, agreed to allow the parliament- including the opposition parties, the opportunity to review the legislation.

But the events of the fall of 1997 soon dramatically changed the international environment. As the economic collapse of

President Kim Young Sam

Southeast Asia began to impact in South Korea, the economy, already faltering, went into a tail spin(see The Economy below). With the nation's confidence crashing, a long awaited presidential campaign began which would be among the most dramatic of Korea's long history.

Kim Dae Jung: Korean President

The election campaign opened up with President Kim Young Sam's popularity in tatters and his government unable to take decisive action to deal with the nation's growing economic crises. Given the new situation it now looked like Kim Dae Jung, the three time presidential candidate, frequent political prisoner and life-long opponent of the military regime, might finally have a real chance of winning. Recognizing that this was his last chance at the presidency, the former political prisoner, so long labeled a leftist radical by his opponents, moved decisively toward the political center and sought out allies on the middle and right of the South Korean political spectrum.

Not giving up, South Korea's long time ruling party, the Grand National Party nominated Lee Hoi Chang as its standard bearer who not surprisingly worked to distance himself from the extremely unpopular Kim Young Sam.

A third candidate, Rhee In Je, angry that the ruling party had not nominated him, emerged to turn the struggle like that of 1987, into a three way one. But this time, unlike in his previous efforts, the momentum was behind Kim Dae Jung the long time political dissident. When he won in

Korea

South Korea's National Assembly in session. Housed in the nation's new building, legislators enjoy all modern technological innovations including electronic voting.

Courtesy: Embassy of Korea

December 1997's vote it was as astounding a political transformation as when Lech Walesa had become president of Poland or Nelson Mandela of South Africa! The final vote tally gave him 40.3% to Lee's 38.7% and Rhee's 29.2%.

Having waited a life time to lead South Korea and then at 73 winning power as his country experienced its worst economic collapse in a generation the new President had his work cut out for him. Much to the relief of many he seemed ready to begin. Recognizing he'd been elected by less than a majority and knowing the importance of unifying the country he named as his Prime Minister, Kim Jong Pil long time supporter of the former ruling party, a man who had even played a decisive role in bringing about the long years of military rule. If that move did not endear him to some of his long time supporters the new President's decision to grant general amnesties not only to imprisoned political prisoners but to those who had been convicted of traffic violations certainly was. It was all part of a concerted effort to create a sense of a new beginning as the country took on the challenge of dealing with the economic crises it found itself in.

Unfortunately for the new president 1998's economic crisis turned out to be far more difficult to manage. While Kim was able to replenish the country's foreign ex-change reserves which had been dangerously low in the months before he took office, real reform seemed far off. Initially successful in obtaining promises of cooperation from the labor unions, he soon found their leadership was quite unwilling to accept layoffs to strengthen the nation's businesses.

Thus by summer of 1998 Korea was once again experiencing major labor unrest. Nor were the nation's economic leaders any more willing to cooperate with the government's plans for restructuring and thus despite considerable rhetoric on the new president's part little real economic reform has been accomplished.

One problem that also appeared to weaken the President's efforts were accusations that he was not only favoring his own political supporters but carrying out an anti-corruption drive against supporters of the previous regime. Not that his efforts were not warranted. One former director of the previous regime was even convicted of seeking to have the North Koreans take provocative acts that might have affected the results of the previous presidential election! Nevertheless, there were those who felt that the corruption drive was hurting the economic recovery effort. And those accusations of corruption were not merely the problem of members of previous regimes. Over the last few years some of President Kim Dae Jung closest colleagues and friends were accused of similar crimes and he found his party, the National Congress for New Politics, loosing ground politically. The situation became so bad that by late 1999 Kim Dae Jung felt it necessary to personally apologize for the scandals in his administration.

Reacting to the weakening of his power base, President Kim also began planning

President Kim Dae Jung

to organize a new political grouping, eventually known as the Millennium Democratic Party which, it was hoped, would do well in the spring 2000 elections. Unfortunately for Kim, when the elections actually occurred his new party came in a relatively distant second, 115 seats, to the 133 seats won by the former ruling party, the Grand National Party.

Economy

The late 1990s have brought increasing levels of economic frustration to South Korea but the drama that unfolded after the summer of 1997, when the Asian economic crisis began, was quite unprecedented. Still, it was hardly a surprise to closer observers of the Korean economy. After spending a heady period as one of the exciting Asian "Tigers," South Korea, like Japan before, saw its economic vitality lessen as the 1990s unfolded. South Korean wage bills had been going up faster than their Asian competitors and the growth of productivity had not kept up either. They were losing markets to the newer emerging economies like that of the People's Republic and the smaller but until recently vibrant economies of Southeast Asia.

As we have seen, late in 1996, hoping to inject new life and flexibility into the system, then President Kim Young Sam, the first elected civilian president in a generation, reverted to a very undemocratic method of decision making. In the early dawn hours after Christmas his party arranged for a secret parliamentary meeting where it used the absence of opposition delegates (who had not been informed of the meeting) to pass legislation that would have given Korean employers more flexibility in firing workers.

The act, which on purely international economic grounds might have been defensible, only further undermined the repu-tation of the government while doing little to add strength to the economy. These moves may have strengthened democracy in the long run but they did nothing to make South Korea more economically able to meet the demands of the 21st century nor compete with other Asian economies with lower wage demands. But though President Kim Young Sam's motives might have been understandable his methods were in violation of the new more democratic mood of the country. Moreover, the economic situation was not yet critical enough to allow the sort of dramatic economic reforms necessary to reinvigorate the economy. But that too soon changed.

By the fall of 1997 the economic crises that had begun in Thailand, a relatively minor player in the international economic arena, had hit Korea, one of the

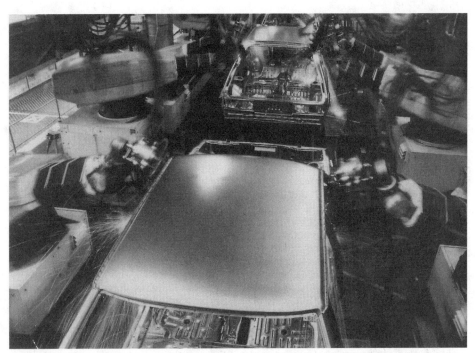

Assembly line at the Hyundai automotive company in Seoul—the *Excel*

largest economies in the world. With confidence much weakened in the currencies of the entire region the Korean currency, the *won*, went into a slide making it all the more difficult for Korean businesses to meet their international debt. All this came at the worst possible time as the country moved into a presidential election campaign.

Unable to meet its international loan obligations South Korea was forced after so many years of economic growth to request an enormous aid package of around $60 billion in loans from the International Monetary Fund. Korea had as well to accept stringent IMF demands that it institute major changes in its economy. Many of those demands, which would see unemployment rise considerably within the country, were very difficult to accept but given the circumstances Seoul had little choice.

And the problems have persisted. Recent headlines have been filled with stories of once powerful conglomerates like Hanbo Iron & Steel starting to go bankrupt. But it was only among the best known of the many firms that started to go under. These firms had been using powerful political connections to over burden themselves with debts they simply could not meet.

For the first time in a generation the South Korean economy had begun to shrink and unemployment for 1998 doubled to 7.4%. Nineteen ninety-seven had seen the country grow by more than five percent but 1998 registered a 5.% contraction.

Fortunately, the new President, Kim Dae Jung, after some initial hesitancy, heroically decided to accept the necessity of dramatic reform and took them on as his own. In sharp contrast to President Kim Young Sam's strong arm tactics of the previous winter, the new president used his long term ties to the labor movement to help gain their initial cooperation. Those efforts were not though as successful as the new president might have hoped.

By late 1999 there were finally signs of recovery and some even predicted a growth rate over 8% for 1999. But despite the good news there was still plenty of work ahead given the fact that over the last few difficult years the annual per capita income of Koreans has fallen from a high of $12,000. a year to the current $6,500!

Foreign Relations: Relations: With North Korea

In the years since the collapse of the Soviet Union and the more recent death of Kim Il Sung the long time leader of North Korea, people in the south have been divided about how to deal with their northern neighbor. On one hand it has been clear that the North Korean economy has been failing and the regime losing its grip on the minds of its citizens. That the regime is likely to continue to weaken seems apparent but how the south should react remains less clear.

Basically three different approaches seem to be in the forefront of public thought. First that the northern regime

Korea

might collapse suddenly. That such an eventuality might please those in the south who have spent their lives struggling against the north is certainly likely. On the other hand such a collapse would leave the Republic of Korea the enormous and sudden burden of integrating the much less sophisticated infrastructure of the north into that of the south. The financial burdens would be enormous as demonstrated in 1990 when West Germany had to do the same thing with East Germany. But South Korea does not have the same resources as Bonn did and its current economic weakness would only make the burden more difficult.

Others have hoped for a smoother transition, a so called easy landing to North Korea's assumed collapse, emphasizing those programs which allow a smoother and less dramatic transition. Lastly, some aware of the enormous complexities of following either strategy have understandably hoped for a simple stabilization of developments on the peninsula. But that is often difficult as incidents keep occurring that highlight both the tensions and the North's weakness. Most prominent among those incidents in recent years were the landing, and discovery of two different North Korean mini-submarines in South Korea.

In the first incident, in September 1996 a mini-submarine was accidentally beached in South Korea. Recognizing the dangers of their circumstances the sailors on board appear to have killed themselves or perhaps been murdered while the soldiers among them set off into the interior of South Korea. Before the incident was over 26 North Koreans and several people from the South were dead.

Eventually the North apologized for the incident but not before another round of incrimination had developed between the two sides. But the North's attempt to infiltrate the South even while it accepted its food aid was only one more example of the North's inconsistency regarding its relations with Seoul. Happily, things were looking up a bit when in March of 1997 the two sides met for the first time in a quarter of a century in New York to discuss opening further talks. On the other hand the North Korean regime makes decisions on a regular basis that at times suggest they are more interested in confrontation than dialogue. Most dramatically during the summer of 1998 they test fired a missile which passed over Japan. That gesture came close to jeopardizing what limited trans-peninsula calm had been realized and inspired South Korean efforts to expand their own missile program.

Since he came to power Kim Dae Jung, the former democratic activist, has believed that a more open policy dubbed a "sunshine policy" would help improve relations with the North. And over the years progress has been made. Recently the North, in need of cash, allowed some South Korean tourists to make very controlled visits to its territory, and the leader of Hyundai delivered much needed herds of cattle to Pyongyang.

But the most dramatic development was the announcement last spring that Kim Jong Il of North Korea had agreed to meet with Kim Dae Jung in June of 2000. Such a meeting would be quite unprecedented in the entire history of Korea since the end of the Second World War.

Relations With the United States and Japan

A large number, although not a majority, of South Koreans, have become strongly dissatisfied with the status of the relationship with the United States. The major issues are the American responsibility for the partition of Korea in 1945 (even given that the alternative was communist domination of the entire peninsula), earlier American support for a series of authoritarian governments in South Korea, and the alleged lack of American enthusiasm for reunification of the country. Somewhat less serious irritants are American control of the Combined Forces Command, under which South Korean forces serve, American pressures to increase Seoul's financial support for the American forces in South Korea and to open its markets further to American products, especially agricultural commodities.

The recent weakening of North Korea has added to the differences which divide these two long time allies. Chief among them is the ambivalence among the South Koreans regarding the appropriate policy to take towards the North. For some Koreans this is believed to be the best time to push toward a complete collapse of the Northern regime regardless of the short term difficulties involved in absorbing the communist government. Washington however, with thousands of troops on the peninsula, has been much more interested in lowering the level of rhetoric and moving toward a smoother transition toward the future. These two views have often dictated different attitudes toward events and decision-making on the peninsula.

Not surprisingly the frustrations associated with the economic collapse and some of the demands of the IMF, within which the U.S. is quite influential, added a level of tension to the relationship as well. But Kim Dae Jung, unlike some of the region's other leaders did not succumb to the temptation to lay the blame exclusively on outsiders. This stance kept some potential tensions to a minimum.

Relations with Japan, Korea's former colonial master, improved over the last year as both countries worked to resolve continuing tensions over the occupation years. Especially important were the mutual statements issued by the two countries. Japan's government finally issued an official apology for their behavior toward Korea, and President Kim of South Korea officially forgave Tokyo. Going further than previous South Korean presidents, Kim even promised to ease the barriers against Japanese cultural imports into the republic. These moves of course all helped ease the way for Japanese help to the ailing Korean economy.

Culture and Society

Korean culture, although distinct from that of Japan, resembles it in many respects. And of course they have both also been exposed to Chinese influences over many centuries. Not surprisingly there are many cultural features that all three Confucian-influenced communities share in common. Nevertheless, Korea like Japan has also developed along its own unique cultural lines.

The ancient pre-Chinese aspects of Korean culture, such as shamanism—the belief in occult sorcerers and worship of demons—have a Northeast and Central Asian derivation. On this base the ingredients of Chinese culture, including Buddhism and Confucianism, were superimposed as a second layer. Since the 19th century there have been many conversions to Christianity. In fact, due to the support many foreign Christian missionaries gave to the Koreans during their years as a Japanese colony, the religion has an association with Korean nationalism not generally found elsewhere in East Asia. Today, the Christian community is a large and influential group which exerts a profound influence in the peninsula.

Korean Women

Like most of Asia, Korean society remains a strongly patriarchal society. Traditionally some women's roles as shaman-like priestesses in the traditional religion of the peninsula did give them levels of influence not always possible elsewhere. In recent years, partly as a result of women's activism, laws have been passed improving their status within society. In 1991 the South Korean Family Law was amended to give women more property and divorce rights. Of those college educated Korean women less than 20% are actually employed and usually in non-professional positions. Today, they have access to higher education as do young men though few hold positions of execu-

A railroad station plaza in downtown Pusan.   Courtesy: CALTEX Petroleum Corp.

tive level responsibility in the country's businesses. Still the situation is improving. The number of women in more senior management positions has doubled over the last decade though in real terms the numbers remain small.

Women have served in positions of influence in the government bureaucracy and as elected officials and more efforts have been made to expand the opportunities available to them. The Korean Military has even been involved with efforts to have women serve as pilots.

North Korea: Political System

The Democratic People's Republic of Korea (DPRK) is one of the world's few remaining hard line communist states. The constitution was adopted in 1948 and was revised most recently in 1992. The legal system is built on communist legal theory and German civil law. The judiciary has no authority to review acts of the legislature. Suffrage is universal for everyone 17 years of age and older. The government has both a head of state and a Premier. The Supreme People's Assembly is the national legislature and has one house. Candidates for office are chosen by the Korean Workers' Party (DWP) and run unopposed. The National Defense Commission has emerged as the supreme decision making body.

For most of its history the state was dominated by one individual, Kim Il Sung who died in 1994. Since then his son, Kim Jung-Il, has assumed the mantle of authority. Hong Song Nam is the prime minister.

Politics and Government

The 1990s have been a disaster for North Korea. The decade began with the collapse of its long time supporter, the Soviet Union and even now Beijing, its only significant international friend, insists that North Korea dramatically transform its economy to survive. Despite North Korea's long time reputation as the most isolated of national states, evidence of its dramatically faltering economy are everywhere. Recent years have seen disastrous floods that have devastated important farmlands while the once proud regime has had to request enormous amounts of food aid from outside agencies. Visitors report as well that the country's electrical system is failing also. Very credible reports of famine have been widely reported—some authorities have even suggested that as many as two million people or ten percent of the population have died. The regime's usual bluster aside, the defection of respected leaders and the departure of thousands of refugees to China in search

Korea

In protective gear, making microchips in Seoul.

of food all attest to the desperate situation Pyongyang finds itself in.

In 1994, Kim Il Sung, the long time exalted leader, died just before he was to meet with South Korean President Kim Young Sam. Then, in a fashion more reminiscent of an imperial dynasty than a modern socialist state, his son Kim Jong Il assumed power. Since then the younger Kim seems to have solidified his authority and slowly assumed many of his father's official titles. Most recently, Kim Jong Il was named the official head of state. But how powerful the new leader really is remains uncertain as some have suggested that recent events suggest a strengthening of the military's influence over events.

Economy

Obtaining authoritative data for the government of North Korea is a very difficult matter indeed. Massive floods and mismanagement of the economy were responsible for a disastrous year. The health care system has collapsed and the hospitals have none of the modern medicines necessary to keep the population healthy. Surgeons have been forced to operate without anesthetics. Some have estimated that several million people could face starvation in the near future. It is a situation that has simply grown worse over the years.

The South Korean watchers claim that the North's economy has shrunk by 3–4% for each year of the 1990s. Last year the government itself claimed the economy had shrunk by 50% over the last five years! But really reliable figures are not available. The only thing that is certain is that the collapse of the socialist economies of the USSR and Eastern Europe hurt North Korea greatly.

Far too late, North Korea has slowly begun trying to follow the path long ago trodden by the People's Republic, that of opening the country to global trade while liberalizing the economy. Following

China's lead North Korea has finally established a free trade zone at Rajin-Sunbong. Like those established a generation ago by China near Hong Kong, the goal has been to attract foreign investment with promises of cheap labor and tax incentives. However, the new special economic zone has attracted little international interest. This effort at reform by opening up the system is hampered as well by the perception that the introduction of capitalist reforms had helped bring about the collapse of the Soviet Union, a road Pyongyang has no interest in following. Still, the state has tried to find ways to enhance government revenues.

The effort to find new funds has ranged widely from agreeing to allow international flights over North Korea in order to earn overflight fees from the airlines to the more controversial offer to accept some of Taiwan's nuclear waste. That deal which might have brought millions of dollars into North Korea called for Pyongyang to accept and bury on its territory thousands of barrels of radioactive material from Taiwan. While not of potential use for military purposes the agreement aroused considerable tension within South Korea which was especially unhappy with the decision to place the material in mine shafts near their common border! Unfortunately some recent events seem to also suggest that the search for funds now includes involvement in the international heroin trade.

The tensions between North Korea and South Korea have made it much more difficult for southerners, the most logical investors, to play a part in the new economic zone. Theoretically though, the North is in a good position to arrest its drastic economic circumstances. After all, just to their south lies the Republic of Korea with which they share a common language and heritage. Economically the two are a fine match reminiscent of the relationship between China's Guangdong province and Hong Kong. The south has international economic sophistication but is burdened

by wage bills that are moving ahead faster than both their competitors and their own productivity. In theory an economic accord between Seoul and Pyongyang would help both, but examples of such logical cooperation are few. Daewoo, the huge South Korean industrial giant has set up a textile facility in North Korea. But tensions on the peninsula have made this potential avenue of recovery quite unlikely.

Foreign Relations

North Korea has few options as it attempts to survive in the post Cold War world. It needs to stabilize the economy and improve its relations with outside powers. Its efforts though in that direction have been at best inconsistent. On one hand it has made gestures toward improving relations with both South Korea and the United States yet concurrently it has carried out provocative acts from firing missiles over Japan to sending more mini-submarines into southern waters.

It has also refused to play the "beggar" it has actually become in recent years. Instead it continues to play the "nuclear card," i.e. threatening that it will move toward developing nuclear weapons unless the outside world supplies it with needed supplies and facilities and most prominently a new series of more modern nuclear reactors. This strategy has worked.

After long planning and difficult negotiations, ground was broken in the summer of 1997 for the two new nuclear power plants that the international community had agreed to build in the north. The project which was expected to cost around five billion dollars was designed to help North Korea phase out its older Soviet style nuclear reactors. The ground breaking ceremony occurred after the U.S. and North Korea had reached an agreement in 1994 which provided for the building of two light-water reactors. The reactors are being built by a U.S. led consortium with South Korea paying the bulk of the costs. These new facilities will not produce by-products which can be used in the manufacture of nuclear weapons grade material. North Korea has however, refused to publicly acknowledge South Korea's central role in the construction and financing of the reactors. The agreement, despite many difficult moments—most prominently reports that the North had begun building another nuclear facility (apparently erroneous)—has largely remained on track.

The U.S. has also delivered tons of fuel oil to North Korea. But despite the real progress already made, the regularity of incidents usually provoked by the North Koreans, keeps derailing efforts to lessen tensions on the peninsula. Clearly North Korea wants to improve its relations with the outside world, if only to strengthen the regime but its inconsistent behavior and frequently aggressive tone accomplishes very little. The most positive development of 1999 was the agreement negotiated by the special U.S. envoy to North Korea, William Perry, within which Pyongyang was said to have agreed to curtail some of its weapons programs for aid and improved economic relations with the United States.

The Future

South Korea faces many challenges in the decade ahead. Its most immediate challenge is to keep up the economic momentum it appears to have regained over the last year and to more dramatically transition into a more open democratic society. Under Kim Dae Jung they seem to have made a good start. And time may be limited. South Korea not only has the burden of its own economy to deal with but it might soon have to face the enormous challenge of integrating a far less sophisticated North Korean economy into its own as West Germany did before it.

Whether North Korea continues to limp along, suddenly collapses or simply withers over time, it will be South Korea that will have the principal responsibility for picking up the pieces. There are also those who fear that the North in a desperate effort to enhance the leadership's credibility may actually provoke some sort of confrontation with the South. While they would be unlikely to benefit from such aggression it will still be South Korea that would bear the principal brunt of such a move.

North Korea, in contrast, is clearly in major trouble. The economy is a disaster and major supporters have been defecting. The drama of early 1997 was the spectacle of the chairman of the Foreign Affairs Committee of the North Korean Workers Party, Hwang Jang Yop, defecting to South Korea's Beijing embassy. By early 1999 even the well known film star Kim Hye Young had managed to depart with her entire family for Seoul. There were even reports from refugees in China that discipline was breaking down among the ranks of the army.

It may well be too late for the regime to reform itself sufficiently to survive long in the 21st century. One major factor preventing North Korea from joining the international community is an exalted sense of "pride." Yet to survive it needs to stabilize relations with South Korea and that it is very reluctant to do though the planned for Korean Summit of June 2000 does bring some hope in that regard.

Pusan's bustling harbor.

Courtesy: CALTEX Petroleum Corp.

Mongolia

Celebrating the 750th anniversary of the 13th century volume, *The Secret History of the Mongols,* **a book devoted to the Mongolian Empire and to the exploits of Chingis Khan**

Courtesy: Government of Mongolia

Area: 604,247 sq. mi. (1,564,619 sq. km., somewhat larger than Alaska).

Population: 2.5 million (estimated).

Capital City: Ulan Bator (Pop. 450,000, estimated).

Climate: Dry, with bitterly cold winters.

Neighboring Countries: Russia (North, Northwest); China (South, East).

Official Language: Mongolian.

Other Principal Tongue: Russian.

Ethnic Background: Mongol (about 97%); Turk (about 3%).

Principal Religion: The Lamaistic sect of Buddhism; religious practice is not discouraged.

Main Exports (to Russia): Beef, meat products, wool, minerals.

Main Imports (from Russia): Machinery, equipment, petroleum, building materials, clothing.:

Currency: Tugrik.

Former Colonial Status: Tributary of the Manchu Dynasty of China from end of the 17th century until 1912; Soviet influence since that time. Nationalist China recognized Mongolian independence in 1946, but withdrew recognition in 1952. Communist China recognized the Republic in 1949.

National Day: July 11th, in recognition of a communist revolution in 1921.

Chief of State: Natsagiyn Bagabandi, President (since May 1997).

Head of Government: Rinchinnyamyn Amarjargal, Prime Minister

National Flag: Three vertical bands of red, blue and red. The band closest to the pole has a set of traditional symbols with a five–pointed star at the top all in yellow.

Per Capita Annual GNP: US $360.

Mongolia is located in an area of extreme contrast in terms of geography. The arid rocks of the Gobi Desert in the southeast region of the country support almost no vegetation, and have a variation of temperature that splits the craggy rocks which interrupt the monotonous landscape. Proceeding northward there is a gradual change, punctuated by the presence of mountains rising to heights of more than 13,000 feet. The desert gives way to mountainous forest which ceases its thick growth in the heights where continuously present snow dominates the landscape.

Water also becomes more abundant in the north, but the rivers are uncontrolled and rough, descending in cascades over rocky beds and resembling the swirling waters of the Pacific Northwest and Alaska.

It is in this somewhat inhospitable part of the country that most of the people live in a thinly scattered existence devoted to animal husbandry. Their dwellings are constructed of felt from their animals stretched over rickety frames. Although possessing an international currency, the rural people still think that one horse, yak or ox equals seven sheep, fourteen goats or one–half of a camel.

History

Prior to the 16th century, the people who inhabited Mongolia had an aggressive, warlike character which enabled them periodically to conquer vast areas as far away as eastern Europe. This was principally due to the greatly superior horsemanship and cavalry techniques of the Mongols, acquired as a necessity due to the organization of their society which was traditionally nomadic. This pastoral existence contributed to the superior stamina of the fierce horsemen.

Mongolia

Several Mongolian leaders became well–known; the most famous was Chingis (Genghis) Khan; he and his successors were able to lead his men in the conquest of vast areas of eastern and southern Asia as far as Baghdad, now the capital of Iraq. However, the Mongols were eventually "conquered" by the people they had subdued. Their empire broke up in the 16th century and they were converted to Lamaist Buddhism, a pacifist religion, by contact with Tibet. At about the same time, they became dominated economically by the industrious Chinese, who possessed skills in manufacturing and trading unfamiliar to the Mongols. They soon found themselves trapped between Russia and China, two large wealthy empires, equipped with newly discovered firearms and other instruments of modern technology which rendered the skills of horsemanship and prowess in cavalry warfare obsolete.

The Mongols were soon reduced to the status of a tributary of the mighty Manchu Empire which had come to power in China. Russian interest in the area awakened to a greater extent in the 19th century; considerable economic and political power was gained In what was then called *Outer Mongolia* by the end of that century.

The numerous and hard–working Chinese pressed northward in the first decade of the 20th century, settling what was Inner Mongolia to the edge of the Gobi Desert, and creating a threat to the people of remote Outer Mongolia. For this reason, when the Chinese Manchu Empire collapsed in 1912, the princes and lamas of Outer Mongolia refused to recognize the claim of the Republic of China to the lands within the region.

In order to gain support for their independence, they appealed to the Russian tsar for protection. An agreement was reached in 1913 whereby China was to administer Inner Mongolia, and its legal "sovereignty" over Outer Mongolia was "recognized," but actually the region was to remain autonomous under local administration.

China took advantage of the collapse of the government of the Russian tsar in 1917 and attempted to seize absolute control of Outer Mongolia in violation of the 1913 agreement. This attempt was initially successful, but in 1921 Outer Mongolia was invaded by a force of White (anti–Bolshevik) troops from Russia. Control was then wrested from the White Russians by the Bolshevik (communist) forces, who remained until 1925.

The Russians quickly organized a communist regime, built around Mongols who were either communist or pro–communist—Mongolia became the first satellite of Soviet Russia. From the Soviet point

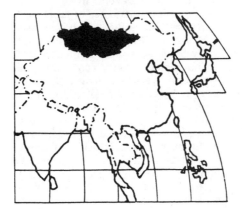

of view, Mongolia served as a buffer against an increasingly powerful Japan, and now also serves as a buffer state, separating it from any threat posed by China to the south.

In the succeeding decades the communist regime brought the nomadic tribes and lamaist monasteries under increasingly centralized control. Occasional resistance was easily crushed by Soviet troops armed with modern mechanized equipment. State services, previously unknown in the region, were provided, including badly needed shelters for livestock to provide protection from the bitter winter wind and snow.

A defensive alliance between Mongolia and Russia, signed in 1936 and renewed every ten years since, was used by the Russians in 1939 to drive a force of invading Japanese from eastern Mongolia. Military units from both nations joined in 1945 to fight Japanese troops remaining in Inner Mongolia; at the same time, Stalin was able to obtain the promise of the Chinese to recognize Outer Mongolia's independence if a vote of the people showed that this was their desire. The plebiscite was held under carefully regulated conditions in October 1945, resulting in a unanimous vote for independence from China. The Nationalist Chinese subsequently recognized Mongolia's independence in 1946, but withdrew this in 1952, claiming that the Soviet Union had violated the commitments made to the Nationalist Chinese under the treaty of 1945.

The communist Chinese, with some hesitation due to their reluctance to abandon traditional claims of sovereignty over Mongolia, recognized Mongolia in 1949, and subsequently signed a boundary

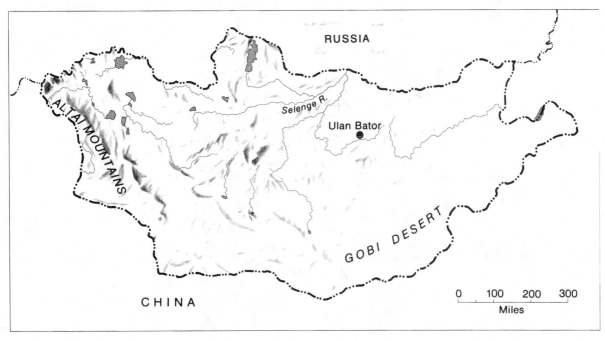

91

Mongolia

Former President Ochirbat's oath–taking ceremony   Courtesy: Government of Mongolia

treaty with it in 1962. But China has occasionally shown some signs of wishing to increase its influence. These pressures caused Mongolia to cling to Russia for protection—it sided with the Soviet Union in all phases of the ongoing Sino–Soviet dispute. It received in return substantial economic aid, which permitted the beginning of industrialization in the country.

Mongolia sought and was granted admission to the UN in 1961, and at about the same time it started to establish diplomatic relations with a small number of "neutral" nations such as India and Indonesia. Japan recognized the Mongolian People's Republic early in 1972.

A boundary treaty with the Soviet Union was signed in late 1976. But because of tensions along the Sino–Soviet border, Soviet troops had entered Mongolia ten years earlier. In 1981, as a gesture to Mongolian nationalism, a Mongol cosmonaut was allowed to take part in a Soviet space flight.

Tsedenbal, Mongolia's long–time leader, was removed in 1984 allegedly because of age and illness, but also apparently because of his colleagues' discontent over his autocratic behavior and his subservience to the Soviet Union. Jambyn Batmunkh succeeded him later in the year.

As part of its effort to improve relations with China, the Soviet Union began in late 1986 to withdraw one of the estimated five divisions it had maintained in Mongolia. Diplomatic relations with the US were established at the beginning of 1987; Mongolia opened its embassy in Washington in 1989, and the U.S. had already rented office and residence space in Ulan Bator.

New Directions

Under the influence of developments in the Soviet Union, especially the ascendancy of Mikhail Gorbachev, the Mongolian leadership had begun to move toward political liberalization in 1985. By the end of 1989, the dramatic events in Eastern Europe led to the emergence of an opposition party in Mongolia, which calls itself the *Mongolian Democratic Union (MDU)*. Led by Soviet–educated intellectuals, it demanded an end to the communist monopoly of power. Surprisingly, this position won increasing acceptance from the communist leadership, beginning with an official statement in early 1990. This decision was the outcome of a debate within the Politburo during which some members urged the use of force against the demonstrators. When Batmunkh said he would agree only if all members signed the order, the idea collapsed.

In early 1990, Batmunkh promised free elections for April. The *MDU* tried to maximize its appeal to the voters by emphasizing nationalism, including praise for the medieval conqueror, Ghengis Khan, in opposition to communism. A few weeks later the entire five–man Politburo of the ruling *Mongolian People's Revolutionary Party* resigned and was replaced by reformers; Batmunkh remained as chief of state for the time being. The ruling party formally gave up its monopoly of power at that time. The new General Secretary, Gombojavyn Ochirbat, was a relatively unknown figure.

In July, while the communist ruling party won about two–thirds of the seats in an election for the Great People's Hural, the opposition parties achieved a recognized place in Mongolian politics. The beginnings of a new era of reform seemed imminent. Changes came quickly. By 1992 a new constitution was in place that allowed for multi–party voting and even the term *People's Republic* was dropped

and the country was renamed simply "Mongolia."

Political ferment and liberalization continued after these dramatic events. Freedom of the press brought a mushrooming of new newspapers and magazines. Freedom of religion led to a widespread resurgence of Buddhism and even to some extent of Christianity.

The constitution provides for a popularly elected president and a Western–style parliamentary system of government, with a 76–seat unicameral legislative chamber, the *Hural*. The president may introduce legislation before the *Hural*, and has a veto. The prime minister is the leader of the dominant party or parties in coalition, which control the *Hural*. A Constitutional Court has the authority to review the legality of laws.

The new constitution also allows for private property, but pastureland continues to be under public ownership. After the mid–1992 elections, the former *Communist Party (MPRP)* still controlled 71 of 76 seats in the *Hural*. But their domination was beginning to weaken.

In mid–1993, Mongolia held its first presidential election. Candidates for the post had to be over forty–five years of age and only political parties that held a seat in the parliament could select a standard bearer. The old line *Mongolian People's Revolutionary Party* (MPRP) nominated L. Tudev, over the incumbent President Ochirbat. The opposition *Mongolian National Democratic Party* (MNDP) formed a coalition with the *Mongolian Social Democratic Party* (MSDP) and selected President Punsalmaagiin Ochirbat, himself, who had been turned down by his own *MPRP*, to be their candidate.

In the election, Ochirbat was elected president with 58.7% of the vote. Perhaps as high as one–fourth of the *MPRP* supporters defected to support their old president. The newly reelected president promised to speed privatization but also to protect those who were hurt most by the process.

During 1994 the *MPRP* continued to rule under Prime Minister Puntsagiyn Jasray, but not without challenges. Street demonstrations broke out in April. The primary issue was apparently corruption in the *MPRP* which reached as high as the prime minister. Demands that the government resign were ignored. Perhaps as a way of making peace, the *MPRP* sat down with the opposition parties in the Great *Hural*, the *Mongolian National Democratic Party* (MNDP), and the *Mongolian Social Democratic Party* to create important reform–oriented legislation. One part of the agreement between the three parties was to require electoral reform to allow for a fairer representation among the parties in the Great *Hural.* The *MPRP* also agreed to the creation of an independent media, not under government control.

A Non-Communist Start

The weakening of communist control which had been going on since the early 1990s was finally fully realized during the 1996 elections when a coalition of democratic parties swept the communist Mongolian People's Revolutionary Party from power. The *MPRP*, which had been in power since 1921, saw its legislative control destroyed as its opponents won 48 of the 76 seats in the parliament! With that vote Mongolia took its place along side other former socialist states who have attempted to find a new future beyond their communist past.

The new prime minister was the 41-year-old M. Enkhsaikhan, leader of the Democratic Union Coalition. Moving beyond the economic liberalization which had already begun, the new prime minister promised to reform the economy to attract more foreign investment.

And the new prime minister certainly had his work cut out for him for within months of his election, in May of 1997, Mongolian voters frustrated by recent economic problems, elected Natsagiyn Bagabandi, leader of the former dominant People's Revolutionary Party, into office as president. More recently, during the spring of 1998 Prime Minister Enkhsaikhan resigned as the leader. Tsakhyagin Elbegdorj then became the temporary leader of the country but the latter was unable to establish his own leadership and throughout much of the fall of 1998 served merely as a caretaker prime minis-

President Natsagiyn Bagabandi

ter as a new leader was sought. Eventually, after more than six months of delay the popular mayor of Ulan Bator, Janlaviin Narantsatsralt, became the new prime minister only to fall from power a mere seven months later when he was replaced by Rinchinnyamyn Amarjargal. Clearly Mongolia's political elite were having problems maintaining political stability. And if the difficulties of maintaining a consensus about the office of prime minister was not serious enough, Mongolia was traumatized recently by the murder of Sanjaasurengiin Zorig, a long time democratic activist.

More important than the problems over finding a suitable individual to hold the position of prime minister has been the on-going competition between the market reformers and the former Communist Party members who made up the Mongolian People's Revolutionary Party, the *MPRP.* Pushed from leadership by the results of the 1996 election, the party has been gaining greatly from the reformist government's inability to cope with unemployment and inflation. Moreover, the MPRP willingness to boycott the national assembly made it difficult for important work to be accomplished. Moreover, during the last year Mongolian politics were even more complicated by the controversies surrounding Mongolian-Russian economic relations. One can assume that all these political battles were likely to play an important role in the elections which were planned for June of 2000.

Foreign Relations

The new Mongolia has been moving to improve its relationship with the outside world. Meetings have been held with Bill Clinton, François Mitterrand and Boris Yeltsin. Not surprisingly relations with Russia have been especially important though not always as smooth as one might want. Officials from both countries have met to discuss the terms under which Mongolia would repay its debt to Russia. The two parties disagree on the amount and the terms. One estimate puts the debt at about $15 billion. A second ongoing problem, cross-border smuggling and rustling, is being addressed jointly.

Without doubt, the most prominent visitor to Mongolia in recent years was the 1995 visit of the Dalai Lama. People came from all corners of the country to hear him speak. His presence signaled a re-

Ulan Bator—modest modernity comes to a proud, isolated society

Mongolia

A factory worker packs camel wool for export

Courtesy: Government of Mongolia

birth of a part of the country's culture which had been suppressed under communism. During his 10 day visit the "God King of Tibet" conducted a mass initiation to replenish the dwindling number of Buddhist monks. One source estimated a crowd of 37,000 people or about 2% of the population greeting the former leader of Tibet. And the Dalai Lama was not the only distinguished religious figure to visit Tibet recently. During mid 1999 the aging ninth Javzundamba Lama arrived for a very controversial visit which saw him enthroned at the Erdene Zhu monastery. The visit attracted not only popular interest but also considerable religious and political controversy within Tibet. Eventually the newly enthroned "living Buddha" departed when his visa ran out.

Another more mundane problem has been fish poaching by Chinese who have entered Mongolian territory. One clash between Chinese poachers and Mongolian border guards in 1997 left more than thirty Chinese dead. But if the Dalai Lama's visit and border incursions have not improved relations between Mongolia and the P.R.C. relations were not weakening either. The two countries have signed a defense cooperation pact and Chinese officials have also reiterated their respect for Mongolia's sovereignty and territorial integrity.

For several years Mongolia has been attempting to reach out beyond Northeast Asia internationally. A major foreign policy initiative of 1995 was launched when Natsagiyn Bagabandi, then chairman of the People's Great *Hural* (national assem-

bly) publicly expressed Mongolia's desire to join the Asia-Pacific Economic forum. The country's former and current leadership feels APEC membership is essential to open the door wider for foreign investment and economic cooperation. That same year an agreement was reached in Washington, D.C. for military assistance for Mongolia. More recently, in the spring of 1998 Mongolia was finally admitted to the ASEAN Regional Forum and by the next year, having paid up its back debts, Mongolia took up its seat in the United Nations' General Assembly.

Society and Culture

The nomadic pattern of life of the Mongols, reflecting a need and desire for mobility, has slowed the growth of substantial cities until recent years. Likewise, there have been no buildings of any great size except for the monasteries within the country.

The traditional literature of the people is ancient—it first consisted mainly of oral epics passed down from generation to generation. In the 13th century the Mongols developed a system of alphabetical writing based on the Tibetan script which served to record the epics as well as being a tool for later literary efforts.

The indigenous religious tradition was relatively simple until the advent of Lamaist Buddhism in the 16th century. Though the communist era no doubt weakened the religious establishment the recent visits of the Dalai Lama and the ninth Javzundamba Lama demonstrates a clear and continuing interest in their religious heritage.

While the processes of industrialization and modernization intrude into the solitude of the people with increasing frequency, the Mongolians are still excellent horsemen, fond of festivals which stress the traditional skills of horsemanship, particularly racing, archery, wrestling and physical stamina. Even as the 20th century came to a close at least half the country still worked in the agricultural sectors of the economy.

Today's Mongolia is undergoing the severe stresses common since the collapse of communism around the world. During this transition, as efforts have begun to build economic systems based on more open markets, the day to day lives of people have been shaken by the increase in unemployment. In the last several years the numbers of people living below Mongolian poverty standards has risen sharply as have related problems such as alcoholism and spousal abuse. The figure for the percentage of households living in poverty was 17% for 1996 and by 1997 had risen to 20%, an ominous sign to those hoping to improve living standards in the country.

Women

Women have long been respected in traditional Mongolian society. The socialist state carried out proactive efforts to raise their status further. Today, the vast majority are literate and they constitute almost half of the graduates of higher education. Women play important roles in the professions and represent the majority of the physicians and academics and over forty percent of the agronomists, public servants, economists, and engineers.

Although recent years have seen a greater openness in the country's political system the end of the formally free health care system has especially hurt women, particularly pregnant and nursing women. Not surprisingly the maternal mortality rate has risen. Moreover, as with other collapsing socialist regimes, the withdrawal of state child care facilities have added additional burdens on women.

Economy

Agriculture and livestock production have been and remain the backbone of the Mongolian economy. Much of the country's industry, including wool production, clothing and leather goods is tied to this sector. The mining of gold, coal, copper, molybdenum, tin and tungsten also figure significantly in today's economy. In recent years the production of copper has been particularly problematic as world prices have fallen and Mongolia's copper enterprise has been unable to fulfill some of its contract obligations. Inflation also remains a significant problem but does appear to be calming. In 1996 alone it had reached over 50% but was reported to be only about 17.5% for 1997.

The transition from communism has not been easy. The break-up of large collective farms has had a negative effect on livestock production—in 1995, livestock production (28.6 million animals) was only slightly larger than the previous record set in 1941. Happily, in 1998 it had gone up somewhat to 31.3 million. Despite the economic problems, efforts at privatization have continued. Most recently the decision was made to privatize housing without cost to the owners. The sale of small shops to private owners continues as well. By the end of 1996 there were over 30,000 private firms which employed hundreds of thousands of people. According to the government the private sector now generates 60% of Mongolia's GDP and the new prime minister remains committed to furthering the private sectors of the economy.

Because of the privatization movement, some one million Mongolians own stock. Because the exchange is starting from scratch, it is likely that the new state-of-the-art systems will be far more advanced than exchanges in many developed countries. The director of the newly installed exchange, Naidansurengen Zolzhargal, an American trained Mongolian is said to be working on a cellular phone system which will allow herdsmen to trade directly with the exchange from horseback!

Still, the economy remains dependent on international organizations and foreign countries. International donors from the United States, the PRC, Japan and Russia are deeply involved in Mongolia's economy as are organizations from the World Bank to the International Monetary Fund. Private foreign investment though has been slow to come into the country because of the uncertainty of government regulations. Mongolia has managed to attract limited international investment from over 58 countries including South Korea, the United States, Russia, Japan and the People's Republic. In fact, the government remains confident that it will be able to replace the need for foreign aid with hopefully more productive foreign investment.

The Future

Mongolia has made remarkable progress in the last year toward the goal of creating a politically more open society. Unfortunately, the economic transition from a communist economy to a more open market society is likely to be slower and the rewards less obvious for quite some time to come. Still there is reason to be somewhat optimistic.

The country has been experiencing reasonably positive growth rates, 3.5% in 1998 and was predicting even better rates for the first years of the new century though the terribly harsh winter Mongolia went through last year (which killed larger numbers of live stock) is said to have dramatically hurt the country economically. The government has even speculated that it might take three years to recover from the damaging winter.

Externally the challenge will probably lie just across the border. Maintaining good relations with the increasingly powerful People's Republic, especially in the face of Russian weakness, is likely to occupy much of the leadership's energy over the next few years.

The pastoral life of Mongolian sheepherders

Brunei Darussalam

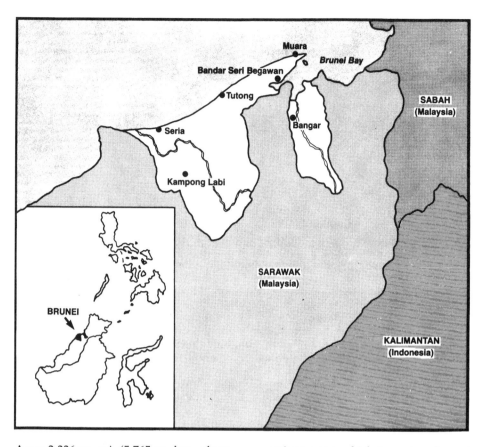

Area: 2,226 sq. mi. (5,765 sq. km., about the size of Delaware).

Population: 306,000 (1999 estimate)

Capital City: Bandar Seri Begawan (named in honor of the present Sultan's father, Pop. 64,000.

Climate: Tropical.

Neighboring Countries: The East Malaysian states of Sarawak and Sabah enclose Brunei on the large island of Borneo, also known as Kalimantan, two thirds of which is Indonesian.

National Language: Malay. English is the second language.

Other Principal Tongue: Chinese.

Ethnic Background: Malay (64%), Chinese (20%), Other (16%).

Principal Religion: Muslim (60%, official State religion); Buddhist, Christian, traditional native beliefs.

Main Exports: Crude petroleum, liquefied natural gas, and wearing apparel.

Main Imports: Aircraft, electronics, other manufactured goods, and foodstuffs.

Currency: Brunei dollar.

Former Colonial Status: Previously independent, it was a British protectorate (1888–1983).

Independence Day: January 1, 1984.

Chief of State: His Majesty the Sultan and Yang Di–Pertuan of Brunei Darussalam, Sultan Hassanal Bolkiah Mu'izzaddin Waddaulah (b. 1946).

National Flag: A yellow field crossed diagonally by single white and black stripes upon which is centered a red crest.

Annual Per GDP Capita Income: U.S. 16,683 (1995est.).

Brunei *Darussalam* (meaning "abode of peace") is one of the most unusual nations in the world. Having two distinct parts, with Malaysia's state of Sarawak plugging a 15–mile gap between the two, it is also one the wealthiest sovereign nations *per capita* on earth.

Much of inland Brunei is dense jungle scattered with remote villages and alive with brilliantly–plumaged birds, but its gleaming capital city, Bandar Seri Begawan, on the Brunei River about nine miles from its mouth, is sleekly modern, has several international–class hotels—and no slums! The country's main port is bustling Muara.

Malays form the majority of the population, but there are also about 70,000 non–Malays, most of them Chinese involved in trade and commerce. In 1961 Brunei passed a law allowing non–citizen Chinese to become Brunei citizens if they had resided in the country for 20 of the previous 25 years and could pass a Malay language test. There are also small groups of British, Dutch, American and Australians associated with the oil and gas industry. Education is free up to a doctorate if one's scholarship takes him that far. There are three "streams" in the educa-

tional program—Malay, English, and Arabic; students may pursue advanced studies at schools at government expense. Over 2,000 students are enrolled in foreign universities.

Brunei has many splendid beaches, and hotels provide excellent service and delectable foods, often combinations of rice, meat and vegetables. The country's cattle are raised on a ranch in northern Australia, which as it turns out, is larger than Brunei! The cattle are flown into the country and slaughtered according to Muslim customs. Television is common in most households.

History

From the 14th to the 16th century, Brunei was the cornerstone of a powerful Muslim empire which encompassed most of northern Borneo and the Philippines. However, the advance of the Dutch and the British, internal corruption, and warfare took their toll as the 17th century dawned. Brunei's rule was confined to an area today formed by Sarawak and part of Sabah. Towards the middle of the century, in 1841, in a rather desperate move to secure military help against marauding South China Sea pirates, the Sultan ceded to the English adventurer Sir James Brooke the entire region of Sarawak. Brooke styled himself *Rajah* ("prince" or "king") of the area and was succeeded by his nephew and the latter's son until 1946. By 1847 the British secured from the Sultan the island of Labuan off the northwest coast of Borneo, which they speculated could become an important naval base, although the plan never came to realization.

There were further concessions and further treaties. In 1865 the United States government under President Lincoln's administration, concluded a treaty with the Sultan. The *American Trading Company of Borneo* was created and granted vast land holdings, but this venture was soon thought worthless and was abandoned. Sixteen years later the British set up the *North Borneo Company*, which acquired the assets of the U.S. firm and pushed further land concessions from the Sultan who had little power to refuse the mighty British Empire. Brunei was thus reduced to its present size.

With a fragile economy and no way to defend itself against the many European powers which were continuing to colonize the entire area, Brunei chose British protection in 1888 and, later in 1906, permitted a British commissioner to take up residence in the country; the Sultan was required to take his advice in all matters involving defense and foreign affairs, but not the Islamic faith and Malay customs.

During the next few years the country's economy began to grow, first with the cultivation of rubber. Then the economic picture drastically changed as vast oil reserves and natural gas were discovered in the 1920s in the western part of the nation followed by offshore deposits in the 1960s. Brunei was on the road to enormous wealth.

Brunei's 1959 constitution allowed for a measure of shared political decision making beyond the royal family, but that experiment in more open politics was short-lived. In the aftermath of a 1962 rebellion led by a pro-Indonesian leftist, a state of emergency was imposed which allowed the banning of all political parties. The state of emergency allowed the Sultan to reestablish absolute control. That mandate has continued until the present. In fact, those powers were last renewed in July of 1996 more than thirty years after they were first imposed.

When the Federation of Malaysia was established in 1963 to be composed of Malaya, Sabah, Sarawak and Singapore, the Sultan of Brunei was urged to join. The then sultan rejected the plan, fearing for the erosion of his political position and determined that Brunei's oil and gas revenues would be reserved for the benefit of native Bruneians rather than becoming available to the proposed federation at large.

Brunei regained its independence after almost a century of colonialism on January 1, 1984. A member of the British Commonwealth, Brunei has since joined the UN and the Association of Southeast Asian Nations (ASEAN) among others. At the Sultan's request, the Gurkha army units from Nepal stationed in Brunei while it was under British protection have stayed on to aid the Royal Brunei Armed Forces. The government continues to pay for their maintenance, but they are still under British command. Given the end of

His Majesty The Sultan of Brunei, Hassanal Bolkiah Mu'izzaddin Waddaulah

the British control over Hong Kong, where the Gurkhas also served, the role of the Gurkha units in Brunei is now being reevaluated.

The present Sultan, Hassanal Bolkiah, heads the government, serving as prime minister, defense minister and more recently as finance minister. Other key government posts are held by members of his immediate family. The Sultan, born in 1946, has, as Muslim custom allows, two wives; he has three sons and six daughters. Educated in Brunei and Malaysia, the Sultan then enrolled as an officer cadet at the Royal Military Academy at Sandhurst, England.

He was crowned the 29th ruler of Brunei by his father in 1968 upon the latter's abdication. Easily one of the richest men in the world, the Sultan controls the finances not only of his own family but that of the state itself. With such resources he can be quite lavish. For example, in 1996 to celebrate his fiftieth birthday, the Sultan threw a party that cost over $25 million dollars and included Prince Charles, an old friend, as a guest, and the American performer, Michael Jackson, as the entertainment.

Politics and Government

According to its constitution Brunei is a "democratic Islamic Malay monarchy." However, while it is clearly a monarchy it does not constitute a true democracy. The Sultan and his family completely dominate the political life of the country. Although the constitution of 1959 did allow some sharing of political decision-making, much of it has been suspended since the early 1960s. Additional modifications have occurred since independence in 1984. Freedom of speech is limited and political activity severely restricted.

Sultan Hassanal Bolkiah, chief of government and head of state, rules the country with the help of the Council of Cabinet Ministers, most of whom are family members. The unicameral legislature, *Majlis Masyuarat Megeri*, has been an appointed body since 1970. The traditional system of village chiefs was modified in 1992 to allow all adults to vote for them by secret ballot. It is through these chiefs and their various organizations that the government expects the population to present their concerns.

After his father's death in 1986, the present Sultan devised an ideology designed to reinforce the monarchy. Known as *Malaya Islam Beraja* or *MIB* it is mainly an affirmation of Islam and the monarchy. The

The Omar Ali Saifuddien Mosque

Brunei

A marketplace in Bandar Seri Begawan

Sultan's new ideology, *MIB,* was brought into the secondary schools in 1992. Undoubtedly, the country's leadership sees *MIB* as a mechanism for strengthening its continued leadership role.

For a time, Brunei politics appeared to be moving toward a more pluralistic form. In February 1995, Haji Abdul Latif Chuchu, a political activist, was elected president of the *Brunei Solidarity National Party,* the country's only legal political party. Haji Latif and other party officials then called for democratic elections in a meeting with the Sultan. That effort did not accomplish much. Haji Abdul Latif Chuchu was banned from all political activity and now his former party appears inactive.

For now, Brunei's internal politics remain within the royal family though there has been talk of a new general election which would be the first one since 1962! Over the last year the Sultan has also been emphasizing a more religious tone in some of his public talks—reminding his subjects of the importance of adhering to their Muslim duties.

But though there may be little "public" politics within Brunei there is certainly controversy within the ruling family which occasionally becomes more publicly known. Over the last few years an open conflict broke out between the Sultan and his brother Prince Jefri Bolkiah, who was accused of financial mismanagement and removed from his direction of Brunei Investment Agency (BIA). Quite surprisingly the break became very public and Prince Jefri even went into self-imposed exile. During the same period the Sultan officially decided to name his twenty-four year old son, Prince Billah, a recent graduate of Oxford, his heir.

Defense

While tiny in size, Brunei has a modern and capable defense force. Internal and external security are under the control of the Royal Brunei Armed Forces (RBAF), the Royal Brunei Police, the Gurkha Reserve Units, and the British Army Gurkha Battalion. Recent defense expenditures have been around 10% of the national budget. The RBAF has about 4,000 personnel and includes several hundred women who were recruited beginning in 1981.

The air force and navy are small but well equipped. Joint military exercises have been held with Malaysia, Thailand and Singapore. The latter trains its troops in Brunei's jungles. An option for Brunei would be to join the Five Power Defense Agreement (Singapore, Malaysia, New Zealand, Australia and Britain). A Gurkha Reserve Unit of some 900 men is directly under the control of the Sultan and is composed of retired British army personnel. The Royal Brunei Police Force of approximately 2,000 is the fourth component of national defense.

Negotiations over a Memorandum of Understanding (MOU) with the United States on national defense matters were initiated in the early 1990s. The United States may be interested in using the country as a staging point for air surveillance in the region.

Foreign Relations

Brunein foreign policy stresses the security of the nation. A true mini-state, the country must rely to a considerable extent on the goodwill of its neighbors. The fact that it is surrounded by its two Muslim brother states, Malaysia and Indonesia, is advantageous. Brunei joined the Association of Southeast Asian Nations (ASEAN) just after independence in 1984. Membership has helped the country establish close diplomatic and military ties with the other ASEAN states. Brunei also takes part in the ASEAN Regional Forum (ARF). The ARF is a consulting body which focuses on Asia-Pacific security matters.

Brunei was the first Muslim state in the region to recognize Israel. Earlier on it had established ties with the Palestine Liberation Organization and opened an embassy in Iran. More recently Brunei has been strengthening its ties to other Muslim Middle Eastern states from Saudi Arabia to Morocco.

During the fall of 1997 the Sultan attempted to use his vast financial resources to shore up the collapse of his neighbors' currencies though even his efforts failed to stem the tide of the currency debacle that hit the region. In years since the Asian economic crisis settled in, the Sultan, despite weaknesses in his own economy—caused by then falling oil prices—has vowed to take a more active role in helping the region progress. Not only has he been significantly involved in helping Malaysia and Indonesia recover financially, the Sultan set out recently for his first official visits to his northern neighbors Burma, Laos and Vietnam.

Culture and Society

The country is ruled by the royal family. The royal line goes back some twenty-nine generations farther than any of the other twenty-eight monarchies in existence today. Brunei Malays are similar to the Malays of Malaysia and Indonesia. All are followers of Islam and speak the Malay language. They differ significantly from other ethnic groups in Brunei. Traditionally, Brunei Malays were fisherman, traders and craftsmen.

Today's generation is seeking more "modern" means of employment. About ten percent of the Brunei Malays claim royal blood, having been descended from one of the Sultans. Many of the Malays live in Kampong Ayer, the Malay community consisting of about thirty-five villages. Marriages were once arranged by the village headman and the family. Now, however, more modern methods prevail. Although under Muslim law, a man is permitted to have up to four wives this is actually rare in Brunei.

Contemporary life in Brunei for its citizens is one that many would envy. Perhaps to keep dissatisfaction with the Sultan's political control to a minimum the state has used its oil resources to create a cradle-to grave social security system. Almost every urban family owns at least one car, often more, and there is no income tax. Both education and health care are free. Though given recent financial setbacks it might be wrong to assume these circumstances will continue indefinitely.

The Kedazans are the second most populous indigenous group. They are similar to Malays in their practice of religion, language and appearance. The greatest difference is that they have tended to be rice farmers. They do not have the same status in society as the Malays. Other smaller indigenous groups include the Bisayas, who follow indigenous religious traditions; the Penans, nomads of the jungle; the Muruts, who once populated the military for the Sultan; and the Ibans, whose numbers are increasing compared to the other smaller groups and who are known for their past head hunting activities.

The Chinese are far more important than their numbers would suggest. They dominate the Sultan's commercial sector. They also provide the managerial and technical talent for the country. The older generation follows Taoist-Buddhist traditions. Less than ten percent of the Chinese in the country have been granted citizenship. Still, their importance was recognized last year by the government's agreement to allow the founding of a Chinese language newspaper in the kingdom.

Women

As is the case elsewhere, the experience of women in Brunei is a mixed one. While no women hold leading positions in the bureaucracy, large numbers hold positions at the lower levels. Today nearly two-thirds of the student body at the national university are women. They also serve in the military though not in combat positions.

However, since Brunei is officially a Muslim society, Islamic domestic law governs the life of women. Women have fewer rights in such important areas as divorce and inheritance and, as is common in the region, they can not pass on their citizenship to their children. Men also have considerable advantages over women in the government's civil service jobs.

Economy

Oil and gas provide Brunei with more than 90% of its export earnings; it is the third largest oil producer in Southeast Asia after Indonesia and Malaysia. The Seria oil field was discovered in 1929 and by the 1950s it was producing 115,000 barrels a day. Offshore production began in 1964 and there are today hundreds of oil rigs operated by Brunei Shell Petroleum Company, jointly owned by the government and Shell. Actual oil production is carefully watched since Brunei wants to conserve this source of income for the future. Most oil is exported to Japan—almost half, and the rest goes to other nations, the United States receiving about 10%. Brunei uses only about 3% of its production for domestic use.

Brunei is also the world's fourth largest supplier of liquid natural gas, a venture owned by the government, Royal Dutch Shell Group and Japan's Mitsubishi Corporation. Millions of tons are exported annually to Japan alone. The petroleum sector still accounts for around 50% of Brunei's gross domestic product (GDP). This figure was over 80% in the 1980s. Unfortunately, the recent lowering of oil prices due to the world economic slowdown and consequent reduction of demand has hurt the nation's economy significantly.

Another source of revenue is foreign investment which is now producing almost as much money as the petroleum sector. Nevertheless, under the circumstances the nation's GNP has been slowing. In 1997 it was around 4% and by 1998 it was only around 1%. Last year's figures were expected to be even lower prompting plans for economic restructuring on the part of the government.

Overall, the government has spent much of the 1990s working on various plans to diversify the economy and more recently even moving toward privatizing some government agencies. One goal has been the plan to steer the economy away from dependence on oil and natural gas. However, this attempt to diversify the economy has been less than a smashing success. It is made especially difficult because the government employs more than half of the labor force. A new joint-venture garment manufacturer was forced to import Philippine and Thai workers because locals were either too few in number or not interested.

The government has frozen civil service pay in an attempt to make state employment less attractive. However, in a country where health care and education are free, and where subsidized loans are readily available, there is little pressure to change. There may be some ambivalence on the part of national leaders concerning economic change. An influx of foreigners and new ventures will surely disturb the comfortable and traditional environment of this Islamic mini-state. Nevertheless, in June 1995, Brunei applied for membership in the World Bank and the IMF. It is unlikely that Brunei needs to borrow funds. But it clearly does believe that it is important to play a role in the emerging global economy.

The Future

With a per capita Gross Domestic Product (GDP 1995) of over $16,000 per year, the country faces no serious economic problems. The discovery of new oil deposits insures that the country will be pumping petroleum for many decades to come. Self-sufficiency in food is a worthy but not essential goal. The country's wealth has spawned growing environmental problems. Local waterways are being clogged with Styrofoam, old refrigerators, and even cars. This is a serious problem that can only get worse until the government takes action. The primary economic challenge remains to diversify the economy to prepare it for the day when the oil lines run dry. Thus far the nation's limited growth levels, now hovering around 1%, do not bring a lot of hope that Brunei will be ready for that day.

Although Brunei has good relations with its neighbors, long term defense requirements need attention. Finally, domestic tensions could rise if *MIB* is forced too aggressively. Like Malaysia and Singapore, Brunei is a multiethnic society which can only survive with a good bit of tolerance and acceptance of diversity. For the foreseeable future, political reform is not likely. If it does occur, it will originate in the royal palace and not in the streets of Bandar Seri Begawan.

An early morning traveler swings through the towering trees in Bardar Seri Begawan
Courtesy: Sarah Cassell

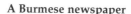

A Burmese newspaper

The Union of Burma
(The government has renamed the country *Myanmar*)

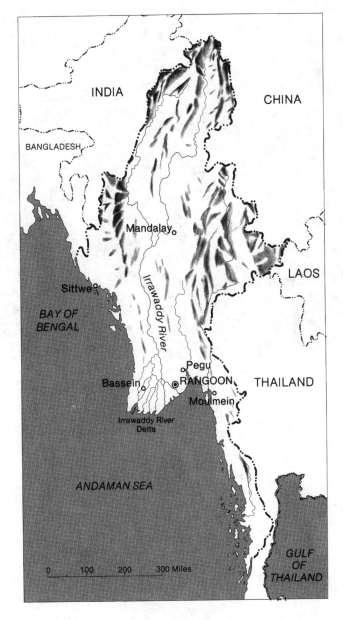

Area: 261,700 sq. mi. (676,600 sq. km., almost as large as Texas).

Population: 50 million (estimated).

Capital City: Rangoon (Yangon, Pop. 3.8 million, estimated).

Climate: Tropical, with torrential rains during the summer monsoon (June–November) in the coastal areas.

Neighboring Countries: China (North and East); India, Bangladesh (West); Laos (East); Thailand (East and South).

Official Language: Burmese.

Other Principal Tongues: English, Chinese, Karen, Shan.

Ethnic Background: Oriental Mongoloid mixtures, including Burman (72%) in the central valley area, Karen (7% in the Pegu Yoma and Karen States), Shan (6% in the Shan Plateau and Chindwin Valley), Chin and Kachin (5%) in the western mountain and extreme north, Wa (2%), a group along the Chinese border; Chinese, Indian, Bengali and other (8%).

Principal Religion: Buddhism.

Main Exports (to Singapore, China, Thailand, India and Hong Kong): Beans, teak, rice, hardwood.

Main Imports (from Japan, China, Thailand, Singapore, Malaysia): Machinery, transportation equipment, chemicals, food products.

Currency: Kyat.

Former Colonial Status: British dependency (1886–1947).

Independence Day: January 4, 1948.

Chief of State: General Than Shwe, Chairman, State Peace and Development Council (since April 1992).

Secretary, SPDC: Kin Nyunt.

National Flag: A red field with a blue union in the upper left–hand corner containing a large white gear (representing workers) superimposed with a sheaf of rice (representing peasants) surrounded by 14 small white stars symbolizing the states and divisions of the country.

Annual Per GNP Capita Income: U.S. $841 1993 estimate.

The long western coastline of Burma faces the tropical waters of the Bay of Bengal in the North and the Andaman Sea in the peninsular southern regions. The northern part of the country is actually a moist and hot basin—it is separated from India and Bangladesh by high, forested ridges and lower valleys, and from China, Laos and Thailand by the mountains and by the Shan Plateau, which combine to form a crescent enclosing Burma.

The mountains of the plateau region are not particularly high when compared to those in other countries of southern Asia; they reach a maximum height of about 9,000 feet. The Irrawaddy River originates in the mountainous region of the north, turbulently descending to the lowlands where it is transformed into a sluggish, muddy stream of water. It is along this river and also along the Sittang River that the largest cities of Burma are located, including Rangoon and Mandalay.

The northern mountains are inhabited thinly by people who are mostly non-Burman; they live principally in the thick forests where teak and other valuable trees grow.

The great majority of the people live in the crowded central valley where great quantities of rice are raised each year, much of which is exported. The comparatively cool and dry season, which starts in November, ends in about mid–February when the wind changes from the north and begins to blow from the Bay of Bengal. The air becomes hotter during April and May, and periodic storms appear on the horizon.

101

Burma

Rush hour in Rangoon with Longgyi-clad men clinging to bus entrance

AP/World Wide Photos

In June the full force of the southwest monsoon rains inundate the coastline. It is in this region that an average of 200 inches of rain fall each year, but the further inland regions receive less rain as their distance from the coast increases. The rains abate in late October; the wind again comes from the North, providing a cooler and drier relief from the oppressive moisture of the preceding months.

History

In the early centuries of the Common Era, the fertile coastal region of Burma was inhabited by the Mons, who had cultural characteristics quite similar to those of India. In about 1000 A.D. they became converted to *Hinayana* Buddhism which had come from India by way of Ceylon (Sri Lanka); they in turn transmitted this sect to other people living in the region, including the Burmans.

The adjective "Burmese" is used by Americans to describe all of the people living within the country; "Burman" is used to designate the largest ethnic group; the British usage is exactly the opposite. Burmans are closely related in terms of language and appearance to the Tibetans, and seem to have moved southwest into Burma from the remote regions of eastern Tibet beginning about 800 A.D. Although they have oriental features, they usually do not have the eyelid fold of their Chinese neighbors; the color of their skin varies from deep brown to extremely light in color.

The Burmans emerged as the most powerful force in the country by the mid-11th century under King Anawrata, who established a national capital in the central city of Pagan, from which most of the country was subdued. The Shan (Thai) people, who lived in the northeastern part of Burma, disliked Burman rule, and in the late 13th century requested the protection of the Mongol empire which ruled China. The emperor Khubilai Khan sent a large force of cavalrymen who invaded Burma, totally destroying the Burman kingdom.

The Mongols did not remain for any great length of time; when they left the Shan established a number of states which were under Burman influence, but which governed the nation. From about 1300 to the mid-18th century, Burma's history is one of repeated destructive civil wars among the Burmans, Mons and Shans. No one emerged victorious; these wars served only to limit the development of Burma.

European merchants and explorers appeared along the coast after 1500; although the Dutch had trading bases for a brief period, there was no early colonization of Burma. In 1753 a new Burman kingdom emerged, rapidly reuniting the several small states into which Burma had been split by civil war. This warlike kingdom raided Thailand, fended off two invasions by the Manchu dynasty of China and in the early 19th century invaded Assam to the west.

The British East India Company, which was in control of Assam at that time, sent British troops to push the Burmans out of the area in the First Burmese War (1824). The British took over the Arakan and Tenasserim coasts and advanced up the Irrawaddy River. Faced with defeat, the Burmans surrendered those coasts and permitted the British to maintain a minister at the Burman capital of Ava. However, relations with the British were tense which eventually led to the Second Burmese War of 1852. Trade relations were established in a commercial treaty in 1862 giving the British the right to trade throughout Burma.

Thibaw became king in 1878, and rapidly alienated the British by again interfering with their trade and establishing relations with the French. This resulted in the Third Burmese War (1885–1886) which ended Burman rule. The country was then governed as a province of British India until 1937 when it became a Crown Colony.

The emphasis during the British colonial period was on profitable trade and not on the welfare of the various ethnic groups in Burma. In depriving the Burmans of control, the British aroused the hatred of this the largest group. The minority Karen, Shan, Chin and Kachin peoples however looked to the British for protection from the Burmans, and thus were less antagonistic towards their colonial rulers. The British also undermined the influence of the Buddhist monasteries and imported large numbers of Indians to perform skilled and semi–skilled tasks rather than training the Burmans for these jobs. Thousands of Chinese also entered to engage in trade. These foreign minorities caused anti–Indian and anti–Chinese riots in 1931. The anti–foreign Burmans resisted adoption of European skills and cultural patterns more successfully than the people in almost all of the other British colonies.

There was considerable economic growth during the colonial period. Burma became the chief rice exporter of Southeast Asia; the lower Irrawaddy valley was cleared of its dense forests and brought under cultivation. Burmese labor was used for the cultivation of the huge crops.

The British granted a degree of self–government to Burma in 1937 which included an elected legislature and a cabinet. The lack of experience in government on the part of the Burmans created a basic instability in the government; there was little support among the people for the elected members and officials.

Thus, when the Japanese invaded Burma in 1942, they were welcomed by the people, including many Buddhist monks. Chief Minister Ba Maw of the colonial government accepted leadership in a puppet government established by the Japanese in 1943. Even though the people had welcomed their conquerors, the Japanese quickly set up a very oppressive administration designed to exploit Burma's capacity to produce rice. Active resistance soon formed around the *Anti–Fascist People's Freedom League (AFPFL)*, a political movement composed of left–wing nationalists and some communists, leading a guerrilla army under the Burman popular hero Aung San. The Allied forces, in an effort to establish a supply route to southwest China, in order to support the war against the Japanese in that country, slowly fought their way through Burma in 1944–45. The country was eventually liberated by mid–1945. The British then tried to establish a government along prewar colonial lines, but friction erupted immediately with the *AFPFL* led by Aung San. Happily for Burma the British were then living under the anti-colonial *Labor Party* government of Prime Minister Attlee, which was in the process of giving up its control over India and Pakistan. It agreed in 1947 to give Burma its independence; the *AFPFL* chose then to leave the British Commonwealth entirely.

Sadly, Aung San was assassinated in 1947. U Nu, an attractive and fervently Buddhist member of the *AFPFL*, took control of the government. Burmese communists threatened the government of Burma in the years following 1948—in 1949 the government controlled little of the nation outside Rangoon. The lack of cooperation among the insurgents though enabled the Burmese army under Ne Win to reduce the rebellion to a much lower level by 1951.

China, Burma's largest neighbor, fortunately was not involved in the civil strife. The Burmese, although independent, were not experienced in operating an effective government; the *AFPFL* split and became a coalition of parties with a high degree of inefficiency, corruption and factionalism. The leftist–socialist group was led by U Nu; the more conservative wing was led by Ba Swe. The split between the two factions resulted in the forced resignation of U Nu in the fall of 1958; Burma was then ruled by the military commanded by Ne Win until February 1960. Little progress was made toward solving the political problems of the country, or toward getting the sluggish economy moving during this period of military rule.

Elections were permitted in 1960 which resulted in U Nu's faction being returned to office, but in 1962 adverse political and economic conditions again caused the military to intervene. This time, Ne Win abolished the existing political parties, imprisoned a number of political leaders, including the highly popular U Nu, and established a military dictatorship under the *Union Revolutionary Council* which he led. He then dramatically announced that he would make Burma a completely socialist—although not a communist—state. Meanwhile the internal revolts had continued, particularly in rural areas during the post–independence years. Ne Win was unsuccessful in negotiating an end to these revolts despite new military operations and the jailing of a number of communist leaders.

Ne Win invited some of the former political leaders in early 1969 to advise him on Burma's political future. They urged a return to elected government instead of military rule. When Ne Win refused, U Nu went into exile and announced that he would try to lead a political movement for the overthrow of Ne Win; however, he eventually gave up the plan and returned to Burma. Ne Win meanwhile launched a process of making Burma a one–party state, controlled by the *Burma Socialist Program Party*, a leftist movement with some communist elements, headed by himself. Over the years the army has proved unskilled and ineffective in managing the economy.

A new constitution was adopted by referendum at the beginning of 1974. Burma was renamed the *Socialist Republic of the Union of Burma*. Real power was exercised by a 29 man Council of State, chaired by President Ne Win. However, the government remained repressive, unpopular and inept.

Inflation, shortages of rice, and floods contributed to political unrest in the mid 1970s. In December 1974, the funeral of U Thant, former Secretary General of the United Nations, provided the occasion for Buddhist and student organized riots which were quickly suppressed by the military. In 1983, Burma found itself dragged into the violent politics of the

Lord Louis Mountbatten, supreme allied commander in Southeast Asia (1943–46), later *Earl Mountbatten of Burma*, talks with British troops near Mandalay in April 1945

Burma

Korean peninsula when North Korean agents planted a bomb in a public monument which killed 17 visiting South Korean officials and journalists on October 9th. High Burmese officials were narrowly spared from this terrorist attempt. Infuriated, Ne Win again shook up security services and broke diplomatic relation with North Korea.

Domestically the army improved its position against insurgency somewhat in 1985 as China reduced its support for the communists in the Wa and Shan states and as a number of Karen insurgents were driven across the border into Thailand. On the other hand, the so–called Shan United Army, which in addition to defending the interests of the Shan tribes in Burma and Thailand was involved in the opium trade, transferred its operation from Thailand to Burma in 1982.

Meanwhile the *National Democratic Front,* a coalition of ethnic insurgent groups, attempted to engage the government in talks on the key issues of ending military rule, restoration of parliamentary government and autonomy for ethnic minorities.

In August 1987, Ne Win made an unprecedented public admission that he and his government had made some mistakes. These included authoritarian policies that led to demonstrations which in turn caused the closing of all educational institutions at the secondary and higher levels.

An Epic Struggle for Democracy

In March 1988, a long series of massive demonstrations against the ruling regime by students, monks, and urban residents seemed to promise a democratic or liberal revolution like those in the Philippines and South Korea. But the army proved too strong and determined, however, to permit such an outcome. An of course, unlike similar struggles elsewhere it did not have the world's press to worry about. Rangoon was neither Manila nor Seoul and it was far easier to use brute force with impunity. The long time dictator, Ne Win officially resigned in July as chairman of the ruling *Burma Socialist Program Party,* but nevertheless stayed in the Rangoon area and continued to give orders to the army from behind the scenes.

At the end of July, Ne Win was succeeded by a close associate and tough former general, Sein Lwin, who also became president of the Union of Burma. He proclaimed martial law in Rangoon and tried to control the democratic demonstrations by military force but failed.

The leadership then turned to a relatively moderate civilian, Maung Maung, who pledged multi–party elections in which none of the current leaders would run for office. There was great popular joy

Aung San Suu Kyi (1991 Nobel Prize Winner)

Photo by Leslie Kean, The Burma Project USA

at this, but also a widespread demand for an immediate interim government. In September of 1988 Former Prime Minister U Nu proclaimed such a government, composed largely of opposition leaders.

The nation's military leaders had other ideas. Defense Minister Saw Maung seized power on September 18 and assumed both the chairmanship of the ruling party (the *State Law and Order Restoration Council (SLORC)* and the presidency of the state.

Protest demonstrations were then violently and brutally suppressed by the army. Thousands of people died as the army drove the democratic crowds from the streets. The military assault that followed was even more brutal than the more publicly viewed repression which occurred in the People's Republic of China the following year. Thousands of refugees eventually headed for Thailand and various border areas beyond the control of the government. For the moment, efforts to end the generation long military dictatorship had failed but Burma's democratic activists soon had another opportunity to expand the nation's democratic base. The opposition, calling itself the *National League for Democracy,* discarded U Nu as its head and selected as its new leader the increasingly popular, Aung

San Suu Kyi, the daughter of national hero Aung San (assassinated in 1947). She benefited not only from his name and memory but from the atmosphere surrounding the funeral of her mother on January 2, 1989, which amounted to a peaceful demonstration against military rule.

In preparation for the supposedly free election scheduled for May 27, 1990, the military leadership disqualified the most prominent opposition figure, Aung San Suu Kyi, from running (January 1989) and placed her under house arrest in July of that year, together with other leading members of the opposition.

Nevertheless, the opposition parties won over 80% of the vote for the National Assembly in the May 1990 elections. But the army refused to surrender power and intensified its campaign of repression. Attempting to assert themselves, Aung San Suu Kyi's party and the Karen guerrillas then symbolically proclaimed a coalition government in opposition to the army–dominated one.

In spite of the brutal repression by the military, unrest continued to grow, both in the cities and in the rural areas. The government responded by closing the universities in December 1991. The army,

Burma

strengthened by purchases of more than $1 billion in arms from China, launched a series of offensives in ethnic minority areas. One result was a stream of refugees out of the country, including Muslims fleeing to Bangladesh.

In 1994 and early 1995, the State Law and Order Restoration Council (SLORC) neutralized much of the opposition by signing individual ceasefire agreements with rebel groups. Their support was thus denied to anti–government democratic forces in urban areas. Supporters of democracy had to go underground. Over the years, the government has been more and more effective in militarily dealing with the ethnically based rebellions thus creating a steady stream of refugees out of the country.

Government and Politics

After independence from the British at the end of 1947, the Burmese political system which emerged was nominally a parliamentary democracy under the leadership of Prime Minister U Nu. However, the multiethnic nature of the state, the lack of experience with the Western-style government and the inability to confront important political, social and economic problems, led to the entry of the military into government in both 1958 and again in 1962. The early assassination of the country's popular independence leader also complicated the situation. The independence struggle had been led by Aung San, the man often spoken of as the father of modern Burma. Aung San had been an effective leader of the nationalist movement and was expected to lead the first post-colonial government but his death ended that possibility. Later, of course, his memory would help galvanize Burmese behind the pro-democracy movement of his daughter Aung San Suu Kyi, the 1991 winner of the Nobel Peace Prize. Today the country is best characterized as a military dictatorship. The dominant political figure has been General Ne Win, who still commands great loyalty though apparently no longer holds any direct power. He ruled from 1962 through 1987 through the country's only political party, the *Burmese Socialist Program Party (BSPP)*. This was, however, only a front for military rule. The period from 1988 to the present, as described in the previous section, was one of crisis, in which the military sought a way to maintain control and regain legitimacy even going as far as ignoring the results of the 1990 election which had been overwhelmingly won by the country's democratic party, the *National League for Democracy*.

The political culture of the country is both hierarchical and paternalistic. There is almost no real experience with democratic institutions despite the strong public support for Aung San Suu Kyi's efforts to create a democratic Burma. Effective control of the government rests with the military junta which was officially known as the *State Law and Order Restoration Council (SLORC)*, until it renamed itself the more benign sounding "*State Peace and Development Council*" in late 1997. But a military junta by any other name is still a military junta and no real political openings have followed the change of names. In fact, the transformation appears to have indicated more of a generational change among the country's military leaders than any movement toward a greater political opening.

Power within *SPDC* officially rests with its chairman, General Than Shwe, who also serves as Prime Minister. However, Intelligence Chief Lt.-General Khin Nyunt is thought to be the most powerful person in the government.

The People's Assembly (*Pyitha Hluttaw*) was never convened after the May 27, 1990 elections because of the victory of the democratic forces. The judicial branch is subject to the power of the government.

The major political event of recent years was the 1995 release of Aung San Suu Kyi, the most famous opposition figure in the country. She had been under house arrest since 1989. But despite Aung San Suu Kyi's release from formal house arrest it has been clear that the government has no interest in allowing her to carry out her political activities. Throughout the late 1990s her efforts to address her supporters were constantly interfered with and confrontations between students, monks and the government forces were a constant feature of life in the capital. During the fall of 1996 the *NLD* even attempted to hold an official meeting within Burma which not surprisingly resulted in hundreds of arrests. Attempts in 1997 and 1998

The pavilion of the Shwe Dagon pagoda, Rangoon

Burma

Worshippers inside the Shwe Dagon pagoda

Photo by Jon Markham Morrow

for the surrender, Khun Sa was apparently assured that he would not be extradited to the United States. Amnesty from Rangoon and the right to maintain control over part of the Shan state with a downsized army may have also been part of the deal. The Burmese government has also signed agreements with the *New Mon State Party (NMSP)*. The military agreement gave Mon rebels control over 20 designated areas in their home state in return for a cease-fire. Rangoon has also been militarily successful against the *Karen National Union*. Overall these agreements are a clear indication of Rangoon's determination to put an end to rebel activities in the country. Happily, from the perspective of the ruling junta, considerable progress has been made and only remnants of the once strong ethnic armies still resist Rangoon.

The military situation along the Thai-Burmese border remains tense. Rangoon has at times accused Thailand of providing sanctuary and help to the Karen rebels. Burmese military forces have also conducted raids against refugee camps across the Thai border. Most recently, Thailand's forced return of thousands of illegal workers to Burma as well as incidents associated with anti-Burmese junta activists in Thailand have strained relations between Rangoon and Bangkok.

In contrast, relations with the People's Republic of China are quite positive. Since the early 1990s Burma has reportedly received huge amounts of military equipment from China and trade between the two countries has become a very important factor in Burma's economy.

Not surprisingly the growing ties between Burma and China have aroused concern among regional neighbors. Both India and Indonesia as well as the other ASEAN states appear concerned about Chinese access to three strategic islands (Ramree, Coco, and St. Matthew's), off the Burmese coast.

fared no better and the *NLD* supporters found themselves under major pressure from the government which jailed many. *SLORC* even refused to allow the former president of the Philippines, Corazon Aquino, to visit her!

The junta also created the *Union Solidarity Development Association (USDA)* as a front organization. The *USDA* has set up branches throughout the country in an effort to channel support to the government. *USDA* appears to be modeled after Indonesia's *GOLKAR*, which until recently dominated Indonesian politics. And those efforts have proven successful. As Burma entered the new century its military government was stronger than ever and the National League for Democracy led by

Aung San Suu Kyi was barely surviving as an organization.

Defense

Until recently much of Burma's defense policy was internally directed against the various ethnic groups which sought either total independence or some degree of autonomy. Progress though has been made in recent years. On January 14, 1996, *SLORC* improved its hold on the country when Khun Sa, the number one opium and heroin producer in the Golden Triangle, surrendered his 10,000 man Mong Tai army to Burmese officials. The "triangle" refers to the area where the borders of Burma, Thailand and Laos meet. In return

Foreign Policy

As Burma emerges from its self-imposed isolation, it faces a complicated international environment. Moreover, that effort is especially complicated by a split between many Western states and Burma's more immediate southeast Asian nations on the question of relations with Burma and its controversial military government.

External to the region, her international support has practically vanished. The fame of Aung San Suu Kyi is spreading throughout the Western world, no doubt helped by the success of the film "Beyond Rangoon." In early 1997 she even made it on the cover of the influential *Parade Magazine*, a newspaper magazine that reaches millions of Americans every Sunday. In the eyes of many Westerners, Burma may be emerging as the 'South Africa' of contemporary human rights concerns. Within the United States, individual states like Massachusetts have moved to bar their governments from working with any corporation active in Burma and efforts to boycott the developing tourist trade have begun as well. Furthermore, the United States government in April of 1997 officially banned all new American investment in the country.

The United States, along with other Western nations has become even more critical of Burma's military government. Madeleine Albright, when she was still United States Ambassador to the United Nations, visited Rangoon and delivered the message that there would be no significant change in U.S. policy toward Burma until the government changed the way it treats the Burmese people. Since she has become the first American woman to serve as the Secretary of State, Dr. Albright has not indicated any change in this position and the regime is clearly concerned about this weakening of its international position. In fact, it has even hired Western public relations firms to try to improve its image.

Not surprisingly, Burma's relations with its neighbors are even more complicated. Overall the closer nations, especially those in ASEAN, are interested in a policy of "constructive engagement" which finally allowed Burma to enter ASEAN as a full member during 1997.

The decision to allow Burma to enter ASEAN not unexpectedly aroused considerable concern in the Western world and created tension between the European Economic Community and ASEAN. ASEAN itself is keen on bringing Burma into the organization as a means of providing Rangoon with other alternatives to China which has established strong ties within the country. And while Burma's rulers wanted to enter ASEAN they have probably not appreciated the widespread criticism they have received from many regional colleagues who have often been quite outspoken in their negative comments about Burma's human rights practices.

Chinese influence in Burma is already significant through the military assistance described above and because of significant immigration and trade from the provinces north of Burma which created other complications. India for example is concerned about the Chinese presence in Burma and especially on Burmese offshore territories. Recently, India even attempted to warm relations with the junta perhaps to balance Chinese influence. Interestingly, Pakistan, India's arch rival has explored the possibility of building an air base in Burma—a development which is only likely to complicate even further foreign relations in the area.

Society and Culture

While Burmans constitute the largest ethnic group in the country, other groups such as the Karens, Shans, and Kachins are important. Much of modern Burmese history has been dominated by the efforts of these groups to gain greater autonomy from the Burmese Government.

Hinayana Buddhism pervades almost every aspect of Burmese culture. In fact, the military junta in recent years has made efforts to link itself to Buddhism as a way to reinforce its legitimacy. Monks are numerous and influential; most Burmese males spend at least part of their lives in monasteries. The countless temples and shrines have been constructed with great care and with precious materials which combine to create structures of exquisite beauty; the best known of these is the huge and ornate Shwe Dagon in Rangoon. Although the Buddhists teach the usual traditions of Buddhism, there is also among the people a widespread belief in animism, especially with respect to the existence and activities of "nats" which are spirits within objects. But Buddhism is not the only tradition found in Burma. Christian and Muslim groups both exist though they operate under heavy controls imposed by the government.

But while these religious traditions reinforce Burma's ties to its cultural tradition, today's political policies carried out by the current government are hurting the country's ties to the future. The regime is so concerned about the thousands of students who have so often protested against its rule that most of the nation's colleges have been closed to keep the opposition under control. The result of course has been a generation of Burmese who have either failed to gain the higher education they and their country need to move into the 21th century or the departure of the very people Burma needs for the challenges of the new century. The regime thus has literally been sacrificing the nation's entire future, for that future will require trained Burmese professionals, to ensure its own survival.

Women

In clear contrast to the customs of both traditional India and China, Burmese women have enjoyed a high degree of freedom and social equality; they can inherit property, keep their native names after marriage and have equal rights in

Young monks contemplate lottery tickets, Rangoon. Photo by Jon Markham Morrow

Burma

contracting marriage and suing for divorce. Reports of spousal abuse are infrequent. Nevertheless, for many young Burmese women, especially among minorities that live near the borders, life can bring great trials. There are frequent reports of young women lured across the border to Thailand for jobs, which in contrast to the original claims see these young women forced to work as prostitutes in Bangkok's brothels. Moreover, the government's policy of demanding forced labor from its citizens often leads to abuses. Politically, there are no independent women's rights organizations nor government ministries responsible for women's issues. With the exception of Aung San Suu Kyi, women play almost no role in the political life of the nation.

Economy

The government's initial success in trying to transform the economy from its earlier centrally planned socialist style economy into a market orientated one has lost enormous momentum. By 1997 the economy, having done somewhat better during the early 1990s, was again a disaster. Currently the more open economic policies of the early 1990s seem to have lessened and a new tone of corruption and patronage reestablished. All this was made worse by shortsighted government manipulation of the currency which only served to collapse further public faith in their country's money system. Inflation has become rampant with figures for 1998 at 45%! Most significantly, the World Bank has ended its relationship with the regime and thus sent a clear message that investment there should be considered especially risky.

Tourism, often an important industry for the region, has not played its usual role either. The government had dubbed 1996 as "visit Myanmar year." Unfortunately for the junta, their marketing campaign was weakened by the efforts of Aung San Suu Kyi and her supporters around the world to discourage tourism so as to avoid inadvertently helping the junta in its domination of the country.

The bottom line is that Burma remains a very poor country with an economy that seems to be getting worse by the day. These problems include a significant foreign debt, a continuing trade deficit, high inflation, an unrealistic exchange rate, a very poor infrastructure, a failed educational system, and the prospect of no immediate assistance from the international community as a result of the junta's anti-democratic behavior. And many Western companies, including Eddie Bauer, Pepsi, Carlsberg, Heineken Beer, Liz Claiborne, Apple Computer and Levi Strauss have discontinued or lessened their operations because of the country's international reputation. Investment from the ASEAN states, which was growing for a time, has also lessened.

A new Burmese middle class may be emerging but the average cash income is between two and three hundred dollars a year and few get any advanced education. Forty percent of its children never attend school and 3/4 never get past the fifth year of schooling. As mentioned above, especially significant is the country's failure to produce enough college educated professionals to meet the new economic challenges of the globalized world economy.

Really significant economic gains though have been made in the illegal but lucrative narcotics trade. Since *SLORC* came to power, Burma has become the world's main producer of opium and heroin and more recently has added the production of methamphetamine to its infamous production schedules. The government itself though claims it has been actively working to reduce the production of opium and even forcibly relocating peasants to areas where they can cultivate crops other than opium.

Actual growth figures remain difficult to gauge. The figures issued by the Burmese government differ dramatically from those offered by the Asian Development Bank by almost two to one. The former, for example claims that Burma grew by close to 6%

Rangoon: Procession in front of the Shwe Dagon pagoda

Photo by Jon Markham Morrow

108

in recent years while the Asian Development Bank sites numbers around 3–4%.

The Future

Burma's integration into ASEAN may help the regime emerge out of its isolation but nothing is certain. Certainly, Southeast Asia does need an independent and economically stable Burma; however, it is as an even more repressive and economically weak nation that Burma enters the larger international community. For the moment the government has strengthened itself through its ties to the People's Republic. Democracy is more distant than at any point in the recent past.

What is possible though is that Burma, which has for so long remained on the "back burner" of Western human rights campaigns, is likely to become a more pressing issue in the future than it has been in the past. But even that role is less certain as Western human rights activities have tended to turn their attention more toward Tibet than Burma. For the immediate future Burma can be considered the most controlled society in Southeast Asia, a regime in many ways not that different from that found in North Korea.

Two young boys in Buddhist ceremonial attire

Photo by Jon Markham Morrow

The Kingdom of Cambodia

The temple of Angkor Wat built by Khmer warrior kings a thousand years ago

AP/World Wide Photos

Area: 68,898 sq. mi. (181,300 sq. km.; slightly larger than Missouri).

Population: 11,360,000 (1999 estimate)

Capital City: Phnom Penh (Pop. 450,000, estimated).

Climate: Tropically hot with a rainy monsoon season during the summer from May to October.

Neighboring Countries: Thailand (North and West); Laos (Northeast); Vietnam (East).

Official Language: Khmer (Cambodian).

Other Principal Tongues: French, Chinese, Vietnamese.

Ethnic Background: Cambodian (Khmer, about 80%) Vietnamese (semi–permanent or permanent, about 12%), Chinese (5%), other, including primitives, (about 2%).

Principal Religion: Buddhism (Hinayana sect, but religious observances have not until recently been permitted.)

Main Exports (to China): Natural rubber, rice, pepper, wood; export trade is almost nonexistent.

Main Imports (from China, North Korea, Vietnam and Russia): International food aid and some economic development.

Currency: Riel.

Former Colonial Status: French protectorate (1863–1949); Associated State within the French Union (1949–1955).

Independence Date: November 9, 1953.

Head of State: Norodom Sihanouk, King (Sept. 24, 1993).

Head of Government: Hun Sen, Premier (since 1985).

National Flag: A plain red field upon which is centered in gold the ancient temple Angkor Wat.

Per Capita Income: GNP per Capita $270 (1995 estimate)

Cambodia has a rather short coastline which runs about 150 miles along the warm waters of the Gulf of Thailand. The land stretches from this coast in a wide plain, which is traversed in the eastern part by the broad waters of the lower Mekong River. The western part of the plain is dominated by a large lake known as Tonle Sap, twenty miles wide and one hundred miles long—a body of fresh water that produces a heavy annual harvest of fish needed by the Cambodians, who do not eat meat because of Buddhist beliefs.

The borders with Laos and southern Vietnam run through thickly forested foothills that rise to highlands at the demarcation lines. The greater part of the northern border with Thailand consists of a steep series of cliffs; the part of Thailand closest to Cambodia is a plateau which is situated about 1,500 feet above the plain. The western border with Thailand and most of Cambodia's coastline is occupied by the Cardamom, Kirimom and Elephant

110

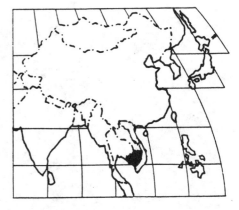

Mountains, which rise to heights of 5,500 feet.

Much of the central plain, which is the largest by far and is economically the area of prime importance in Cambodia, is regularly flooded by the mighty Mekong River in an uncontrolled fashion—there are no elaborate dikes to contain the waters such are found along the Red River in northern Vietnam. The rains which begin in May are the first cause of flooding; melting snows in Tibet and China in July add to the volume of water, which is also joined by monsoon waters from Thailand and Laos. By mid–September the flood water may cover as much as 8,000 square miles of land. These are not violent waters—they deposit a fine silt which enriches the land and they also bring huge quantities of fish to the Tonle Sap lake, permitting annual harvests of up to 15 tons per square mile of water surface.

The waters recede in October and the winter season begins in November, bringing slightly cooler and much drier weather except in the western and southern mountains, where there is sporadic rainfall.

History

The civilization of Cambodia first emerged as a product of indigenous communities of peoples and their interaction with peoples from South Asia. The Khmer people, from whom the modern Cambodians (Kampucheans) are descended, first organized themselves under a state usually known by its Chinese name of Funan, which emerged about 500 A.D. in southern Cambodia. This was apparently a result of trade with, and immigration from, India to Cambodia via the Kra Isthmus, which is now the southern part of Thailand. These early contacts were brought about by Southeast Asia's geographic location on the trade routes between South Asia and China. More significant for the development of society in Southeast Asia was that the region's powerful monsoon rain storms often forced the ships to spend long periods on the peninsula itself waiting for weather conditions to change. It was under these circumstances that the spread of Indian culture, including traditions like Hinduism and Buddhism, could spread widely.

Although Funan was not a centralized state as would later develop, it did have tributary relations with the Chinese to its north. But it would be Indian, not Chinese, society that would have the most profound influence on the region during these years. Just as Koreans would in these years model themselves after Chinese society, the Cambodian elites in these first centuries of the modern era strove to become more like their Western neighbors. They took Indian names and developed literary works in Indian languages. Hindu Gods, from Shiva to Vishnu, were worshiped, and local leaders strove to associate themselves with these powerful Indian images.

The Khmer Civilization of Angkor Wat

From the era around the early 9th century through much of the fifteenth century, Cambodia was home to one of the world's most impressive civilizations. Located in Cambodia and parts of today's Thailand, this civilization, associated most with the extraordinary building structure at Angkor, has left us an enormous amount of information to try to understand it. Early leaders of this civilization were strongly influenced by Hinduism and associated themselves with the Hindu god Shiva. Because the temples were made of stone, many of which can be studied today, we tend to know more about elite religious society and less about the average "Cambodians" of the era. What we do know is that they were used by the monarchy to supply labor to the building projects of the empire. And their labor was impressive indeed! Angkor Wat, built in the 12th century, remains the largest religious building in the world today.

The people were converted after 1000 A.D. to the older school of Buddhism referred to as *Theravada* Buddhism. Mahayana, or Greater Vehicle Buddhism, was also influential but less so as the more austere *Theravada* (the way of the elders) Buddhism which prevailed over time. At its height in about 1200, the Khmer Empire controlled much of what is now Vietnam, Thailand, Laos and Burma. One of the main features of Angkor Civilization as we now understand it was a very attractive commitment to religious toleration.

Externally, in the later years of Angkor Civilization, the Cambodians were much influenced by the arrival of Muslim traders from India who not only converted many southeast Asians to Islam, but played a significant role in reorienting the inward-looking rice based economy of Angkor to one that was also interested in international trade.

In foreign affairs, the Angkor Civilization found itself by the twelve hundreds under pressure from the Thai forces as

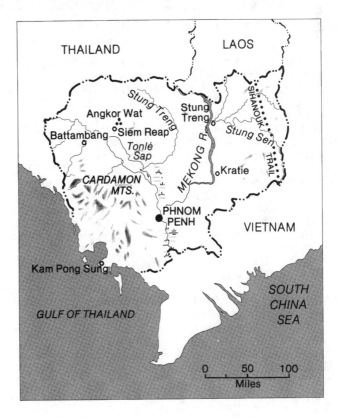

Cambodia

Days of the monarchy: young King Norodom Sihanouk, 1946

well as the Vietnamese, a community whose tensions with Cambodia lasted well into the modern era. Sadly, having flourished so dramatically in early centuries, the Khmer Civilization of Angkor had collapsed by the 15th century and its people dispersed. The city itself lay forgotten until the 19th century when it was rediscovered.

For the next three and one-half centuries, Cambodia was sandwiched between the Annamese of Central Vietnam and the Thai to the north and west, and was almost continuously dominated by one or the other, or both.

The Arrival of the West

By the 1500's the Western missionaries had begun to arrive in Cambodia seeking converts to Christianity and influence for the Spanish Empire. They were not terribly successful and unlike their brethren in the more southerly Philippine Islands, had little success in attracting converts. But while Western missionaries from the Iberian peninsula were the first to show themselves in Cambodia, the Indochinese peninsula's more fundamental encounter with colonialism would come from the forces of imperial France.

The beginning of formal French influence in Indochina was initially an offshoot of their activities in China during the Second Opium War. Once the Anglo-French forces had captured the city of Canton in southern China, French officials made the decision in 1859 to send a fleet to Vietnam to establish a presence there. From the French perspective, it was a way to successfully compete with their arch rivals, the English, in the rush to establish themselves in East and Southeast Asia. French-specific interest in Cambodia was stimulated in the late 1850's by British advances in Burma. Both powers thought of Southeast Asia principally as a stepping stone to the supposedly vast treasures and markets of southwest China.

Although it established a protectorate over Cambodia in 1863, France did not dethrone the reigning family; the area was

increasingly drawn into the Indochinese colony created at the end of the century in an attempt to rival the much larger British Indian Empire. The French prevented the Thais from moving against Cambodia and protected it also from its other traditional overlord, the Vietnamese, who had also become part of the French Indochinese empire. This protection was welcomed by the Cambodians, and as a result, there was not the violently anti-French attitude that existed in neighboring Vietnam during the same era. Nevertheless, when the French in the early 1880s attempted to modify tax rates and introduce other administrative changes they provoked a revolt in 1885 which lasted for more than two years and required large numbers of French troops to suppress it.

During those early years of the French presence they ran Cambodia as a trusteeship and allowed the indigenous monarchy and its officials to largely administer the countries. Nevertheless, the French held the ultimate strings of power and were usually instrumental in choosing who actually held the Cambodian throne during their years of colonial control. The hands-off policy was abandoned by the late nineteenth century as French officials began to more directly interest themselves in internal developments and to more directly control it as a colony.

As in other parts of Southeast Asia, the existence of a stable colonial administration attracted a sizable number of Chinese immigrants, who quickly emerged in a virtually dominant position in profitable ventures as commercial middlemen. Many Vietnamese also immigrated to Cambodia during these years, and because they were more likely to speak French they were more able than the native Cambodians to advance themselves through links with the French.

Initial French enthusiasm for Cambodia lessened after it became clear that the colony itself lacked the rich mineral resources many had hoped for nor provided a convenient "back door" to the southern provinces of China. Nevertheless, by the interwar period, the Cambodian economy, like many of its neighbors in southeast Asia, was increasingly integrated into the world economy. For Cambodia this meant producing rice for the world markets and becoming, under the control of French companies, a major exporter of rubber.

The Second World War

Japan quickly overran Cambodia in 1941, and as a token of appreciation, two of the Cambodian border provinces were awarded to Thailand, by then an official ally of the Japanese. Although they were returned after World War II, the Cambodians have a lingering suspicion that the Thai still covet them.

Politics in Cambodia were dominated after the return of the French in 1946 by a popular and unpredictable man who ruled until 1970: Prince Norodom Sihanouk. He had been made king by the French in 1941, but became impatient with the conservative traditions of the monarchy and increasingly interested in the liberal political movements within the country. During the early 1950s he successfully convinced the French to grant full independence for Cambodia, an effort that gained him even more public appreciation. He abdicated the throne in 1955 in favor of his father so that he could organize his own political movement, the *People's Socialist Community* which he expected to have replace the existing political parties. Building on his widespread support among the population, Sihanouk dominated Cambodian political life for the next generation.

He skillfully used this popularity to cope with what he regarded as major domestic problems—the traditional aristocracy, the partly westernized intellectuals, the businessmen, the small communist movement and a segment of right-wing opponents whom he believed were supported by Thailand. Initially, his efforts were almost uniformly successful. He continued to lead the *Sangkum*, or the *People's Socialist Community* which was the only significant political party. Sihanouk's sense of his own talents are difficult to exaggerate. During the same years he wrote, and produced a number of feature films which featured himself as the leading man.

But for the popularity of Sihanouk at home, Cambodia would never have been able to deal with the external pressures with which it was faced. In order to keep open the largest number of possible alternatives, Sihanouk remained "neutral" in the international "Cold War" and aloof in the hot war in Asia. He engaged in active and skillful diplomacy which often puzzled the most astute foreign ministries. His view after independence was that Cambodia was largely surrounded by potentially hostile forces and neighbors.

To counter-balance the threat of North Vietnam, he established close relations with the People's Republic of China which was itself not anxious to see Ho Chi Minh's Vietnam dominate Cambodia.

Clearly Sihanouk hoped he could play off the powerful forces around his country to keep Cambodia safe and independent. But given the tensions of the Cold War era, Sihanouk's efforts to find a middle ground between the contending forces was complicated indeed and aroused the suspicions of the United States which saw him as an impediment to their own plans for the peninsula.

He was, for example, supplying goods to both sides in the Vietnamese struggle during the early 1960s while allowing the North Vietnamese to use Cambodian territory in their efforts to supply their troops in South Vietnam.

For this reason, relations between Sihanouk and the U.S. were strained after the early 1960's. Complaints by the U.S. increased sharply in late 1967 as the fighting in South Vietnam became more intense. Clearly the United States wanted to pursue the communist Viet Cong into the eastern provinces of Cambodia. At one point Prince Sihanouk announced he was willing to discuss the possibility of the Americans pursuing the Viet Cong with a U.S. emissary, but when the diplomat later arrived back in the U.S., he was denounced by the Prince, who proclaimed that the only item on the agenda was the "territorial integrity of Cambodia." The whole situation was made even more complicated by Cambodia's claims to areas in South Vietnam, claims he put forth at the bargaining table repeatedly when dealing with the U.S. Eventually Sihanouk did secretly agreed to allow the Americans to bomb North Vietnamese supply lines in Cambodia.

The ever-changing diplomacy of Sihanouk worked to the extent that its Asian neighbors did not constitute a direct threat to the survival of Cambodia. Nevertheless, the unity of Cambodia and Sihanouk's direct control were weakening. There was a significant increase in communist-led revolts in the provinces bordering Thailand and Laos in the latter part of 1968, as well as the number of Viet Cong illegally present within Cambodia.

The displeasure of anti-communist Cambodians grew so great that in 1970, while Sihanouk was out of the country, major anti-Hanoi demonstrations broke out in Phnom Penh. General Lon Nol and Prince Sirik Matak, an older cousin of Sihanouk, proclaimed the ouster of Sihanouk and a new government under their leadership. The communist problem, however, was not the only issue—there had been disputes over Sihanouk's socialist economic policies which were thought to be hurting the economy as well.

Recognizing the more pro-American tone of the new Cambodian administration, the North Vietnamese and Cambodian communist forces, now supported by the ousted Sihanouk, promptly began to expand their military activities in various parts of the country. That same year, in April of 1970, twenty thousand American and South Vietnamese soldiers entered Cambodia to attack the communist bases along the border from which the communists had been conducting raids into South Vietnam. To their disappointment

they found the bases had been abandoned weeks before. The Americans soon pulled out but their bombers would return in coming years to carry out a massive bombing campaign against leftist forces within Cambodia.

The country suffered severely as a result of this military campaign. Although in poor health and under heavy military pressure from communist forces, Lon Nol remained in power until 1975. Long before that Lon Nol dissolved the National Assembly and began to rule by decree. He then proclaimed himself President, reshuffling his cabinet drastically and excluding Sirik Matak from it. But little helped. Public confidence in the government eroded badly. Meanwhile the expansion of the Vietnam War into Cambodia had further outraged many Americans and by mid 1973 the bombing partly undertaken to support Lon Nol's pro-Western government was halted.

The Coming of the Khmer Rouge

Meanwhile the communist forces of Cambodia, dubbed the *Khmer Rouge* by Prince Sihanouk, who was himself quite publicly working with them, were growing stronger. Although fiercely nationalistic they initially also had the support of the North Vietnamese. The Khmer Rouge's most influential leader was Solath Sar, better known as Pol Pot, a Western educated Cambodian whose family had earlier had significant ties to the Cambodian court.

The Cambodian Genocide

Communist *Khmer Rouge* military efforts came close to isolating Phnom Penh by early 1975. Undermined by his own shortcomings, political bickering, and uncertainty about American support, Lon Nol's government evaporated. The rebels refused to negotiate with it, leaving it no alternative but to surrender amid ominous proclamations of a collection of "blood debts" from the leadership. The final collapse came in mid-April 1975, when Phnom Penh fell to the *Khmer Rouge*. It was to be the first step in the darkest chapter of Cambodian modern history.

The policies of the new *Khmer Rouge* regime, which was pro-Chinese and soon became anti-Vietnamese, reflected the ideological mentality of its leaders and personnel. Once in power the *Khmer Rouge* set out to brutally transform Cambodia, which they now renamed Kampuchea, into a classless agrarian society. It was to be an experiment in social engineering more radical than ever tried in modern human history. Going beyond the social reorganizations of Asian groups like the

Cambodia

Jakarta, Indonesia, July 1988: Another fruitless meeting with (l. to r.) *Khmer Peoples National Liberation Front* leader Son Sann, Cambodian Prime Minister Hun Sen, and Prince Norodom Sihanouk

AP/Wide World Photo

famous Chinese Taipings or what had gone on elsewhere in the communist world, the *Khmer Rouge* was determined to remold all Cambodians to fit their "idealistic" images. Those who were not perceived as "appropriate" for the new order were simply murdered. Over the next several years civil society as Cambodia had known it simply disappeared. Money and wages were abolished, the cities largely emptied and all forms of religious life, freedom of the press and much of the middle class were simply eliminated from the life of the nation.

To build their new classless agrarian society the *Khmer Rouge* closed down institutions from hospitals to educational facilities and even monasteries. Private property, down to the most personal hygiene supplies, were communalized and a bloody and systematic series of factories of death were created to force compliance. It was to be a genocide that rivaled the horrors of the Armenians and Jews earlier in the century or that experienced by others in Central Africa later on. As one writer has put it, Democratic Kampuchea was less a nation than a state prison camp!

The major cities, including Phnom Penh, were forcibly evacuated, allegedly on account of food shortages. There were executions of supporters of the former regime and widespread atrocities, mainly against persons of middle class background. Anything, even the wearing of eye glasses, could mark someone as too bourgeois and thus bring on a death sentence! Cambodians found themselves brutalized by one of the harshest governments of the 20th century. A veil of secrecy shrouded the once

great nation. The formerly beautiful capital of Phnom Penh with 1.3 million was left with 90,000. Boarded-over store fronts and virtually deserted streets told the story. The new regime wanted to stifle religion, wipe out any education system conflicting with the hopes of the "new order," and stamp out family ties.

Families were driven from the cities to labor from dawn to dusk in the fields. First priority was the destruction of the intelligentsia and middle class. Although estimates regarding the number of dead vary widely, the best scholarly estimates now put the number of victims at between 1.5 and 1.7 million people dead from execution, starvation and overwork. Of the seven to eight million Cambodians before the genocide began, some have estimated the death toll to have ranged from 15 to 40% of the entire population!

The regime's atheistic and racist mentality was particularly devastating for the nation's Buddhist community whose monks and properties were regularly singled out for destruction. Although much of the killings were of Cambodians by Cambodians, the nation's ethnic minorities were not spared; hardly surprising given the vehement racist/nationalist mentality the *Khmer Rouge* usually displayed. Previous to the *Khmer Rouge's* arrival to power the largest ethnic communities in Cambodia were the Muslim Chams, the Chinese and the Vietnamese. Together these minorities had traditionally made up about 15% of the nation's population but once in Cambodia the new leadership was determined to change the situation. The Vietnamese, who were particularly hated, were com-

pletely eliminated with many dead and others fleeing to Vietnam. Recent researchers have failed to find a single Vietnamese who survived the assault on their community in Cambodia. The Chinese, whose traditions as city dwellers made them particularly unpopular with the new rulers, saw more than half, about 200,000, of their numbers die during these years. The Muslim Chams faired no better. After first experiencing the *Khmer Rouge's* efforts to destroy their Islamic traditions, their people were systematically massacred after they attempted to resist.

The new leader's preferred method of execution even saved the cost of a bullet: a skull-penetrating blow to the rear of the head by a pick axe used on a kneeling person. Silent, massive piles of bones throughout the country attest to this grisly activity. Others simply starved to death.

Once Lon Nol's government was overthrown, the still popular Prince Sihanouk returned home. *Khmer Rouge* run Cambodia was not though run by Sihanouk, but by a shadowy leadership of the *Cambodian Communist Party* known as the *Angka* ("organization"), of which Pol Pot was Secretary General. An election held in 1976 filled 250 seats in the People's Representative Assembly. All 515 candidates were picked by the *Angka*. Sihanouk then resigned, together with the rest of the government. The former king was placed under house arrest. An entire communist government was announced, with Pol Pot in actual control.

Given the vehement nationalism of the new regime it is not surprising that it almost immediately provoked friction with its neighbors. The most serious case was with Vietnam. A continuing border warfare erupted between the two nations until late 1978 when a massive assault was launched on Cambodia by the Vietnamese.

Cambodia's Vietnamese Interlude

The new Cambodian regime had immediate friction with all of its neighbors, the most serious with Vietnam, which erupted into continuing border warfare from early on until late 1978 when Vietnam invaded. By early January 1979, Pol Pot had fled to western Cambodia, and a new pro-Vietnamese government known as the People's Republic of Kampuchea had been set up in Phnom Penh. Despite their defeat, Pol Pot's forces would then carry on a guerrilla war against the Phnom Penh government until the late 1990s.

Though Hanoi probably viewed its invasion as both a reaction to the *Khmer Rouge's* assaults and as an effort to free the Cambodians from Pol Pot's murderous regime, few in the international community viewed the invasion in that light. In

Cambodia

general the world community viewed the invasion as an unprovoked Vietnamese aggression and responded negatively. Ironically, the world reaction produced some very strange informal alliances as both the United States and the People's Republic of China condemned the invasion and to various degrees were supportive of the defeated Khmer Rouge.

The Chinese, long unhappy with Hanoi's ties to the USSR, staged a brief invasion across the Vietnamese border in early 1979 with the announced purpose of "teaching Vietnam a lesson." Unfortunately for the PRC the only "lesson" learned was their own forces were ill prepared to deal with Hanoi's experienced troops. The attack had no impact on Vietnam's control of Cambodia.

For the next decade regular fighting went on in western Cambodia between Vietnamese troops and Pol Pot's forces. Tension also arose between Vietnam and Thailand over the Cambodian refugees grouped near the border. A coalition under Sihanouk, including what was left of Pol Pot's regime, emerged in opposition to the Vietnamese-dominated government in Phnom Penh. This group retained Cambodia's seat in the UN.

The Phnom Penh government, while hardly the genocidal regime of the *Khmer Rouge* was itself repressive and continued to be dominated by the Vietnamese which scarcely endeared it to the Cambodian population. For a time the government attempted to carry out socialist agricultural policies somewhat similar to those common during Pol Pot's years and within Vietnam itself, but these were eventually phased out. The anti-religious policies of Pol Pot were also ended and once again Buddhist activities were allowed. Monks could once again, despite some restrictions, retake their traditional place in Cambodian life. Though many Cambodians had been very relieved to have the Vietnamese drive out Pol Pot's murderous regime, the new Vietnamese-backed government was hardly popular. Thousands of Cambodians continued to flee the country.

It was during these years that Cambodia's later "strong man" Hun Sen emerged in importance. Originally from a middle class family, Hun Sen had initially been part of the Cambodian Communist resistance to Sihanouk's government. He later joined the *Khmer Rouge* only to break with the regime in 1977. Two years later he returned home as part of the Vietnamese invasion force and rose quickly in power becoming prime minister in 1985.

Eventually, in May 1988, the Vietnamese Government announced that it would soon withdraw its troops from Cambodia. By 1979 Hanoi had done so. The reasons for this major policy shift included the dis-

mal state of the Vietnamese economy, the small chances of attracting aid from abroad while the Cambodian occupation continued, and Soviet pressure, or at least persuasion. It is probably not a coincidence that only the month before Moscow had formally agreed to remove its troops from Afghanistan by February 15, 1989. Hanoi also wanted to improve its relations with the United States, something that its continuing hold over Cambodia made impossible.

The prospect of a Vietnamese withdrawal naturally accelerated the pace of political and diplomatic activity relating to Cambodia, both within and outside the country. Hun Sen's government was faced with the necessity, having lost its more immediate Vietnamese support, of building a strong popular base of its own within Cambodian society. It was thus during this era that he moved to reintroduce private property and expand further the role of Buddhism which had been allowed to revive in the years after Pol Pot's defeat.

The main problem though that the Vietnamese evacuation created was the fear that it might lead to another seizure of power by the blood thirsty *Khmer Rouge*.

The other contenders for power were, of course, Hun Sen's government in Phnom Penh, the Royalists around the former king, Prince Sihanouk, and a non-communist resistance group directed by the former Prime Minister Son Sann. The latter two in fact had received international recognition as a Cambodian government in exile but represented little of practical importance within the country.

The U.N. Sponsored Elections

As the 1990s unfolded a complicated series of international negotiations took place with the goal of establishing Cambodia on a more healthy and stable road to recovery. On October 23, 1991, the Paris International Conference on Cambodia adopted an agreement on a Comprehensive Political Settlement of the Cambodia Conflict, which created the United Nations Transitional Authority in Cambodia (UNTAC) with a force of 16,000 military and 6,000 civilians which began arriving in Cambodia in early 1992. UNTAC's function was to disarm the Cambodian warring factions and create a political climate where free elections could take place.

H.R.H. Samdech Krom Preah Norodom Ranariddh

Cambodia

Their Majesties the King and Queen of Cambodia

The long awaited free elections took place in 1993 but unfortunately the victory of the royalist forces under Prince Ranariddh, the son of King Sihanouk, was overturned by Hun Sen, whose military forces remained the stronger. Refusing to accept his party's political defeat at the polls, Hun Sen forced the creation of a very convoluted political system with two prime ministers.

Thus from 1993 through 1997 Cambodia operated under the coalition government formed in the aftermath of the 1993 United Nations sponsored election. After more than a generation of civil war and totalitarian governments this was a remarkable improvement. Officially its government was a constitutional monarchy headed by the long time Prince Norodom Sihanouk who was once again officially sworn in as monarch in September of 1993.

Sihanouk's sons directed FUNCINPEC, the "royalist" party and Prince Norodom Ranariddh held the position of 1st Prime Minister. Hun Sen, the long time leader of Cambodia held the title of 2nd Prime Minister though he actually held more power than his rival. The cabinet also featured dual ministers representing both parties.

The country operated as a parliamentary system though the judiciary was not as independent of the government as the constitution required. The unusual system of two prime ministers certainly helped get the government operating though the more common pattern of having rotating prime ministers as has occurred in Israel and Turkey might have worked more efficiently.

From the start the two prime ministers were frequently estranged and actual fighting often broke out between their supporters. Only the most optimistic believed the unstable coalition could survive. Norodom Sirivudh, half brother to King Norodom Sihanouk, was "encouraged" to go into exile for allegedly planning to kill co-prime minister Hun Sen. Many believed the Prince was framed in an attempt to silence his criticism of the government. The murder in 1996 of Hun Sen's brother-in-law was another example of the level of tension. Nevertheless, the coalition might have survived if the third factor in Cambodian politics, the blood thirsty *Khmer Rouge*, had not complicated the situation enormously.

The *Khmer Rouge* and what to do about it had, of course, long been the major issue which faced the government. Attempts to end the fighting took different forms over the years. The approach ranged from fighting to occasional efforts to reconcile with the *Khmer Rouge*, despite its bloody record of mass murder. Of those contending for power it was the royalists who were most willing to associate themselves with the *Khmer Rouge*. For example, in May 1994, the King called for peace talks with the *Khmer Rouge* which had refused to go along with the

United Nations' election efforts. There was also a move to have Sihanouk form a provisional government of reconciliation which would have included the *Khmer Rouge*. Hun Sen's supporters though opposed the plan and Sihanouk withdrew his offer. Nevertheless, by the late 1990s the dynamics of Cambodian politics started changing dramatically.

The End of the *Khmer Rouge*

1996 saw major progress in the government's efforts to end the long time insurrection of the *Khmer Rouge*. In August, Ieng Sary, a long time senior leader of the *Khmer Rouge*, said to be second only to the infamous Pol Pot, broke ranks and offered to end his role in the insurrection. The offer, while greeted as an important step in the final reconciliation of the country, was complicated by the former *Khmer Rouge* officer's direct role (vehemently denied) in the genocide of the 1970s. After complicated negotiations, he was granted a royal pardon.

That Ieng Sary's defection indicated a weakening *Khmer Rouge* was highlighted by the remaining leadership's allowing of a formal radio talk show discussion on maintaining *Khmer Rouge* solidarity— a remarkable step to take for a party with one of the most totalitarian records of the 20th century. These developments highlighted a blow to the *Khmer Rouge* as profound as their earlier loss of power after the Vietnamese invasion of 1979 and which later events showed they would not recover from. By early 1999 the last of the major *Khmer Rouge* leaders had fallen into the hands of the government though it was unclear how many of the actual killers would ever come to trial before either a Cambodian tribunal or one organized by the international community. Thus far the Cambodian government has resisted calls for international trials by claiming that such trials might destabilize the admittedly new and fragile peace that Cambodia has been enjoying in recent months.

Search for Political Stability

Meanwhile, even as the government operated through an unstable coalition, opponents of the regime often had even greater difficulties. Sam Rainsy, the former head of the Ministry of Finance, has tried to lead the *Khmer Nation Party* (KNP) despite considerable pressure from the government, especially Hun Sen's allies. For example, at one point, after Rainsy's party had successfully worked out an alliance with the Royalists, grenades were thrown into the crowd as Rainsy led a demonstration march. More than a hundred people were killed or wounded.

The unstable coalition government which had operated since the United Nations's sponsored elections collapsed during the summer of 1997. The actual break was caused not by tensions with Sam Rainsy's group but, as so often in the past, over relations with the then weakening *Khmer Rouge*. In early July, Hun Sen's forces carried out a coup against the supporters of his rival Prince Ranariddh. The second prime minister claimed that the Prince had finalized an alliance with elements of the *Khmer Rouge* and was planning to integrate them into his own forces. All this took place in the middle of a "circus" of international media attention as the *Khmer Rouge* itself seemed close to collapse and rumors abounded that the notorious Pol Pot might become available for trial at an international tribunal against genocide. What was actually going on behind the scenes was quite uncertain. What was clear was that after the dust settled Hun Sen's forces had driven the Royalists from the capital and Prince Ranariddh was in exile.

By mid July 1998 most of the major aid donor countries had temporally halted aid to Cambodia in protest against the coup and the country's hopes to join ASEAN were dashed as the leaders of the Association of Southeast Asian Nations decided to postpone the planned admission of Cambodia. Apparently the proposed alliance between the Cambodian Royalists, assuming we accept Hun Sen's claims, caused major political waves within the *Khmer Rouge* as well for by the end of the month the movement's long time leader Pol Pot had fallen from power, denounced by his former followers! Later that summer the world got its first glimpse in a generation of the fallen leader when Pol Pot was given a "show trial" by his former colleagues and sentenced to life imprisonment. Within months word came that the former ruthless dictator had died, *apparently* by his own hand.

In the months after the coup Hun Sen worked to establish his authority throughout the country even while claiming he was ready to allow the continuation of parliamentary elections. He even retained the title of second prime minister while allowing a one time Royalist, Ung Huot, to replace Ranariddh as the first prime minister. As for King Sihanouk, the man who had spent his entire life trying to retain his influence within the Kingdom he had inherited, there was little room for hope and his comments seemed to suggest an exhausted leader who had lost faith in the future.

Given the international community's negative reaction to Hun Sen's actions Cambodia's strong man found himself still required to present to the world a

Cambodia willing to continue the process of democratization. Well aware that the long planned parliamentary elections of mid 1998 would not be accepted as valid unless Prince Ranariddh took part, the world was entertained in the months before the election with a show of the former First Prime Minister and his associates being tried for smuggling weapons and plotting a coup against Hun Sen. After being found guilty, the Prince was then sentenced to thirty-five years in jail and fined millions of dollars. Once that was done, the plan, arranged in advance, was carried out. The Prince's father, King Sihanouk, granted him a full pardon that allowed the ousted first Prime Minister to compete in the elections of July 1998!

Cambodia's election of the summer of 1998 did not though improve conditions much. Once again, the players remained largely the same, the supporters of Hun Sen, the Royalists led by Prince Ranariddh and Sam Rainsy's followers. As expected Hun Sen's' backers dominated the country's media outlets making it hard for the opposition to get their electorial message out to the voters. Discouraging to supporters of the opposition was the decision by both Ranariddh and Rainsy to attack Hun Sen by stirring up anti-Vietnamese sentiment. Certainly, it was a tactic that could be effective against Cambodia's long time leaders who had initially been installed in power by Hanoi. Nevertheless, given Cambodia's recent history of ethnic based genocide, few could find the decision an admirable one and it eventually caused several deaths among the local Vietnamese community.

Once the voting took place a new controversy exploded over the counting of votes which eventually saw both opposition parties refusing to cooperate in the creation of a new government. And their cooperation was needed because Hun Sen's supporters had failed to gain enough seats in the national assembly to form a government on their own.

A young Buddhist monk

Cambodia

A Khmer classical dancer rehearses.

Officially the vote tally had given the government party, the CCP 41.1% of the vote to 31.7% for the Royalists and 14.3% to Sam Rainsy's party. Whether the actual vote counting had been corrupted or not the result was more months of political strife and public demonstrations before it was agreed that a new coalition government would be formed. Not surprisingly the compromise left Hun Sen as the main political leader and prime minister with Prince Ranariddh as the new president of the National Assembly. Sam Rainsy's party, although holding 15 seats in the assembly, was not included in the new coalition.

Foreign Relations

Throughout its history, Cambodia has been in the unfortunate position of being caught between contending forces beyond its borders. In the pre-colonial era both the Thai and Vietnamese empires occupied parts of Cambodia. The country was also caught between the United States and the Vietnamese during the Vietnam War. The North Vietnamese used overland routes through Cambodia to transport war materials to the south to carry out the war against the South Vietnamese and their U.S. allies. The U.S. used the North Vietnamese supply lines through Cambodia for target practice. Prince Sihanouk could neither prevent the North Vietnamese

from using his territory, nor satisfy the United States that his policies were not pro Hanoi. During the Vietnamese occupation which was backed by the Soviet Union, Cambodia was again a pawn between the Vietnamese and their Soviet ally on the one hand, and the Chinese, who backed the *Khmer Rouge* on the other. And even to today relations with Vietnam remain difficult as both nations continue to argue over where the border should be between the two states.

The most important development for Cambodia in recent years has been the slow improvement of its relations with its neighbors throughout Southeast Asia. In 1995, Cambodia secured "observer status" within the Association of Southeast Asian Nations (ASEAN) and was soon expected to become a full fledged member, but the 1997 coup delayed Cambodia's entrance until 1999 when it finally gained full membership.

Hun Sen himself may have felt justified in acting to keep the *Khmer Rouge* from again reasserting its influence in Cambodia, but many in the international community were less than pleased. International supporters from the United States to Japan, condemned the 1997 ouster of Prince Ranariddh, and began partial cutoffs of their aid programs. At the United Nations, Cambodia lost its representation as arguments over who would represent the government broke out. Although Cambodia's

neighbors were apparently more inclined to continue Phnom Penh's official entrance into ASEAN, tensions between Hun Sen and the organization led to the decision to temporally delay their entrance.

As with Burma, Cambodia's isolation from its Southeast Asian neighbors has strengthened its ties with the People's Republic of China, a development ASEAN members are said to be interested in countering by greater integration among the Southeast Asian nations themselves.

Society and Culture

The art and culture of the Khmer Empire, based largely on its Indian, Hindu and Sri Lankan Buddhist origins, were an elaborate and highly developed combination to which distinctly local elements were added during the centuries which have passed. The surviving specimens of the Empire are mainly of stone and bronze which display highly stylistic and ornate techniques. The modern Cambodians are justifiably proud of their historical heritage. The Khmer (Cambodian) language was spoken prior to the arrival of Indian influence and is now written in a script derived from India. Sadly for Cambodia's cultural heritage, an enormous percentage of the country's cultural leaders were killed by the *Khmer Rouge,* a blow few countries could survive.

And more than the nation's cultural heritage will take years to recover from the recent decades of strife. Cambodia today remains a country where the ratio between men and women has been distorted by years of civil war and genocide. There are for example only 93 males for every 100 females in contemporary Cambodia and that is even more pronounced among the older generation where the loss of males to warfare and violence has been even more dramatic.

Women

Women are the majority of the population and the largest percentage of the work force in most sectors, from agriculture to business, industry and service sectors. Because of the years of violence women today head a quarter of the households in Cambodia. They do not, however, hold many significant positions of influence. Men continue to dominate decision making.

The country's new constitution very explicitly contains language offering women equal rights but in practice these are not normally carried out. Cultural traditions which emphasize male authority are still strong. There are, however, many nongovernmental organizations which are quite active and emphasize improving the lives of women. As with other Southeast Asian countries stories of the trafficking in women are very frequently reported. The unfortunate young women and girls far too often end up as part of the region's well known sex trade.

Economy

A major challenge for the new government is to establish a national economy. Two decades of conflict and revolution have destroyed much of the country's infrastructure. The presence of UNTAC, the United Nations force, also caused distortions in the economy. The Asian economic crisis also affected Cambodia though it had, one might say, less far to fall given the long term weakness of the economy compared to its neighbors.

Cambodia also continues to have severe problems with deforestation although raw log exports were supposedly banned in 1992. Still both Thai and Japanese entrepreneurs continued to operate in 1993 and additional contracts were signed in 1995, in spite of the ban. About half of the country's operating budget comes from foreign

aid. And, as might be expected, the military commands about 20% of the entire budget though plans are now being made to scale back the military.

The country has continued to receive substantial amounts of aid and loans from individual donor countries, the International Monetary Fund (IMF), World Bank, and the Asian Development Bank (ADB). One bright spot for the Cambodian economy in recent years was the jump in foreign investment which included several major hotel chains. Unfortunately, the bloody struggle between the two prime ministers during 1997 set back much of this momentum for a time though by the new century Cambodia's tourist industry was again clearly on the mend.

Fortunately for Cambodia's new found stability, the end of the *Khmer Rouge* has allowed for Cambodia to begin to heal economically. Inflation has lessened and economic momentum has once again begun. Some were even anticipating that Cambodia might record a growth of around 4% for 1999. Very good news for a country that has experienced the tribulations Cambodia has in recent years.

But not all growth is positive. The growth of Cambodia's role in the world drug market is discouraging. Cambodia is rapidly earning a reputation as Asia's newest "narco-state." In early 1996, Washington placed Cambodia on its "watch list" of trafficker states.

The Future

The collapse of the coalition government in 1997 was a dramatic setback for those who have hoped for a more democratic Cambodia to emerge. The convoluted political deals that saw Prince Ranariddh both tried and pardoned in order to allow him to run in the elections set for the summer of 1998 suggest some of the damage may have been repaired. More importantly, the collapse of the *Khmer Rouge* over the course of recent years and Pol Pot's own death, does change the political balance in Cambodia in an extraordinary fashion. For the first time in many years it is again possible to feel somewhat optimistic about Cambodia's future.

Boat racing at the Water Festival in Phnom Penh.

Photo: Serge Corrieras

The Republic of Indonesia

Tea pickers have their daily bundles weighed

Area: 741,040 sq. mi. (1,906,240 sq. km., covering an expanse equal to the width of the U.S. coast–to–coast.)

Population: 200 million.

Capital City: Jakarta (Pop. 7.2 million, estimated).

Climate: Tropical, with a monsoon season from November to March.

Neighboring Countries: Malaysia and the Philippine Republic (North); Australia (South); Papua New Guinea (East).

Official Language: Bahasa Indonesia (a formal version of the Malay language).

Other Principal Tongues: Malay, Common Malay (a dialect), and about 250 other Malayo–Polynesian languages and dialects, such as Sundanese and Madurese, Japanese, Dutch, Chinese.

Ethnic Background: Malayo–Polynesian (a mixture of Polynesian, Mongolian, Indian and Caucasian many centuries old, about 95%); Chinese (about 3%); other (including European, about 2%).

Principal Religion: Overwhelmingly Muslim, with small groups of Christians, Hindus and Buddhists.

Main Exports (to Japan, Federal Republic of Germany and other European nations): Petroleum, liquefied natural gas, carpets, fruits, nuts and coffee.

Main Imports (From U.S.): Aircraft and equipment, cotton textile fibers, engines, civil engineering equipment, pulp and waste paper.

Currency: Rupiah.

Former Colonial Status: Dutch Colony from about 1625 to 1949.

Independence Day: December 27, 1949. (August 17th, the anniversary of the 1945 date when revolutionaries proclaimed the Republic of Indonesia.)

Chief of State: Abdurrahman Wahid, President (since October 20, 1999).

National Flag: Two horizontal bands; the top is maroon and the bottom is white.

Per Capita GDP Annual Income: U.S. $792-probably not reliable.

Stretched along the Equator between Australia and the Asian mainland for a horizontal distance of about 3,000 miles, Indonesia consists of some 13,000 individual islands. The largest are Sumatra and Java; Kalimantan occupies the southern portion of the Island of Borneo, and Irian Jaya is the western portion of the island of New Guinea. About one–fourth of the land is covered with inland waters.

If Indonesia did not have a great variation in elevation, its climate would be uniformly oppressive because of its equatorial location. The heat and humidity of the coastal areas give way to more moderate temperatures as the altitude rises to breathtaking heights. Although Irian Jaya is predominantly low and swampy, as is Kalimantan, there are mountains that are snow–covered throughout the year on New Guinea.

This is an area of volcanic peaks—some dormant and some active—which have enriched the soil greatly during their centuries of destructively explosive activity. Krakatoa, located on a tiny island between Java and Sumatra, exploded with such force in 1883 that it produced a tidal wave which was felt around the world, and which inundated parts of nearby seacoasts. In other areas of the world, torrential rainfall such as occurs during the monsoon season is the enemy that washes valuable topsoil to the sea, exposing infertile land to the sun. In Java, the downpours are welcome—they wash away old soil and expose even richer volcanic ash and dirt which is fertile almost beyond belief.

The wildlife of Indonesia is more interesting and varied than almost any other country of the world. The Komodo dragon, ten feet long and a remnant of prehistoric times, inhabits the island of Komodo east of Java. The Javanese rhinoceros makes increasingly rare appearances in the Udjung Kulon ("western tip") preserve on the end of Java, where successive governments have tried to maintain the natural setting of plants and animals. The gibbon, most agile among the primates, swings overhead in the tall trees that pro-

Indonesia

vide thick shade for the banteng, a native ox with white legs that resembles an ordinary dairy cow. Although crowded by a multitude of species adapted to its character, this area, as well as most of the interior of the Indonesian islands, is extremely inhospitable to modern man.

History

Fossils and other prehistoric remnants of human skeletons indicate that Indonesia was the scene of one of the earlier areas of the world to be inhabited by man. The present population of the area acquired its somewhat uniform appearance about the second millennium B.C., a time when there was gradual intermarriage and mixture between native Polynesians and people from the Asian mainland. This combination, relatively stable since that time, is now referred to as Malayo–Polynesian.

Early Indonesian history is best seen as a regional history of diverse communities rather than as a unified early state directly tied through time to modern Indonesia. In fact many different communities existed though there were several commonalities among them, especially the presence of Hinduism and Buddhism, and their role in early international trade.

The arrival of Indian cultural, religious and commercial influences about the first century A.D. greatly influenced the people. Hinduism and Buddhism mingled with the ancient animist background of the Indonesians and produced an extremely complex, varied and unique culture, especially on Java and nearby Bali. The advances brought by the Indians and

the availability of good harbors in the Malacca and Sunda Straits were the basis for the rise of two powerful commercial and naval empires at the beginning of the 7th century, A.D. Srivijaya was based on the island of Sumatra; Sailendra arose on neighboring Java. The empires thrived on a lively trade centered on the production of spices treasured throughout the rest of the world, though available only here. Especially important was these islands' control of the trade routes between India and China and, in Srivijaya's case, its ties to imperial China. Taxes were imposed on passing ships based on the number of passengers and the cargo carried.

But if Hinduism and Buddhism were prevalent in the early traditions of these island kingdoms, their modern heritage lies elsewhere. Indian merchants also brought Islam to the islands at the beginning of the 11th century, but it did not have much influence at first. The development of the Indonesian empires was briefly disrupted in the 13th century by a naval expedition sent by the powerful Mongol emperor of China, Khubilai Khan. Shortly afterward, a new empire, known as Majapahit, became dominant, and seized control of the valuable spice trade. Majapahit was the last major Indonesian kingdom headed by a Hindu.

After their departure from the scene, Islam became more and more common. It had long been spreading, and by the end of the 16th century the vast majority of the people had become Muslims. In a sense the early South Asian influence continued, but now in its Islamic, rather than Hindu form. Today only Bali, the famous tourist attrac-

tion within Indonesia, remains deeply committed to its traditional Hindu heritage.

The Colonial Period

Though Europeans had longed for the spices of the East for centuries (European spices were limited to salt, garlic and vinegar), the profits from those valuable commodities were largely in the hands of Muslim middlemen during the pre–modern era. What the Europeans wanted was to gain access to those profits themselves. This explains the push in the 15th century to find new trade routes to the East. These images of fantastic wealth to be earned in the spice trade first brought Europeans to the East Indies, or Dutch East Indies as the islands were later called. The spices were, and now are, grown principally in the Moluccas (Spice Islands) and on Java.

There was a keen interest in the area on the part of Portugal and Great Britain, but it was the Dutch who were ultimately successful in dominating Indonesia, controlling the area through a commercial organization, the Dutch East India Company. By then the Majapahit Empire was already in decline leaving the island of Java as a relatively easy conquest. It was quickly identified as the most strategic and fertile of the islands and one which could produce coffee, indigo and some spices. The local leaders were either militarily defeated or intimidated by the Dutch, who compelled them to deliver produce to the Company.

The colonial experience of the East Indies, as Indonesia was then known, was-

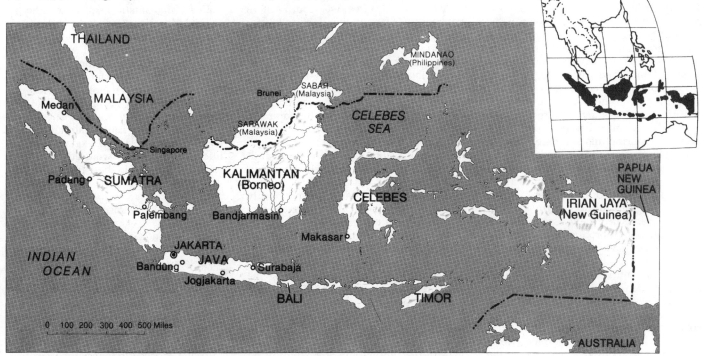

121

Indonesia

much the same as in other parts of the colonized world: centered around the process of extracting wealth from the colony. As was so common during colonialism, this was often carried out without any concern for the welfare of the indigenous peoples themselves. Thus for example, in an effort to drive up prices, the Dutch actually destroyed some island communities' ability to produce spices, devastating their economies and people in the process.

With the wealth gained, Holland emerged as one of the most powerful European countries of the early modern period and one which supported an impressive navy. But as would be the case in the 20th century their control over the East Indies was temporarily interrupted in the nineteenth century due to developments back in Europe.

The Napoleonic Wars resulted in a brief period of British occupation of Java from 1811 to 1816. But once the Napoleonic war was over the Dutch were able to reestablish their control partly because the British themselves, wanting to maintain a balance of power on the European continent, knew that Holland would need Indonesian wealth to contribute to that European stability. It would not be the last time the states of Southeast Asia were sacrificed to the needs of internal European politics.

By then the East Indies had passed from administration by the Dutch East Indies Company to that of the Dutch crown. But direct crown control proved difficult as it undertook administrative and judicial changes that challenged the power of the Javanese aristocratic class and provoked a war in the 1820s. The Dutch won but only after great loss of life. An especially exploitative economic system known as the *Cultivation System* was designed to gain maximum economic advantage for Holland from their control over the islands. This system added further to the hardships of the native Indonesians.

Eventually, in the last part of the 19th century there was a return to free economic development based on private investment. During this era there was considerable Western investment and the introduction of railroads. Large amounts of new land were put under cultivation. Indonesia emerged in this era as the world's largest producer of tin and rubber. The islands became so associated with the production of products such as coffee that the term "java" became synonymous with the drink itself.

By the late nineteenth century, feelings against Dutch control were growing in both Indonesia and the Netherlands itself. Responding to these new sentiments, the colonial government adopted the "Ethical Policy," under which strenuous efforts were made to promote the welfare of the Indonesians through public works and health measures. The government even announced that it would no longer take any surplus revenues generated by Indonesia and canceled the colony's debts.

Nevertheless, direct control over the East Indies grew during the early twentieth century even as new transportation methods allowed the Dutch themselves to become increasingly more remote from Indonesian society. They could, after all, send their children to schools in Europe and develop their own society more distant from that of the Indonesians they ruled. The phenomenon was a common one throughout much of the colonial world.

Not surprisingly local education was neglected and little serious effort toward preparation for self–government occurred despite the more general calls in the post World War I era for national self–determination. There was thus a rapid growth of both nationalism and communism in the interwar period in spite of increasingly harsh Dutch police measures.

World War II

When the Pacific War began in December 1941 Indonesia was, due to its great natural wealth, a prime target for the Japanese offensive in Southeast Asia. Weakly defended by a Dutch government–in–exile which had been driven from its own European homeland by the Germans, the islands rapidly came under Japanese control in early 1942.

As was the case elsewhere, many Indonesians warmly greeted the Japanese and sincerely believed Japanese claims that they had come to free Asia from Western colonialism. Many Indonesians, either for convenience or commitment, made the decision to work with the Japanese. Sukarno, the long term Indonesian nationalist, was among those who decided to use the occupation as a tool to help realize Indonesia's goal of national freedom. Eventually, he even managed to convince the Japanese authorities to help arm and train Indonesians in the struggle against the West.

The initial enthusiasm not withstanding, the Japanese administration soon convinced many Indonesians, as was to occur elsewhere in Asia, that they were hardly liberators, but merely new conquerors come to exploit the resources of Indonesia as the Dutch had before them. But if the Japanese hoped to build a new colonial base in Indonesia, their real impact was rather in fundamentally destroying the old colonial mentality rather than building a new one.

Moreover, although they were foreign conquerors, the Japanese not only destroyed the prestige of the Dutch in the eyes of the Indonesians, but in addition gave the latter valuable experience in political activity and public administration.

A New Nation

As soon as the war was over, Sukarno and fellow nationalist leader Mohammed Hatta, immediately proclaimed the independent Republic of Indonesia. This move had widespread support of other leaders and among the population of the outlying islands. And of course, it paralleled similar anti–colonialist developments elsewhere such as those of Ho Chi Minh in Vietnam. But declaring independence and actually winning it were not the same thing.

British forces soon arrived and used their power to help the Dutch reestablish themselves, though not before a massive public outbreak of anti–Dutch feelings and considerable violence. For the moment the Dutch would be able to reestablish themselves, but over the next four years a major independence struggle took place, which eventually saw the Dutch withdraw.

A settlement was reached at the end of 1949 that recognized the independence of Indonesia, which was supposed to be linked to the Netherlands through the Dutch Crown. West Irian, part of the island of New Guinea, was not included in the agreement; Dutch–owned industry and investment were to remain intact.

The new Republic of Indonesia, based on Java, promptly abolished the federal system created by the Dutch administration and established a unitary republic which later cut all ties with the Netherlands. Over the first several years it would operate as a parliamentary democracy with the charismatic Sukarno at its head.

The Indonesians faced independence under almost insurmountable difficulties. There were geographic and cultural differences, poor communications between the islands, and the dominant power of the Javanese, resented in the other islands—referred to as "Outer Islands." The political turmoil left by the years of Japanese occupation followed by battle against the Dutch, and the primitive state of economic and political development, were adverse influences. In addition to these liabilities, there was the leadership role of Sukarno himself.

The Sukarno Years

Flamboyant, popular, unpredictable, self–indulgent, articulate, dictatorial and lovable are all adjectives that have been used to describe Sukarno. During the years of his control he moved Indonesia from a parliamentary system to a more authoritarian one called "Guided Democracy." Denouncing Western democratic traditions, he practiced a political leadership that stressed Indonesian nationalism

Presidents Sukarno and Eisenhower enter the White House, May 1956

above regionalism and non–alignment in the Cold War between Washington and Moscow. Although not a communist, he frequently worked closely with the *PKI*, the *Indonesian Communist Party*. The U.S., alarmed by this, arranged a tryst for Sukarno with a beautiful woman at his hotel in New York while he was appearing at the UN. Cameras recorded the whole event in detail. When confronted with it, accompanied by threats of being disgraced, he was delighted. He asked for a copy to play publicly in Indonesia to visually demonstrate his sexual prowess!

Politics in those years became a complicated mixture of *PKI* communists led by the young and energetic Aidit, the army and Sukarno. The charismatic Sukarno was usually able to command the support of both the communists and the army. But his economic policies weakened the country. Promises had been given to leave foreign investment intact, but these were not kept. Dutch assets were seized in 1957. Some Chinese investment was nationalized in the following years. Most American assets were confiscated in 1963–1964.

Supported by Soviet diplomacy, Sukarno, in 1962, threatened West Irian, today known as Irian Jaya, with a substantial Soviet equipped military force. Under American pressure and mediation, the Dutch finally surrendered that western portion of New Guinea which they had until then continued to hold.

Sukarno then turned his attention toward Malaysia. This area of Southeast Asia was formed by the British when they united Malaya, Singapore and North Borneo (Sabah and Sarawak) into a single, independent nation in 1963. The British, unlike the Dutch in West Irian, were willing to fight to protect Malaysia.

The confrontation with Malaysia, launched in 1963 by Sukarno, led the *PKI*, which already had achieved considerable power, to demand the arming of communist–led "workers and peasants." This demand was resisted by the army, but endorsed by China and given an increasingly enthusiastic reception by Sukarno in 1965.

The events that followed remain unclear to this day though their impact transformed the country. What we do know is that a group of dissident military officers plotted to overthrow their more senior commanders. The exact relationship between the *PKI*, Sukarno himself, and the plotters remains uncertain. The results though are not.

As dramatized in the famous film, "A Year of Living Dangerously," events moved quickly during the fall of 1965. The coup attempt failed and the army, now under the leadership of General Suharto, emerged in power. Suharto then crushed the rebellion. Resentment against the *PKI*, which had been smoldering in the islands for years, erupted into a massive slaughter that resulted in the death of hundreds of thousands of people suspected of being communists or their sympathizers. While the army itself was directly involved, a large percentage of the deaths seem to have actually been carried out by civilians with the military's encouragement. The total number killed remains unclear. The *PKI* was almost annihilated and was outlawed as a political party. The army soon stripped Sukarno of all power. He died in 1970.

Suharto

If Sukarno had led an authoritarian government with leftist leaning nationalist sentiments, Suharto would now offer his own version of authoritarianism but one that was more open to the West and based on the military. Ideologically it had been built around the idea of *Pancasila*. This state ideology incorporated the five principles of national-

ism, democracy, internationalism, social justice, and belief in one God. All political parties were required to accept them and the armed forces had been given a legitimate role in the political process through the official government party, *GOLKAR*.

After the 1965 coup, the appointed *Provisional People's Consultative Congress (MPRS)* was purged of pro–communist elements. Later in March of 1967 it proclaimed Suharto president for five years.

Having achieved effective control of Indonesia, Suharto and the army ended the "confrontation" with Malaysia and began to tackle Indonesia's massive economic problems. Steps were taken to rejoin the UN, from which Sukarno's government had withdrawn in 1965. An interest was shown in resuming normal economic relations with the non–communist world, including the Netherlands and the United States.

Communist China, in contrast, denounced the new military regime as a gang of fascists, particularly after there was some anti–Chinese violence following the military seizure of power. The Soviet Union had more mixed feelings; it did not wish for communists to be slaughtered, but since the *PKI* had adopted the Chinese side of the disputes in international communism, the Soviets undoubtedly were gratified by the example of its failure—an example to other communist movements of the world which sided with Beijing.

Unlike his rejection of Sukarno's anti–Malaysian foreign policy, Suharto's regime continued the latter's interest in West

Former President Suharto

Indonesia

Irian. When the Dutch withdrew from West Irian in 1962, the UN promised that a popular vote would be taken to determine the will of the people. The alternatives were independence or union with Indonesia. However, Indonesian military officers present in West Irian in 1969 rigged a unanimous vote for union with Indonesia. Thus the region, known today as Irian Jaya, came to be part of Indonesia though even through the 1990s problems of anti–Jakarta regionalism have continued.

After the failure of the 1965 coup in Indonesia and the end of the "confrontation" with Malaysia, Indonesia joined with Malaysia, Singapore, Thailand and the Philippines to form the Association of Southeast Asian Nations (ASEAN). Brunei joined in 1984. The original purpose of this organization was to help stabilize regional power, develop the area economically and support the American struggle in Vietnam.

Its main visible functions were to maintain easy access for its members' raw materials to the markets of the developed countries, and to cooperate to a limited extent against communist insurgency. After the Vietnamese invasion of Cambodia at the end of 1978, ASEAN, with Thailand as the "frontline" state, began to play an important role in trying to negotiate an end to the struggle on terms that would include a Vietnamese military withdrawal.

It was announced in late 1969 that general elections would be held in mid–1971 in Indonesia. The result was an overwhelming victory for the government party, the Sekber GOLKAR, a federation of about 260 trade, professional and regional groups which enjoyed an overwhelming advantage over the other legal parties.

Nevertheless, widespread discontent over the lack of political freedom and social justice erupted in serious riots in early 1974. Most of the anger was nurtured by inflation, commodity shortages and was mainly aimed against the government. Other elements included dissatisfaction with the growing economic influence of Japan, and the commercial influence of local Indonesian Chinese whose preeminent role in the economy has often led to outbursts of anti–Chinese sentiment.

In the wake of the riots, President Suharto made some changes but government corruption, food shortages, a weak educational system, tensions between the Indonesian majority and the important Chinese minority continued to dog the country.

Nevertheless, In Indonesia's third general election in 1977, GOLKAR won 230 out of 360 seats in the House of Representatives. A few years later, in 1982 GOLKAR was again predictably victorious. Overall the system allowed the appearance of a more democratic system while really remaining a military dominated one which limited the number of parties that could compete and greatly favored its own creation GOLKAR.

Despite the authoritarian and military nature of the regime, Suharto's generation-long control over the country was economically very successful until quite late in his career. In fact, the government specifically defended the lack of political progress made over the years precisely on the grounds of economic development. And those boasts were not without merit. Very real social and economic progress was made in Indonesia during the last quarter of the 20th century. The Suharto government, despite its many faults dramatically improved the educational level of the In-

donesian people. Real wages went up as social conditions improved markedly. Per capita GDP had, for example, risen more than 4% annually for the first twenty years after 1965 and after 1988 the figure for the last decade of Suharto's control was closer to 7%–impressive figures indeed.

These changes occurred in part because Suharto's regime was committed to integrating Indonesia into the world economy and he did so very successfully until his last months in power. During these important years Indonesia was able to successfully offer its services as an assembly area for products produced in the dynamic Asian economies of its neighbors from South Korea and Taiwan to Singapore and Hong Kong. Indonesia had long had the advantage of having considerable oil, gas and timber reserves. Now these additional efforts at diversifying the economy were quite effective and improved the lives of Indonesians a great deal.

Still, Suharto's rather heavy-handed rule had naturally aroused opposition. There were two small legal opposition parties: the *Indonesian Democratic Party* and the *United Development Party* (the latter is Moslem-based). Interestingly those parties were not even officially allowed to call themselves "opposition" parties nor were they in a position to seriously challenge GOLKAR and the military due to the latters' overwhelming political and financial advantages.

Administratively the general trend from the 1960s was toward a greater centralization of authority at the national level in Jakarta. But, perhaps under the impact of democratic developments in the Philippines and South Korea there was during Suharto's last decade in power some liberalization of the authoritarian political system. One form this trend took was through a lessening of some central control—at least in the politically less sensitive areas of fiscal and technological authority. Another form was the revival of unofficial, as well as official, interest in the personality and career of the late President Sukarno, a development which has played a role in the recent prominence of his daughter.

One feature of the tensions which became more evident in recent years was anger at the ability of well connected individuals and groups to dominate the economy. This was hardly new. Both the Dutch colonial system as well as that employed during the years of Japanese occupation and under Sukarno had seen the economy tightly controlled by those with special advantages. But in recent years expectations had changed and these long established economic controls were no longer as acceptable.

The long-time domination of Suharto's family and friends in the Indonesian economy particularly aroused concerns that

Children at play in a poorer part of Jakarta ...

124

. . . while the capital's business district plays the stock market.

their activities were actually stifling the economy. These concerns were so significant that they, at times, even provoked challenges to Suharto from within the ranks of the usually supportive Indonesia military. Most of these tensions however remained fairly subtle till the crises of 1998.

Suharto's government also kept the pressure on the media. In 1994 it arrested three members of the Alliance of Independent Journalists for slandering the government through their publication *Independent*. The government even set up an Association of Indonesian Journalists which all reporters were required to join. But things have not always gone as smoothly as the government wanted. In fact, Suharto's regime was already looking vulnerable even before 1998's crash.

The Fall of Suharto

Indonesian politics, after the blood bath of 1965, remained reasonably calm until the economic turmoil that developed in late 1997. The military and its partner, *GOLKAR*, allowed the impression of political harmony while maintaining a tight grip on political power. Nevertheless, even before the famous economic meltdown of the region during late 1997 and early 1998 Suharto's grip was being challenged.

The military's long term domination of the country, the growing disparity between rich and poor, the economic domination of Suharto's family and more general frustrations with pervasive levels of corruption all played a role in the developing tensions. But the more immediate cause was the entrance into Indonesian politics of the daughter of Indonesian nationalist hero Sukarno.

Until 1987 Megawati Sukarnoputri, the former president's daughter was not involved in politics. Only in the late 1980s was she elected to parliament. It was somewhat later, in 1993, that she emerged as the leader of the Indonesian Democratic Party, one of the two parties the govern-

ment allowed to exist. But while many had dismissed this college-educated former housewife, President Suharto did not. He moved to weaken the political base of this cautious leader who carries with her the inheritance of a powerful name in Indonesia's national memory.

Not content to harass her, Suharto's government engineered her ouster as leader of the *PDI* by pro-government supporters within the party. No doubt the hope had been to remove Megawati Sukarnoputri's official base but doing so appeared to backfire when, in the summer of 1996, government backed hoodlums attempted to force her supporters from the *PDI* headquarters. Rather than go quietly her supporters quickly gathered and a confrontation ensured which eventually saw several deaths and hundreds wounded. The government's strong arm tactics had done no more than solidify her leadership before her followers and raise the international prestige of her movement. By late fall she was being coupled in the public mind with other Southeast Asian women who have challenged dictatorial governments, women ranging from Corazon Aquino of the Philippines to Aung San Suu Kyi of Burma. In late 1997, as the economic meltdown began to hit throughout the country, Megawati Sukarnoputri even announced she was ready to replace the President when his term ended in March of 1998.

Not surprisingly her offer was not taken up. Rather, the government's political arm *Golkar*, backed by the army proceeded to reelect the 77 year old President once again. The aging president had no interest in leaving office. Far more significant for the nation's future Suharto chose, as long anticipated, Research and Technology Minister B.J. Habibie as his vice-president and presumably his successor.

B.J. Habibie, a 61 year old engineer had the confidence of the president and the technical background Suharto was said to have been looking for. Unfortunately, his reputation among the international finan-

cial community was not very positive—he was seen as a volatile leader and an economic nationalist too infatuated with unrealistic showcase style industrial goals. Nor did the ever influential army have any affection for him. Nevertheless, Suharto favored him and that was enough. By March 1998 newly elected President Suharto and his new vice-president were in place. But by then Indonesian politics were starting to move far beyond Suharto's control.

By mid-May 1998 the loss of confidence in Suharto's regime had become simply too great. Initially aroused by the rising prices of basic commodities, as mandated by the IMF's recovery program, Jakarta and other cities saw dramatic demonstrations by at first students and then others against the regime. After more than a quarter of a century in power, Suharto had lost the confidence of more than just the younger and poorer members of society. By late May even his most trusted loyalists and many of the country's leading political, intellectual and religious leaders had withdrawn their support. After one bloody clash between the students and the army, many even within the army leadership itself, were apparently ready to abandon Suharto and more importantly to help the country transition toward new leadership. With encouragement of General Wiranto, the Chief of the Indonesia Armed Forces, President Suharto finally resigned on the 21st of May and allowed his newly chosen vice-president Habibie to assume office.

We still have much to learn about the details of Suharto's fall but at this writing it appears that members of the Indonesian military, most notably those led by Suharto's son-in-law were quite probably working to bring about a situation which would have allowed the military to suppress the demonstrations and retain its influence. General Wiranto, the Minister of Defense and Security apparently had other ideas and threw his weight behind those hoping for a more peaceful resolution of the crises including the newly installed president.

Indonesia

The 76 year old Suharto had stepped down after 32 years in power. But of course the Indonesian establishment, military, political and financial was still largely in place. And the new President, B. J. Habibie had no popular mandate or even strong support among the military to help him lead. Unfortunately for the new president, nor was he able in the months following the fall of Suharto to develop such a following. In fact, his attitude, relatively cautious and incremental did little to build popular support and merely reminded many of his fundamental ties to the Suharto years.

Habibie did manage to move the country cautiously toward new elections; first parliamentary elections which took place in June 1999 and then the presidential contest scheduled for late 1999. The earlier elections proved to be a vindication for the efforts of Megawati Sukarnoputri, whose party the Indonesian Democratic Party won 34% of the votes and 153 seats in the legislature. Despite those who thought Golkar's strength had totally failed it, the former "government" party came in second with 120 seats. Altogether 21 parties managed to win seats in the 500 seat Indonesian House of Representatives—down from the 200 parties that were competing earlier in the year.

Though Golkar's continuing strength was a surprise to some observers the really big winner in the contest was Megawati herself who seemed to be on a clear path to the presidency. Certainly, she appeared to have the necessary public support, but the presidential election that occurred the following October turned out quite differently from what many expected. Sukarno's daughter may have been very popular with the Indonesian public but winning the presidency required far more than that. Megawati herself was hurt by a reputation for indecision and most importantly she emerged far less able than others to build the necessary support within the legislature. When the vote actually occurred the aging and partially blind Muslim leader Abdurrahman Wahid outmaneuvered not only Megawati but Suharto's chosen successor Habibie to emerge as Indonesia's new President.

That Indonesia had moved beyond Suharto and Habibie was certainly exciting for those who had hoped for a more open Indonesia. Wahid himself had long been known as an open minded and tolerant leader. Nevertheless, Megawati's supporters were understandably very disappointed. Happily, the new president's decision to tap her as the nation's new vice-president satisfied many and the new team was duly sworn in.

In the months since Abdurrahman Wahid became president he has had to

President Abdurrahman Wahid

Vice President Megawati Sukarnoputri

deal with a host of problems from secessionist regions to asserting his own authority over the nation's military. The latter has been an especially critical challenge given the Indonesian military's long domination over the nation. Clearly Wahid's primary task was to support those members of the military who were willing to build a new less politically involved Indonesian military. Wahid's initial confrontation was with the powerful General Wiranto. Thus far the new president has been successful. Over the last few months Wiranto has slowly been pushed from power along with scores of other lower level officers.

But if Indonesia wishes to move beyond its military dominated past, shuffling and removing individuals will not be enough. More important will be to drastically reduce the enormous role of the military in the country's civil administration. True enough, for the moment the Indonesian army has found itself reeling under a bru-

tal public criticism of its activities both during Suharto's administration and in the two years since. Public revelations of its role in suppressing both political and ethnic movements have been very embarrassing and the army has found itself largely on the defensive. Whether the army's new weakness and the government's commitment will be enough to fundamentally alter how Indonesia is governed though is quite another thing.

Indonesia Regionalism & East Timor

When studying the modern history of communities like Indonesia it is important to remember that they were not single ethnic/linguistic/political communities before the colonial era. Rather, it was often the colonial experience itself that helped create the generation of nationalists like Sukarno or Hatta who led the struggle for independence. But like nations throughout the world, whose political borders were shaped by outside colonial powers, it has often been difficult to keep focused on their identities as Indonesians in the face of strong regional and ethnic ties. During the heady days of Indonesia's dramatic economic growth, pride in those accomplishments helped to strengthen Indonesia's national identity. Nevertheless, strong separatist sentiments and movements continued to be influential in regions from Aceh, near Malaysia, to Irian Jaya far to the east. And those sentiments have been strengthened in recent months as the struggle over East Timor prompted both international media attention and outside intervention over the last year.

No Indonesian region though has experienced as much international attention for the level of its struggle and suffering as East Timor. Unlike much of the rest of Indonesia, which had been administered as the Dutch East Indies, East Timor had been a Portuguese colony for hundreds of years. Rather like Portuguese Goa in India or Macao near Hong Kong it was a small reminder of the once energetic Portuguese role in colonization.

But just as India's government had moved into Goa in the early 1960s, and China took back Macao in December of 1999, Indonesia decided to absorb East Timor in 1975. The logic of Indonesian nationalism might have made the move seem appropriate, but culturally Indonesians and the East Timorese were quite different. As we have seen, Indonesia, while it includes many religions including millions of Christians, is largely Muslim, while East Timor, by grace of its centuries as a Portuguese colony, and more importantly the tensions which existed after Indonesia occupied it, is primarily Catholic and animist.

But however significant the religious differences, the real problems were probably the lack of a shared historical experience between the two peoples and especially the brutality of the Indonesian occupation itself. The Indonesian move was resisted by a leftist and Nationalist movement called *Fretilin*, the Revolutionary Front for an Independent East Timor, and widely condemned internationally. In fact, only Indonesia's ASEAN partners and Australia actually recognized the legality of the occupation. Throughout the 1990s, reports of significant human rights abuses continued to be a problem for the Suharto government and aroused the sympathy of an increasingly large group of international sympathizers.

But it was not until the fall of Suharto in 1998 that the situation began to change dramatically. Once in power the new government of President Habibie indicated interest in trying to resolve the long standing struggle. Clearly hoping to move toward some sort of autonomy, the regime made a series of dramatic admissions regarding its own previous role in East Timor and claimed to be withdrawing some of its troops from the region. Not surprisingly leaders in East Timor were more interested in real independence than Jakarta's offer of greater autonomy.

And Habibie himself blundered deeply by not ensuring that the Indonesian military was on board before offering the East Timorese an opportunity to vote on their future. In the months leading up to the August 1999 vote it became abundantly clear that elements of the Indonesian military were supporting a terrorist campaign within East Timor to disrupt the referendum scheduled for August 1999.

Eventually the violence, after the dramatic East Timorese vote for independence was announced, became so blatant that the United Nations supported by a force from Australia and other regional powers assumed control over East Timor from an extremely embarrassed and humiliated Indonesian military leadership.

Foreign Relations

Recent years have been a disaster for Indonesia's relations with the outside world. Not only have Indonesian based forest fires often filled the entire region with choking smoke that hardly endeared her to her neighbors, but her ongoing battles with the International Monetary Fund made the rest of the region less able to begin their own effort to recover economically. And of course the struggle over East Timor not only soured relations with Australia and much of the international community but forced Jakarta to accept a humiliating presence of foreign troops on land she had until recently vehemently insisted was her sovereign territory.

And that was ironic given that Indonesia has usually played an important and respected role in the region. As the fourth most populous country in the world, Indonesia has always considered itself to be number one among equals within the Association of Southeast Asian Nations (ASEAN). And, it is fair to say that the other ASEAN states have usually accepted the "big brother" role of Indonesia. The ASEAN headquarters is located in Jakarta. For its part, Indonesia has worked within the context of ASEAN though Jakarta has often been less enthusiastic about the rapid elimination of trade barriers since it is the least developed of the member states.

In the past Indonesia prided itself on being an arbiter of disputes and a conciliator. Indonesia played a role in the settlement of disputes in Cambodia and was helpful in having the Burmese activist Aung San Suu Kyi released from house arrest during the mid 1990s. Indonesia has also sponsored several seminars on the conflicting territorial claims in the South China Sea, and especially the Spratley Islands.

During the Cold War Indonesia was a key player in the Non-Alignment Movement which traced its beginnings back to the Bandung (Indonesia) conference of 1955. Nevertheless under former President Sukarno, the policy definitely leaned left. Sukarno tried to organize the New Emerging Forces which linked Indonesia to such countries as China, North Korea and Vietnam. After Sukarno's fall, President Suharto placed the country on a much more centrist path and one more tied to Western economic ideas. This generally non-aligned policy was evidenced for example in that

the country did not develop defense treaties with any major outside power or group of powers. This set Indonesia apart from most of her ASEAN neighbors.

The country's territorial waters expanded greatly when the UN Law of the Sea Convention went into effect. Under the convention, all of the waters between the country's numerous islands, officially set at 17,500, now became Indonesian territorial waters.

But Indonesia's important and influential role regionally and economically began to unravel in late 1997 as her economy was struck by the same economic crises that had begun in Thailand and swept on toward South Korea. But unlike the situation both in Thailand and South Korea, there initially seemed no new or alternative leadership ready in the wings to take charge of getting the country back on track.

Unfortunately for Indonesia its long entrenched leadership, led by Suharto seemed unwilling to find a way to work with the International Monetary Fund even as it requested funds from the agency. Thus by early 1998 the world was treated to an ongoing series of major world financial figures each making their way to Jakarta to meet with its aging leadership hoping to encourage a more cooperative stance from the Indonesian government.

Certainly there were reasons for Jakarta to balk at some of the IMF's stringent financial demands for economic restructuring which would only add to the financial distress of the Indonesia people and hurt Suharto's own family's financial interests. Nevertheless, the open struggle with the IMF only added to those doubts about whether Indonesia's leadership would be

Coffee pickers off to the fields

Indonesia

East Timor

The new community of East Timor emerged over the last year in a bloodbath that much of the world witnessed. It was, for this small nation that occupies only part of one island in the vast Indonesian island archipelago the second effort to establish itself as an independent nation. To understand the origins of the region's newest—soon to be independent nation—requires a close look at the centuries of Portuguese and then Indonesian colonial control of East Timor.

East Timor, is about the size of the American state of Maryland and historically included about two dozen different linguistic communities most of which practiced an animistic religious tradition until quite recently.

The colonial history of East Timor began with the arrival of the Portuguese in the first years of the 16th century. Those early arrivals from Europe were initially interested in the sandlewood of the area and had little impact on the lives of the inhabitants who lived largely in small villages in the interior. By the late 16th century Dominican friers from Portugal had begun to establish themselves in the area as did people known as "Black Portuguese" a reference to the peoples of mixed Portuguese and local ancestry from the surrounding area. Long known for the sandlewood produced there the island found itself fought over by both the Portuguese and the Dutch during the era of colonial expansion. Eventually, and that was not until the early 20th century, the present boundaries were established between Dutch administered West Timor, part of the larger Dutch East Indies colony, and East Timor which was controlled by the Portuguese. As with the rest of the area, the British occupied the region during the Napoleonic wars. After the defeat of the French, the Portuguese reestablished their control.

Within East Timor, the Portuguese colonizers made little effort to develop their holdings. In fact, according to one nineteenth century visitor no roads had been developed at all beyond the settlement of Dili itself. Lisbon put very little effort into East Timor until late in the nineteenth century when they feared loosing it to the other, more aggressive, European powers.

As tensions built toward the Second World War a group of Australians landed in East Timor and prepared to resist the advancing Japanese forces. Later as with the rest of the enormous Indonesian archipelago, the advancing Japanese army occupied East Timor. Over the following years Western forces, frequently with the help of the East Timorese, worked to sabotage the Japanese holdings. After the war the Portuguese once again reestablished their control.

A generation later, in the mid 1970s, another even more dramatic trial began for the East Timorese when Portugal's authoritarian government fell from power replaced by a more liberal government less committed to retaining the country's colonial holdings. The new government declared its intention to allow East Timorese to decide their own future in a referendum planned for the fall of 1976.

Unfortunately for the inhabitants of East Timor their own location—within the enormous Indonesian Archipelago—and the then still raging international Cold War made their transition out from under colonialism far more dangerous than it might have otherwise been. Especially important is the timing for as things came to a head within East Timor during mid 1975, the American led anticommunist struggle on the mainland of Indochina was just coming to a dramatic end with the unification of Vietnam under Hanoi and the fall of Cambodia's capital Phnom Phen to the forces of the communist *Khmer Rouge* in the spring of 1975.

From the perspective of the very anticommunist Indonesian military government, which itself had wiped out its own communist party ten years before, the possibility that an independent East Timor led by the leftist and Nationalist movement, *Fretilin*, the Revolutionary Front for an Independent East Timor, was simply unacceptable.

Ironically, given later events it is now known that as early as 1974 the Australian Prime Minister had actually encouraged Jakarta to absorb East Timor rather than let it emerge free. Despite denials in the years since it is also clear that the American government certainly had no objections to Jakarta's decision to invade, and later supplied enormous amounts of military aid to help facilitate the Indonesian army's conquest.

When the Indonesia invasion began in December 7, 1975, the East Timorese were actually more prepared to resist Jakarta than one might have imagined. As a former colony of Portugal—a member of NATO—some East Timorese had had professional military training and the departing colonial power also left weapons behind which were later used effectively against the Indonesians.

But these advantages hardly made them a match for Indonesian forces. Unlike the East Timorese, Jakarta had the military support of the United States and thus the ability to impose its will upon the resisting East Timorese. During the initial occupation and in the years since, scores of thousands have died in the many clashes between the East Timorese and the forces of Jakarta. Estimates on the numbers killed over the years either directly or indirectly as a result of the occupation are around 200,000 people!

Sadly for the people of East Timor there was almost no international awareness of their plight from the mid 1970s through the early 1990s when word of the horror going on there began to be better publicized. Most important in that growing international awareness of the crisis in East Timor were the events which took place in Dili in 1991. On that occasion, hundreds of East Timorese, perhaps emboldened by the presence of members of the international press, openly defied Indonesian authorities while attempting to commemorate the recent death of an East Timorese activist.

At the cemetery, despite the presence of Western reporters, the Indonesian military opened fire killing an estimated 70 to 200 people. Despite the horror the event marked—because of the coverage it received—the beginning of a greater international awareness of events in East Timor. Thus, after a generation of suffering the East Timorese finally found, after what became known as the Santa Cruz Massacre, a growing body of international supporters.

Later the East Timorese nationalists got a much needed boost in 1996 when two of their most prominent members were awarded the Nobel Peace Prize for their efforts. Bishop Carlos Filipe Ximenes Belo, who continued to live in East Timor, and Jose Ramos Horta a militant leader of the movement in exile shared the award which gave the struggle of East Timor much more international attention.

But East Timor's fate began to change most dramatically only in the years after the Asian economic crisis which saw the authoritarian government of former General Suharto finally fall from power. His successor B.J. Habibie, perhaps seeking a dramatic gesture to respond to the long running crisis of East Timor, announced in January of 1999 that the unhappy province would be allowed to have a referendum on staying within Indonesia. Unfortunately, the decision, while greeted enthusiastically by most East Timorese was seen as a disaster by many Indonesian immigrants to East Timor and the Indonesian army which had fought so long to retain the area. And Indonesian attitudes were not surprising. Not only had many Indonesians in the military served in East Timor, many were heavily invested in the region's economy. And there was as well a reasonable and understandable fear that East Timor's freedom

(Continued)

might provoke the many other restless parts of Indonesia to succeed.

The Referendum

The months leading up to the August 1999 referendum were both a time of crisis and excitement for the East Timorese. On the one hand international observers arrived to supervise their long awaited opportunity to vote on ending their relationship with Indonesia. On the other hand, local militia, clearly supported and supplied by the Indonesia military, violently attacked those supportive of independence and threatened a blood bath if the vote resulted in a choice to leave.

The actual referendum went fairly calmly, but as soon as it became clear that the East Timorese had voted against autonomy within Indonesia and more specifically for independence, an explosion of violence racked East Timor as pro-Jakarta militias clearly backed by elements of the Indonesian military went on a rampage that saw unknown numbers of people slaughtered and thousands more flee to West Timor where they ended up in refugee camps often still harassed by the pro-Jakarta militias which have opposed East Timor's desire to be independent.

Eventually, as the international outrage grew and public awareness of the crisis expanded, the Australians agreed to lead an international force, which included troops from Thailand, Singapore, Malaysia, and the Philippines to East Timor to help restore order. Even China sent some of her own security forces to work with the international community in East Timor.

As the most violent of the fighting has ended thousands of East Timorese have returned home from the refugee camps of West Timor though reports of continued harassment and persecution of those still in West Timor are very common. It is also clear that the militias have

made it very difficult for the refugees to actually return to East Timor. And unfortunately, those refugees who have been allowed to return are going home to a devastated land.

Meanwhile the East Timorese under their most popular leaders from Xanana Gusmao to Bishop Bello are attempting to build the rudiments of a future government that would administer East Timor when the international forces known as UNAMET eventually pull out. Currently East Timor is being administered by the United Nations which is using funds from several countries from Norway and Sweden to the Netherlands and Portugal. And such funds are vital since East Timor is not able to generate its own tax funds yet.

Unfortunately in the months since the departure of the Indonesian troops East Timor has not yet received its long anticipated calm. There has been considerable tension between the UNAMET administration of East Timor and the local leaders who have vehemently complained of being ignored by the United Nations professionals. East Timorese leaders have also accused the international aid agencies of underpaying their own workers and being more interested in earning money than delivering aid. East Timorese have also been upset with the number of outsiders the United Nations authorities have been hiring to administer programs there.

Still there are positive signs. Last January the Dili Airport opened again and Australian airlines was one of the first to schedule regular flights there. It will not be easy for East Timor to establish itself as an economically viable nation. Certainly there are some advantages, East Timor has an international community of people concerned about its fate and countries from Australia to Portugal committed to helping out. Nevertheless it will be some time before we can gauge how well the world's newest nation is faring

Men on the way to work

isolated communities. Bali, the island fabled in story and song in the Western world, is the one significant part of Indonesia that still practices Hinduism, the tradition that once dominated the entire region.

Thus, Indonesia is a country of great cultural differences. More than three hundred different specific groups are recognized and over 250 different languages are spoken. The dominant Javanese themselves constitute about 50% of the population. The largest non-indigenous community is the ethnic Chinese who, while constituting only around 3% of the population, are especially dominant in private economy.

The economic accomplishments of the era from the 1970s through the mid 1990s brought into being a new middle class which enjoyed many of the material comforts such groups enjoy elsewhere. Unlike some groups in other parts of East and Southeast they did not appear to be particularly politicized or willing to challenge Suharto's regime until the drama of the late 1990s. Now though the situation is quite different and many have become involved in the fast evolving political environment.

Modern Indonesia has developed as a community that draws sources from many different groups from Javanese and Malay traditions to those from the West and derived from Islamic society. Normally, nonviolence and courteous agreement are a tradition in Javanese culture. Open disagreement is avoided—differences are buried in an atmosphere of agreement, no matter how unreal. Still, once it becomes apparent that differences cannot be hidden, violence has at times become painfully real.

In recent years a revival of an Islamic emphasis by the Javanese has tended to make the Christian and Chinese community feel more insecure than in previous years. And of course, often in Indonesia, the tendency has existed to blame the nation's economic crises on its influential Chinese minority which has sometimes resulted in violent attacks upon that community.

Thus, over the last few years, and especially as Indonesia's economic crisis has

able to make the hard choices necessary to recover and gain the confidence of the world financial markets.

As we have seen, by May 1998 those stresses had simply become too great and President Suharto fell from power replaced at first by his vice-president B.J. Habibie and then by the new more democratically elected team of Abdurrahman Wahid and Megawati Sukarnoputri.

Relations with the People's Republic of China, which were strained by the anti-Indonesian Chinese riots of 1998 have improved. In fact, the new president has even indicated an interest in improving relations

with neighbors from China to India in order to offer a counter-balance to the enormous Western influence in the region.

Society and Culture

Indonesia is a nation of islands which traditionally had mainly indirect contact with each other—a nation more recently ruled in effect by a cultural minority located on the island of Java. The vast majority of Indonesians are Muslims though other important groups of Christians, and Chinese Buddhists are also present. Animism, a common tradition throughout Southeast Asia, is also found among some of the more

Indonesia

worsened, there have been more and more outbreaks of communal violence. Fairly predictable have been the attacks on the financially influential but small Chinese minority. Especially violent outbreaks of fighting between Dayak tribesmen against Muslim Madurese settlers in Kalimantan have also regularly created thousands of casualties and refugees. Dramatic tensions between Indonesia's Christian and Muslim communities have broken out as well. Clearly Indonesia is a country currently in crisis but that is a relatively recent development.

Indonesian Women

As is the case in many countries throughout the world Indonesian women have many disadvantages when compared to men. Officially, they have the same rights as men but reality is often quite different. Those that work in industry usually get lower pay than men and often without the benefits men receive. Traditional Islamic family law prevails, making it legal for men to have more than one wife though President Suharto, to make an example, forbade senior level officials and officers from actually doing so. At the lower levels of the civil service it is allowed but men wishing to take on another wife are required to get the permission of the supervisor as well as the first wife.

Women's lower status is especially evident in the laws of citizenship. Women are not allowed to pass on their citizenship to their children. Thus a woman who becomes pregnant by a non-Indonesian citizen takes the risk of seeing her own children deported! In contrast though to some Asian societies there is much less of a social preference for boys over girls.

Some real improvements were being made in recent years. The number of young women graduating from high school went up enormously in the last generation and the number graduating from college tripled in the years from 1980 to 1990. Additionally, a number of women's organizations have appeared to help improve the lives of Indonesian women.

A Balinese song–and–dance drama

Moreover, at the upper more educated levels the gap between women and men's salaries lessens and many women now work at important mid level positions in both government and the private sector. Unfortunately, the lives of women as with others has been dramatically affected by the economic collapse. Spousal abuse is thought to be up as families experience more tension and women are apparently less able to afford the contraceptives they previously had used to help control their own fertility.

Today's Indonesians can also be proud of the fact that Megawati Sukarnoputri, so recently a democratic dissident is now the country's newly installed vice-president. It is though important as well to note that she might have emerged not as vice-president but as president if prejudice against having a woman as president had not played a role in the final choice of new leadership.

Economy

The last few years have been an economic nightmare for the Indonesian people. Long proud of the steady economic progress they had made over the last generation, Jakarta suddenly found itself caught in the currency collapse begun in Thailand in the summer of 1997. Over the next months as the rupiah lost an increasing percentage of its value, Indonesian businesses became unable to pay their U.S. dollar based international debts. As the crisis grew worse more and more Indonesian firms began failing and laying off their workers. For much of the country and so many of its citizens, all that they had worked so hard for over the previous generation was collapsing around them.

Initially working closely with the IMF, an enormous aid package of 43 billion dollars was arranged and Suharto's government started to act decisively by promising to close various banks that were insolvent and to take "belt tightening" economic decisions. But of course, as the economic crisis grew, social and political cracks within the society, long present, began to add to the tensions. As the century drew to a close more and more riots were breaking out within the country as people protested higher food and fuel prices. Fearing a further growth in the unrest the police cracked down hard on those who demonstrated. All this was in such great contrast to the economic experience of Indonesia over the last generation.

For the previous generation Indonesia had a diversifying economy. Economic growth in GDP (Gross Domestic Product) has averaged about 7% annually since the 1970s. Foreign investment grew enormously. Indonesia's participation in the "growth triangle" with Singapore and Johore state in West Malaysia appeared to prove the merits of the private sector in

the development process.

But despite the enormous economic growth and social improvements accomplished over the last generation some 26 million of the country's 200 million were said to be living in poverty as defined by the World Bank even before the economic problems of 1997–1998. But now with the onset of the Asian economic crisis which has hit harder in Indonesia than anywhere else the situation has grown far more dire. Millions have been pushed back into poverty as unemployment has soared and more than two thirds of the population appear to be falling below even the most modest Indonesia poverty line.

Word of violent communal strife which made international headlines during 1999 is hardly likely to improve matters as investors are much more likely to invest elsewhere in the region than within Indonesia itself. In fact the only industry that seemed to be experiencing growth was the Indonesia insurance industry as frightened property owners afraid of further violence tried to buy policies. For the moment Indonesia, unlike many of its neighbors, shows few signs of recovering economically from the Asian economic crisis.

Future

Indonesia has come a long way since the days of Sukarno. Continued growth appeared about to put Indonesia firmly into the mid-level developing nations category by the end of the century but the 1997–1998 economic crash and resulting political transformation and uncertainty ended those hopes. Now the real issue will be how to successfully deal with the coming year's social, political and economic challenges. That Indonesia's new leadership does so is critical to the region and important to the world.

As the fourth most populous country in the world Indonesia is simply too large to become an example of yet another of those "failed nations" that made the last years of the 20th century so complicated. The only thing that is certain is that Indonesia's leaders have an enormous challenge ahead of them. Given the reports of economic collapse and rioting, some have even suggested that Indonesia itself might break up, but the most experienced observers seem reasonably convinced that Indonesia will survive relatively well even these latest challenges.

And those challenges are considerable for Indonesia faces the necessity not only of retaining territorial unity but of repairing the economy while building a new more democratic political system. And on top of that the nation's long term future is at risk as more and more families are unable to afford to send their children to school to acquire the education Indonesia will need in the twenty-first century.

The Laos People's Democratic Republic

Area: 91,400 sq. mi. (234,804 sq. km., somewhat smaller than Oregon).

Population: 4,800,000.

Capital City: Vientiane (Pop. 230,000, estimated).

Climate: Tropical, with a rainy monsoon from May–October and a dry season from November–April.

Neighboring Countries: China (North); Vietnam (East); Burma (Northwest); Thailand (West); Cambodia (South).

Official Language: Lao

Other Principal Tongue: French.

Ethnic Background: The majority of the people, living in the Mekong Valley, are the Lao, of Thai ancestry. There are a number of tribes, including the Meo, Yao, Kha and Lu, some of which are Thai, but most of which are Malay, Chinese and Vietnamese ancestry.

Principal Religion: Buddhism; animism is predominant among the tribes.

Major Exports: Electric power (to Thailand), timber and textiles.

Main Import (from Thailand, Russia, Japan, France, China, Vietnam): Rice, petroleum products, machinery.

Currency: Kip.

Former Colonial Status: French protectorate (1893–1949); member of the French Union (1949–1954).

National Day: December 24, 1954.

A Laotian newspaper

Laos

Chief of State: Khamtai Siphandon, President (since February 1998).
Head of Government: Sisavath Keobounphanh, Prime Minister (since February 1998).
National Flag: Two red stripes (top and bottom), a wide blue stripe between them upon which is centered a white circle.
Per Capita GNP Income: U.S. $400.

Laos is a landlocked, country largely covered with mountains and tropical forests interrupted by patches of low scrub vegetation in the areas where the soil is poor. From one point of view it is an extremely backward country with almost no roads, but from another point of view it is an area of the world where the natural beauty has not been greatly altered by the presence of man.

Most of the fertile land lies along the valley of the Mekong River, where it is eroded and flows as silt to the rice paddies in the Mekong Delta in southern Vietnam. The land receives ample rainfall, but the sandstone soils have little capacity to retain the moisture. In the last part of the dry season from November to May, the air becomes oppressively hot and very dry—this is the time when the tribesmen living in the mountain forests burn the trees to clear the land. This practice, coupled with natural forest fires, robs the land of much of its fertility; when the farmer ceases to cultivate the land it becomes choked with a primitive, ugly scrub vegetation.

History

The Lao people moved into northern Laos from the southwestern Chinese province of Yunnan beginning in the 11th century A.D. During the succeeding centuries they slowly expanded toward the south, founding two communities in central and southern Laos. In their efforts to settle these additional lands they came into frequent conflict with the Burmese and Thai who were also active in this part of Southeast Asia.

The French established their colonial authority over neighboring Vietnam by 1893. When there was a dispute between Thailand and Laos over demarcation of the border, the French proclaimed a protectorate over Laos in 1893, making it a dependency within the French Indochinese Empire. Because of its remoteness and lack of natural resources, the French did almost nothing to develop Laos; they did succeed in ending the payment of tribute to the kings of Thailand, however.

When the Japanese soldiers conquered Southeast Asia in 1942, Tokyo supported their Thai ally in taking some border territory from Laos. A nationalist movement,

known as the *Lao Issara* and directed mainly against the Japanese occupation forces, arose during World War II. When the French re–entered after the defeat of the Japanese, Thailand was forced by Britain and the U.S. to return the territory it had acquired while allied with Japan. The *Lao Issara* promptly started anti–French activity from bases in Thailand. Preoccupied with resistance movements in Vietnam, the French granted Laos internal self–government within the French Union in 1949; thus splitting the resistance movement. The non-communist majority took a leading role in the new government, but the communist and pro–communist minority formed itself into a party known as the *Pathet Lao*.

This communist movement opposed the new government and came increasingly under the influence of Ho Chi Minh's communist movement in Vietnam. Following invasions of northern Laos by communist Vietnamese in 1953 and 1954, the *Pathet Lao* completely controlled the provinces of Phong Saly and Sam Neua on the Vietnamese border. Under the terms of an agreement reached in Geneva in 1954, it was allotted these provinces for "regrouping."

After prolonged haggling, the government, which had achieved full independence from France in late 1954, and the *Pathet Lao* agreed on political and military unification in 1957. The strong showing however of the *Pathet Lao* in the elections of 1958 alarmed the Laotian government, as well as the Americans. The situation became critical when the government tried in 1959 to integrate two battalions of the *Pathet Lao* forces into the army and to demobilize the remainder of the communist–oriented forces. The result was a confused, small–scale civil war in which the North Vietnamese seized the opportunity to give increasing aid in personnel and equipment to the *Pathet Lao*. The U.S. then

President Khamtai Siphandon

increased its assistance to the government to meet the threat.

By 1960 a military *coup* replaced the right-wing government with a neutralist regime under Prince Souvanna Phouma. When the Prince was later driven from Vientiane by right–wing forces in December 1960 he appealed for Soviet military aid. Russia promptly airlifted arms to the neutralist forces, but also sent an even larger shipment to the *Pathet Lao*, with whom Souvanna Phouma was cooperating. North Vietnam meanwhile sent its own forces into the mountains of eastern Laos at the beginning of 1961 in order to improve its access to South Vietnam via the "Ho Chi Minh Trail." This was done to assist the revolutionary war against South Vietnam which was then in full bloom. Hanoi also increased aid to the *Pathet Lao*.

Evidently realizing that a war could not serve the aims of either side, U.S. President Kennedy and Soviet Premier Khrushchev agreed in 1961 that Laos should be neutralized. In spite of this, following intense jockeying for position, the *Pathet Lao* withdrew from the coalition government which had just been set up. The result was continuation of a highly complex and somewhat obscure, undeclared civil war. It included Thai volunteers and operations managed by the U.S. Central Intelligence Agency.

During the following years until 1971, military activity was related directly to the Ho Chi Minh Trail, vital to the North Vietnamese war effort in South Vietnam. The communists sought to keep it open, while the South Vietnamese, assisted by the U.S., sought periodically to close it. As part of the accord supposedly settling the Vietnamese conflict reached in Paris, an agreement was reached in 1973 regarding Laos. It included many of the *Pathet Lao*

**Prime Minister
Sisavath Keobounphanh**

Lane Xang Hotel, Vientiane

demands and tended to lessen the influence of the right wing in the central government.

A coalition government was not installed until April 1974; which then became a means whereby the *Pathet Lao* greatly strengthened its political influence. Prince Souvanna Phouma's age and ill health reduced his role, and Prince Souphanouvong, the leading *Pathet Lao* in the coalition government, assumed the chairmanship of the Political Council. He in effect made it, rather than the National Assembly, the real legislative body. Although the *Pathet Lao* military located themselves in the government areas, non–communists were not allowed to function politically in or even to enter areas held by them. North Vietnamese troops remained in the highlands after the coalition government was formed.

A heart attack suffered by Premier Souvanna Phouma in mid–1974 made things easier for the *Pathet Lao*. The early months of 1975 saw demonstrations by pro–communist elements (students, etc.) in some towns, as well as fighting in remote areas. But the fall of South Vietnam and Cambodia in the spring of 1975 made a *Pathet Lao* takeover inevitable; the right–wing members of the government resigned in May. Soon there was a shift in favor of "hard-line" communism. The monarchy was abolished and a new government was created with Souphanouvong as President. By 1977 the ex–King was under arrest.

In 1976, the political "education" of the

people was widespread, involving several thousand "advisors." A sizable Soviet aid program, including the building of an airfield on the Plain of Jars, was made available. Vietnamese influence was also very great, and their troops remained on Laotian soil. Using "yellow rain" (Soviet-made natural poisons) for a time, they fought Lao insurgents, some of whom were supported by China.

By the mid 1980s the situation had begun to evolve again. At a congress of the ruling *Lao People's Revolutionary Party* held in November 1986, there were some leadership changes, with a tendency toward younger and better trained men rising to the top. The change clearly reflected new attitudes on economic development. The party, in line with developments elsewhere in the communist world, and troubled by the poor state of the Laotian economy, called for better relations with China, Thailand and the U.S., and began to move away from a rigid communist economic system in favor of a more open system along the model of the People's Republic of China and other former hard line communist systems.

Politics and Government

Under the 1991 Constitution, the Lao People's Democratic Republic (LPDR) continues to have a Marxist-Leninist style political system, though in reality its economy is far more open to capitalist style practices. Political power rests with the

Pasason, the central organ of the Lao *People's Revolution Party* (*LPRP*). The party Chairman is Vongphet Xaykeuyachongtoua.

The unicameral Assembly, with 99 members, operates under the principle of democratic centralism, which allows the leadership of the *LPRP* to control the legislative process. Khamtai Siphandon is the LPDR President and the most influential leader of the country. Sisavath Keobounphanh serves as the Prime Minister.

The *LPRP* also controls the electoral process. Candidates for the National Assembly are approved by the *LPRP* and in some cases picked by government departments. Assembly members also receive political training before assuming their responsibilities.

As has been the case in communist countries elsewhere the *LPRP* has moved the country closer to a market economy and away from socialism.

Like their Vietnamese and Chinese neighbors, the Laotian leadership apparently wants economic reform while maintaining their hold on political power. Nevertheless Laos, like so many of the East Asian political systems, may be moving toward an internal confrontation between the demands of an emerging economy and the wishes of an outmoded political leadership.

The *LPRP* maintains firm control—there is no real political opposition in the country. The National Assembly has been trained to avoid politics and tend to other

Laos

matters, including economic development. Nevertheless, during the mid 1990s the political landscape began to change with the passing of 86-year-old Souphanouvong, known as the "Red Prince" and Phoumi Vongvichit, a leader of the *Pathet Lao*, who died in 1994. Virtually all of the founding members of the *LPRP* have now either died or retired and the general trend of Laotian politics has since them moved rather dramatically away from its recent history. In the immediate aftermath of the Asian economic meltdown the most obvious political change in Laos was the lessening influence of more modern technically trained administrators. But that was not the most dramatic of recent changes.

In 1998 a military leader, Khamtai Siphandon, became President and as we have seen the dominant leader of the country. But his promotion is more than a personal gain. Equally important is the recent rise of various generals, who have taken over many of the cabinet portfolios and other key positions. Relative to the party, the army itself appears increasingly powerful. In fact, some have suggested that Laos is moving toward the sort of military government common in Burma and during Suharto's term in Indonesia. And like elsewhere the military has become a major player in Laos' economic development. Dividing the country into three regions, the military has been deeply involved economically in everything from tourism to timber products.

The military may well be the only organization with the skills necessary to administer the process of economic modernization. Nevertheless, their control is hardly likely to allow the sort of vigorous economic growth that a more open system might offer. But given the recent economic failures of so many of Laos' neighbors the attractions of a more open system may seem rather tarnished these days anyway.

In keeping with the National Assembly's emphasis on economic rather than political issues, the principal concern lately has been how to deal with the growing gap between rich and poor which has emerged in recent years as well as with tensions between the nation's different ethnic groups.

Although the general commitment toward market economics has continued, many influential Lao conservatives have also been concerned about their impact on Lao society. Increases in crime have been noted with fears that the reforms may have gone too far. Those concerns were acted upon during 1999 as the government made a conscious effort to emphasize what it called "traditional Lao values" as a counterweight to the growing obsession with making money. Consider-

ing the economic distress that hit the region over the last few years, those that have remained more skeptical about market reforms probably feel vindicated.

Foreign Relations

LPDR foreign policy had a decided "look East" orientation for years. The country has had a long-standing relationship with Vietnam. In 1977 the two countries signed the Treaty of Friendship and Cooperation. The agreement gave the Vietnamese, among other things, the authority to enter Laos whenever it is deemed necessary. Still, the Vietnamese troops were withdrawn from Laos in 1989. Laos is also especially involved with its neighbor to the West, Thailand, which has been a major investor in the Laotian economy. The recently opened Mitraphap bridge spans the Mekong River, and links Vientiane, the capital of Laos, to Nongkhai, Thailand. As the economic significance of this new link increases, the political influence of Bangkok will become stronger. Given Laos' interest in selling the energy from its hydroelectric industry to Thailand, these ties are likely to become even more important over the years, though they are of course dependent on the strength of the Thai economy. And internal Laotian problems

also impact on this important relationship as well as Vientiane has accused Bangkok of allowing anti-government Hmong tribesmen shelter in Thailand.

Relations with the United States have been on relatively good terms in recent years. The two countries have worked together successfully in the areas of refugee repatriation and curbing the production of opium for export. Washington and Vientiane have also worked to resolve the status of Americans missing in action since the Vietnam War. Today, reasons for cooperation are obvious as Laos struggles with decisions about opening the country more and attracting outside investment. There was even talk recently of the U.S. granting Laos "most favored nation" status which would make it much easier for Laos to export her products to the United States. Nevertheless, Laos also has strong ties to the People's Republic and thus Laos-American relations are also tied to the success of Sino-American relations as well.

Laos has also signed an agreement for foreign assistance with North Korea. However, in recent years it seems Laos, despite all its problems, is in a better position to give assistance then receive it from that beleaguered state. The most obvious sign of Laos' emergence from the isolation it long held itself in is its finally

Lane Xang Avenue in Vientiane

Lao Buddhas

becoming an official member of *ASEAN* during the summer of 1997.

As elsewhere in the region the influence of the People's Republic has grown in Laos as well, though that relationship has not always worked out well. China's Yunnan airline recently took a controlling interest in the Lao National Airline, but within a few years relations went bad and Lao Aviation withdrew its cooperation.

Culture and Society

In physical appearance and culture, the Lao are generally and accurately regarded as cousins of the Thai. They are an extremely easygoing people; their country was relatively peaceful in modern times until the turmoil brought about by the Vietnamese revolutionary struggle nearby.

Religious festivals, derived from very old traditions of southern Buddhism which had migrated from the island of Sri

Lanka, are frequent, colorful and very similar to those of Thailand.

Although the government abandoned formal communist economic controls for a more open economic system after 1986, real changes in people's living standards are only just now beginning to be felt. Some wealthy urban dwellers now have the money for cars and TVs, and electricity now reaches 15% of the population. The capital, Vientiane, has itself seen important changes. For example, foreign newspapers are now available along with a new local paper *Vientiane Times*. Laos is now even available on the Internet and has its own e-mail service provider! Nevertheless, 86% of the population still live as subsistence farmers and in a world far beyond Vientiane.

And not surprisingly the growth of recent years is uneven. Half of the people remain at below the World Bank's poverty line. Illiteracy is still very high, and malnutrition is common among children.

Women

The new constitution provides equal rights for women though the traditional culture still favors males. Today women occupy positions of responsibility in business and government and have improved their representation in the latter recently. The government, working through women's organizations, has also moved to educate young women about the dangers of labor recruiters who lure women and girls to the sweatshops and brothels of Thailand. As is frequently the case, the more educated urban women have more opportunities than the majority of the women who live in the countryside where many remain illiterate.

Economy

From the standpoint of economic geography, Laos falls into two clearly divided areas. In the Mekong Valley, agriculture

135

Laos

centered on rice prevails. In the hills, the remote tribesmen sporadically cultivate the poor soils in a migratory fashion. Predictably, the poorly developed infrastructure of roads and other means of communication and transportation around the country holds back development. Like the adjacent highlands of Burma, Thailand and China, the Laotian mountains are among the main opium producing regions of Asia. Most of this narcotic substance is smuggled out by air.

In the years after the communists came to power they enforced a socialist economic system but by the mid 1980s that system began to be modified. The People's Democratic Republic (*LPDR*) launched the New Economic Mechanism (NEM) in 1986, in an attempt to modernize the country's economy. Since 1990, reforms include the introduction of a new accounting system for production and domestic trade, assigning a permanent staff to monitor budgetary revenue, creation of central banking laws, and the integration of official and parallel exchange rates. More recently serious efforts have begun to train civil servants in English so they can more easily work with their counterparts in *ASEAN*.

Foreign investment regulations were also liberalized in 1989 and again in 1994. In fact, Laos now has one of the most liberal environments for foreign investment in Asia.

In 1994–1995, the country attracted significant foreign investment for the development of hydroelectric power. The second largest sector for investment is tourism, followed by mining and manufacturing, including clothing. One of the hydroelectric projects will be built by an Australian concern and will be the world's second highest concrete-faced, rock-filled dam. The government plan has been to sell much of the newly generated power to Thailand.

Between 1990 and 1996, the economy averaged 6.5% growth. Unfortunately, that growth was uneven with poorer production in the agricultural sector. Inflation has also been high in relation to the growth rates of recent years. Laos still remains among the poorest countries in the world with a per capita income well under $400 and a life expectancy of only fifty years.

Considering the limited state of its involvement in the larger international economic community, Laos was initially somewhat less vulnerable to the economic crisis of 1997. Nevertheless, given how tied her economy was to that of Thailand, she too has been badly hurt by the dramatic fall in Thai economic vitality. And within Laos itself poor economic policies as well as a major problem with the state owned banking sector has made the situation even worse. Foreign investment has dropped from a high of $1.2 billion in 1995 to far lower figures over the last year. Still, the effort to attract outside income goes on. The country's first casino is now up and running hoping to attract gamblers with Thai Baht to spend! Over the last year there has finally been some cause for optimism as the economy has started to improve somewhat and tourism, often an important revenue source in Southeast Asia, has begun to pick up. Nevertheless Laos, like the rest of the region, will have to face the future knowing that the world financial community is no longer quite as enthusiastic about the region as it once was.

The Future

Though Laos faces many challenges, the future is still reasonably bright. Relations with Thailand have improved with the signing of a Treaty of Amity and Cooperation in early 1992. Laos is now a member of ASEAN and likely to benefit from those improved ties. The government acceded to the organization's Treaty of Amity and Cooperation in July 1992. Laos is also attempting to broaden its relations by strengthening links with other countries, especially of late, the People's Republic of China and Vietnam. If the entire region continues its slow climb out of the 1997 Asian economic collapse, Laos will be part of that growth and gain from it.

Transplanting rice, Laos

Malaysia

The modern skyline of Kuala Lumpur

Courtesy: Embassy of Malaysia

Area: 128,775 square miles.

Population: 21 million (estimated).

Capital City: Kuala Lumpur (Pop. 1.2 million, estimated).

Climate: Tropically hot and humid.

Neighboring Countries: Thailand (North); Singapore (South); Indonesia (South and Southwest).

Official Languages: Malay and English.

Other Principal Tongues: Chinese, Tamil.

Ethnic Background: Malay (about 48%); Chinese (about 36%); Indian (9%) plus other indigenous peoples' languages.

Principal Religions: Islam, Buddhism, Hinduism, Christianity.

Main Exports (to Japan, Singapore, U.S.): Natural rubber, palm oil, tin, timber, petroleum.

Main Imports (from Japan, U.S.): Machinery and transportation equipment.

Currency: Ringgit.

Former Colonial Status: British commercial interests acquired the islands of Penang in 1786 and port city of Melaka in 1824. The various states of Malaya entered into protectorate status from 1874 to 1914; they remained British colonies or protectorates until 1957 with the exception of the Japanese occupation from 1942 to 1945. Sabah was administered by the British North Borneo Company from 1881 to 1941, occupied by the Japanese from 1942 until 1945 and was a British Colony from 1946 to 1963. Sarawak was granted to Sir James Brooke by the Sultan of Brunei in 1841; it became a British protectorate in 1888; after the Japanese were expelled in 1945, Sir Charles Vyner Brooke, the ruling Raja, agreed to administration as a British Crown Colony, which lasted until 1963.

National Day: August 31st.

Chief of State: His Majesty Sultan Salahuddin Abdul Aziz Shah Alhaj (Sultan of Selangor), Yang di–Pertuan Agong, meaning King, or Supreme Head of Malaysia.

Head of Government: Dato' Seri Dr. Mahathir Mohamad, Prime Minister.

National Flag: Fourteen horizontal stripes of red and white with a dark blue rectangle in the upper left corner containing a yellow crescent and a 14–pointed star.

Per Capita GNP Annual Income: U.S. $4,370.

Located at the southern end of the Malay Peninsula, the mainland portion of Malaysia consists of a broad central belt of forested mountains. In the areas of Malaysia where the mountains give way to low plains the vegetation turns into a thick green jungle situated on swampy plains, particularly in the coastal area. The climate is uniform during the year because of the closeness to the equator—hot and humid.

The Borneo states, also known as East Malaysia, contain wide coastal lowlands which have basically poor soil and are interrupted by frequent rivers. The altitude rises in the South as the border with Indonesia is approached. The division between the two occupants of the island straddles a scenic range of rugged mountains the highest of which is Mt. Kinabalu, towering majestically to a height of 13,000 feet. Few people of the western world have penetrated Borneo to view this remote area, which is inhabited by an indigenous people who have advanced little beyond Stone Age life. The people of Malaysia are quite similar to their Indonesian neighbors—a mixture of Polynesian, Mongol, Indian and Caucasian origins. There is also a large minority of Chinese who are descendants of laborers brought in by the colonial British.

History

The history of Malaysia, as a country, really begins during the colonial period, when the British started to establish their holdings in the area. Before that, the various regions that today are associated with Malaysia were part of several different political communities ranging from the mainland based Siamese kingdom to the north to the various commercial empires in what later became Indonesia.

The Malay language was prominent enough in the region's early life to have had it serve as the principal language for commercial activities until the early modern era. In fact, throughout the region, regardless of a person's ethnicity, a knowledge of Malay was absolutely necessary to take part in the international trade of the region.

Malaya would probably have been colonized sooner than it was if the Dutch had

Malaysia

not focused their attention on the fabled riches of Indonesia. The colonial history of both nations is very similar. The absence of Dutch control permitted the British to enter the area without opposition. In order to protect their trade routes the British compelled the rulers of the small individual states of Malaya to accept "protection." This included the presence of a British advisor at each Malay court to insure that British goals were achieved. Four outlying, impoverished states of Siam (Thailand) in the North, were added to Malaya in 1909.

The rubber tree was brought from Brazil and planted in the rich soil to grow in an almost ideal climate. Drawn by the natural resources and the stability of the area, British capital poured in. There was also a mass influx of Chinese and Indian laborers to work the rubber plantations and the tin mines. In many cases these Chinese soon entered commerce and some became extremely wealthy and influential.

The arrival of immigrants from China and India created the ethnic mix which has been the most fundamental feature of modern Malaysian social and political life, the tripartite division of the population between native Malays who constitute around half the population and the Chinese and Indian communities who make up very significant minorities. In fact the Chinese, in contrast to their numbers which usually average around 10% throughout the region, make up closer to 40% of the population in Malaysia.

During the British rule the later "division of labor" also began to appear as Chinese moved into the economy with the Malays largely remaining less urbanized or in some cases becoming part of the British civil administration of the area. The British often favored the Malays, often at

**His Majesty
The Yang di-Pertuan Agong**

**Her Majesty
The Raja Permaisuri Agong**

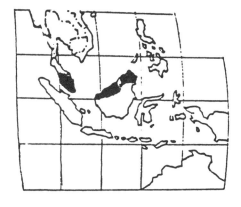

the expense of the Chinese, a preference that more recent Malaysian governments have also followed. More importantly, British rule not only saw the evolution of the region from one that was relatively homogeneous to the more multi–ethnic society of modern Malaysia. As elsewhere British policy was to retain its authority by "divide and rule" processes which have certainly contributed to the problems which have affected Malaysia in later years.

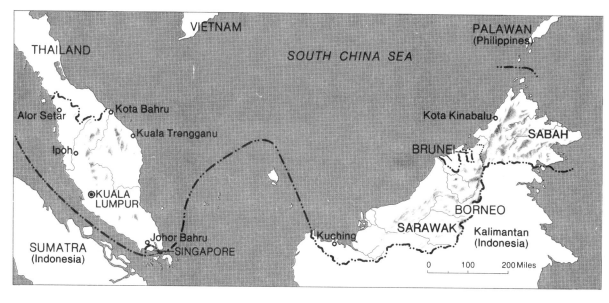

World War II

When the Japanese arrived in 1942, they treated the Chinese with much greater brutality than they did the Malays. In reaction, the local Chinese, whose own politics were more tied to developments within China itself, developed an anti–Japanese guerrilla force of Chinese, most of them communists, which operated from bases deep within the thick jungles. Receiving weapons smuggled in by the British, the guerrillas fought their non–communist rivals as well as the Japanese. In contrast to the Chinese community, there was some sympathy among Malayans for the Japanese activities. That is not very surprising considering that many people in Southeast Asia had been attracted to the Japanese calls to free the region from Western colonialism. That the Chinese themselves, well aware of the atrocities the Japanese had committed in China, did not view Japan's forces so positively is hardly surprising!

After the war, the British moved to unify the various regions which would later come to form modern Malaysia. A major problem though was the indigenous Malay concerns about maintaining their own dominance in a future independent Malay state. The eventual compromise offered freedom within a constitutional structure which included clear support for the traditional Malay leaders, the recognition of Malay and Islam as the official language and religion respectively, and an overall structure that clearly favored the Malay over non–Malay peoples.

The arrangement as it was called included an understanding that while the Malays would dominate politics, the economy would be dominated by the non–Malay citizens. Nevertheless, not all members of the Chinese community were happy with the agreement, and for the next decade a major insurrection developed led by local Chinese communists who had earlier been active in the resistance against the Japanese. While the entire period, known as "The Emergency," was very traumatic for the region, the rebellion was never able to draw much popular support and especially not from the Malay community itself. The British mounted a huge military effort which reduced the rebellion to almost nothing within a few years.

A New Nation Emerges: 1957

The British granted Malaya internal self–government in 1955, and full independence in 1957. Under the able leadership of Prime Minister Tunku Abdul Rahman, head of the dominant *Alliance Party*, (now known as *the National Front*) which

included then and now, a dominant Malay party known as the *United Malay National Organization (UMNO)* as well as other parties representing the Chinese and Indian communities. *UMNO*, which has dominated Malaysian political life ever since, originally emerged as a reaction to British efforts to grant more rights to non–Malays. The party has not in the years since, lessened its commitment to strengthening the position of Malay peoples within modern Malaysia. As we will see below, *UMNO* has dramatically improved the social and economic standing of the average Malay citizens but tensions over such favoritism continue to plague the country.

By the early 1960s Malaysia's chief problem, though, was not over indigenous ethnic tensions but with their immediate neighbors, especially with Sukarno,

**The Prime Minister
Dato Seri Dr. Mahathir Mohamed**

the fiery nationalist leader of Indonesia. Faced with Sukarno's increased interest in dominating the region, and a marked swing to the left in Singapore politics, Rahman and the British devised a plan to unite Malaya, Singapore, Sabah and Sarawak into the Federation of Malaysia. (The tiny, oil–rich Sultanate of Brunei was also invited to join, but declined). After many complicated negotiations the federation came into existence in September 1963.

Sukarno in Indonesia, encouraged by his success in acquiring West Irian, (now Irian Jaya) from the Dutch without a fight, was furious about the federation's formation. A "confrontation" with Malaysia was started, which involved sporadic fighting in the remote parts of Borneo, and unsuccessful attempts to land Indonesian guerrillas in Malaya. The "confrontation" was quietly discontinued in the mid–1960s af-

ter General Suharto seized power from Sukarno.

The new Malaysian Federation faced significant domestic problems as well. There was continuing tension between the Chinese and Malays, especially over the role of Singapore, whose population is overwhelmingly Chinese, and which resented Malay domination of the central government. When Prime Minister Lee Kuan Yew of Singapore engaged in efforts to increase his party's influence and power beyond Singapore and within the Malaysian Federation at large, a crisis erupted which led to the expulsion of Singapore from Malaysia in August 1965.

A Challenge to the System

But if Singapore's expulsion from the federation only two years after its formation had lessened tensions between Kuala Lumpur and Singapore, the core issues of Malay, non–Malay relations continued. As will be recalled, the compromise of the late 1940s has seen emerge a political system which favored ethnic Malays while allowing the non–Malays to dominate the economy. But the elections of 1969 challenged that arrangement.

In the years leading up to 1969 the Malay political leadership had been able to successfully dominate the country's political system. But the elections of 1969 challenged the political and economic compromise which had been at the root of the new nation's stability. In the elections non–Malay parties won more votes than those of the Malay allies. While no dramatic change in government direction was immediately in the offing, it clearly aroused the concerns of the Malay population and hundreds died in the resulting communal violence.

This led the government to proclaim a state of emergency and to suspend the constitution; parliamentary government was, however, restored in early 1971. In the following years the government committed itself to a major effort to improving the status of Malays, economically and socially. The hope was that if Malays were more integrated into the economic life of the community there would be less cause for the sort of social tensions that so commonly existed.

In the general elections of 1974 the *National Front* (the *Alliance Party* plus some smaller ones) won a sweeping victory. During the elections, strong precautions were taken to avoid the violence of 1969. In fact, to preserve social peace it became literally illegal to even discuss the issues which separated the different ethnic communities or the various programs designed to promote the economic life of the Malays.

Malaysia

A Hindu wedding in Kuala Lumpur

Photo by Jon Markham Morrow

A New Voice for Asia

In the mid 1970s a new political activist emerged who would eventually dominate Malaysian politics over the next generation. First chosen as Prime Minister in 1981 Dr. Mahathir Mohamad, a physician by training, was the first non–aristocrat to become first minister and a man whose political views have led him, along with Singapore's Lee Kuan Yew, to be seen as one of the most articulate spokesmen for an "Asian Voice" in world affairs.

Mahathir originally gained public attention with a series of articles and then a book dealing with what he called the *Malay Dilemma*, which dealt with what he described as the second class status of Malays. A fervent nationalist, who wrote in English and even addressed such controversial subjects as the emancipation of women, his work was banned by the authorities when it came out in 1970. For a time he even had to go into hiding from the authorities for his outspoken comments against the leadership.

But given his support among younger Malays he was eventually invited back into *UMNO* and by the mid 1970s began his assent toward the premiership. In the years since, Dr. Mahathir has become one of the most outspoken leaders of his generation and a frequent and regular critic of the West even as he has successfully worked to integrate Malaysia itself into the modern industrialized world economy. In fact, Mahathir, along with Vice President Gore of the United States, are probably among the most committed and involved world leaders in the use of the Internet. He even has his own web site!

In the years after his arrival to power Mahathir managed to grow increasingly influential. He has consistently prevailed over his opponents within his own party, *UMNO,* and over other centers of power within Malaysia.

The Mahathir government has even over the years tried to curb the constitutional powers of the various Malay Sultans. In January 1984 it was successful in abolishing the Yang di–Pertuan Agong's power to veto legislation.

Several political problems of fairly serious proportions appeared in the last decade. One was leadership struggles within both the main components of the ruling coalition which governs the country: the dominant *United Malay National Organization (UMNO),* and the less powerful *Malayan Chinese Association (MCA).* The sec-

PENINSULAR MALAYSIA
The nine states with hereditary rulers, and Penang and Malacca

ond was a rise in the activity of militant Islam, especially among the 20,000 Malaysian students in the United States and in Sabah (North Borneo), where there were violent Muslim demonstrations early in 1986 against the state government.

There were serious tensions within *UMNO* in 1987, reflecting a leadership struggle, a generational gap and a growing feeling that the party was strong enough to govern without the inconvenience of a coalition with other parties representing different races. Prime Minister Mahathir won a close vote for the party leadership in April and then purged some of his rivals. The relatively passive *Malayan Chinese Association* was troubled not only by a leadership problem, but also by a challenge from outside the National Front by the *Democratic Action Party (DAP),* a younger and more vigorous party.

The government cracked down on opponents of several types in October 1987, some of them *UMNO* members, but more of them belonging to the *DAP,* in a series of sudden arrests which were strongly criticized within and outside the country.

In a shocking ruling a judge held in February 1988 that because of structural problems at the regional level, *UMNO* was an illegal organization. This was a bizarre conclusion that had the main effect of intensifying the power struggle within the party. Mahathir, responding quickly, reorganized *UMNO* on a "legal" basis and strengthened his hold on it, and on the country.

Prime Minister Mahathir had long admired the economic dynamism of Japan and South Korea and has sought to use them as models for Malaysia, though given their recent weaknesses, they no longer seem to hold the keys to success that some once felt they did.

Overall, Mahathir has emphasized a "Asian" approach to economic issues. He has spoken enthusiastically of an economic organization (the East Asian Economic Grouping) that would include the ASEAN states, China, South Korea, Taiwan, Hong Kong, and Japan, but would exclude everyone else, especially the United States. During the most recent economic problems it was Mahathir who was most ready to suggest regional solutions to the area's problems from the use of local currencies for trading to a regional equivalent of the International Monetary Fund.

Not surprisingly, Dr. Mahathir's ideas have not usually been well received in either Australia or the United States nor even among his Asian economic partners. Nevertheless, he himself has often been increasingly admired as an outspoken voice for the "non-Western" and specifi-

Malaysia

Parliament House, Kuala Lumpur

cally Asian communities well beyond Malaysia itself.

Contemporary Politics

Malaysia, a member of the British Commonwealth, is a parliamentary democracy with a bi-cameral legislature composed of the Senate, Dewan Negara; and House of Representatives, Dewan Ra'ayat. The parliament in Malaysia is not an effective institution for the discussion of public policy. The opposition has limited time to speak and often receives bills for consideration the same day on which they are to be voted. The Standing Order of Parliament prohibits treasonable or seditious words, the interpretation of which is left up to the Speaker of the Dewan Ra'ayat who is appointed by the government (Prime Minister).

Certain topics such as the special rights of Malays are not subject to discussion. Tough questioning by the opposition is rare and would not be widely reported in the media in any case since it is either owned or licensed by the government. Overall, the Prime Ministership under Mahathir has evolved into a particularly powerful position.

The country has a very unusual system for selecting the Yang di-pertuan Agong (King). The Yang di-pertuan Agong serves for five years and is selected on a rotational basis from among the hereditary rulers from nine of Malaysia's 13 states.

Elections in Malaysia have generally been clean, unlike those in many other developing countries. The single-member district formula benefits the government as does the fact that districts are often gerrymandered to favor the Malay voter.

Until recently, although important opposition parties existed, Malaysian politics was dominated by the Malay-dominated *United Malay National Organization (UMNO)* which ruled in coalition with other small parties. In practical terms, really significant political issues and the fate of individual governmental leaders was determined more within the political struggles of *UMNO* itself rather than between *UMNO* and her coalition partners.

One of the most significant issues of the 1990s was the question of who would assume the mantle of Prime Minister Mahathir's authority after the long dominant leader leaves the scene.

The most significant effort to answer that question began in November 1993

when the *United Malay National Organization (UMNO)* was involved in selecting a deputy president. This post, within Malaysia's dominant political party, was tantamount to a guarantee of gaining the post of deputy prime minister, and eventually the prime ministership. The contest involved the Minister of Finance, Anwar Ibrahim, and the then Deputy Prime Minister, Ghafar Baba. The Prime Minister, Mahathir Mohamad, seemed to prefer Ghafar Baba, but Anwar won a decisive victory.

Thus on December 1, 1993, the prime minister appointed Anwar Ibrahim as deputy prime minister. Thus began a complicated relationship which has seen Anwar over the years become the most obvious heir to Mahathir's leadership and then later the powerful prime minister's most implacable opponent. Over the years the strong minded Mahathir showed confidence in Anwar but there were also frequent signs that the relationship was a very complicated one.

For example relations with the more activist Islamic community have often been problematic. One significant challenge for the government in recent years came from the radical Islamic group, *Al-Arqam*. The sect was eventually banned by the government which had become fearful when it learned that the *Al-Arqam* was successfully recruiting among the Malay middle class. As many as 7,000 civil servants may have joined the movement. *Al-Arqam* operated 257 schools and many businesses throughout the country.

As with other issues, the style of Dr. Mahathir and Anwar differed. The Prime Minister has at times seemed to go out of his way to challenge conservative Muslims by suggesting that a too rigid adherence to Islam might impede economic growth. Interestingly the question of whether one wears a beard or not has became an important issue in measuring the growth of Islamic influence on party politics. Here again, Anwar, a former Muslim activist, wears a very discrete goatee, while Mahathir goes clean shaven. A subtle difference but one that carries considerable symbolism. The issue is reflected as well in the clothing choices of their wives. Mrs. Mahathir wears her hair uncovered while Anwar's wife covers her head in public.

Until recently Mahathir's leadership had been largely unquestioned. Nevertheless, in October 1996, the party's convention saw very real competition between followers of the Prime Minister and Anwar Ibrahim. For a time it even looked like Anwar's supporters were pulling ahead of those of Mahathir, but that was only temporary. By the time the polling had been completed a balance had been maintained between the two groups and Mahathir's power to sway his party's loyalists again confirmed.

Malaysia

Then the following year, as the full brunt of the economic crises hit Malaysia, the long outspoken Mahathir lashed out at those he felt had brought on the crisis. His primary target was international currency traders and while many perhaps more objective economists have come to the same conclusion, Mahathir's comments, especially his coupling them with suggestions about controlling the financial markets with new laws seemed only to make the situation worse. Fear that such laws might hamper international currency movement caused Malaysia's currency to drop even further. Meanwhile provoked by the worsening situation Anwar stepped forward to calm the markets by denying any such plans. Anwar was wrong. Mahathir not only introduced controls on some currency and stock exchanges but also imposed price controls on a limited number of commodities as well. As for his long time deputy, while Anwar's monetary policies as the nation's long time finance minister had put him largely within the range of international opinion on economic decision-making, they contrasted dramatically with those of his boss Prime Minister Mahathir.

Thus over the summer of 1998 it was clear that behind the scenes the Prime Minister was moving against Anwar's supporters including important members of the media. By early September the strong minded leader had driven his most important financial advisers from power including his long time heir, Finance Minister and Deputy Prime Minister, Anwar Ibrahim.

In fact over the next week Anwar found himself not only imprisoned, but beaten by his jailers and charged with an enormous range of sexual offenses and charges of corruption. The arrest and subsequent conviction of Anwar on charges of corruption sparked considerable international media attention and inspired large pro-Anwar demonstrations throughout Malaysia. And while Prime Minister Mahathir seemed still able to control the situation, many of the most acute observers began to believe that the entire struggle had dramatically lessened his influence and perhaps shortened his tenure in power.

Those observations proved more debatable when the results of Malaysia's tenth general elections were announced last year. At least in the short run the election results showed Mahathir's ruling National Front Coalition doing quite well—winning 148 seats of a possible 193. Nevertheless, it was clear that significant problems were brewing below the surface. For the first time most Malay voters voted against Mahathir's own UMNO organization. In fact, Mahathir's larger coalition had largely won due to the support of Indian and Chinese voters some of whom were apparently nervous about the influence of Islamic groups among the opposition. Prime Minister Mahathir, himself, will now have to rely on his non-Malay coalition partners far more than he has had to in the past. Obviously the days when controlling UMNO meant controlling Malaysia appear to be drawing to a close, and the struggle between Mahathir and his long time deputy Anwar Ibrahim had much to do with the transformation.

Foreign Relations

Malaysia has been an effective actor in international politics for some time. In fact, Malaysia has increasingly taken the liberty of speaking for the developing countries in the world community and particularly in international forums like APEC and the WTO. For years, Malaysia, along with Singapore, have emerged as the most effective representatives of an Asian vision for the future and one which was strongly backed by the economic accomplishments of both regimes over the last generation. More recently the government has also moved to strengthen its ties to the People's Republic of China.

Malaysia also maintains strong ties with the Islamic countries of the Middle East but has also officially attempted to improve relations with Israel. On a more practical level, that has not always been easy. A visiting Israeli cricket team was greeted with major protests during its spring 1997 visit to this heavily Muslim country.

Curiously, the Prime Minister seems at times to have gone out of his way to arouse the concerns of many in the United States, the last superpower and an important Malaysian market. Not only did he charge that Western financial speculators had caused the economic meltdown, but went on to make charges that Jews were somehow behind the attack against Muslim countries like Indonesia and Malaysia. And if that were not enough to arouse the ire of many in Washington, he subsequently led a large entourage to Cuba to encourage trade with the Castro regime!

The Americans returned the "compliment" when U.S. Vice President Albert Gore chose the fall 1998 meeting of APEC, which took place in Kuala Lumpur, to denounce the Malaysian government's treatment of Anwar Ibrahim and to speak favorably of those who were demonstrating in his favor. Though some might have wondered if the Americans were more upset about Mahathir's anti-democratic activities or his effort to impose currency controls! In either case, having Gore act as

if Anwar were a hero not unexpectedly turned to the Prime Minister's advantage as many Malaysians clearly resented the American interference. But Gore was not the only world leader to be critical. There was a considerable amount of criticism over the Anwar affair regionally as officials from Indonesia to the Philippines made negative comments.

Other issues also affected regional relations. Disputes continue over the many islands that dot the area. The disagreement with Indonesia over Sipadan and Ligitan islands off the coast of Sabah, East Malaysia, remained causes of concern during the 1990s. The dispute over Pulau Batu Putih ("White Rock Island") with Singapore was referred to The Hague by mutual agreement. The claims and counter claims continue throughout the region. For example, China, Malaysia and four other countries claim all or part of the South China Sea and the Spratley Islands.

Malaysia has agreed to purchase 18 Russian MIG19's for $500 million thus becoming the first non-communist state in Southeast Asia to operate Russian military equipment. India will train Malaysian pilots and technicians as part of the deal and Russia will set up a technical service center in Malaysia. Malaysia previously agreed to purchase F18's from the United States. Some analysts have wondered about the wisdom of purchasing two totally different fighter aircraft for a relatively small defense force.

In general, the last few years have been relatively successful for Malaysian foreign relations especially with respect to ASEAN. Singapore and Malaysia came to a permanent agreement on their territorial waters boundary. They also reached agreement over Malaysian restrictions of the importation of Singaporan petro-chemicals. Still as often in the past, issues such as water can make relations between Singapore and Kuala Lumpur complicated. Relations with the Philippines and Thailand also improved somewhat. The promising idea of a Malaysia-Indonesia-Thailand northern growth triangle was still on track (Singapore-Malaysia and Indonesia have been highly successful with the "first triangle" which encourages free trade and makes special concessions to attract foreign businesses).

Most recently Prime Minister Mahathir was particularly incensed by the United Nation's decision to have Australia lead the peace keeping force sent to East Timor in the aftermath of the August 1999 referendum there. Mahathir had not opposed the necessity of intervention but made it abundantly clear that he felt it would have been better if the entire force came from Indonesia's Asian neighbors.

Society and Culture

Malaysia's population is very young—about 45% are under the age of 15! A high percentage of the people are literate; primary and secondary school education is provided for all, and there are a number of colleges and five universities. Although Islam is the State religion and Muslims enjoy certain special privileges by law, there is complete freedom of worship for other faiths.

Malaysians are also great sports enthusiasts, and although more traditional ball game forms have dominated in the past, soccer is now the nation's most popular pastime. There is also tremendous interest in horse-racing as seen by the country's five first-rate turf clubs.

The majority of the Malay community used to live in a fairly traditional manner, principally engaged in farming and fishing, but modern Malays are increasingly entering the trading, professional and other sectors of the modern economy. Today, Malaysia has a significant Malay middle and upper-middle class. There are also a significant number of very wealthy Malays, some of whom have made fortunes by having access to lucrative government contracts. With the exception of Singapore, Malaysia also has the highest percentage of Chinese found in Southeast Asia. The community is divided into several linguistic groups which reflect the origins of their ancestors who migrated from China, they tend to remain apart except in economic activity—they dominate in the business community. Many educated Chinese, particularly among the younger generation, learn English and Malay. The more educated Malays usually speak English.

Despite the recent crises the impact of sustained economic growth over the last generation remains very visible. Longer life, improved health care, a significant increase in the number of people owning telephones, and an expanding national highway system were all indicators of the country's economic success over the last decade. Sadly, one effect of the recent economic problems is the reduction of the number of Malaysian families able to send their children abroad for higher education. And while staying at home to save money might be a logical option, Malaysian universities have not been able to accommodate the larger numbers of potential students.

Women

In Malaysia, Muslim women are subject to Islamic legal codes. In contrast, non-Muslim women are subject to the more secular civil code. For Muslim women that means that practices such as polygamy are allowed. On a practical basis of course the situation is more complicated. While at least one Malay state has made it somewhat easier for a man to meet the requirements to take more than one wife (not, for example, having to gain the first wife's permission) Prime Minister Mahathir has made it clear he disapproves of the practice as have other national leaders elsewhere in the region. Mrs. Mahathir won't even welcome second wives into her home! And Dr. Mahathir's daughter has also made her opinions known. The prime minister's daughter, Marina Mahathir has emerged as a well known AIDS activist and human rights and democracy advocate. She has also spoken out against a too strong emphasis on Islam in Malaysian life. Nevertheless, Islamic domestic law is employed and it favors males in matters of inheritance, but its application in Malaysia has varied from that practiced elsewhere. In fact, in 1989 the Islamic Family law was revised to give Muslim Malaysian women more rights in such personal matters as divorce. Nevertheless, in some regions, where Islamic parties have been influential, in Kelantan, for example, their rights have been lessening lately.

Looking at today's Malaysia, women are still under-represented in decision making positions and their role in the professions is only recently growing. Happily, as has been the case so often elsewhere, the next generation of Malaysian women seems well situated to gain more control over their lives than women of earlier generations. Today's civil law gives them equal rights in work and education and today they are well represented among university student ranks. Women have served in cabinet level positions and they represent between 6 & 7% of those who serve in the various regional and national legislatures.

Rural life, Penang

Malaysia

Economy

Until the economic crash of 1997, Malaysia had one of the strongest and fastest growing economies in the Asia-Pacific region. Many expected Malaysia to become the "fifth tiger," joining Hong Kong, Singapore, South Korea, and Taiwan in the developed country ranks. Under Dr. Mahathir, the country had even developed enormously ambitious plans from the erection of the world's tallest building to hopes of turning Malaysia into a center for world telecommunications. The Malaysian national development plan had called for the country to achieve fully developed status by 2020. Under an earlier economic policy, the government was able to substantially raise the level of Malay (rather than Chinese) participation in the non-agricultural sectors of the economy. Although the precise goals were not achieved by the target date, the success of the policy was such that Prime Minister Mahathir was able to announce that there was no longer a need to stress the fulfillment of targets or quotas for specific ethnic groups.

When 1997's economic crises hit, Malaysia suffered the same fate as so many of her neighbors. Her currency value dropped dramatically as did the local stock market. Initially, the government seemed confident it could manage the crises and unlike so many of her neighbors, Malaysia chose to confront the economic crises without borrowing funds from the International Monetary Fund. Given how strongly Malaysia's leadership has felt about the continuing Western influence within the world's financial institutions such as the IMF and the World Bank, this was a fairly predictable decision. Nevertheless, the initially optimistic financial projections of the government were not working out. 1998 saw a real decline of 7.5%.

To response to the deteriorating situation, the government finally decided to cut its budget by a fifth and delayed some large infrastructure projects like the 550 million dollar monorail system that had been planned for Kuala Lumpur. By the fall of 1998 Mahathir, as we have seen, had decided to go much further. Defying the international trend toward greater economic liberalization, he decided to impose controls against the trading of Malaysian currency or stocks outside the country. His goal of course was to shield the country from the sort of outside financial speculation he deeply believed caused the crisis in the first place. The problem is that such a move can also end any hopes for outside investment—something most countries have felt necessary to help growth. As we have seen, the

Early morning fishing

move caused enormous and immediate political problems for the prime minister.

Despite the controversy, economic and political, Malaysia's economy in the following months did respond favorably. Although it was not clear if Malaysia's economy started to recover because of or despite the financial controls Dr. Mahathir imposed—improve they did. Early 2000 has seen reports of significant growth once again and interest rates have fallen. Overall confidence seemed to be returning as Malaysia entered the new century. Still Malaysia's leaders could not rest on their laurels.

Like the rest of the region, environmental problems are also increasingly plaguing the country. The Science, Technology and Environment Ministry reported in late 1995 that two out of three rivers in Malaysia were polluted and that those unpolluted (28%) were deteriorating fast as a consequence of industrial waste. It was estimated that 7 million fish died off the coast of Perak state from exposure to potassium cyanide. Malaysia was not scheduled to have a treatment

plant capable of handling toxic waste in operation until 1998.

Another problem, which one finds throughout the region is deforestation. A shocking estimate is that by 2005, the rain forest in the East Malaysia state of Sabah will have no marketable timber left. Native peoples are losing their lands to greedy state politicians and Japanese plywood manufacturers.

It will also have to continue to make progress on the social/economic front. One third of Kuala Lumpur's people still live in slums and the country is producing too few technically trained college graduates to keep up with the demands of the economy.

The Future

Given the election results it is clear that it will be some time before the damage done by the "Anwar Affair" is repaired. Nevertheless, for the moment, the economy is doing well and Malaysia and its long time leader Dr. Mahathir Mohamad have considerable reason to be satisfied.

Shipping at Port Moresby

Photo by Ray Witlin

Area: 178,260 sq. mi. (475,369 sq. km., somewhat larger than California).

Population: 4,705,000 (1999 estimate)

Capital City: Port Moresby (Pop. 193,000 1991 estimate).

Climate: Tropical.

Neighboring Countries: Australia (South); Indonesia (West).

Official Language: English.

Other Principal Tongues: There are over 800 indigenous languages, and a pidgin English is spoken in much of the country.

Ethnic Background: Mostly Melanesian and Papuan, with a small minority of Australians and Europeans.

Principal Religion: Traditional tribal beliefs, with an overlay of Christianity.

Main Exports (to Japan, Germany, Australia): oil, copper, gold, timber, coffee, rubber and other tropical products.

Main Imports (from Australia, Japan, Singapore): Machinery, consumer goods.

Currency: Kina.

Former Colonial Status: Until 1975, a United Nations trusteeship administered by Australia.

National Day: September 16, 1975.

Chief of State: Her Majesty Queen Elizabeth II, represented by Governor–General Sir Silas Atopare.

Head of Government: Sir Mekere Morauta, Prime Minister (since July 14, 1999).

National Flag: Divided diagonally from top left to bottom right, the top a red field upon which is centered a yellow bird of paradise, the bottom a black field showing five white stars in the Southern Cross.

GNP Per Capita GDP: U.S. $1,150.

Occupying the eastern half of the large island of New Guinea, the western portion—*Irian Jaya*—being part of Indonesia, the nation was formed from Papua, the southeastern quarter of the island and the Territory of New Guinea, the northeastern quarter plus the nearby Admiralty, northern Solomon and Bismarck island groups.

The terrain is covered largely with very high mountains, swamps and jungles. The climate is uniformly tropical except in the more temperate altitudes of the mountains. There is an extremely small European minority; the indigenous inhabitants belong either to the Papuan group (on New Guinea) or to the Melanesian people (on the islands).

History

Prior to the late 19th century, apart from missionaries, New Guinea attracted two main types of Europeans: explorers and investors, lured by its supposedly substantial mineral resources. Dutch influence based on Indonesia became dominant in western New Guinea. The northeastern part of the big island and the smaller islands to the east were annexed by Germany in 1884. The southeastern part of the island known as Papua was placed under British protection in the same year, during the greedy scramble for colonial possessions that was then underway worldwide. Britain soon changed its policy toward Papua to a less possessive one and later transferred the area to Australia.

The German holdings in northeastern New Guinea and the nearby islands were seized by Australia during World War I and then were awarded to it under a League of Nations mandate which after World War II became a United Nations trusteeship.

In reality, Australia administered the entire dependency until 1974 from Port Moresby without regard to the legal distinction between the status of Papua, a direct Australian dependency, and New Guinea, the trusteeship.

In 1942 the Japanese conquered the islands east of New Guinea and invaded parts of the large island itself, including both of the eastern regions. Some of the bitterest fighting of the Pacific war occurred during the next two years as Australian and American forces drove the Japanese out of all but a few strongholds. Following the end of the war, Australian civil administration was restored. In response to UN criticism and a growing de-

Papua New Guinea

mand for self–government, an elected assembly was established in 1968.

In elections in 1972 to the House of Assembly (the parliament), the *National Coalition*, led by Michael Somare was victorious. His program, which called for full self–government in 1973, was accepted by Australia soon afterward, even though it was opposed by many of the European inhabitants who were understandably concerned about the changing political environment.

Politics and Government

The political system of Papua New Guinea is a federally based parliamentary system that offers universal suffrage for its citizens. The judiciary is independent from the executive branch of the government. Unfortunately, though democracy has been successfully maintained, too little has been accomplished in terms of the daily living standards of PNG citizens in the decades since full independence.

The vast majority of the population (around 85%) still lives at a subsistence level in isolated villages. Little headway has been made in developing the more industrial sectors of the economy or helping the villagers compete in the world agricultural market. More recently, things have actually weakened still further due to drought conditions caused by the famous El Nino phenomenon which caused the worst drought of the century and even more recently a devastating series of tidal waves that killed over two thousand people in July of 1998. Especially damaging until recently was the struggle over the island of Bougainville.

In fact, the bloody struggle there led to an especially dramatic crisis in PNG's governing system. In addition to the almost decade long revolt on Bougainville Island, the government has also been dealing with independence demands from the New Guinea Islands.

A major governmental reform was recently undertaken which resulted in the elimination of the country's nineteen provincial parliaments. Non-paid local government officials along with the national parliamentary representatives formed local assemblies. They took the place of some 600 paid politicians who composed the provincial parliaments. The MPs in the new assemblies with the largest representation became Governors. They are to be the primary link between the local assemblies and the capital. The move may also have some impact on the unstable political party system, where new parties appear frequently, and where members shift from one party to another regularly.

In spite of the severe economic problems and demands by the World Bank for reform, former Prime Minister Chan, who came into power in 1994, was able to keep as a part of the national budget $250,000 for each of the country's 109 parliamentarians which they could spend as they pleased for their constituents. Initially Prime Minister Chan appeared to be in firm control of the government but lost support for having made a very questionable decision regarding the insurrection in Bougainville.

Hoping to end the revolt once and for all, Prime Minister Chan in early 1997 arranged for the hiring of a foreign mercenary contingent to deal with the rebels. But his own military refused to go along. Led by Brigadier General Jerry Singirok, the military demanded the termination of the mercenaries' contract and forced Deputy Prime Minister Haiveta from office. In the ensuring brouhaha Prime Minister Chan himself was forced temporarily from office only to then lose his own political seat in the July 1997 elections, the first sitting Prime Minister to do so.

Chan was followed in office by the flamboyant Bill Skate, who successfully held off a challenge by the nation's first prime minister, Sir Michael Somare, to return to office. Skate, the former Port Moresby governor, took office in July of 1997. His primary accomplishment, during what turned out to be a very short lived administration, was without question finally ending the fighting in Bougainville by signing a peace treaty in January of 1998. Unfortunately for Skate, by early 1999 his tenure in office had become very rocky and by the following July he was ousted from his position by a whopping 99 to 5 parliamentary vote! His successor was the well known economist and businessman Sir Mekere Morauta who promised a more stable financial and international administration.

Foreign Policy

The most controversial aspect of PNG's foreign policy in recent years was former Prime Minister Chan's decision to resolve the Bougainville crisis by employing a mercenary contingent. The effort, which failed, was roundly condemned by the government's neighbors. The incident temporarily soured relations with Australia which had been especially angry about the employment of the South African mercenaries. Matters were not helped later on when a confidential Australian government document, which negatively evaluated PNG's leadership, was leaked to the press during the summer of 1997.

Nevertheless, Australia-PNG tensions have not gotten in the way of Canberra's helping PNG with major contributions of food to help deal with the food shortages caused by the *El Niño* based drought.

PNG's southwestern neighbor New Zealand also played an important role in trying to reconcile the opposing sides in the on-going Bougainville crises. Later, PNG's neighbors contributed to the resolution of the problem by agreeing to supply troops from not only New Zealand, but Australia, Tonga, Fiji and Vanuatu. Since the peace was signed, calm has returned to the area and relations with many of PNG's neighbors have improved though discussions are still going on.

The last months of Prime Minister Skate's tenure also saw some dramatic gyrations in Papua New Guinea's international position as the weakening prime minister decided to switch his nation's recognition from the mainland based People's Republic of China to that of the Republic of China for a generous payment from Taiwan. The change did not last long and PNG's new government has restored ties to Beijing.

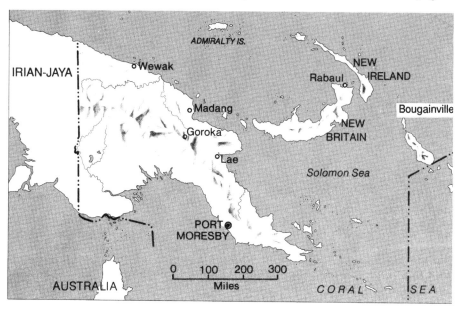

Society and Culture

The vast majority of the peoples of Papua New Guinea live in the rural area and practice a traditional form of agriculture with many living at a purely subsistence level. Most of them practice some sort of Protestant Christianity with the majority Lutherans. About one third are Roman Catholic. Traditional religious practices are also an important part of the religious environment. Western missionaries, many of them American, are quite active in the area.

PNG has not, unfortunately, been able to improve the longevity of its people as much as one might have hoped. Its citizens live twenty years less long lives than those in Australia and even ten years less then their neighbors in Indonesia.

A small portion of the indigenous inhabitants still live at an Old Stone Age level, hunting and gathering for a living. Unfortunately for PNG, the general impression that all of its citizens live under such traditional circumstances has at times made it difficult to attract foreign investment. Additionally, in recent years the combination of the growth in the urban population and significant levels of unemployment in PNG has seen a major growth in crime which has made it even more difficult for the country to attract many tourists to its shores.

Women

Although government legislation gives women extensive rights, they are in practice still discriminated against and some of the traditional cultural values which once offered women some protections have broken down in recent years. Polygamous marriages are allowed and often are at the root of domestic violence. It is for example, not uncommon for women to be imprisoned for attacking another of their spouses's wives. Most recently the government has banned new polygamous marriages though the legislation does not effect previously established unions.

Only 63% (male literacy is around 81%) of PNG women are literate and a third do not attend primary school. Still, some women have established themselves in many upper level positions in business and government. Nevertheless, traditional practices still tend to treat women as property which adds to the perception of them as second class citizens or even less.

Recently the traditional expectations of rural women were dramatically and publicly challenged. The drama began when a young rural woman refused to cooperate when her family agreed to turn her over to another clan in compensation (along with $15,000 and 25 pigs) for the killing of a clan leader. The young woman fled to Port Moresby where she gained legal support for her refusal to cooperate.

Economy

The economies of the two areas, Papua (in the south) and New Guinea (in the north) are basically similar, except that most of the mineral deposits (copper, gold and silver) so far discovered are located in New Guinea. The external trade of Papua New Guinea is largely with Australia, the United States and Germany. Almost 70% of PNG's exports come from mining. The country is now the world's sixth largest producer of gold. There are also substantial oil and gas deposits. In recent years production has been disrupted at several sites throughout the country by bandits and local armed gangs backed by land owners who want an increased share of the benefits from the country's resources.

Of late the World Bank and other international observers have been concerned over how the country's budget was being handled. A new Investment Promotion Authority was initiated with the power to allow increased foreign equity in designated national industries. Giving foreign investors a greater share of ownership is a common mechanism to induce increased foreign investment.

In spite of the country's political difficulties, economic growth was impressive in the early 1990s but has weakened dramatically in recent years. In 1995, the country narrowly avoided financial collapse. In mid-year the government was forced to accept a World Bank-IMF structural adjustment package involving some $350 million.

More recently the country has faced extraordinary challenges. Though its economy was less directly affected by the Asian economic crisis than some of its neighbors, the *El Niño* weather system devastated the country's farming community. Hundreds of thousands of people died from a famine caused by a drought and then almost as soon as that crisis eased the country was hit by devastating tidal waves.

Moreover, during the Asian economic crisis PNG itself was hurt as the economies of its neighbors went into decline. Its logging industry which had thrived on the needs of the growing Asian economies largely collapsed. Nineteen ninety seven saw the nation's growth rate drop by over 5% with 1998 dropping by another 3%. The situation through 1999 was no better with inflation particularly damaging.

But all the news is not negative. Especially important for PNG's economy will be the recent agreement to build a natural gas pipe line to Australia. The 3.5 billion dollar deal will certainly be very helpful to the nation's future. Clearly the new prime minister, Mekere Morauta, who has a record of economic accomplishment behind him, will have his work cut out for him in improving PNG's economic situation. Most immediately he has moved to reform government spending with a goal of reducing national debt.

The Future

PNG's biggest problems are both natural and political. Resolving the conflict on Bougainville was terribly important for bringing a measure of stability to the country. Now, the goal will be to make sure the fighting does not begin again. Certainly the best news for PNG is that the entire region is starting to show significant signs of recovering from the recent Asian economic slowdown and with any luck PNG might gain some advantage as well as growth renews.

An alert "cowboy" in Papua New Guinea

Papua New Guinea

Mekeo Tribesmen in ceremonial dress

The Republic of the Philippines

Majestic Mayon volcano, the most symmetrical mountain on earth, looms mistily over Legaspi City at the southern tip of Luzon. Still active, a curlicue of smoke issues from its summit.

Area: 115,700 sq. mi. (300,440 sq. km., occupying an area somewhat smaller than New Mexico).

Population: 66 million (estimated).

Capital City: Manila (Pop. 7.5 million, estimated).

Climate: Tropically warm with rainy monsoons in the summer.

Neighboring Countries: The Philippines' closest neighbors are Nationalist China on the island of Taiwan (North) and Malaysia (Southwest).

Official Languages: Filipino (a formal version of Tagalog) and English.

Other Principal Tongues: Tagalog and tribal dialects of principally Malay origin, including Visayan, Ilocano and Bicol.

Ethnic Background: Malayo–Polynesian (about 93%) Chinese, Negritos, mixed and European (about 7%).

Principal Religion: Christianity, predominantly Roman Catholic (about 91.5%), Islam (about 2.5%), animist and other (about 7%).

Main Exports (to the U.S. and Japan): A variety of coconut products—copra, oil and fibers, abaca—Manila hemp used in rope making, timber, Philippine mahogany, sugar, iron ore.

Main Imports (same trading partners plus Saudi Arabia): Industrial equipment, wheat, petroleum.

Currency: Philippine Peso.

Former Colonial Status: Spanish colony (circa 1570–1898); U.S. colony (1898–1946); occupied by the Japanese (1941–1945).

National Day: July 4, 1946. (June 12, the anniversary of the proclamation of independence from Spain in 1898, is a national holiday).

Chief of State: Joseph Estrada, President (since June 30, 1998).

National Flag: The left edge is the base of a white equilateral triangle containing a yellow sun and three yellow stars; the rest of the flag is divided into two horizontal stripes with blue on the top, red on the bottom.

Per Capita GNP Income: US$1,160.

The land which makes up the territory occupied by the Republic of the Philippines consists of a portion of a mountain chain running from northern Siberia in Russia through the China Sea to Borneo and New Guinea and the small islands of eastern Indonesia, and then southward through eastern Australia. Countless ages ago the sea invaded the lower part of these mountains—the Philippines are a small portion of the top of this mountain range that has sufficient height to rise above the surface of the tropical waters of the Southwest Pacific.

This nation includes eleven larger islands with more than 1,200 square miles of land on each island: Luzon, Mindanao, Samar, Negros, Palawan, Panay, Mindoro, Leyte, Cebu, Bohol and Masbate. More than 95% of the nation's land and people are located on these islands.

The remaining islands, around 7000 islands are desolate, jungle–infested and mostly uninhabited. Few have an area of more than one square mile, and about 4,500 of them exist as land masses in the 20th century only because it is impossible to sail across them—they are dots on navigation charts not even possessing the dignity of a name.

The temperature is consistently warm. Much of the terrain lies above an altitude of 1,600 feet. Almost all of the islands are mountainous, containing a multitude of dead and active volcanoes. The eastern slopes receive ample rainfall during all months of the year. The westward–facing parts are moistened by the southwest

Philippines

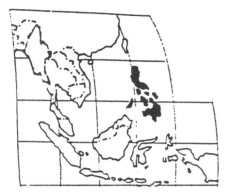

monsoon from May to October. All areas of the islands have periodic, often devastating, visits from typhoons of the region, which bring torrential rains.

The land is covered with vast expanses of thick jungle which grows with incredible rapidity and contains among its taller trees the timber from which Philippine mahogany is marketed to the world. The part that has been tamed by the population varies from a thick growth of poor grass which supports grazing to plantation production of coconut, rubber, pineapple and other tropical crops.

History

Unlike some of the communities discussed in *East, Southeast Asia, and the Western Pacific*, the Philippines did not have a unified history before the arrival of the colonial powers. Rather, like Indonesia, it is made up of widely diverse groups of communities that had largely gone their separate ways before the conquerors, first the Spanish and later the Americans, forced them into a single administrative unity. What we know of the years before colonization is relatively limited.

Research has shown that about two centuries before the Common Era a fairly advanced people from what is now northern Vietnam and southern mainland China migrated to the large islands of the Philippines. They practiced a system of communal agriculture based on irrigation. Many of their descendants live in the islands today as small non-Christian communities. The larger number of Filipinos, who are of Malayo-Polynesian origin, arrived in the islands from the 8th to the 15th centuries from Java and the Malay peninsula. Their migrations occurred principally during the period of the strong Srivijaya kingdom in the Indonesia-Malaya area and during the Majapahit kingdom on Java, which dominated a large area up to the beginning of the 13th century A.D. Muslim traders and pirates later arrived during the 14th century. There has also long been a small Chinese community.

The Arrival of the Spanish

Ferdinand Magellan, the famed Portuguese explorer who, sailing under the Spanish flag, directed the first successful voyage around the world, was killed in the islands in 1521. Nevertheless, there was no serious attempt by the Spanish to establish a colony until fifty years later when the Spanish forces, based in their colony of Mexico, dispatched an expedition to the Philippines. The initial settlement was small, and had as its only contact with the European world the annual visit of the "Manila Galleon" sent to Mexico once a year. This is not very surprising because, unlike many of the other island communities to their south and east, the Philippines did not produce many of the spices that had attracted the Europeans to Asia in the first place.

Nevertheless, as they had done in Cen-

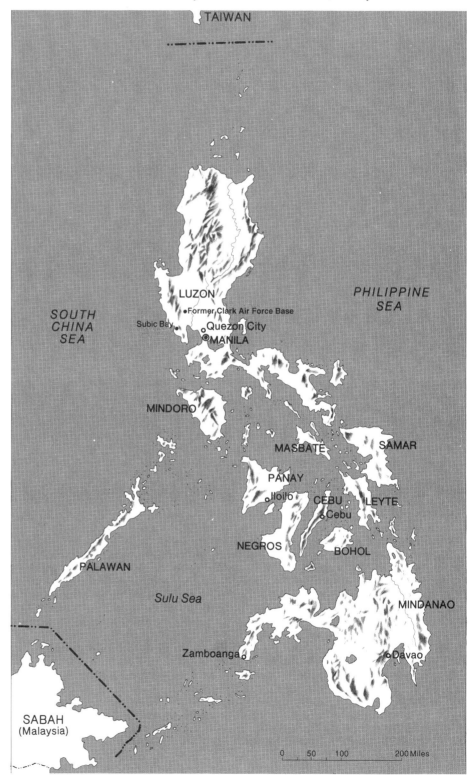

tral and South America, the Spanish gave large tracts of fertile land to prominent Spaniards who had almost complete authority over their domains, and exploited the native inhabitants without interference. Many of the native Filipinos, driven from their farms by the Spanish, went to the more hilly and mountainous areas of the islands to continue farming. Faced with the steep slopes of these regions they developed new agricultural plots based on intricate stone terracing of the steep sides to allow their crops to grow on artificially "level" land.

Given the especially harsh treatment the Filipinos received from their Spanish military occupiers, the best friends that the Filipinos initially had among the early Spanish were the Catholic monks who protested their treatment by the secular authorities. Eventually the harsh treatment of the natives reached even the ears of King Philip who by the mid 16th century granted primary responsibility for the islands to the Catholic monastic orders. Unfortunately, over the next centuries, the various Catholic orders acquired huge estates and become themselves especially resistant to efforts at reform.

Compared to the Spanish civilian officials the friars had far more power and influence, the most obvious example, their successful conversion of the islands over the centuries to their current status as the most Catholic country in Asia. Nevertheless, in sharp contrast to the Americans who later made the teaching of English a major priority during their own colonial years, or even their own brethren in Latin America, the Spanish religious authorities actually discouraged the teaching of Spanish which it was felt would make the Filipinos more difficult to control. Moreover, even as they converted many Filipinos to Catholicism, they resisted the ordination of native priests.

The Catholic religious establishment was involved in all aspects of the colony's civilian administration from collecting taxes and doing budgets through control over the recruiting for the army and the police.

Predictably, the tight control of the ecclesiastic authorities eventually aroused tension with the indigenous Filipinos. Over time various leaders arose to challenge the Spanish Friar's authority, frequently over the latter's unwillingness to ordain Filipino priests.

A particularly unlucky trio of reformists, accused of questioning Spain's authority, were publicly executed by the authorities in 1872 in front of a huge crowd that watched the unhappy prisoners being slowly strangled to death!

Spain's attitude toward the islands had evolved during the century. After Spain lost its colonies in Central and South America during the first part of the 19th century, the Philippines assumed an even more important position. Nevertheless, efforts to develop the colony's economy to serve the Spanish were largely unsuccessful, as were the efforts to subdue the warlike Moros (Muslims) in the southern islands, who had lived there for many decades without interference. Nevertheless, the slow but steady growth of education, the spread of European political ideas such as nationalism and unrest caused by oppressive economic policies of the Spaniards, slowly gave rise to a small group of educated Filipinos who demanded independence from Spain.

Among the best known of these Filipino nationalists was Jose Rizal, a passionate Filipino intellectual whose fictional portrayal of life in the Philippines, in a novel published in 1887 and smuggled into the islands, aroused considerable public sentiment and the anger of the Church authorities. Eventually, associated by the government with another revolt that had broken out, Rizal was executed in 1896, yet another martyr to the Philippine nationalist cause.

But his death hardly ended the cries against Spanish control and a late nineteenth century insurrection would emerge

Jose Rizal y Mercado

even as international events beyond the Philippines were soon to transform the circumstances of the islands almost completely.

The Arrival of the Americans

Taking advantage of Spain's preoccupation with Cuba during the Spanish-American War of 1898, local Philippine nationalists proclaimed an independent Republic of the Philippines and quickly adopted a European-type constitution.

Given the well known American feelings against colonialism, the Filipino leaders, assuming the United States supported them in this independence move, joined the Americans in a combined assault against the remaining Spanish forces in the islands. Their assumption about America's intentions were wrong.

To the frustration of the Philippine nationalists, the American government, partly out of fear that some other power such as Germany would seize the Philippines, and influenced by the young American assistant secretary of the navy, Teddy Roosevelt, decided to keep the islands for itself.

Feeling understandably betrayed by the Americans with whom they had fought against the Spanish for the previous six months the rebel forces led by General Emilio Aguinaldo immediately went into armed revolt against the United States.

During the Spanish American War itself, the Philippine struggles had merely been a side show to the American war with Spain over Cuba. Few Americans, save the young Teddy Roosevelt and his colleagues, were even interested in following the European powers in the exercise of empire building. In fact, when the clash over the Philippines actually came, even the President of the United States had to locate a map to find out where the islands were!

Nevertheless, once the decision was made to conquer the islands, the United States committed itself to put down the forces of the Philippine nationalists. The resulting struggle was carried out in a fashion very similar to the Vietnam struggle generations later.

As the struggle began, Aquinaldo, the leader of the Philippine nationalists, declared his nation free and independent and moved to occupy as much territory as possible before the Americans established themselves. The goals of the movement were quite impressive for their age. They envisioned a democratic Philippines, which would even include votes for women, something that was not yet a reality in the United States at that point. But Philippine aspirations were of little interest to the Americans who by then had their own plans for the islands' future.

The inevitable clash finally occurred in February of 1899 as fighting broke out between the American and Philippine forces. Over the next few years the United States was forced to commit three-quarters of its entire military, about 75,000 soldiers, to the struggle.

Before it was declared over by then President Teddy Roosevelt in 1902, approximately 200,000 people had died— most of them Filipino civilians, but a figure that also included more than four thousand dead American soldiers as well. It was a bloody affair that included atrocities on both sides that sound ominously

Philippines

General Emilio Aguinaldo

familiar to later generations who came of age hearing horror stories of the Vietnam struggle. In the end though American power and divisions among the Philippines themselves weakened Aguinaldo's effectiveness. His capture after a daring American raid, determined the fate of the islands. Among the most prominent of the Americans who commanded there during the struggle was Arthur MacArthur, father of Douglas MacArthur whose boyhood experiences in the islands would affect the rest of his career.

Though the Americans had fought hard to establish their control over the islands, there was enough ambivalence about the blatantly imperialistic effort for Washington to also commit itself to preparing the islands for eventual independence. Unlike some of the other colonial powers the United States did make a clear effort to share administration with the Filipinos from the colony's earliest years. In fact, the American-sponsored assembly that was soon formed had the distinction of being the first elective legislative body in the entire region. But while the United States increasingly turned over internal decision making to the Filipinos, control over defense and foreign policy remained tightly in the Americans' hands.

Education was a major goal of the islands' new administration and large numbers of young Americans were recruited to serve as teachers, especially English teachers. It was in many ways rather like the Peace Corps efforts later in the century. The major emphasis on education and English soon had a considerable impact. Literary rates improved markedly and English became in more common use among the island's inhabitants.

By 1916 the United States had formally committed itself to a goal of eventual independence for the islands and begun the creation of internally self-governing insti-

Mindanao's Maria Cristina Falls pounds out its dramatic message

tutions. The colonial administration also made efforts in the fields of communication, public works and education.

Nevertheless, the emphasis was on creating areas for profitable American investment, and little was done to develop the economy as a whole for the benefit of the Filipinos, especially the poorer classes. A foreign trade emerged that was almost totally linked to and dependent on the U.S. market. And sadly, while the Americans were quite influential in moving Filipinos into governing position and improving literacy rates, their economic policies did little to address the economic domination the land-owning elite held over the population.

Feudal systems of sharecropping in the rural areas, which had arisen under the Spanish as a result of land grants, continued and became an even worse problem. The local elected governments permitted by the colonial administration drifted toward control by Filipino political machines and bosses who bore a remarkable resemblance to some of their contemporaries in Latin America.

In the 1930s, Manuel Quezon, who formed and led the Nationalist Party, emerged as the leading politician and eventually President. Political idealism was one factor that prompted the United States to adopt legislation providing for an almost fully self-governing Commonwealth to be established in 1935. The other was pressure from U.S. sugar interests for protective tariffs against Philippine sugar, which were impossible unless it was independent.

Toward World War II

The growing threat of the Japanese in Asia in the late 1930s lessened the desire for total independence on the part of the more radical Filipinos, who saw the need for U.S. protection. Partly as an assurance of further American support, Quezon hired Douglas MacArthur, son of the island's late military governor and more recently the American army's Chief of Staff to serve as the Philippine armies new "Field Marshal." But despite MacArthur's famous reputation as a military strategist the Philippines were not at all prepared for the assault they were to experience as the forces of imperial Japan attacked in December of 1941.

The islands were quickly overrun by a force of well-trained Japanese soldiers who inaugurated in 1942 the same harsh military rule that was their policy in the other areas of Southeast Asia they conquered. Nevertheless, as was the case elsewhere, many Filipinos, including the father of the later martyred hero Benigno Aquino took the Japanese at their word about freeing Asia from the Western colo-

nialists and collaborated with them. This was often especially true of the Philippine elite which had earlier worked first with the Spanish, then the Americans, and now the Japanese occupiers. Many other Filipinos eventually took up arms against Tokyo's forces.

This resulted in a limited guerrilla movement operating clandestinely in the rural areas to sabotage the military installations of the Japanese. Quezon and his government went into exile in the United States, where he died in 1944. His successor, Sergio Osmena, was eventually able to return to the Philippines as a result of the progress of General Douglas MacArthur's forces in liberating the islands.

Unfortunately for the future of the Philippines, MacArthur, in sharp contrast to his later role as a social revolutionary in Japan, chose to reestablish the Philippine landowning elite in power even overlooking their role as frequent war-time collaborators with the Japanese. Not surprisingly, that enraged many of the leftists guerrillas who had fought Japan and had long harbored hopes for a more equitable land distribution after the war. Sadly, given American concerns about socialism and fear of communism the likelihood that the U.S. would have supported their war time guerrillas in efforts at significant land reform was small indeed. Most groups, like the leftist Huks, were simply demobilized and sent home only to emerge in later years as a new threat to the government. On a political level though, the United States did officially grant the islands their independence on July 4, 1946.

The economy had been devastated by the war, and it was necessary for the United States to pour in huge sums for relief and rehabilitation and to grant duty-free status to Philippine exports in the American market until 1954. Much of the aid, unfortunately, did not reach those who needed it. Osmena died in 1946. For the next twenty years the Philippines was ruled, with one exception, by a succession of colorless, corrupt and inefficient leaders, and behind the scenes the United States remained especially influential.

Ramon Magsaysay, who served as president during the mid 1950s was, for example, especially close to the American intelligence community which had sponsored his rise in Philippine politics. Once in power he not very surprisingly maintained a consistently pro-U.S. policy and took the Philippines into SEATO, the Southeast Asia Treaty organization in 1954. In spite of his strenuous efforts the power of the small group of families who dominated agriculture, industry and trade—the descendants of the Spanish aristocratic class, continued. Unfortunate-

ly for the Americans, who so valued their ties to him, Magsaysay was killed in an airplane accident in 1957.

The next few years saw little change in the Philippines though there was a limited growth of anti-Americanism as some of her leaders dabbled in an active, anti-U.S. foreign policy intended to make the Philippines more popular, powerful and acceptable in the Asian community.

The Marcos Years

Ferdinand Marcos of the Nationalist Party was elected president in 1965 amid a general sense of an urgent need for change among the people—change toward better performance by their rulers. His election had been helped by his claim, later disproved, to have been an influential leader in the anti-Japanese guerrilla movement. Marcos embarked upon a reform platform similar to that of Magsaysay, but met the same intractable obstacles as his predecessor. Corruption remained a virtual custom among minor government officials and employees for the next twenty years. The *Communist Party (PKP)* abetted by discontent among the poverty-stricken rural people, also resumed its guerrilla activity against the state. Traditional rivalry between the *Nationalist Party* and the *Liberal Party* continued.

President Marcos was reelected in 1969 over a *Liberal Party* opponent by a large majority and became the first Philippine President to win a second term. Nationalist majorities in both houses of the Assembly were sizable. But student and labor demonstrations in Manila, which occurred in 1970, were symptoms of the country's malaise; some of the dissent had an openly anti-U.S. tone.

Among Marcos' most outspoken opponents was the young Benigno Aquino, a former journalist and popular politician. Aquino and his later internationally famous wife Corazon Aquino both came from very important elite Filipino families. Having been unable to run against Marcos in the 1969 election it was expected that Benigno Aquino would run for president in the next elections but those elections never came about. Ferdinand Marcos, already the first Philippine president to serve two full terms, had other plans.

Marcos had no intention of running for office again. Rather, after staging a series of violent incidents which added to the sense of crisis in the country, he declared martial law and canceled the upcoming elections. Large numbers of his political enemies were imprisoned. Aquino himself was to spend the next seven years in jail where much to Marcos' displeasure he came to be seen as the principal martyr of

Philippines

the developing dictatorship. Marcos himself justified his action by claiming the islands were threatened by communism and needed authoritarian government for the moment. Despite these actions, both the influential Americans and the local business community as well as much of the population approved of the move. Economically these years turned out to be a successful period with recognizable gains.

In the ensuing years Marcos had some success in improving the state of law and order except in Mindanao, where an ongoing Muslim revolt had been in progress for years. Of greatest importance, however, he received approval by rigging a referendum on a new constitution under which he awarded himself virtual dictatorial powers for an unlimited period.

Principal opposition to the Marcos regime came from the Catholic Church and insurgent Muslims in the southern islands. The latter received support from other Muslim countries. Little progress though was made dealing with these problems until years later by Fidel Ramos who began to reduce the level of tensions on the southern island. Under Marcos, martial law delegated great political power to the armed forces which became repressive and corrupt, even while providing a semblance of order.

Imelda Marcos, the flamboyant wife of the president, became Governor of Manila and announced ambitious plans for its redevelopment. Even as she set up her own power base, she remained loyal to her husband. Still, her plans to succeed him were widely known. For a time the powerful couple seemed to offer themselves up as a Philippine equivalent of the glamourous Kennedys of American political life.

As might be expected, the militant wings of the opposition groups began to resort to terrorist bombings in 1980. Insurgency, particularly Muslim and communist, became a continuing problem as well.

Despite the lifting of martial law in 1981 there was little improvement in the political situation. The country continued to be run by an alliance led by an aging Marcos, his wife Imelda, the armed forces, the ruling *New Society Party* and rich and powerful men close to the president who operated for their own benefit in an economic system known informally as "crony capitalism."

By the early 1980s more and more of the Philippine elite had lost faith in Marcos's government and its ability to deal with the economic crises brought on by the rise in oil prices in the mid 1970s.

Fairly predictably, Marcos often talked of forcing the U.S. out of its huge air and naval bases in the Philippines, but this was almost certainly to divert popular at-

Ferdinand and Imelda Marcos at their zenith in 1972

tention from his domestic policies as well as to get greater concessions from the United States, including higher rents. In addition, he was determined to appear at home and abroad as entirely independent of the United States and as the leader of a truly Asian nation. Partly for this purpose, he visited and granted diplomatic recognition to the People's Republic of China in June 1975; another consideration was that he wanted, and apparently thought that he got, a pledge from Beijing not to support the small Philippine communist in-

surgent movement, the New People's Army. Marcos also established diplomatic relations with the Soviet Union in 1976.

Despite the occasionally nationalistic rhetoric, relations with the United States were reasonably good; President Ford visited in late 1975. During the late 1970s the United States' primary concern in the Philippines, especially after its loss in Vietnam, was to maintain its access to the bases. Marcos knew that and often offered himself to the Americans as their only guarantee that the bases would be maintained—assuming the Americans were willing to pay enough. An agreement concerning the base leases was finally concluded with the United States in 1978 and a second in late 1983.

The Aquino Challenge

Nevertheless, the forces of opposition to Marcos' rule continued to grow. Had he been able, as were other southeast Asian rulers of the era, to preside over a continuously strong economic growth his authoritarianism might have been tolerated. But that was not the case and, as in the early 1980s, other regional economies started to take off; the Philippines lagged behind, mired in economic problems.

Sensing an opportunity, longtime opposition leader Benigno Aquino, probably encouraged by false reports that Marcos was about to undergo surgery in August 1983, decided to return to Manila from the United States where he had been serving as a fellow at Harvard University. Sadly, he had misjudged just how dangerous his decision was. As he was getting off the plane Aquino was summarily gunned down.

Minutes after an earthquake in northern Luzon, a huge boulder crashed down the mountainside to block the highway

The opposition blamed the government, and more specifically, the armed forces, for the assassination. Huge demonstrations occurred in the cities against Marcos and in protest at the sham official investigation of the murder. The confusion led to a cancellation of a visit to Manila by President Reagan scheduled for late 1983.

The opposition *United Nationalist Democratic Organization (UNIDO)* did succeed in early 1984 in getting the constitution amended by referendum so as to restore the office of vice president, the purpose being to reduce the chances that the widely-disliked Mrs. Marcos might succeed her husband to the presidency. The document even permitted the election of a vice president from a different political party than that of the president.

Nevertheless, events in 1985–1986 showed anything but unity. After an unnecessarily lengthy inquiry, armed forces Chief of Staff General Fabian Ver and 25 others were indicted in January 1985 for complicity in the assassination of Benigno Aquino. The trial began in February and continued for months. But when all the evidence was in and after the jury had retired to deliberate, the Philippine Supreme Court took the unheard of step of dismissing the charges on the ground that there was insufficient evidence!

Despite their success in dealing with the events surrounding the assassination, the Marcos regime seemed to be unraveling. Nevertheless, Marcos still had some major advantages, the ever influential Americans were, as always, more interested in the security of the American bases than the welfare of the Philippines themselves. And they still believed Marcos' continuing power was their best defense against losing the bases.

In fact, even as many officials among the Americans had lost faith, Marcos's long-term relationship with Ronald Reagan kept the United States from openly siding with his enemies until his regime was almost completely spent. Nevertheless, under American pressure, in early November, Marcos called a presidential election for February 7, 1986.

By then though, the opposition had managed to unite behind the widow of Benigno Aquino, Corazon. Her candidacy, which had the support of the Philippine Catholic hierarchy and its influential Archbishop of Manila Jaime Sin, soon attracted widespread support, especially in the cities. She also had, at least for the moment, the support of her vice-presidential candidate, Salvador Laurel's powerful political organization.

Although Marcos was officially declared to have won the election — which had been monitored by large numbers of official and unofficial observers, mainly Amer-

ican — it soon became obvious that his supporters were guilty of massive fraud, and that Mrs. Aquino had actually won.

The United States government was by now finally convinced that Marcos' time had passed and switched its support from Marcos to Mrs. Aquino. A group of army officers belonging to a military reform movement usually known by its acronym *RAM* then began to plan a coup against Marcos.

Hearing of the plans for a *coup*, Marcos concluded that it was the work of Defense Minister Enrile and Vice Chief of Staff Fidel Ramos and began to move against them. They and their supporters, now in-

Hon. Corazon Aquino

cluding many Americans, promptly came out in support of Mrs. Aquino. Privately, the Americans supplied important intelligence to the insurgents. Cardinal Sin, meanwhile, urged the Catholic faithful to block the streets of Manila to prevent the movement of troops loyal to Marcos. This tactic was effective and later came to be known to the world as a famous example of "people power." Marcos had lost. After gaining an offer of asylum from the United States, provided he did not use force against his own people, Marcos went into exile in Hawaii and Mrs. Aquino was inaugurated President.

As President Aquino repealed Marcos' repressive regulations and released his political prisoners. She also initiated steps to recover the enormous wealth—put at ten billion dollars by the C.I.A.— that he had stashed abroad, mainly in the United States and Switzerland. President Aquino and her middle class cabinet, faced with a pro-Marcos majority in the Assembly and the

Supreme Court, then declared a "revolutionary" government in order to be better able to eliminate the legacy of Marcos' rule.

About six months after her election, President Aquino began to move on her major challenges. She visited the U.S. in September, and the American Congress voted an extra $200 million in aid for the Philippines. She began then to work on an ambitious and difficult land reform program, which was badly needed. In late November she broke with her former supporter Defense Minister Juan Ponce Enrile, who had apparently been threatening a military coup against her. At that time, Chief of Staff Fidel Ramos ensured that the armed forces remained loyal to President Aquino. Aquino's most important military supporter, Ramos, later president, also pressed her at the time to take a stronger line against the communists and their *New People's Army (NPA)*.

After long negotiations, the communists agreed to a 60-day truce, beginning December 10, 1986. The *PKP* used its interlude of legality to make energetic propaganda in the cities, but it ended by probably alienating more people than it impressed. Accordingly, it refused to renew the cease-fire and resumed its offensive. President Aquino countered with an offer of amnesty to any insurgent who surrendered. In January 1987 another dissident movement, the (Muslim) *Moro National Liberation Front* (based in Mindanao), signed a peace agreement with the government. Unfortunately, it hardly solved the ongoing problems in the largely Muslim island.

There were also some serious disorders just before a referendum was to be held on a new constitution, but they were suppressed. Despite these problems President Aquino's constitution got an unexpectedly high vote (about 75% of those casting ballots). It limited the president to one six-year term, created a bicameral legislature, granted the courts the power of judicial review of laws and provided that the U.S. bases be non-nuclear and could be continued after 1991 only on the basis of a treaty approved by at least two-thirds of the Philippine Senate.

President Aquino's supporters won a sweeping victory in elections for the Senate and House of Representatives held in May 1987. But in August of the same year, in the most serious of several attempts made to overthrow President Aquino, a colorful paratrooper, Colonel Gregorio (Rambo) Honasan, led an attempted coup against her. It failed due to energetic action by loyal forces under Chief of Staff Ramos (made Defense Secretary in January 1988). For a time it appeared that President Aquino's position might be untenable. Increasingly, her former political allies were moving against her.

Philippines

Workmen cut the bananas from the stalk and place them in a washing vat.

Despite the great hopes that had accompanied her arrival to power, the new president had great difficulty living up to those expectations. The army disliked her efforts to reconcile with the long running communist insurgents. Those that hoped she would move against the entrenched land owners and institute true land reform were equally unhappy.

Given the unequal land distribution of the Philippines it is hardly surprising that the communist insurgency continued to grow to the point where, for a time, President Aquino was apparently considering proclaiming a state of emergency. Frequently brutal anti-communist vigilantes emerged also in many areas.

Despite the victory of the democratic forces, Philippine political life, nevertheless, remained riddled with corruption and factionalism on the part of elected and appointed officials. From Aquino's perspective, actually accomplishing something was quite difficult. The lower house of Congress was subservient to the popular President Aquino, whereas the Senate, whose members were elected by the national electorate, rather than from local constituencies, was highly independent.

In June 1988, the Philippine Congress finally voted a moderate land reform pro-

gram that managed to please neither the landlords nor the land hungry tenants. Social unrest and communist insurgency continued.

During these years, the presence of the U.S. bases, holdovers from the years when the Philippines were an American colony, became especially controversial in the eyes of the Philippine political elite and intellectuals. After difficult negotiations, an agreement was reached in October 1988 under which the U.S. was to give $481 million in economic aid (one-third of what the Philippine side had been demanding) in 1990 and again in 1991, when the current base agreement was set to expire.

Under the new constitution, any new agreement would have to be ratified by the Philippine Senate, and perhaps by a popular referendum. In May 1988, the Senate voted a ban on storage of nuclear weapons on the bases, but it appeared that in practice they could still be taken through in transit. No one, Philippine or American, showed any interest in a vague proposal by General Secretary Mikhail Gorbachev that the U.S. give up its Philippine bases in exchange for a Soviet withdrawal from Camranh Bay, Vietnam.

A series of developments in late 1989 and early 1990 heightened the general im-

pression that under President Aquino's indecisive leadership, the country was drifting or even regressing. In early December the sixth and most serious attempted military coup against her was quelled, but mainly because U.S. combat aircraft unprecedentedly flew over the rebel positions. The fact that the United States had effectively used its Philippine-based military resources to intervene in local politics added a new and complicated dimension to the base issue.

The American side wanted continued access even after the bases passed to Philippine control. Manila wanted to get as much money as possible out of the entire transaction and, of course, Philippine nationalists found the presence of the bases themselves to be a source of national shame. Understandably, those Filipinos who were employed at the bases were concerned about their continued employment.

Political unrest and attempted military coups continued to be a serious problem. As the end of President Aquino's term approached, various political figures began to jockey for succession. One of these figures, surprisingly, was Imelda Marcos, the widow of Ferdinand Marcos. She returned from exile in November 1991 and gained government permission to bury her husband in his native province, Ilocos Norte. Although facing criminal proceedings on charges of corruption, she soon began to campaign as the champion of the poor, notwithstanding her vast fortune. But while the return of Imelda Marcos was something of a distraction, much more important issues demanded the government's attention.

In 1991 the Philippines suffered a series of natural disasters, — a storm that struck the central islands in November and caused unusually heavy damage (runoff and mud slides) because of heavy illegal logging in the area and more dramatic, a volcanic eruption!

Mt. Pinatubo, a volcano about 55 miles north of Manila and only 10 miles from U.S.-controlled Clark Air Force Base erupted in June of 1991 and ironically determined the outcome of the long and complex negotiations between Manila and Washington on the future of the U.S. bases in the Philippines.

Before the eruption, Manila had been demanding $825 million per year for seven years in aid, in exchange for continuation of the base agreement. The American Congress was unwilling to appropriate that much, and Washington had been offering $520 million per year over 10–12 years. Certainly there were lots of reasons the Americans wanted to keep their bases in the Philippines. The bases were very valuable for repair and refueling of ships and aircraft and for training of personnel; Filipino labor was plentiful, cheap, and skilled.

But as someone said at the time, the volcano had its own agenda, and it was clearly not the same as that of the negotiators. The eruption, apparently the most powerful anywhere in the twentieth century, not only heavily damaged the town of Angeles, near Clark, but covered the base with about a foot of ash, rendering it virtually useless; Subic Naval Base and its environs also suffered some damage.

After the eruption, some haggling continued between the two sides, but the negotiations were basically over. The bases had also become much less important to U.S. strategic interests since the collapse of the Soviet Union, the main regional threat.

In September of 1991, the Philippine Senate, in a nationalistic mood, voted not to ratify an agreement incorporating the U.S.'s final offer (Clark to be turned over, Subic to be kept for ten more years for $203 million per year). American forces then began to withdraw. The most graphic reminders of the American occupation of the Philippines were now to fade into history.

Politics and Government

The Philippine political system resembles that of the United States. Prior to 1987, the Philippines was governed under the U.S.-modeled 1935 constitution. The constitution provided for a bill of rights, a bicameral legislature, an independent judiciary and a president with a four year term.

A new constitution was approved on February 2, 1987. The president is now limited to one 6-year term. Close relatives of the president cannot be appointed to public office. Both the legislature and the judiciary may review the legal reasons for the imposition of martial law. The constitution also provides for civil liberties and is very democratic in form.

The country has a House of Representatives and a Senate. Under the constitution congress has the power to declare war, restrict presidential emergency powers and control the appropriation of revenue. The Senate has twenty-four members with six year terms with a limit of two consecutive terms. The house can have up to 250 members elected from legislative districts apportioned by population. Twenty percent of the seats are filled through a party-list system.

The Philippines has historically been a two party system. The *Nacional* and *Liberal* parties traded control of the government between 1946 and 1972. Both parties tended to serve the interests of the political elites in the country. During much of the Marcos era there was no effective political party opposition. Strong opposition began to emerge around 1980 with the formation of *UNIDO* which had the backing of anti-Marcos elites. Benigno Aquino Jr. established *LABAN* ("Fight") as a vehicle for his political ideas. The political party landscape fragmented somewhat during the Aquino years. Politics continues to be highly personalized. Support is given to individuals, not platforms, programs or ideologies.

Like many other communities in Asia and elsewhere, Philippine politics are much influenced by the presence of influential "patron-client relationships." Essentially, this means that political life centers on relationships that are personal and hierarchical. Political relationships are also built on the concept of *"utang na loob,"* obligations of indebtedness. Politics is therefore frequently dominated by personal loyalty to a hierarchical group. Patrons must provide resources to their clients to keep their loyalty. This is a major cause of corruption in the Philippines. The client in the relationship is concerned only with what the patron can deliver.

In this type of environment, institutions like interest groups, political parties and other organizations that could unite large segments of society are less effective than they might be. Thus, the institutions which have at times been so effective in countries from South Korea to the United States, are of less value in the personalized political culture of the Philippines.

A New Beginning for the Philippines

Fidel V. Ramos was elected president of the Philippines in May 1992. However, as one of seven candidates, Ramos, in winning, received only 23.4% of the vote. To make matters more complicated, his closest challenger, Miriam Defensor Santiago, claimed fraud and managed to have the Supreme Court consider the charge. Ramos, in short, did not start off with a lot of support, though Mrs. Aquino backed him strongly. Nevertheless, for most of his term, he was quite effective.

During the first years after his election President Ramos and his government faced several significant challenges: the need to establish law and order, opposition to the current political process by groups including the *National Democratic Front* (representing the communists), the *Muslim National Liberation Front, the Muslim Islamic Liberation Front*, the military officers' group *RAM-YOU* and the continuing entrenched position of the old political elite. By his last year, of course, he also had to face the challenges of the Asian economic crises of 1997, but that was much later. Initially, he was quite successful in dealing with the issues that faced him.

In fact, by early 1996, most of these challenges were still present but somewhat diminished. Yes, there were still plenty of problems but also signs of improvement. President Ramos and the *MNLF* leader, Nur Misuari, finally concluded an agreement that would hopefully contribute to ending the generation-long struggle which had taken more than 120,000 lives. Overcoming the opposition of minority Christian communities in the south, Ramos and Misuari agreed to form a special presidential council headed by Misuari which would have responsibility over development issues in fourteen of the southern provinces. The deal, part of a larger plan that included the formation of a more autonomous Muslim-dominated region after three years, marked a major breakthrough for efforts to reinforce Philippine stability. Sadly, it was later to prove less successful in bringing in Misuari's more militant Muslim co-religionists.

Ramos even managed to gain an agreement with the *Communist National Democratic Front* in early April 1998 which projected a series of negotiations intended to end the generation long communist rebellion. Economically, the Ramos administration had moved dramatically to reform the Philippine economy and further integrate it into world.

But, despite a very impressive record for most of his administration, President

Philippines

Ramos's last year in office was dramatically hurt both by forces he controlled and those he did not. Although Ramos never publicly said he wanted a second term—a clear violation of the new constitution— Ramos let his followers try to modify the constitution in order to allow him to do so. The decision was very inadvisable and he soon found his former allies, President Aquino, Cardinal Sin and much of the population aroused against the idea. In the end he backed down and disavowed the idea but not before he had hurt his reputation. Then President Ramos, understanding his time at the helm was really up, chose House Speaker Jose de Venecia as his successor.

But while having Ramos' support was important, de Venecia nevertheless still had to win the election for himself. And that turned out to be a very daunting task, especially when facing the Philippine Vice President Joseph Estrada. Estrada, a former actor, wanted the job for himself and campaigned hard to get it. In contrast to the organizational skills of de Venecia, Estrada, despite his origins in the Philippine elite classes, campaigned as a populist and was much more flamboyant as a public campaigner, a skill especially important in the May 1998 election which included not only Estrada and de Venecia but nine other candidates.

In the end, as the polls had long predicted, the Philippine people chose Joseph

Former President Fidel Ramos

Estrada. Estrada may not have had the support of many Philippine elites. In fact much of the leadership, from the military to the church, was skeptical; nevertheless, he won the presidency with an impressive 40% of the vote and drew his support from a wide range of voters. It was a far better performance than Ramos himself had

done in his own earlier effort. It was an impressive showing and coupled with both President Ramos's ultimate willingness to accept the end of his term, and Estrada's decision to continue Ramos's economic policies, the Philippines now seem to have a far brighter future than anyone might have imagined a few years ago.

Unfortunately, for President Estrada, his initial popularity did not last as long as he probably hoped. Over the two years since he came to power his poll ratings have dropped steadily lower as his administration has been plagued by rumors of economic corruption, inattention to detail, favoritism and unpopular policies.

Foreign Policy

Until recently Philippine foreign policy long focused on strengthening its relationship with the United States. But that has been modified in recent years. It has now become more common to favor downgrading relations with the United States, and emphasizing stronger ties with Asia. During his term in office President Ramos made it a personal priority to strengthen ties with his regional neighbors and traveled extensively to do so. All this is a logical development considering the withdrawal of the American forces in 1992.

Particularly important for the Philippines has been improving relations with other members of ASEAN, the Association

A panoramic view of the Sierra Madre slopes.

of Southeast Asian Nations. President Ramos, for example, visited Indonesia to discuss the possibility of links between Mindinao, in the southern Philippines, and Indonesia. Eventually, the Indonesian government offered important help to President Ramos in his efforts to bring the confrontation with the *MNLF* Muslim leadership to resolution.

Over the last few years Manila has experienced strained relations with China. By far, China's occupation of Mischief Reef in the South China Sea constituted the most serious problem. In early 1995, Manila discovered that one of the small islands in the Spratley chain about 150 miles off the Philippine coast had been occupied by members of the Chinese navy. Mischief Reef is in Philippine territorial waters.

In May 1995 the Philippine military officials tried to take a boatload of journalists to see the reef. A Chinese patrol boat blocked their path. The Philippine navy then detained a number of Chinese fishermen who were illegally in the country's territorial waters. Later, at the ASEAN Re-

President Joseph Estrada

gional Forum, ARF, the ASEAN states spoke with one voice in raising concern about the Chinese occupation. Beijing subsequently agreed to deal with the conflicting claims in the South China Sea multilaterally. Thus, Manila would have its fellow ASEAN member states as partners in negotiations over the Spratley Islands. This was far more preferable than going one-on-one with the PRC.

Somewhat to Manila's embarrassment, the struggle has at times turned out be rather embarrassing for the Philippines. During the spring of 1997 the Philippine navy dramatically arrested some Chinese fishermen and drove a few Chinese ships from Scarborough Shoal to the west of Lu-

zon Island. Unfortunately, for Philippine authorities, upon closer inspection it became clear that particular shoal was beyond Philippine territorial waters! By the spring of 2000 nothing significant had been accomplished on resolving these issues.

As for the important relationship with the United States, the last few years did not go particularly well. The primary problem was with tensions between the two countries over whether American servicemen were liable to Philippine local prosecution for criminal acts. The United States reacted quite strongly, canceling joint military exercises when Manila decided to end the exemption for the American troops. Eventually a compromise was worked out to offer immunity for servicemen engaged in "official acts" but that required ratification by the Philippine Senate—a complicated issue in itself.

Culture and Society

Like so much of the developing world the contrasts in society are dramatic. Manila, a busy, modern city, has a sophisticated cultural atmosphere which can compare with most western cities. In recent years, a building boom has made it look even more like some of its more economically vibrant East and Southeast Asian neighbors. But many of the peasants live in poverty as extreme as anywhere in the world. The Philippines remain one of the most stratified countries in the world, a society where forty percent of the population can not meet their basic nutritional and other needs while the richest 10% hold 36% of all personal income.

The Filipino language, a refinement of the Tagalog spoken by many Philippine people, serves as the official language. Spanish is spoken by a dwindling number of descendants of the older aristocracy left by the Spaniards. English is well known and many educated Filipinos, unable to find work in their homeland have left the country. For example, many Filipino medical doctors and nurses have settled in the United States.

The influence of the Catholic Church is also very important. The church controls enormous holdings, and, Archbishop Jaime Cardinal Sin, who was instrumental in helping to end the Marcos dictatorship and making sure President Ramos honored the constitution by not running again, is very influential. Here again, President Estrada has managed to weaken his political base by antagonizing the church officials by supporting population control programs and the death penalty.

The church has also played an important role in condemning corrupt political practices and campaigning for greater support for the poor. Not surprisingly the church's

strong stand against birth control has made it very difficult for the Philippines to limit the country's soaring population though President Estrada has attempted to do so by supporting contraception programs.

Women

Philippine women have not been influential in their country's politics, and the careers of women such as Imelda Marcos or Corazon Aquino are more representative of the power of family connections than women's influence. In the workplace their salaries are often one third that of men. Philippine women often travel abroad to find work to support themselves and their family, They go to places like Singapore and the Persian Gulf States to serve as domestic servants and, as often in the United States, as nurses. In fact, the Philippines supply more female overseas workers than any other country.

In the late 1980s a new family code was introduced in the Philippines that replaced the older more traditional code that had reinforced inequality between the sexes. Women gained the right to practice professions without having their husband's permission. Women also gained more rights over their children and remarriage. As is the common case in East and Southeast Asia Muslim women are covered by separate legal codes that allow polygamy. Catholic practice is understandably also very influential in the Philippines, thus divorce is not legally available (though annulment is) and abortion is available only to save the life of a mother.

Former President Ramos made a significant contribution to the rights of women

**His Eminence
Jaime Cardinal Sin**

Philippines

when he signed a new anti-rape law that offered considerable more sensitivity to the rights of the victims. Still domestic violence against women, as elsewhere, is common. In contrast to most Asian countries, Philippine women go to college more often than men do and around 10% of all women are college graduates. The figure is only around 7% for men. By 1992 women began to be admitted to the Philippine military academies.

About one-third of the workforce is female though women predominate at the lower levels earning the lowest wages. Women have made considerable gains in the field of law. They make up 26% of the trial court judges. They are also very involved in teaching at both the primary and secondary levels and outnumber men in government civil service though not at the highest levels.

Politically women have served both in the country's parliament and as cabinet level ministers though in relatively small numbers as yet. During the most recent election, Gloria Macapagal-Arroyo, daughter of a former leader and a college classmate of Bill Clinton's at Georgetown University, was elected vice-president.

Economy

The Philippine Republic is fairly rich in natural resources and, with the exception of the Manila plain, not overpopulated. Sadly, the post-World War II economy was quite weak until the mid 1990s when it started showing signs of the sort of economic vitality that many of its neighbors had demonstrated during the 1980s.

Still, much of the wealth winds up in the hands of a small group of rich individuals and families. Corruption and inflation have been a continuing problem. Under former President Marcos's "New Society," a limited land reform program was in progress. Landlords, as part of the establishment, were well compensated by the government for what land they had lost, and this further inflated the economy. President Marcos sold highly profitable monopolies of such commodities as coconuts and sugar to his friends, a system known to the opposition as "crony capitalism."

Under President Aquino, a less stifling, but still harmful version of the "crony capitalism" that had flourished under Marcos emerged. Happily, her successor, President

Fidel Ramos, was much more successful with economic reforms and carried out a significant amount of land reform and other economic efforts. Called "Philippines 2000," the government strove to change its traditional agrarian-based, paternalistic economy to an industrial and market driven one. They have moved, for example, to liberalize rules for investment, trade and banking among other economic activities.

During the mid 1990s the economy was finally showing signs of strength. If the 5.1% growth figure of 1994 pales compared to double digit numbers of some of its neighbors, economic indicators were finally showing substantive growth. By 1996 the growth rate was recorded at a much more impressive 7%.

Even more impressive, despite earlier fears, the economy has also weathered well the departure of the Americans. The former American Clark Air Force Base, now recovered from the volcano eruption, is operating as a civilian charter airport and the former naval base at Subic Bay is serving as a successful tax free port and industrial base. The American-based FEDEX company even made it its regional hub! By the mid 1990s, tourists were starting to flock to the base to enjoy the amenities built for the departed servicemen.

By the time President Ramos hosted the APEC, the Asia-Pacific Economic Cooperation, forum meeting in November 1996 he had plenty of reason to be pleased. And the facilities at the Subic Bay were ready to convince the arriving dignitaries that the Philippines, so long the laggard in the regime's economic spurt, was ready to make its own effort to become a new "Asian Tiger!"

Unfortunately, when the Asian economic crisis hit in mid 1997 the Philippines was as vulnerable as many of her neighbors and saw her own currency take a plunge. But unlike many of her neighbors the Philippines initially weathered well the international economic stresses and began not only to recover but pull ahead. Clearly the Philippine economy was helped by former President Ramos' economic reforms and especially by the political stability that seemed in place. Since the overthrow of Marcos, smooth political transitions have occurred regularly and international investors are clearly noticing. Money that might have gone to Indonesia a year ago seems to be moving toward the Philippines.

Over the last year the economy has shown a modest growth rate and inflation has lessened—two factors which contribute to the generally improving situation. Unfortunately, news of scandals, financial and otherwise, have become more and more common since President Estrada assumed office which does not help matters economically.

Students relax in a courtyard of Santo Tomas University in Manila. Founded in 1611, it is one of the oldest universities in the world.

Courtesy: Jon Markham Morrow

The Future

The Ramos government had a chance to bring about significant change to the country. Unlike Mrs. Aquino, the president was not from the aristocracy and made a lot of progress with reform. It is encouraging to note that the Ramos administration turned over more land to the peasants than had been done in the previous 20 years. Real progress was even made in dealing with the Muslim and communist rebellions. And, of course, his years in office saw a steadily improving economy until the very last months of his administration. All of these activities have paid off.

President Estrada had taken some bold moves like supporting population control and expanding the right of outside firms to purchase Philippine companies in order to expedite the country's entrance into the globalized world economy. Nevertheless, he has squandered much of his popular support which will most probably leave him politically weakened during his remaining years in office.

The Republic of Singapore

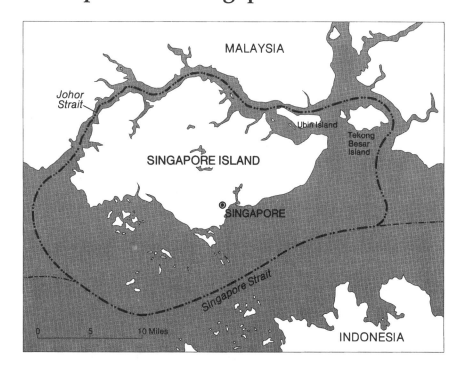

MALAYSIA

Johor Strait

Ubin Island

SINGAPORE ISLAND

Tekong Besar Island

SINGAPORE

Singapore Strait

0   5   10 Miles

INDONESIA

Area: 239 sq. mi. (618 sq. km., somewhat smaller than New York City).

Population: 3.4 million.

Capital City: Singapore (Pop. 2.79 million, estimated).

Climate: Tropically hot and humid.

Neighboring Countries: Malaysia (North); Indonesia (South).

Official Languages: Chinese (Mandarin dialect), Malay, Tamil, English.

Ethnic Background: Chinese (about 77%); Malay 14% Indian (about 7%).

Principal Religions: Buddhism, Hinduism, Islam, Christianity.

Main Exports (to Malaysia, U.S., Japan): Rubber, petroleum, tin, manufactured goods.

Main Imports (from Japan, U.S., Malaysia): Manufactured goods, petroleum.

Currency: Singapore Dollar.

Former Colonial Status: Possession of the British East India Company (1819–1867), British Crown Colony (1867–1958), occupied by the Japanese (1941–1945), internally self–governing (1958–1963).

National Day: August 9, 1965 (Independence Day).

Chief of State: Ong Teng Cheong, President (took office September 1993).

Head of Government: Goh Chok Tong, Prime Minister (1990).

Dominant Political Figure: Lee Kuan Yew, Senior Minister.

National Flag: Divided horizontally, with a white crescent moon and five white stars on a red field at the top and a white bottom.

Annual Per Capita GDP Income: U.S. $23,565.

The small island of Singapore is separated from Johor State at the southern tip of West Malaysia by a narrow strait of water; road and railway bridges provide access to the mainland. Although tropical, the island is highly urbanized. The city occupies the more agreeable part of the island on the southeast coast. Its harbor is naturally a good one, and it lies at the crossroads of Southeast Asia at one end of the Straits of Malacca. This is the best and shortest passage between the Indian Ocean and the South China Sea, and Singapore has been an important naval base and commercial port for almost two centuries.

History

Prior to the arrival of Europeans, Singapore was a small insignificant part of the Malay world, inhabited by a few fishermen but not much more. Sir Thomas Stamford Raffles of the British East India Company occupied the island in 1819 after realizing the commercial possibilities of the harbor given its very strategic location. The decision to make it a free port was quite important to the city's later growth. By 1867 it had been made a British Crown Colony. In spite of Dutch competition based on neighboring Java and Sumatra, the colony began to achieve the size of a major commercial port. The opening of the Suez Canal in 1869 attracted even heavier traffic from Europe to the Straits of Malacca.

This commercial development also resulted in the migration of many Chinese to the island. They quickly became the majority ethnic group as they labored to process rubber and tin. Over time, Singapore became the principal British stronghold in the region.

A large British naval base was constructed in the 1920s equipped with coastal defenses designed to protect it from attack by sea. Unfortunately, the new defenses were not finished by the start of World War II and the Japanese assault. When World War II began British plans came to naught. Three days after the attack on Pearl Harbor in 1941, Japanese torpedo planes sank the Prince of Wales and the Repulse, two mammoth British war-

Prime Minister Goh Chok Tong

Hon. Lee Kuan Yew

Urban Singapore

ships which had been dispatched to Singapore to help in the defense of the port. An invasion of Malaya was promptly undertaken by a large Japanese army highly trained in jungle warfare. It fell to the invaders within four weeks and the siege of Singapore began. The British held out for two weeks before the Japanese finally captured Singapore and 60,000 prisoners on February 15, 1942, in one of the worst military defeats ever suffered by Great Britain.

As elsewhere in Southeast Asia, the Japanese often mistreated those they had conquered, particularly those of Chinese origin. Ultimately, of course the Japanese were isolated from Singapore and other holdings in Southeast Asia by American

sea and air action. The British peacefully returned to the island when Japan collapsed in 1945.

After the war Britain used Singapore as their headquarters in the region. Overtime, Britain began to slowly withdraw. It did retain its bases, but decreased their size as it embarked on a pullout. During the process the U.K. maintained control over Singapore's external relations, but permitted increasing degrees of internal self–government. The government nurtured by the British was faced with serious civil strife in the mid–1950s which was promoted by labor unions and student organizations, both communist controlled.

After a new constitution was adopted,

the leftist *People's Action Party*, the *PAP*, came to power in an electoral landslide in 1959. The new Prime Minister, Lee Kuan Yew, though, he himself had ties to the communists, quickly moved to lessen their potential influence. Sensing British and Malayan concerns over his election, he made strenuous efforts to improve relations.

A widespread and ambitious program of centralized economic development and social welfare programs was instituted which caused the communists to redouble their efforts to seize control of the government—they feared a possible increase in popularity of the *People's Action Party*. During those early years of the new state the principal tensions were within the *Peo-*

Singapore

ple's Action Party—between the moderate socialists who favored more ties with Malaysia and their more extremist communist allies. Eventually the PAPs principal leftists quit to form the *Barisan Sosialis Party*, which did well in local elections held in 1961.

The apparent strength of the left in Singapore was a major source of concern to Britain and Malaya. Thus, Prime Minister Tunku Abdul Rahman of Malaya immediately proposed that Malaya, Singapore and the Borneo territories of Sabah and Sarawak be joined into the Federation of Malaysia. His purpose was twofold: to protect the stability and progress of the entire region and to control the leftist trend in Singapore; his plan was vigorously supported by the British. Prime Minister Tunku Abdul Rahman had reason to be concerned, for had Singapore become a communist state, Malaya would have suffered a serious economic blow since the island processed and shipped the bulk of the rubber and tin which produced most of Malaya's foreign exchange, it would as well have posed a political threat.

In spite of opposition by the *Barisan Sosialis Party*, the *Malayan Communist Party*, and the vehement opposition of Indonesia's President Sukarno, the Federation of Malaysia came into existence in 1963. Sukarno immediately declared that Indonesia was in a state of "confrontation" (a sort of undeclared, irregular war) with Malaysia, severing all trade relations. Singapore suffered somewhat from this step, since Indonesia had been one of its most important trading partners, but Indonesia suffered as well. Actually, the economic needs of both gave rise to a widespread smuggling operation which helped to offset the effect of the official boycott.

The short–lived union of Singapore with the Federation of Malaysia came to an end in 1965. The Federation may have solved the immediate problems of a potential communist takeover, but it did not resolve the more basic antagonism between the Malays and Chinese which has long been the greatest internal problem within Malaysia. The Malay–dominated government of the Federation preferred to deal at arms–length with the Chinese–controlled regime on the island rather than add more Chinese to the Federation's population. Lee Kuan Yew's vision of a more multi–cultural Malaysian Federation was clearly threatening to the Malay leaders of Kuala Lumpur. When he energetically tried to extend the activities of the *People's Action Party* to mainland Malaya and to exert greater influence throughout the Federation, matters came

to a head. Singapore was forced out of the Federation, left to survive on its own.

Birth of a New City

Although the separation of Singapore from the Federation of Malaysia was described as a matter of mutual consent, in reality Singapore was confronted with a demand to withdraw—it had no choice but to do so. Within Singapore leaders like Lee Kuan Yew had serious doubts that the newly independent country could survive on its own. There was, though, little choice but to try.

Over the next years the immediate problem for Singapore was survival itself, but happily the new city–state had the advantages of excellent leadership under Lee Kuan Yew and a population committed to accomplishing that goal.

Over the next years, under the paternalistic leadership of Prime Minister Lee and *PAP*, Singapore did more than survive. It prospered and became one of the most successful economies of Southeast Asia with a major commitment to improving the living standards of its people. By late century its population enjoyed the highest standard of living in the region and was one of the safest societies. Some though have come to believe in recent years that Singapore's citizens have paid a high price in political freedoms for *PAP*'s economic successes.

Political developments during the early 1960s also complemented *PAP*'s ability to dominate the new nation's political life. In elections held in 1963, the *People's Action Party* elected 39 representatives to 23 from the *Barisan Sosialis Party*. But even then Prime Minister Lee Kuan Yew so dominated the political scene in Singapore that the members of the opposition party angrily stalked out of the Parliament in 1966.

Since then the *People's Action Party* has been almost completely in charge. A new leftist opposition party formed in April 1971 and was successful in electing one member in 1981. In 1984 it doubled its holding to two, but that has hardly made a dent on the *PAP*'s monopoly of political power.

In 1986, the debates in parliament began to be televised. This gave wide publicity to the speeches of one of the only two opposition members, an articulate ethnic Indian, J.B. Jeyaretnam, who in September of that year was expelled from the body for having allegedly defamed the impartiality of Singapore's judiciary.

Over the years, the government, which maintains a limited amount of censorship, has tried to punish foreign publications which contain articles it does not like. These punishments have ranged from financial pressures to outright law suits.

In 1995, Christopher Lingle, an American academic teaching at the National University of Singapore (NUS), and four *International Herald Tribune* employees, were charged with criminal defamation for writing and printing an article in that influential daily newspaper which referred to intolerant Asian regimes and questioned the independence of their judiciaries. The *Herald* was eventually found guilty of libel and fined $674,000!

As concerns about Singapore's immediate survival have given way to economic success, Prime Minister Lee, who ran the country directly till 1990, began to concern himself with slowing the spread of what he believed were negative Western values. Distressed by the materialistic outlook of Singapore's "yuppies," he has tried to revive a modern version of Confucianism. He and other government officials have enthusiastically embraced Confucianism's more communal values and hierarchal perspective as more suitable for Singapore's predominantly Chinese population than Western individualism.

Nevertheless, while this emphasis on a Chinese approach to values has also encouraged the study of Mandarin Chinese in the schools of Singapore, the government has treated with considerable disdain and hostility those it perceives as pushing multi–cultural Singapore too far in the direction of being an exclusively Chinese nation. Important as well has been Lee Kuan Yew's concern that Singapore's population continue their commitment to learning English, an increasingly important language throughout the world.

Over the years Prime Minister Lee has viewed Singapore as fragile because of its ethnic diversity and vulnerable because of its small size when compared to its neighbors. Accordingly, he and his colleagues have done whatever they considered necessary for domestic and external security in the face of these threats. The armed forces are large for the size of the country and are impressively modern. The Internal Security Act, inherited from the British, is used by the political police, known as the Internal Security Department, to control dissent and the press.

Government and Politics

Lee Kuan Yew, in office since 1959, retired as Prime Minister in November 1990 in favor of his hand-picked successor, Deputy Prime Minister Goh Chok Tong. The change though made little difference in the political realities of Singapore. Lee Kuan Yew remained in the government with the title of "Senior Minister" and has continued to be influential. The Goh Chok Tong government has followed the path of the previous government.

Singapore

The elections, in January 1997, saw Prime Minister Goh more genuinely emerge out from under Lee Kuan Yew's shadow. This time *PAP* even won a greater electoral victory than previously. In fact, they won 65% of the votes. The election though was more than a triumph of Prime Minister's Goh's new authority. *PAP* and the government used all their powers to ensure a victory. They even announced that the government planned improvements in the city's housing infrastructure within which most of the city's citizens live and often own apartments. Interestingly, the government warned that those districts that voted against *PAP* would be last on the waiting list for improvements! The most intriguing recent development has been the emergence of the son of Lee Kuan Yew, Lee Hsien Loong, into the political limelight. He now serves as the nation's Deputy Prime Minister and has indicated interest in a "promotion".

The government's heavy hand is not the only thing that impedes the growth of a more inclusive political system. *PAP* has been in power so long and has been so suc-cessful in improving living standards that few Singapore citizens actually trust the opposition. Well aware of that sentiment, the opposition parties have been careful not to field a full list of candidates during elections. For example, in the elections of early January 1997 the opposition only contested elections in 36 of the possible 83 electoral seats. The logic has been that if the voters know that *PAP* would win regardless of how they voted, the electorate would be more willing to allow an opposition to emerge within the parliament. But that apparently did not work well enough to make a difference. As mentioned previously only two opposition politicians made it into the parliament.

As of the spring of 2000 the *PAP* holds 81 of the 83 elected seats in the nation's legislature. Indeed, the government has made it quite difficult for its opponents to build support for their causes. One opposition politician, Chee Soon Juan, has been at times both fined and jailed for publishing and giving speeches the government did not support. Last year Chee actually spent twelve days in jail for giving a political speech without a permit.

Foreign Policy

Singapore, as an independent mini-state, cannot hope to survive without friends. The strategy has been to make the country so valuable to the region that no one would wish its booming economy destroyed because of the repercussions which would be felt throughout the area. This strategy has succeeded. Singapore is one of the world's busiest ports and is the center of economic activity in Southeast Asia. It intends to keep its value high by always being the best.

Relations with Malaysia, though, can at times be complicated. Singapore has though come to an agreement with Malaysia on its international sea boundary. A flap over a Malaysian tariff on Singapore petro-chemicals was recently put to rest also. Unfortunately, more problems surfaced early in 1997 when Senior Minister Lee Kuan Yew made disparaging remarks about crime problems in one of the Malaysian cities closest to Singapore. The comments were not welcomed and Lee later apologized. Nor were relations improved when Lee later published the first

Rush hour in Singapore

WORLD BANK Photo

165

Singapore

A young boy in Singapore
WORLD BANK Photo

volume of his memoirs about the early years of the city. Many in Malaysia were unhappy with his comments about some of their previous leaders. The reality is Malaysian-Singapore relations are often tense. And considering that Singapore gets most of its food and water from Malaysia, having a good relationship is especially important.

The most important challenge of recent years has been to help Indonesia through the economic and more recently political challenges it faces. Singapore had good relations with Suharto but with the dictator's departure a new and stable relationship needs to be developed. Here again, the outspoken Lee Kuan Yew had complicated matters by making disparaging remarks about Suharto's designated vice-president and then successor, B.J. Habibie. And of course Singapore's citizens could hardly remain indifferent to the fate of so many Indonesian ethnic Chinese who found themselves threatened by the violence unleashed during Suharto's fall from power. And while Singapore did not send troops to East Timor during the crisis and intervention of the summer of 1999 it did send a medical team to lend support to the effort.

In the months since Abdurrahman Wahid came to power in Indonesia Singapore has attempted to improve relations with him, and Wahid's government has reciprocated by asking Lee Kuan Yew to serve on a panel of outside advisors for Indonesia.

Until recently perhaps the most profound aspect of Singapore's foreign relations was the influence it has had on the region as a model of economic and social growth under a non-communist but authoritarian regime. Despite Western preferences and claims that a free and vibrant economy can not exist without a politically open system, Lee Kuan Yew and the *PAP* long seemed to have demonstrated that they apparently can. It is an example that countries as close as Malaysia and as far as the People's Republic have watched closely.

Culture

Despite impressions held elsewhere, Singapore is a more multi-cultural city than many people realize. The vast majority of the population is certainly Chinese, but they immigrated from several parts of southern China and thus tended to speak mutually unintelligible dialects until the government began its emphasis on learning "Mandarin" Chinese. That is also one of the reasons English has long been used as the official language of instruction, business and in government. Moreover, the community includes a significant minority of Malays and South Asians as well.

The central feature of society in Singapore today is that it is centered around the industry of a bustling port and its very urban citizens who enjoy the highest standard of living of the region. Rather than living in the countryside, they live in apartments that the government built and that they have been encouraged to purchase.

An Engineered Society?

Singapore's leadership has made extraordinary improvements in the life of its citizens. It has done so at a price that some might find excessive. The government has intervened in many aspects of the lives of its citizens, thus creating an astoundingly regulated society. There are rules for practically everything from selling gum to landscaping and cleanliness. Still, as a result of the government's almost puritanical attitude, Singapore is one of the safest and cleanest places in the world. Economic prosperity, however, has not been sufficient to keep the country's best and brightest at home. Significant numbers of highly educated young citizens have left the country in search of greater political freedom. While some have returned, the fact that prosperity alone is not sufficient should give the government cause to ponder how much authoritarianism is appropriate for a modern, well-educated society.

Education is highly admired in Singapore and the society is moving smoothly into the computer age. Increasing numbers of households have personal computers and more and more of them are connected to the Internet. Unfortunately for the government, that has opened up yet another vehicle of potential disruption that the government would rather avoid.

Overall, the island has acquired a genuinely cosmopolitan atmosphere with people from all over the world present. The city-state serves as a major international port which lies at the crossroads of Asia. For a modern urban society Singapore is also a very safe city whose crime rates are quite low—certainly lower than in many urban centers in America or many other places in Asia. In fact, until recently it could boast that the crime rate had gone down every year for the last nine! Unfortunately, no doubt tied to the recent economic stresses, it has begun to climb again.

Nevertheless, no matter how much Singapore's leaders might strive to engineer their community's environment and social system, something intervened recently to show the limits of their power. The society that prides itself on being especially sanitary found itself gasping for air as its very atmosphere was choked by the haze and smoke caused by out of control fires begun in Indonesia.

Women

Women in Singapore have the same civil rights as men, and these were written into law in the early 1960s when the Women's Charter was enacted. In contrast to some other parts of Asia the local minority population of Muslim women are covered by most of the provisions of the Charter, though, in matters of polygamy and divorce Islamic law prevails. The government has also mandated that women should get equal pay for equal work and no longer allows separate pay scales.

Inequalities do exist. For example, women do not have the same rights males do in passing on their citizenship automatically to their children. Moreover, medical benefits available to the families of male civil servants are denied to families of female employees.

Economy

In a fashion similar to that pioneered in Japan, Singapore's economy has been developed along the lines some refer to as "Asian Capitalism" though without the corruption often associated with the term. Most importantly, the government, in contrast to "Anglo-American capitalism"'s ever present suspicions about government, Singapore's government has tried to play an important role in guiding the nation's economy. Employing institutions like the Economic Development Board and the Trade Development Board, the leadership has helped guide and set priorities for the economic evolution of Singapore. Such institutions have been especially helpful as Singapore has moved through various economic stages from the processing of primary products to the new information technologies.

Singapore is heavily dependent on foreign trade and investment which it is doing its best to promote. Since the mid-1980s the economy had been growing at a rate of about 8% a year. In 1988, because of its high level of development and its various contributions to the U.S.'s trade imbalance, and much to its annoyance, Singapore lost its preferential tariff status under the U.S.'s Generalized System of Preferences (GSP). Still in the mid 1990s the growth rates averaged around nine percent and Singapore has among the highest annual per capita GNPs in the world. Nevertheless, its economy was becoming sluggish as the 1990s grew to a close.

Even before the onset of the economic crisis of 1997 the island suffered a glut of empty retail spaces and very high rents. Wages were high and rising because labor was chronically short. Not surprisingly there had been a slump in retail sales within the city and some big retailers have pulled back on their operations.

It was in the context of these problems that Singapore, along with its neighbors, experienced the many economic problems 1997 brought. Not only did its currency plunge but tourist arrivals—no doubt frightened by the stories of the choking atmosphere a few years ago—dropped significantly.

Acting pro-actively the government has continued its effort to develop new industries such as those in information technologies and electronic commerce. And Singapore's leaders have reason to be pleased. As the island nation entered the new century the economy appeared largely on track again with a predicted growth rate of 5% for 1999 even as some sectors in the economy were still experiencing retrenchments.

The Future

The success of Singapore may have less to do with the distinct values its leaders talk about than it does with the country's manageable size and optimum location. Some educated youth already find the tradeoff between the general economic prosperity and restricted political and social freedom difficult. This will probably only become intensified over time.

For example, the arrival to adulthood of a generation that takes the material advantages of life in Singapore for granted and is thus not so afraid of losing them may soon demand greater political participation than the government will be willing to grant.

For the immediate future, the most important goal will be to play a positive role in helping its regional neighbors, especially Indonesia, draw back from the economic abyss they fell into over the last few years.

Traffic system at rush hours to reduce congestion

The Kingdom of Thailand (before 1935 known as Siam)

Bustling traffic in Chiang Mai

Courtesy: CALTEX Petroleum Corp.

Area: 198,455 sq. mi. (514,820 sq. mi., more than twice the size of Oregon).

Population: 60 million (estimated).

Capital City: Bangkok (Pop. 5 million, estimated).

Climate: Tropically hot with a wet monsoon season (May–October), dry and increasingly hot (November–April).

Neighboring Countries: Malaysia (South); Burma (Northwest); Laos (Northeast); Cambodia (Southeast).

Official Language: Thai (about 75%).

Other Principal Tongues: Chinese (about 14%); other (about 11%).

Ethnic Background: Thai (about 75%); Chinese (about 14%); Malay (about 4%); inland tribal groups (about 2%); Cambodian refugees (about 2%); other (about 3%).

Principal Religions: *Theravada* Buddhism, Islam.

Main Exports (to Japan, U.S., Singapore): Rice, sugar, corn, rubber, tin, timber.

Main Imports (from Japan, U.S., Saudi Arabia): Machinery and transport equipment, petroleum, chemicals, fertilizer.

Currency: Baht.

Former Political Status: Siam avoided becoming a European colony; it was a nominal ally of Japan during World War II.

National Day: December 10th (Constitution Day).

Chief of State: His Majesty King Bhumibol Adulyadej (b. 1927).

Head of Government: Chuan Leekpai, Prime Minister (since 1997).

National Flag: Five horizontal stripes from top to bottom; red, white, blue (wider than the others),white and red.

Per Capita Income: GNP income $2,960.

The broad central plain of Thailand, through which flows the Chao Phraya River, is the most fertile and productive area of the country and contains the principal cities, including Bangkok. Viewed from the foothills which are found on the western edge of the plain, the land resembles an almost endless window with countless "panes of glass" when the precisely divided rice paddies are flooded with water.

The North and Northwest are more mountainous, and are covered with jungles containing timber and mineral resources. Valuable teakwood is still brought from the jungle on the tusks of the Asian elephant. The northeast region is dominated by the arid Korat Plateau. Ample rainfall occurs in the plateau, but it is not absorbed by the sandstone soil—it quickly collects into streams and rivers and runs to the sea instead of enriching the land. More people live here than can be supported by the limited agriculture that is possible.

Thailand

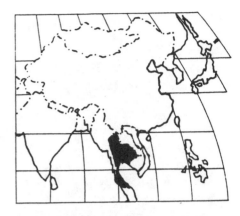

The southern region consists of the narrow Kra Isthmus which is hot and very humid, and the coastal belt, where quantities of rubber are produced by Thailand's Malay minority.

History

People of Thai origin today not only inhabit Thailand but also live in the adjacent regions of all of Thailand's neighbors with the exception of Malaysia. The original home of these people was in southwest China, where they were ruled by a highly organized kingdom in the 7th century A.D. The pressure of the Chinese and later the Mongols caused a migration of the Thais southward; they founded a state in what is now northern Thailand.

In sharp contrast to governmental traditions in China, the Thai kings ruled as autocratic divine beings. Although, they have not ruled directly for much of the 20th century, elements of this earlier tradition continue in the on–going reverence the Thai people still hold for their monarchy.

During centuries of slow expansion they were eventually able to crush the Khmer Empire in neighboring Cambodia. In the 16th century, Siam, as it was then called, was conquered by the Burmese. Apart from sporadic contact by French merchants, the Europeans did not enter the area during the early centuries of exploration and colonization.

There was another Burmese invasion in 1767, but shortly thereafter Burma was invaded by the Manchu empire of China, enabling the Siamese to expel them. The present reigning dynasty came to power in 1782 and moved the capital city to the more secure location of Bangkok. Siam again emerged as a strong state. But though Siam's relations were already complicated, they were about to get much more so.

The Arrival of the West

Early in the 19th century, Siam began to have more extensive contacts, commercial and otherwise, with Westerners. Moreover, the British gradually established control over Burma and the French asserted their power over Vietnam. Laos and Cambodia had formerly been tributary states of Siam, but the French were ultimately able to combine them with Vietnam in their colony of Indochina. Thus, Siam was surrounded by the British on the west, the French on the east and the Manchu empire of China on the north.

Nevertheless Siam managed to avoid becoming a European colony by a lucky combination of factors, first, the advantages of having not one but two European colonial powers on their borders (who could then be played off against each other) and enlightened leadership which moved to strengthen the country through an increasing degree of modernization. It was a combination too few other non–Western states enjoyed.

In Siam's case, two important monarchs, during the critical late nineteenth and early 20th century, helped shield them from the worst of imperialism. The first was Mongkut, who reigned in the critical period of the mid–nineteenth century, and his son Chulalongkorn who followed him in power. It was Mongkut who was the monarch described in the book *Anna and the King of Siam* and in the musical *The King and I*.

Phra Maha Chulalongkorn, his son, was king from 1868 to 1910, and gained fame not only by abolishing Siam's feudal system, but by modernizing the government, the army and by introducing such conveniences as the telegraph and railroad. He also paid an extended visit to the European capitals.

Both monarchs, father and son, recognizing the seriousness of the Western

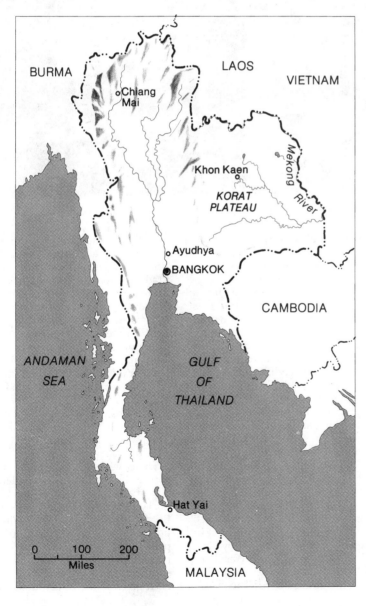

Thailand

The Grand Palace, Bangkok

threat, took significant efforts to educate themselves in Western issues and to find ways to lessen the growth of Western power in Siam. Overall their policies were a combination of tactical acceptance of various legal and territorial demands made by the Europeans while working overall to maintain the ultimate sovereignty of the Siamese state.

There were some later treaties in 1904–1907 which adjusted the borders with Laos and Cambodia. Under these treaties, regions were traded back and forth between France and Siam. In order to keep other colonial powers out of Siam, France and Britain established "spheres of influence"—the French east of the Chao Phraya River and the British west of the river.

As a result of its somewhat limited, but significant, modernization program, and the fact that it escaped being a colony of a European power, Thailand today lacks the sense of resentment toward the industrialized nations that many people feel in the countries of the former colonial world.

A New Political System

After World War I there was a period of extravagant spending by the royal government, which was followed by a world–wide economic depression. This created tensions and discontent within Thailand and gave rise to intense political activity. The result was a bloodless overthrow of the autocratic monarchy in 1932 by a combination of civilian politicians and military leaders.

The two groups cooperated in the adoption of a constitution which limited the power of the king and established a parliamentary form of government. The first Prime Minister was a brilliant lawyer named Pridi Phanomyong. The king, dissatisfied with this system, abdicated in 1935, and was succeeded by his ten–year–old nephew and a regency council. This and other unsettling conditions, including the increased power of Japan in Asia, led to the overthrow of Pridi by Marshal Pibul Songgram. As World War II approached Marshal Pibul would prove to be especially nationalistic and pro–Japanese.

In theory the country continued to be governed by a coalition consisting of the Prime Minister, the military and Luang Pradit, the foreign minister. As the military acquired increasing political power, they displayed their nationalism by such means as legislation aimed at curbing the role of the Chinese commercial community and changing the nation's name from Siam to Thailand, meaning "Land of the Free." In the years since the 1932 coup the Thai military, like the later Burmese and Indonesian military, would insist on an important place for itself in national decision making.

The Pacific War

Three weeks after the bombing of Pearl Harbor by the Japanese, Thailand signed a treaty of alliance with Japan. War was declared on the United States and Great Britain on January 25, 1942. With the support of Japanese troops, Thailand compelled the French to cede some border territories in Laos and Cambodia. The four southern states of Thailand, which had been given to the British in Malaya at the turn of the century, were now returned to Thailand by the Japanese after they seized the British colony of Burma. Thailand probably had little choice in cooperating with the armies of imperial Japan. The Japanese certainly had the means to impose their will on Thailand and had demonstrated their strength in early clashes with the Thai forces.

As the war began to turn against Japan, the Thai government, which has a long history of protecting itself through power politics, began to change sides. An anti-Japanese guerrilla movement arose, and American military intelligence officers were able to operate almost openly in Bangkok during the last months of the war.

Pibul, himself, the pro-Japanese premier, resigned in 1944. At the end of the war, Britain took the position that Thailand was an enemy country and compelled payment of reparations in the form of rice, which was sent to Malaya. The U.S. however viewed Thailand as a more reluctant Japanese ally, and was able to persuade the British to adopt a similar policy.

The Postwar Years

Thailand's most immediate problem in the postwar years was to reintegrate itself into the world community after having been allied with Imperialist Japan and to establish a stable government. The former proved easier than the latter. The lands taken from France and Britain during the war were returned and Thailand was admitted to the UN in 1946.

Political stability however proved more difficult. The king, who had only recently been enthroned, was found dead of a gunshot wound in 1946. Premier Pridi, who was accused, apparently falsely, of having played some part in the slaying, was deposed. The army, still led by Pibul, again seized power. It was a pattern that was to continue through the 1990s.

The Cold War

Initially it appeared uncertain as to what position Thailand would take in the Korean war. Once it decided to support the American-backed UN troops, it began to receive U.S. military aid. This further strengthened the political position of the army in domestic affairs, making it more and more powerful within Thailand and, given the economic support of the wealthy Americans, helping to build the country's economic infrastructure.

The early 1950s saw many leaders like Nehru of India and Sukarno of Indonesia attempting to build a non-aligned movement during the height of the Cold War. Some governments accepted this position, but Thailand chose to align itself more di-

rectly with the Americans. Thailand became a founding member of the SEATO, the Southeast Asian Treaty Organization (designed to be an Asian equivalent of NATO) and supported the American war in Vietnam.

Premier Pibul did permit freer discussion of political issues and actually began to encourage a growth of neutralism. Concerned about potential Communist Chinese influence he also took steps against the local Chinese community that traditionally had been involved in the economy but refrained from taking part in politics.

Nevertheless, Communist gains in Laos between 1960 and 1962 created more uneasiness in Thailand, which was dispelled when the U.S. pledged direct assistance in the event SEATO failed to fully support Thailand.

Pibul was overthrown in 1958 by Marshal Sarit, who kept Thailand firmly in an anti-communist posture. The country had an orderly, stable and not terribly intrusive government. As was true in so many nations, the military leaders were able to accumulate vast private fortunes through corruption.

Less effective military leadership continued after 1963 under subsequent leaders. Reliance was placed upon the ability of the popular royal family to maintain the unity of the Thai people, as well as on an increased degree of official respect shown for Buddhism and its various organizations. However, communist-inspired unrest in the poverty-stricken northeast region became more serious. The government treated this as a genuine threat, though perhaps partly to obtain additional American aid.

Once the United States fully committed to the struggle in Vietnam, Thailand permitted the Americans to use its air bases for attacks on North Vietnam and the Viet Cong. Thailand itself sent about 11,000 troops to fight in Vietnam and Laos. Having sided with the wealthy Americans, Thailand was able to gain enormous economic aid which helped in it own development and, as before, especially assisted the Thai military continue to assert itself.

The reaction from the communist side was predictable—as Thailand increased its assistance to the U.S. and South Vietnam, the communists stepped up their guerrilla activities within the country. The increased

Geese raised on a poultry farm south of Bangkok

Thailand

The Royal Family of Thailand

U.S. military buildup in Thailand was thus paralleled by a greater flow of U.S. aid to the Thai armed forces. But if Thailand's clear association with the anti–communist side was clear in these years its own domestic politics were less so.

The National Assembly was dissolved in 1968, and there was no representative body in Thailand. Eventually, a constitution was drafted by a Constituent Assembly and promulgated by the King in mid–1968. Elections of 1969 gave the *United Thai People's Party,* the government party, the victory. The Senate was then appointed by the government.

But, a powerful military, unhappy with developments, suspended the parliament and reshuffled the cabinet. In 1972 a new constitution was proclaimed under which 299 members of a National Assembly were all appointed by the government, i.e. the army.

A Democratic Experience, 1973–1976

But the next year, the army–dominated government was toppled by student demonstrations that had the support of the King and at least part of the Army itself. A civilian government was then ushered in, committed to greater freedom and

reform. It was yet another step, such as in 1932, when the autocratic monarchy had ended, that gave Thailand the possibility of moving toward a more democratic form of government. And in this case, it was partially as a result of the intervention of the monarchy itself which had not played a political role since 1932. As the new government was formed in 1973 Thailand seemed on the verge of taking yet another step toward more inclusive political decision making.

But true parliamentary government was not to develop in Thailand at least not during those years. A combination of insecurity caused by the growing strength of Communism in the region—Vietnam had been unified under Hanoi and Cambodia taken over the *Khmer Rouge*—as well as unhappiness about the open political battles within the new democratic government moved the military to once again reassert itself and stage another coup in 1976. In October of that year, with the backing of the King, the government was overthrown and the democratic constitution suspended.

Over the next years Thailand's politics have been moved by several factors—the emerging democratic movement, which had its first real chance to govern in the

mid 1970s, the ever influential Thai military and the King who has continued to be revered and has demonstrated a willingness to intervene in the governing system when he deems it appropriate.

An informal power sharing arrangement between the army and civilian politicians and officials has been common over the last generation. Army leadership has divided between those willing to work with civilians and those who are not. Rule has shifted between civilian and military–dominated governments, with and without ex–generals in the premiership, and outright military rule. Corruption has been commonplace. One cannot detect any significant change in the most recent events but there have been signs in the 1990s that the military's domination of Thai politics has been increasingly challenged by the growth of a more politically conscious middle class population.

Another civilian government was brought down because of corruption charges by the military in a 1991 coup. Rule then shifted to the military dominated National Peacekeeping Council. In March 1992, a three party coalition favored by the Council won control of the government with 53% of the seats in the lower house of parliament. The NPC then appointed all 270 members of the upper house with most having military backgrounds or connections.

But when agreement could not be achieved on a new prime minister, the leader of the "junta," General Suchinda Kraprayoon, a key figure in the coup, and an individual especially unpopular with those who supported democracy, stepped into the post. Public demonstrations against Suchinda then led to severe repression by the Thai military. The level of violence against the civilian population was unparalleled in the constitutional period (since 1932).

The King stepped in to calm the crisis. On May 20, Suchinda appeared on national television kneeling before King Bhumibol. He was ordered to settle the crisis peacefully. After a short period of "caretaker" government, new elections were held on September 13, 1992. Chuan Leekpai was chosen as prime minister. The constitution now required that the prime minister be chosen from the lower house of parliament. The new government was ruled by a five–party coalition. This made it difficult to proceed with the legislative agenda which centered on constitutional

reform. Nevertheless, the army had been warned. It could no longer assume the civilian population would simply go along with anything it attempted.

In May 1995, Prime Minister Chuan Leekpai was forced to dissolve parliament when the *Palang Dharma* party pulled out of the ruling five party coalition. Elections took place on the following July which saw the Prime Minister's coalition lose. Thai voters then elected the *Chart Thai* party's Banharn Silpa–Archa as prime minister. The Banharn government was built around a seven party coalition led by his party, *Chart Thai*, and the *Palang Dharma* which defected from Chuan's coalition prior to the election. The coalition won 169 seats in the House of Representatives.

But the new government came under fire almost immediately for a kickback scheme involving the Prime Minister's party and a Swedish submarine manufacturer, and for protecting a minister involved in vote–buying.

Moreover, the military's recent reticence to intervene seemed less sure when a military radio broadcast criticizing the government for its management of the economy raised concerns in Bangkok and abroad. A

disagreement over military promotions between the Minister of Defense and the Army Commanding General, Wimol Wongwanich, also worsened civil–military relations. To make matters worse, the King criticized the government for the traffic chaos in Bangkok. By mid–1996 prospects were not looking bright for the Banharn government and by November new elections brought Chavalit Yongchaiyudh, the Defense Minister, from the previous government, to power.

As a former Armed Forces Chief, Chavalit had close ties not only to the Thai military but to Burma's military junta as well. The new leader was 65 and claimed he was committed to cleaning up corruption. That was probably a good idea since his own party, the *New Aspiration Party*, was said to have been the most involved in buying votes during the elections!

Chavalit had his work cut out for him. Even before the economic crises of 1997 his government had to face calls for a new constitution in order to reduce corruption. Unfortunately, political corruption and vote buying have long been a problem. As has been the case in so many other countries, Thai electoral politics has been

Floating market in Ratchaburi Province south of Bangkok

Photo by Karla Allan

Thailand

Prime Minister Chuan Leekpai

driven by money. In fact, enormous sums of money are usually spent to influence elections including even the direct purchase of votes in rural areas.

To address the problem a group of former parliamentary members and legal experts were chosen to write a new constitution. The results of their efforts were presented to the nation's legislature during the fall of 1997. At that point Chavalit, despite his earlier promises, seemed more in support of those who feared the new constitution would hurt their personal interests. Chief among the changes were the direct election of senators, rather than appointment by the prime minister, more regulations to promote public accountability and further guarantees of individual rights.

The rules for election to the senate were particularly creative. To make the election as incorruptible as possible, those running were not allowed to make any public announcements about proposed goals once in office! And later after the early 2000 senate elections occurred it became especially clear that the commitment to ensuring a more honest electoral process was still firmly in place. To the surprise and irritation of many senatorial candidates the electoral commission, citing concerns about corruption, revoked the victories of more than a third of the winners and called for new supplemental elections! Happily for those who support the new constitution, the new charter has had both the support of the population and the military.

It was a difficult fight and in the end one of the few significant accomplishments of Prime Minister Chavalit's term in office, even accepting his somewhat ambivalent support. For even as the battle over the constitution was going on during the fall, the more immediate crises over the economy was raging. In that bat-

tle the Prime Minister, in office for less than a year, would not prevail.

The economic turmoil now known as the "Asian Economic Crisis" began in 1997 with a crisis over the value of Thailand's national currency, the Baht. Unfortunately, the Prime Minister seemed bewildered by the crisis and many in the country quickly concluded he lacked the skills to take on the challenge. Thus Prime Minister Chavalit became the region's first political casualty of the economic crisis that was setting in.

His replacement, former Prime Minister Chuan Leekpai, returned to power in November of 1997. When Chuan Leekpai, 59, assumed office again, many in Thailand voiced a collective sense of relief that he would be better able to deal with the crisis than his predecessor. Certainly no one person could singlehandedly pull the country back from the brink, but Chuan did move quickly to build a strong support team around himself and then set off for an important meeting in Washington where he was successful in improving relations with the United States, and most importantly, resolving a problem over new defense aircraft Bangkok had ordered and no longer could afford. The trip turned out so well that even his opponents seemed satisfied.

Nevertheless, despite the early confidence he had received from the public, Chuan Leekpai's popularity did not last as long as he might have liked. By mid 1999, much of his authority was being weakened by revelations of corruption among some of his political coalition partners. The Prime Minister responded by inviting new partners into the ruling coalition in order to expand his parliamentary majority. It seemed to work, for by the spring of 2000 the prime minister was still firmly in charge of his coalition government.

Governmental System

The Thai political system is a constitutional monarchy. The military is still influential but far less willing than in the past to intervene in the country's domestic affairs. As we have seen, Thailand has struggled to evolve a modern workable political system since 1932. The first four decades of the constitutional period were dominated largely by the military. Civilian led governments though have become more common since the 1970s. But they have not always been very stable. During the last few years Thailand has had several different prime ministers.

In order for civilian government to truly establish itself several things must take place. First, corruption must be curtailed. As Thailand's educated middle class grows, this segment of society, like ele-

ments of the military, will no longer accept the old ways of doing things. Secondly, national politics must be expanded beyond Bangkok to all parts of the country.

For the time being though there is reason to be quite optimistic. Thailand's military has continued to remove itself from politics and the economy is once again on the upswing. It will, of course, take time to judge the results but many have reason to hope that the new constitution will successfully nurture an even more democratic and economically stable Thailand for the future.

Foreign Policy

Thailand's foreign relations are driven by its geographic location and pragmatism. It has a fascinating history of keeping enemies at bay through diplomatic and other means which generally have not involved the direct use of force. The general trend has been toward improving relations with its neighbors including Cambodia, Vietnam and the People's Republic.

Thailand has also moved to involve itself in more international activities. During the crisis over East Timor, Bangkok decided to dispatch around 1,500 soldiers to reestablish stability in that troubled community and a Thai officer became second in command over the entire military effort there.

Thai officials profess not to be worried about China's growing military might. However, there is concern over the potential for large scale Chinese migration into the country and the possible impact from a flood of inexpensive products from the north which could undercut sectors of the Thai economy. These concerns are long term and unpublicized but they are real.

Nevertheless, rather than shut China out, Thailand wants to see relations between the two countries expanded. Over the last year Prime Minister Chuan Leekpai visited the People's Republic, and President Jiang Zemin made a well publicized visit to Thailand.

Because of its well integrated overseas Chinese community which dominates the business sector, Thai officials and businessmen feel they have an advantage over other Southeast Asian states in opening up new economic links with China, and that they can even provide a link for the other ASEAN states to the People's Republic. In contrast to many other Southeast nations, the local Chinese community also takes an active part in politics.

During the 1990s, the huge explosion in the study of Mandarin was also welcomed in Bangkok. Beijing was also particularly helpful during the early stage of the Asian economic crisis when it agreed to buy large amounts of Thai rice and other commodities to help the struggling economy. Beijing also contributed a billion dollars to the IMF bail-out funds that were arranged to help Thailand and avoided devaluing its own currency which would have made recovery much more difficult.

Relations with Burma remain complex. The defeat of the Karen rebels in Burma in January 1995, sent thousands of refugees across the Thai border and altered relations between the two countries. The Burmese believed the Thais were aiding the Karens. Bangkok was upset because of Burmese military raids on refugee camps inside Thai territory. Later that spring, Burmese officials closed a major border crossing at Mae Sod which resulted in a significant economic loss for businesses on the Thai side of the line. Most recently Burmese authorities were quite incensed over what they perceived to be the "gentle handling" of some Burmese dissidents who took over Rangoon's Bangkok embassy for a time during the late fall of 1999. This resulted in yet another border closing.

Other tensions, including concerns over competing off-shore territorial claims, have also impacted in the region. In May 1995, Thai and Vietnamese navy patrols exchanged gunfire off the Thai coast. Thai fishing boats and crews were taken by the Vietnamese. It is worth noting that Burma and Malaysia have also seized Thai fishing boats.

Relations with the United States are also important and at times difficult. During the early development of the Asian economic crisis many felt, probably correctly, that the U.S. had been slow in reacting to the gravity of the economic problems that beset the region. Fortunately, as the crisis developed and the Americans became more actively involved in trying to resolve the situation, these concerns became less significant. By the time the new Prime Minister visited President Clinton in Washington during the spring of 1998, things appeared generally back on track.

Society and Culture

Shortly after their arrival in Southeast Asia, the Thai were converted to the Theravada school of Buddhism, which came from the island of Sri Lanka. The numerous colorful festivals and the participating monks almost completely dominate the traditions of the people. Thai architecture is unique, colorful and particularly elaborate.

The customs and traditions of the larger cities and Bangkok has been modified greatly by increased contacts with the West, particularly with Americans. In fact, Thailand is among those developed countries with the greatest divergence between the very urbanized middle classes of Bangkok and the peasant farmers in much of the rest of the country.

For years visitors to the city have had to put up with some of the worst traffic in the world. Today the situation is improving. Parts of the Bangkok expressway are now open, and it is now possible to get from one part of the city to another without planning an all day excursion.

Women

As elsewhere, Thai women have grown up in a region that generally values boys more than girls. Today, the situation of women in Thailand is especially complex and combines both examples of considerable progress and proof of their continuing lack of control over their own lives.

For Thai women, though the military has allowed a few into their upper ranks, girls are still not allowed to attend the nation's military academies. Women have fewer rights than men in obtaining documents like passports and domestic law favors husbands. Men, for example, have more rights under the divorce laws. Politically, women are less than 10% of those appointed to the Thai senate. On the other hand young women have far more access to education today and half of the college graduates are female. Where the problem is especially acute is not among Thai women themselves, but among the thousands of young women from Thailand's poorer neighbors, especially countries like Vietnam and Burma who are lured to Bangkok with offers of jobs and then find themselves in virtual debt slavery in the brothels of that huge city.

In early 1994 an ominous cloud appeared on the horizon. A report by an international organization revealed that Thailand now has the fastest growing AIDS population in all of Asia. In spite of a very successful birth control program a number of years ago, there has been little public education about AIDS until recently. Figures for young women especially in northern Thailand are very high. In Bangkok, perhaps 50% of the prostitute community is infected. To make matters worse, a new more powerful strain of AIDS was discovered in Thailand in 1995.

The Thai government has attempted to move against the traffickers and various international organizations have attempted to improve the situation of these young women but the situation remains a very tragic one today.

Economy

Until recently the Thai economy had been among the fastest growing in Asia. Many had expected it to become one of

Sculptured topiary elephants on the grounds of the Royal Summer Palace.

Thailand

Carving teak furniture, one of Chiang Mai's cottage industries.

Courtesy: Marilynn and Mark Swenson

the "Asian Tigers" like Taiwan, Hong Kong, Singapore, and South Korea which had so impressed the world over the last decade or so. In fact, according to the World Bank Thailand's growth between 1985 and 1994 was a robust 8.2%, even better than South Korea in those years. Even in early 1997, things still looked fairly good. The huge American company, General Motors, signed a deal for a new car plant said to be worth over $750 million dollars and which promised 1500 new jobs for its people. And though the situation seemed to change suddenly during the summer of 1997, in truth the problems had been building for quite some time.

In the first half of the 1990s, it appeared that the infrastructure of the country was simply unable to keep pace with the rapidly growing economy. Efforts were made to put a mass transit system into place in the horrendously congested Bangkok area but that is not complete. Progress, though, in building up the country's infrastructure in a logical way is being made. New factories are being located outside the Bangkok area in industrial parks. Each is required to have its own waste water treatment plant. The water coming out of these plants today is far cleaner than the water taken in for use by the industries.

Bangkok had been making progress in helping the country deal with its growing involvement in the world economy, and though the economy had slowed down,

few anticipated the developments of July 1997. That summer, international currency speculators aroused by Thailand's huge private foreign debt began to speculate against the value of the Baht. Though the government defended the price of the local currency through the summer, it was forced by July to devalue the Baht. Thailand's economic bubble began to burst. Especially hurt were the many business people who seeking better loan rates abroad had gone heavily in debt over loans pegged in currencies like the American dollar. Whether the loans had been economically viable when they were originally made or not, they became impossible burdens when Thai locals had to buy much more expensive American dollars to repay them.

The economic crisis had begun. Thailand would not be the only nation caught in the collapse. Soon, Thailand had to turn to the International Monetary Fund to gain the financial resources needed to deal with the crisis though as always those funds came with demands for economic reforms and budget cutting that few countries take easily. Nevertheless, by the spring of 1999, Thailand seemed to be gaining the reputation as one of the nations of the region which had most responsibly taken on the challenges of the economic crises.

And Thailand's leaders had reason to be pleased as the nation entered the new century. Once again, the economy was going

strongly. If the growth rates were not what they had been at points during the previous generation—growth rates of 3–4% were being projected. Clearly it looked as if the worst was over.

But even as Bangkok seems determined to crawl back from the brink, basic problems continue to exist. The country faces serious problems with its natural resources and limited technological base. Because so much of the country's timber has been cut, erosion is rampant. The quality of the soil is being negatively affected, and flooding is common. Happily, while the environment remains a critical problem and will be for decades to come, there is now visible evidence of government efforts. One can now see miles of newly planted trees along major highways and the ban on cutting Teak wood is apparently strongly enforced.

Like other countries of the region, Thailand also faces shortages in the personnel needed to run a modern technological society. They clearly need more college graduates with technical training and especially so as the growth of the Internet impacts on Asia as it has already hit in other parts of the world.

The most immediate challenge, of course, is getting the economy back on track in a realistic way that recognizes that the momentum of recent years is probably over. Thailand has made enormous strides but now, even after the current

Boats on the Chao Phya River

crisis is winding down the next steps in development will probably be more demanding. Creating an economic system more able to withstand the challenges of today's global economy will be one of the most important steps.

The Future

For years a basic political question remained: the question of whether the Thai military would remain outside of domestic politics. Increasingly, we appear to have an answer. The military does seem content to remain in the background and perhaps occupy itself with its growing role as a contributor to international peacekeeping efforts such as that in East Timor.

Also important will be the ability of the monarchy to continue its respected status into the next generation. That is important because the current monarch King Bhumibol Adulyadej (b. 1927) has often served as an important symbol of stability during various crises.

Economically the worst of the economic crisis seems over though the country has an enormous amount of catching up to do. Recent studies have shown that since the onset of the Asian economic crisis, Thailand has lost all the gains made since 1981 in reducing poverty! Certainly that in itself is a sobering reality as Thailand now works to regain her lost economic momentum.

The Socialist Republic of Vietnam

Secondary school students being instructed in computer techniques.

Area: 128,190 sq. mi. (329,707 sq. km., about 1/3 smaller than California).

Population: 76,700,000 (1997 est.).

Capital City: Hanoi (Pop. 2.5 million, estimated).

Climate: Subtropical, with cooler weather in the higher elevations. The Mekong Delta area is hot and humid.

Neighboring Countries: China (North); Laos and Cambodia (West).

Official Language: Vietnamese.

Other Principal Tongues: French, Chinese.

Ethnic Background: Vietnamese (about 85%); Thai, Cambodian, Lao, Chinese, tribesmen (about 15%).

Principal Religions: Buddhism, Taoism, Confucianism, subdivided into many sects; Christianity, animism, Islam and syncretistic traditions like Caodaism, a fascinating blend of eastern and western traditions.

Main Exports (to Japan, Hong Kong, Malaysia, Thailand, Singapore, and Indonesia, principally): Agricultural products, coal, minerals and oil.

Main Imports (Japan, Hong Kong, Indonesia, and Singapore): Steel products, railroad equipment, chemicals, medicines.

Currency: Dong.

Former Colonial Status: French colony (1883–1954); occupied by the Japanese (1942–1945); anti–French struggle (1945–1954); civil war (1954–1973).

National Day: July 21, 1954. The government recognizes September 2, 1945 when independence from the French was declared and the Democratic Republic of Vietnam was proclaimed.

Chief of State: Tran Duc Luong, President (since September 1997).

Head of Government: Phan Van Khai, Prime Minister (since September 1997).

Chairman, Communist Party: This post has been vacant since the death of Ho Chi Minh in 1969.

General Secretary, Communist Party: General Le Kha Phieu (since December 29, 1997).

National Flag: A red field with a five pointed yellow star in the center.

Per Capita GDP Income: $270.

The map of Vietnam is shaped like a dumbbell. The northern "bell" is an area formerly known as Tonkin—it is quite mountainous, with peaks as high as 10,315 feet, close to the southern Chinese border. The mountains gradually dimin- ish in height as they approach the plains and river deltas closest to the Gulf of Tonkin.

The Red River originates in the lofty plateaus of the Chinese province of Yunnan, some 8,000 feet above sea level, and forms the border with China for a distance of about thirty miles. When it enters northern Vietnam it is 260 feet above sea level, descending through a narrow gorge until it widens; after being joined with the River Claire it meanders 93 miles to the sea, flowing in a shifting, irregular course that is 140 miles of curving and twisting water.

The two principal cities of northern Vietnam, Hanoi and Haiphong, are situated on the river and flooded by its waters during the wet season each year—waters which are colored red by the silt washing to the sea from the highlands. It is in this river delta region that the food of northern Vietnam is produced by peasants laboring in the fields with limited tools used by their forebears.

The "bar" of the dumbbell is a thin, coastal plain, closely confined on the west by the Annam Cordillera, a north–south range of mountains forming a natural barrier between Vietnam and Laos to the

Vietnam

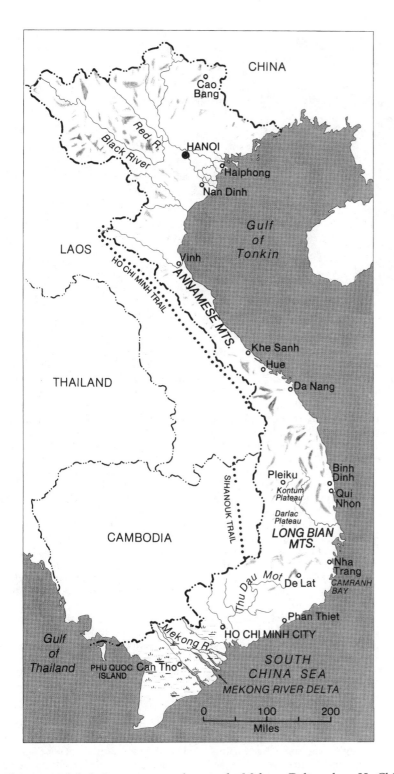

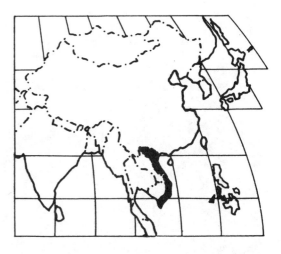

dia during the dry season, and even further upriver during the wet months each year.

Intensive agriculture, dominated by rice production, has enabled the people living in the Mekong River Delta to produce large surpluses of food in the past and present. Traditionally, two harvests of wet paddy rice are possible each year—a feat possible in very few places of the world. In contrast, only dry field rice can be grown in parts of northern Vietnam.

History

Linguistically the Vietnamese speak a Mon-Khmer language which includes a lot of Chinese words. In appearance the Vietnamese most closely resemble other Asian peoples of mongoloid origin. They began to move southward from central and southern China in the last centuries B.C., entering what is now Vietnam shortly before the modern era. Conquered by the powerful Han dynasty of China about 100 B.C., they remained a part of the Chinese empire for the next millennium.

It was natural that during those many centuries the Vietnamese adopted much of the Chinese political system and cultural patterns, but they actually feel a combination of respect, dislike and fear toward the Chinese. Through history, the Vietnamese have tried to simultaneously be "better Chinese than the Chinese" while trying to define Vietnam in terms of what is not China.

After the collapse of the Tang dynasty in China in the early 10th century, the Vietnamese broke away from direct Chinese control. They avoided further conflict with China by acknowledging themselves to be a tributary state until conquered by the French in the late 19th century.

In the late 15th century, the Vietnamese conquered lands to the south occupied by the Chams, who spoke a language similar to that of Indonesia and had adopted many

west. This coastal belt is narrow and somewhat inhospitable. Its lands are not enriched by the silt of any large river, and the typhoons of the South China Sea frequently do much damage.

The lower "bell" starts with an area of central highland plateaus which are heavily forested and inhabited by more traditional peoples who till the limited available land after clearing it by burning. These highlands gradually give way

to the Mekong Delta, where Ho Chi Minh City (formerly Saigon) is located.

The Mekong River starts in remote Tibet where snows gradually melt in the thin, icy air, gathering into small streams. Before reaching Vietnam, the waters travel almost 3,000 miles through some of the most rugged country in the world. The river is yellow and sluggish by the time it enters the country—the tides of the sea are felt as far back as Phnom Penh in Cambo-

Vietnam

Town on the Mekong River

Courtesy: William Garrett Stewart

of India's cultural patterns, including Hinduism and Buddhism. By the 18th century they began to colonize the Mekong River Delta after seizing the kingdom of Funan, also an Indian type of state.

French Colonialism

French interest in Indochina, the name given to the eastern portion of mainland Southeast Asia, began in the 18th century. Initially taking the form of commercial and missionary contacts, the French effort did not become serious until the mid–19th century. Forces of Napoleon III conquered Vietnam in a series of military campaigns, beginning in the South and working slowly northward. Initially, the French navy was far more interested in the region than the French government but over time the national commitment grew. The proclamation of a protectorate over the Annamese (Vietnamese) state in 1883 was followed by a short war with the Chinese to force the Manchu emperors to recognize the end of the tributary status of Annam.

The French divided their newly won possession into three segments: Tonkin in the North, Annam in the narrow middle belt and highland plateaus of the South and the colony of Cochin China in the Mekong Delta. These three areas were ruled by a governor general who also presided over Cambodia and Laos after 1887.

Actual administration of the colonies was by the French during the colonial period, although an imperial court was permitted to exist in Annam. The French introduced a narrow gauge railroad from Hanoi to Kunming in China which allowed them to extract mineral wealth from the North. In addition, intensive cul-

tivation methods were introduced to produce large quantities of rubber.

During the early colonial period the French encouraged the migration of people from Tonkin in the North to the delta of Cochin China; immigrant Chinese were also permitted in the southern colony though at times the European businessmen there resented their competition.

Considerable effort was put into the promotion of French culture among the Vietnamese. As a result, an upper class of Vietnamese eventually emerged that was fluent in French, at home in French culture, and often Roman Catholic, but over time often bitterly resentful of French political domination. It was a pattern that was followed frequently throughout the colonized world.

World Wars and Nationalist Struggles

Shortly after World War I, a nationalist group, composed of people supported by the French–speaking upper class emerged, competing with a communist movement led by a dedicated patriot and communist known as Ho Chi Minh. Both of these movements attempted unsuccessful armed uprisings against the French. In 1930 Ho brought together the various communist groups into a single new movement known as the Indochinese Communist Party.

Once the Second World War had begun, the Japanese took Indochina by default after Germany installed the puppet French Vichy government. Japan demanded the right to land forces in the area, which was granted by the French. Within three months the Japanese controlled all of northern Vietnam. In July 1941 they occupied the south as well.

In contrast to other leaders of anti-colonial Asian movements, individuals like Sukarno of Indonesia for example, Ho Chi Minh did not collaborate with the Japanese. Rather, being a fluent speaker of English, he aligned himself with the allied forces and spent the wars years often working closely with the Americans fighting in the region.

In 1945, the Japanese ousted the local French authorities whom they correctly suspected of being in contact with General de Gaulle and the Allies. Direct Japanese authority though was short–lived—surrender came within six months. At the Potsdam conference in 1945, the Allied powers decided to divide Vietnam at the 16th parallel for the purpose of disarming and evacuating the Japanese. The southern region was to be occupied by the British and the north by the Nationalist Chinese. For Ho, and other nationalists this was a serious development given the long Chinese interest in Vietnamese territory. For the immediate period one of Ho's most important goals would be to make sure the Chinese did not come to stay.

More immediately, for Ho Chi Minh, the moment he had long waited for had finally come. He hastily proclaimed the Democratic Republic of Vietnam at Hanoi at a big public rally on September 2, 1945. Ironically, given later events Ho, an admirer of the United States, began his speech with lines chosen from the American Declaration of Independence!

Shortly thereafter the forces of the Chinese Nationalists moved into the northern region. Meanwhile, Ho expanded his power in the rural areas of the North, eliminating Vietnamese Nationalist rivals and managing to co–exist uneasily with the Chinese occupation forces which gave every indication of hoping to remain in Vietnam. Ho's movement, known as the *Viet Minh* was certainly not the only nationalist movement in Vietnam. Indeed, there were others that were nationalist but not communist. But Ho Chi Minh himself was widely admired and was certainly helped by his reputation for having close ties to the increasingly powerful Americans.

Meanwhile in the south, the British suppressed activity by the *Viet Minh* and quickly returned the area to the French. Seeking a withdrawal of the Chinese in the North, Ho and the French put pressure on them. Fortuitously, the outbreak of civil war in China helped instigate a Chinese withdrawal in early 1946.

Ho permitted the French to re–enter northern Vietnam, promising to keep the Democratic Republic of Vietnam within the French Union, so long as its autonomy was respected and providing it was allowed to control all of Vietnam. He certainly wanted French economic aid, but the chief reason for this attitude was very probably Stalin's desires at the time. The Russians wanted a French communist victory at the polls in France, and did not wish to alienate French voters by supporting a communist revolt in Vietnam.

An Anti–Colonial Struggle

The French colonial regime however refused to allow *Viet Minh* control of Cochin China. But, of course, that is hardly surprising. France was committed to reestablishing its control over Vietnam and Ho and his movement were in their way. By the end of 1946, fighting erupted between the French and the *Viet Minh*, who retreat-ed to the mountains above Hanoi to conduct a guerrilla war. In an effort to find a political cover for their desire to reestablish their former colony, the French selected Bao Dai, the hereditary Emperor of Annam and a descendant of the royal family which had once ruled from a massive palace at Hue, as the new official leader of the country. Bao Dai officially accepted the French offer in 1946. He then became Provisional President and later permanent chief of state of a government obviously organized by the French to maintain their power in Indochina. The arrangement hardly pleased real nationalists like Ho, and the struggle continued.

The American attitude toward Vietnam in the immediate aftermath of World War II was ambivalent. On one hand America had a long–term commitment to anti-colonialism, and FDR himself had long made it clear that he did not favor the simple resumption of European colonies in Asia after the war. These American attitudes were well known. In fact, as early as 1919 the young Ho Chi Minh had attempted unsuccessfully to meet President Wilson at the Paris Versailles Conference to discuss Vietnam with the influential American president who was so associated with the idea of "national self–determination." A generation later, Ho, having just finished working with the Americans during the war still hoped to hoped to gain U.S. support for his fledgling nation.

But in the years after World War II there was also an interest among the Americans in strengthening their erstwhile allies the French. And Paris wanted its former colony back. Thus, those U.S. officials who were concerned about ensuring that France remained strong as an ally in Eu-rope prevailed over those who were more concerned about America opposing the anti-colonial Vietnamese nationalist\communist movement.

As the tensions between East and West grew, American attitudes hardened. As the Cold War set in during the late 1940s, Ho's nationalist credentials loomed far less large in the minds of American decision–makers than his equally strong commitment to communism. Now many American decision makers would develop a strong antipathy for Ho and his movement which in their minds was merely an extension of world communism directed from Moscow. However, it would be another generation before they would act directly on those attitudes.

In early 1950, the *Viet Minh* received diplomatic recognition from newly communist China. With Chinese military aid, they cleared French troops from the border areas of northern Vietnam later in that year. What had been an anti-colonial struggle was evolving into a major theater of the Cold War in Asia, a fact which led to increased involvement of the United States and of the People's Republic.

France, which initially had had trouble convincing the Americans to support their efforts now had little trouble convincing those same Americans that France was now fighting, as the U.S. was in Korea, on the front lines against communist expansion. Ho Chi Minh, a nationalist and communist, had not changed but the context in which he was viewed by the powerful Americans had.

Nevertheless, by the spring of 1953, the French prospects in Vietnam were bleak—the approaching end of the Korean war was expected to enable greater

Ho Chi Minh leaves the French Foreign Ministry, July 1946

Vietnam

Ho Chi Minh

Chinese effort in Vietnam. In desperation, the French granted further political, economic, and military concessions to the non–communist Vietnamese state and substantially increased their own military efforts. Their purpose was not to defeat the *Viet Minh*, since such a goal was unrealistic, but rather to obtain a "face saving" political settlement. The U.S., the Soviet Union, Britain and France decided that a conference should be held in the spring of 1954 at Geneva, Switzerland, to deal with the questions of Indochina and Korea. But developments in the battlefield were moving faster than diplomacy.

Dienbienphu

The French had fortified a position at Dienbienphu in northwest Vietnam in response to a *Viet Minh* thrust into neighboring Laos. The *Viet Minh* then surrounded the French with artillery and mortars supplied by the Chinese and laid siege to the French camp. Although the decision to make Dienbienphu the central symbol of the struggle over Vietnam only grew slowly, the battle eventually grew into one that symbolized the entire Franco–Vietnamese war. Overly confident, the French assumed their position within a valley surrounded by soldiers who held higher ground, would not be a problem. They were wrong. The *Viet Minh* quickly destroyed the air strip to prevent reinforcements and supplies from being sent in, and the siege began in earnest. Even as the battle raged, many within the American administration argued that as the symbolism of Dienbienphu grew, the United States should intervene. Though there was considerable opposition to doing so unilaterally, Washington did go so

far as to approach London about a joint effort to save the French. But Winston Churchill, again the British Prime Minister, declined. The French were left to fight alone. The tiny base fell on May 7, 1954, the day before the matter of Indochina was to come before the Geneva conference.

There were few times in recent history when the fate of a small country so depended on world politics. The French wanted to get out of Indochina on any reasonable basis. The Soviet Union did not want to press France to the extent that it would join the European Defense Community, a multi–country army then being proposed. Russia desired even less a direct clash with the U.S., which had only recently completed a massive series of hydrogen bomb tests in the Pacific. The People's Republic of China also wished to avoid conflict with the U.S. and apparently did not want Ho Chi Minh to achieve too much power.

The Geneva Settlement

Ho Chi Minh's delegation to the conference arrived with a demand that the three nations of Indochina be treated in such a manner that would have produced a communist victory not only in Vietnam, but also in Cambodia and Laos. But the Chinese delegation conceded that a final settlement would treat the three countries separately. Ultimately, the final settlement contained some minor concessions to the communist movement in Laos, but none in Cambodia.

Vietnam was divided at the 17th parallel, considerably further to the north than had been demanded by Ho Chi Minh. Elections were scheduled for mid–1956, to be held in both regions. Military details of withdrawal, etc., were left to the French and Vietnamese. This was a defeat for Ho, who desired immediate elections before a non–communist government could solidify itself in the South. He was sure of victory in the North, since he was credited with expelling the French colonial government. In fact, it was generally agreed by most observers, including the Americans, that Ho Chi Minh, the long time leader of the Vietnamese struggle for independence, would easily win the scheduled elections. Ho appeared poised to win at the ballot box what he had largely won on the battlefield already.

In order to exclude American military forces from Indochina, the settlement enjoined any foreign power from maintaining forces in Vietnam. A general political agreement was included in the final version in which many things were left subject to interpretation. The U.S., unhappy with the settlement which appeared likely to bring a unified Vietnam under communist control into being, declined to sign the agreement. The Chinese, although angered by this refusal, agreed to accept an informal American promise not to "disturb" the agreement by force. The settlement was then "adopted" without actually being signed by the representative of any nation in July 1954.

Ho Chi Minh's regime promptly took over North Vietnam from the French. It began to build a strong and effective regime with large amounts of economic and military aid from the Soviet Union and China. Exhibiting revolutionary zeal, the new government embarked on an extremely brutal program of collectivization which soon cost the party considerable popularity. In fact, the program provoked a peasant revolt in Nghe An, the southernmost province, which had to be suppressed by government troops in 1956. Ho was forced to moderate his programs in order to regain his popular support.

Ngo Dinh Diem and the Americans

Nearly everyone at the Geneva conference had expected South Vietnam to collapse, or to go communist via the ballot box. Bao Dai had no real authority and was under the influence of corrupt military leaders. In mid–1954 however he appointed Ngo Dinh Diem, premier. Diem, an energetic Catholic and committed nationalist, had strong ties to the Americans. In fact he had only just recently returned from an extended stay in the United States. Having appointed the anti-communist Diem, Bao Dai then resumed his luxurious life in France. Diem later deposed him.

In October 1956 Diem proclaimed South Vietnam a republic and assumed the office of president. From the time of his appointment, Diem had enjoyed the support of prominent U.S. officials who hoped to strengthen his position enough to allow him to pose as a non–communist alternative to Ho Chi Minh.

Diem also received the support of the several hundred thousand of his Catholic co-religionists who fled, partially inspired by C.I.A. propaganda, into the South in 1954. Diem also gained the allegiance of the traditionally corrupt army, and managed to oppose his authority over South Vietnamese religious sects which were hostile to his government.

Not surprisingly, the United States backed Diem's 1956 decision against holding the national elections called for in the Geneva Convention and in his efforts to establish South Vietnam as a separate country. For the Americans Diem's regime seemed a way to stop the unification of the country under Ho Chi Minh, which

Vietnam-wide elections would probably have brought about. The U.S. now offered massive amounts of military and economic aid as it had earlier supported the French effort against Ho.

As might have been expected, North Vietnam was furious and called for international action against Diem, but they received no support from the Soviets or the Chinese. Initially hoping that Diem's regime would literally collapse from its own weight of dishonesty and corruption, Ho discouraged the communist guerrillas, who had remained within South Vietnam after the Geneva division of the country, from taking action. But in 1957, calling themselves *Viet Cong*, the rebels undertook a terrorist campaign to force village support of their communist movement.

Diem and his supporters responded as might be expected—a virtual police state was set up to smother all opposition, non–communist and communist. He was able to withstand a military revolt in 1960 and tried to promote the regime's power in rural areas by use of anti–*Viet Cong* measures.

This crackdown against the *Viet Cong* by Diem was successful enough to push them to adopt new, more militant tactics. Initial Southern success though turned into a virtual loss of control over much of the countryside as *Viet Cong* strength swelled and its military activities increased.

In contrast to the conservative American assumption of an unrelenting global conspiracy to spread communism throughout the world, there was no major direct support of the *Viet Cong* by North Vietnam until 1959 because of the reluctance of the Soviets and Chinese to provoke another crisis in the region. Moreover, because of serious economic difficulties in 1960, China sharply reduced its aid to North Vietnam. Nevertheless, despite the international situation Hanoi itself did begin to give substantial and active support to the *Viet Cong* in the South.

In response, the United States, during the first months of the Kennedy administration, increased its aid to the Diem government and raised the number of American military advisers to the South Vietnamese army. The Chinese, in return for Vietnamese support in their ideological disputes with the Soviet Union, also increased their support of Ho's effort to bolster the *Viet Cong*.

The dictatorial Diem government further alienated public opinion in South Vietnam, which resulted in growing support for the *Viet Cong*. Moreover, Diem, whose own background was among the minority Catholics, infuriated the Buddhist community by publicly allowing discrimination against their practices while supporting similar Catholic activities. By the spring of 1963, he had alienated the most influential segment of the public by his harsh measures.

Buddhist demonstrators, aroused by government attempts to ban Buddhist public religious displays, were fired upon by government troops. Soon the international news was filled with images of Buddhist monks burning themselves to death to protest the actions of the American–backed Diem regime.

Predictably, the U.S. government was becoming increasingly embarrassed and disgusted with Diem. An army group, with American support, deposed him in late 1963, resulting in his violent death. Over the next year or so the government of South Vietnam was In uncertain hands. For a time, leadership was held by General Duong Van Minh, but he proved too independent for the Americans and was himself quickly deposed. Power was supposedly centered in Saigon, but local military leaders in the provinces were all but independent of the central government. The U.S., entering an election campaign in 1964, didn't want to disturb the shaky status quo.

But that uncertain period after Diem's death was interrupted in August when news reports indicated that North Vietnamese torpedo boats had attacked a U.S. destroyer in the Tonkin Gulf. Public reports at the time suggested that on two different occasions North Vietnamese boats had threatened the American ships. More recent evidence suggests that though no one was hurt, the American ships operating off the coast of North Vietnam may have provoked one attack and that the second reported assault probably never occurred.

But at the time, given the fact that the United States government had been actively looking for an excuse to step up their efforts, the reports were not questioned. President Johnson manufactured a crisis out of the event and secured a vague resolution from Congress authorizing him to take military action in response. Eventually, the Tonkin Gulf vote would be viewed as the single most important element in U.S. congressional support of the war. In fact it became a *de facto* declaration of a war that never formally occurred.

Because of their opposition to Diem's harsh rule, a great many non–communists also supported the *Viet Cong* and its political arm, the *National Liberation Front*. When he was deposed, this ended. Feeling the need of greater support, and believing it more possible that military action would succeed after the downfall of Diem, the *Viet Cong* embarked on wider military efforts. They were joined by regular units of the North Vietnamese army for the first time at the end of 1964. There was a rapid increase in the area under communist control, particularly in the central highlands of South Vietnam. The Russians, sensing an imminent victory, sent their premier to Hanoi in early 1965 to give assurances of Russian support. The American too feared South Vietnam would soon be lost. For the United States, which had been traumatized internally during the previous decade over the issue of "Who had lost China?," such a development had to be stopped at all costs. More direct action was taken.

The American War

By 1965 the United States was bombing North Vietnam and deploying U.S. Marine and Army combat units. The days of the "advisors" were over. Now American

Gen. Nguyen Cao Ky

troops under U.S. officers would fight the North Vietnamese and their supporters directly. South Vietnam finally had the formal direct support of their major superpower ally, the United States. Given the changing circumstances, Hanoi would need similar help, but developments within the communist world were getting more complicated.

Ideological differences had led to a breakdown in Soviet–Chinese relations. The differences between these two communist giants now included disputes about what role each nation should play in aiding Ho Chi Minh's forces. After 1965, China's leadership resented the superior economic ability of the Russians to

Vietnam

Black smoke covers areas of Saigon during the Tet offensive

buy influence in Hanoi, and limited its own assistance to the maintenance of the Chinese–North Vietnamese rail line and the shipment of infantry weapons. Although there was an agreement to ship Soviet equipment through China to North Vietnam, the trains were often delayed and harassed by "Red Guards" active in Mao's *Great Cultural Revolution*, then in progress in China.

Meanwhile, in Saigon a dashing young Air Force general, Nguyen Cao Ky, emerged as a leading figure in the military establishment of South Vietnam. In mid–1965; he became premier and retained that position for two years. This provided a welcome respite from the seemingly continuous change of rulers in the country. It became clear though that during his rule the armed forces exercised almost all political power—a fact that continued to arouse Buddhist opposition.

The cost to the U.S. rose to more than $30 billion a year, placing a serious strain on the American economy and on its political system. Within the U.S., opposition to the war began to grow more and more significant, especially among college–age students who did not share their leadership's obsession with anti–communism and who were more likely to view the struggle in South Vietnam as a civil war rather than as a part of a world–wide struggle between communism and capitalism. Moreover, the clearly undemocratic nature of the South Vietnamese regime

made it hardly seem worthy of the sacrifices Americans were increasingly being asked to make. Recognizing that last issue, President Lyndon Johnson set out to improve Saigon's image.

Under pressure from Washington to offer at least the appearance of a democratic regime, some political progress took place in South Vietnam. A constitution was enacted and elections were held in 1967 for a new National Assembly. Military intrigue reduced General Ky to the candidacy for vice president and General Nguyen Van Thieu, a Catholic, was elected president though in a relatively poor showing that saw a considerable number of votes going to an anti–military "peace" candidate.

The new government had a broader base, but the habit of jailing political opponents persisted. The military situation, bolstered by a half million U.S. troops, improved. The South Vietnamese army alone could simply not hold its own against North Vietnam and *Viet Cong* units. The government did gain control of half the land area by the end of 1967, but in many cases this control was shaky.

TET: A Battle Won and Lost

As 1968 began, both sides found themselves involved in a terribly costly and bloody conflict. Yet little was being accomplished to seek resolution of the struggle. The U.S. was distracted by the 1968

elections in which President Johnson had declined to run, and the Soviets dared not appear to be less revolutionary than the Chinese. On Tet, the Lunar New Year holiday traditional to the Vietnamese, the communist forces started an unexpected all–out offensive. They invaded most of the provincial capitals, parts of Saigon and held a portion of the ancient imperial capital, Hue, for several days. U.S. encampments and installations were attacked, causing tremendous losses of material and manpower. Moreover monsoon rains prevented effective American defensive air strikes.

In the end the spectacular offensive was dramatically defeated though it had certainly revealed the weaknesses of the South Vietnamese and U.S. forces and driven them back temporarily. The communist goal of generating a popular uprising was also a dismal failure. Nevertheless, the North had proven that, official American claims to the contrary, the war was not being won and that it was likely to go on for many years to come. For Hanoi, committed as it had been for generations to the unification of the country under its rule, that price was acceptable. For the United States, by now more interested in simply finding a way out of the costly but ultimately peripheral struggle, it was not.

Seeking "Peace with Honor"

A somewhat desperate U.S. President Lyndon Johnson suspended the bombing of North Vietnam (except the southern provinces) in 1968 and proposed talks between the combatants. Knowing he could probably not be re–elected, Johnson, as stated, declined to run again. At last, negotiations were begun but organizational issues, such as the status of the *Viet Cong* and seating arrangements at the conference table resulted in endless haggling and little progress. But events within the United States were moving faster than the negotiations themselves.

After a divisive campaign that saw the Democratic Party almost destroy itself over the war, Richard M. Nixon, the former Republican vice president, who had once advocated American intervention at Dienbienphu, was elected president of the U.S. During the campaign, Nixon had spoken somewhat vaguely about a "secret plan" to end the war. Once in power his plans became clearer.

The newly elected President was no longer primarily interested in South Vietnam but in ending the war in a fashion that would retain American influence in the postwar era. Simply pulling out, as many Americans advocated, would not have accomplished that. Rather, Nixon feared, it would send shock waves through the entire American alliance system. Thus, Nixon wanted a way to withdraw that would allow U.S. prestige to continue undiminished.

His method to accomplish these goals came to be known as "Vietnaminization." What Nixon and his soon famous advisor Henry Kissinger had in mind was to transfer the bulk of the ground war to the Army of the Republic of South Vietnam. In their plan, the United States would withdraw to the relatively safer position of offering air support. The goal was to reduce the number of American casualties while building up South Vietnam's ability to defend itself. Certainly a good idea in theory, the plan nevertheless dangerously reduced American military force in Vietnam even as its prestige remained closely tied to events there.

U.S. troop withdrawals thus started in 1969. From Hanoi's perspective their chances of victory probably seemed closer than ever. In mid–1969 they proclaimed a "provisional government" for the South. Nevertheless, 1969 also saw the death of their long time leader Ho Chi Minh.

The Saigon government of President Thieu then turned to what it considered the most reliable elements for support: the armed forces and the Catholics. The economy, spurred by land reform in the South, improved. President Thieu was reelected (unopposed) in late 1971 in a contest his opponents charged was rigged. Although he made an attempt to build an effective government party, disruption came when the northern provinces of South Vietnam were struck by a massive North Vietnam invasion in March 1972.

President Nixon, facing a reelection contest, responded by ordering the mining of Haiphong Harbor. This precipitated yet another international "crisis." The military stalemate was acutely embarrassing to President Nixon as the fall elections approached. Yet, for a time it looked, as Henry Kissinger was publicly quoted "that peace was at hand." But no formal agreement was reached before Nixon's landslide reelection victory of 1972. Once he was reelected, Nixon ordered a resumption of the heavy bombing of North Vietnam in an attempt to persuade Hanoi to accept terms acceptable to the Saigon government.

The End

After the intense December 1972 bombing, the North Vietnamese verbally agreed to end the conflict. The formal agreement was signed on March 2, 1973. The U.S. had already given up its insistence on a North Vietnamese withdrawal from South Vietnam and continued its own withdrawal.

In exchange, it got its prisoners back, although some insist to this day that many were held against their will in violation of the promise.

Hanoi, for its part, accepted a political arrangement that did not guarantee the overthrow of the Thieu government as had been previously demanded. Realistically neither North nor South Vietnam had any genuine interest in abiding by the political provisions of the January 1973 agreement, which called for a vaguely defined coalition government and general elections.

To strengthen its hand, Hanoi, with the help of military aid from the Soviet Union and China, then began to create a "third Vietnam" under the nominal control of the *Viet Cong* in the highlands of South Vietnam. This activity, much of which was in flagrant violation of the agreement, included road building, troop buildups, the stockpiling of weapons and other measures.

Meanwhile Saigon's principal supporter, the United States, was moving deeply into the Watergate scandal which eventually destroyed the Nixon administration. Deprived of American air support by Congressional prohibitions and unwilling to commit its own air force against communist–held areas in the highlands, South Vietnam made no genuine military effort to contain their long–time foe.

In the Saigon–controlled areas, the Thieu government continued its own repressive policies. Although Thieu fired a number of corrupt military and civilian officials, there was no basic change in the style of the regime.

Anti–Thieu protest movements arose in 1974 among both the Buddhists, who stressed liberalization and peace, and the Roman Catholics, who emphasized opposition to corruption. Concessions were promised to both in late 1974, but little happened. By early 1975 five major opposition newspapers were closed down.

Meanwhile, North Vietnam was developing its economy through aid from the Soviet Union and China. The military strength of Hanoi was built up as was that of the *Viet Cong* in the highlands of South Vietnam. A strategy of "accelerated erosion" began against Saigon's military positions in both the highlands and in the Mekong Delta. This approach was obviously inadequate to achieve Hanoi's two principal objectives: imposition of the political provisions of the January 1973 agreement and/or the downfall of Thieu. One reason for this cautious approach was probably the attitude of the Soviet Union and China, which did not want their rapprochement with the United States to be endangered by a major resurgence of fighting in Vietnam.

Nevertheless, the North Vietnamese capture of two provincial capitals in early 1975, and another closer to Saigon, was the beginning of the end. Shocked by the loss of these towns and unquestionably worried by the refusal of the U.S. Congress to vote further large–scale military aid, President Thieu simply abandoned the three provinces in March. What was perhaps meant as a retreat quickly turned into a rout as Hanoi's forces, taking advantage of the dry season and the government withdrawals, moved forward. By the end of March the two important coastal cities of Hue and Danang had fallen to the communists. Saigon fell at the end of April in a morass of confusion as people with close contacts with the Thieu administration or the Americans desperately tried to flee in overcrowded boats and planes.

South Vietnamese President Nguyen Van Thieu decorates soldiers

Vietnam

Harvesting salt in the Central Plain.

The behavior of the leadership during 1975 in South Vietnam demonstrated that their concern was mainly for their personal safety rather than for the future of South Vietnam. Thieu issued military orders which were disastrous, changed daily, and lead nowhere. Many field officers deserted to seek safety for themselves and their families. Ultimately, several hundred thousand refugees fled, most ultimately to the U.S. Thieu, himself, went to Taiwan. Almost the entire leadership was able to depart with substantial wealth, in contrast to most of the refugees who had little more than the clothes they wore. Most dramatically, thousands of South Vietnamese suddenly abandoned their G.I. issued boots to avoid being recognized as former South Vietnamese soldiers.

The reasons for the loss of the war were many, but especially important was the weakness of the southern regime. Despite its access to American support it never developed deep roots among the Vietnamese population, certainly nothing similar to what Hanoi was able to call upon from the populations under its control. When South Vietnam started to lose the support of even the Americans its ability to maintain itself became even more problematic.

A Unified Vietnam

If Hanoi's tenacity had allowed it to finally unify the country under its own control, actually ruling a united Vietnam would require very different skills. And unified Vietnam's new leaders had an enormous challenge ahead of them for the country had been devastated by the years of war.

Over eight million tons of bombs had been dropped. The Vietnamese themselves had experienced some two million casualties—tremendous numbers of whom would have to be cared for for years. And the people hurt and killed by the war were not the only victims. Vietnam's land itself had suffered horribly.

Ten million gallons of Agent Orange had been sprayed over the country by the United States in order to destroy the vegetation cover used by the communist forces. According to the United Nations U.S. chemical warfare created "black zones" within the countryside whose ability to produce crops was dramatically reduced.

And of course, Hanoi's own post victory policies, as it attempted to both centralize authority and move toward building a communist "command economy", often created even more problems.

Not surprisingly the government's initial efforts were thus not very impressive. After its "liberation" from the Thieu regime, South Vietnam was run by men sent from Hanoi, the chief of whom was Pham Hung who, although a southerner, was a member of the top leadership of the *Vietnam Workers Party*, the communist party. Still, imposition of communist controls on the South proceeded fairly slowly, and without the bloodbath that had been widely predicted.

Nevertheless there were executions and forced political "reindoctrination" of more than two million people, many of whom would not be free again for years. Former employees of the Thieu regime often found it difficult to find jobs and even food.

The new regime planned to reduce the population of Saigon, renamed Ho Chi Minh City, through forced resettlement in the countryside. Their reasoning is understandable given how much the city's population had swollen with refugees from the countryside and how little work there was once the free spending Americans left. Nevertheless, the policies caused individual suffering for thousands as they were forced to abandon their lives in the city for the back breaking labor of the countryside.

The party held its Fourth Congress in late 1976, at which it renamed itself the *Vietnam Communist* (rather than "Workers") *Party*. The domination of the North over the South was clear. Soviet aid to and influence on the new regime was also substantial. The Soviets also took over the

huge naval base at Camranh Bay built by the U.S. Chinese influence in contrast was considerably less than that of the Soviets. Clearly Vietnam was tilting toward Moscow as the Sino-Soviet disputes continued.

Meanwhile Hanoi, certainly naively, continued to hope for the $3.25 billion in reconstruction aid Nixon was said to have promised. But no aid was forthcoming as little progress was made on the Missing In Action matter and Hanoi was widely disliked within the United States.

Nevertheless, having finally won its long independence and unification struggle, Hanoi then moved to impose a socialist economy on the South. That effort, though, was not well received by the southerners who passively resisted efforts to collectivize agriculture and redistribute land. When efforts to socialize the urban area brought an end to the free market system of the South, large numbers of indigenous Chinese, the backbone of the urban economy, fled the country creating yet another wave of "boat people" who had already filled refugee camps throughout Southeast Asia.

But these efforts hardly helped strengthen the country and as early as the late 1970s Vietnam's leadership started looking for new solutions to the nation's problems. Hanoi then moved to integrate itself into the world economic community by joining organizations like the World Bank and the Asia Development Bank and sought outside development funds for the exploration of natural resources such as oil.

By 1977 it announced it would honor the former South Vietnamese government's debts to both France and Japan (necessary to build future economic relations). And by 1979 the decision was even made to slow down the process of collectivization of agriculture.

Unfortunately, these early examples of practical economic decision making did not bear the fruit one might have hoped for and other problematic relationships continued to complicate Hanoi's efforts.

The Americans continued to maintain their economic embargo and newly developing tensions with China over Vietnam's role in Cambodia were soon to complicate matters even more.

Vietnam's Cambodia Involvement

In the late 1970s Vietnam developed a border conflict with Cambodia which was then controlled by the murderous and vehemently nationalist Pol Pot regime, a government supported by China. By 1978 Vietnam launched a full-scale invasion of Cambodia. In doing so Hanoi claimed they were responding to the long term border tensions and to end the Pol Pot regime's genocidal killing of so many of its own people. Not surprisingly many Cam-

Vietnam

bodians initially viewed the invading Vietnamese and their supporters as liberators from the hated *Khmer Rouge*. Nevertheless, despite the general hatred of the Pol Pot regime, Vietnam's own invasion was also widely condemned. The Chinese, who had been especially supportive of the *Khmer Rouge*, were outraged and saw Hanoi's actions as an extension of their enemy, the Soviet Union's influence in Southeast Asia. From Beijing's perspective that was unacceptable.

In retaliation for this strike against its ally, China began to pour troops over the Vietnamese border in early 1979, occupying, despite heavy fighting, a portion of its northern territory. Beijing's efforts, though, were clearly less than they had expected. The Chinese troops had not fought in a generation and were hard pressed to deal with the Vietnamese military fresh from its generation-long struggle with the United States. China's efforts to teach Hanoi a "lesson" had failed. After that Beijing directed itself more toward supporting the fallen *Khmer Rouge* and making life "difficult" for the Vietnamese in Cambodia.

Over the next decade, Vietnam's commitment to Cambodia and its allied government would become a major burden on the regime. Predictably, as time went on, the Vietnamese who had initially been welcomed as liberators were themselves seen as aggressive occupiers. Finally, by the late 1980s Hanoi began its withdrawal from Cambodia after a decade which had seen the commitment there contribute to the weakening economic conditions in Vietnam itself and its international isolation.

A New Economic Path

Economically the first decade of independence was a disaster. The most productive citizens had been driven from the country and the socialist economic planning had alienated many others. Moreover the war in Cambodia had added to the economic strains.

The aging, largely North Vietnamese leadership, and its economic policies, had not seen the economy grow. The continuing isolation of the regime due to the American-led boycott had hardly helped. The efforts of many communist states from Eastern Europe to improve ties with Beijing meant less enthusiasm for Vietnam. Hanoi's isolation was growing. Economically, for example, inflation was running at around 700%! By the mid 1980s it was clear that a new direction was required. Not surprisingly this new thinking emerged as China under Deng Xiaoping itself was several years into an economic reform program and even the Soviet Union, under its new leader Gor-

Shopping in Ho Chi Minh City (formerly Saigon)

bachev, was talking of the importance of reform.

A new direction also became more possible with the death in July 1986 of Le Duan, the longtime General Secretary of the *Communist Party* of Vietnam. He was succeeded by Truong Chinh, also elderly but more flexible and with a reputation for being pro-Chinese. Accordingly, at a Party Congress held in December 1986, Truong Chinh, Le Duc Tho and Pham Van Dong "resigned" from the Politburo, although all continued to be "advisors." Chinh retained the presidency of the state and Dong the premiership of the government. A new General Secretary of the party, Nguyen Van Linh, a Southerner and an economic reformer, was elected. In February 1987 there were major personnel changes in the government, although Chinh and Dong remained in place; the newcomers were mostly Southerners with some economic expertise. The new leadership group was clearly interested in moving more decisively away from central control of the economy.

Over the next several years agriculture was decollectivized and many financial reforms were put into place. State factory managers were given more authority, and a partial revival of private enterprise was permitted. By 1989 Vietnam had re-emerged as a major rice exporter. Private businesses such as restaurants and shops were opened and flourished as well.

Not surprisingly, these changes were inspired both by internal developments in Vietnam as well as the influence of the new Gorbachev leadership in the Soviet Union. These changes came to be known as *Doi Moi*, or "renovation" and if they are less well known than the famous *Glasnost* and *Perestroika* of Gorbachev, they were born of the same problems in the socialist world.

A similar relaxation of cultural controls occurred in Vietnam in the late 1980s, which also paralleled developments in both the Soviet Union and the People's Republic of China. It became possible for greater press freedoms, the introduction of Western music videos and even greater religious freedoms for Vietnamese Catholics. Some 6,000 political prisoners were released in September 1987.

The idea of a "new Vietnam," eager for foreign contacts, was energetically promoted by an able Foreign Minister, Nguyen Co Thach. Hanoi expressed an interest in joining ASEAN. In response to foreign concern over the state of human rights in Vietnam, some political prisoners were released and boat people al-

Vietnam

The crowded waterfront of a Mekong Delta town at market time.

Courtesy: William Garrett Stewart

lowed to return. Even official anger at the Vatican's canonization in mid 1988 of 117 Vietnamese martyrs of the seventeenth and eighteenth centuries was not allowed to derail a policy of increased toleration of religion, including Catholicism. Still, Hanoi remained suspicious of the Vatican given the deeply anti-communist reputation of the Polish Pope John II and the church's strong ties to the hated Diem regime.

But even as Vietnam modeled some of its internal policies on developments in the Soviet Union, relations with its patron remained edgy. The Soviets retained major naval and air bases near Camranh Bay and clearly could not afford to alienate Hanoi, the host government. On the other hand, Moscow was unhappy with Vietnamese misuse of Soviet aid and was itself moving to improve its own relations with Hanoi's nemesis, China.

European Communism's Fall & Vietnam

The dramatic developments of 1989–91 in the Soviet Union and Eastern Europe had a serious impact on the Vietnamese leadership. The basic reaction was one of alarm and a determination that the ero-

sion of the ruling party's power would not be repeated in Vietnam. Particularly shocking for Vietnam's leadership was the bloody late 1989 fall of the Ceaucescu regime in Romania.

Political opposition in Vietnam had been almost non-existent. Accordingly, the regime had felt free to proceed along the same lines as in China: minimal political reform combined with some reasonably effective economic reform. But the events of the 1989–1991 era had clearly shown how easily reform efforts in the communist world could swirl out of control. And the Party had no desire to lose its mandate on power. The key appeared to at least make reasonable progress on economically improving people's lives without loosening up on political controls.

One requirement in that effort was the establishment of normal commercial relations with the industrial countries. The 1989 withdrawal from Cambodia helped that process, but Washington was still demanding a full accounting for MIAs. Relations with the U.S. remained difficult. In 1986, Hanoi reneged on pledges that it had apparently given: to resolve fully the issue of American personnel still considered missing in action during the Vietnam

war (the MIAs) and to release several thousand Vietnamese prisoners being held for having collaborated with the U.S. during the war. Thus, Washington, also constrained by anti-Hanoi sentiments in the U.S., continued to withhold diplomatic recognition and trade from Hanoi.

Finally, as time passed Hanoi became increasingly cooperative on the MIA issue and by the end of 1991, the State Department even began to authorize tour groups of Americans to visit Vietnam. The U.S. presidential election prevented earlier action, but in late November of 1992 President Bush permitted U.S. companies to open offices in Vietnam and begin negotiations for future trade relations.

Throughout the early 1990s many signs pointed to the continued opening of Vietnam to the outside world. Vietnamese officials were being trained in contemporary diplomatic practice, a Fulbright program was begun, and American professors were in the country at several institutions teaching business and economic courses. Americans also visited Vietnamese military bases and government offices in search of additional information on American MIA's. Vietnamese were also being trained to aid them in the process of determining the fate of their own MIA's which far outnumber the Americans lost. Unfortunately, Vietnam has lacked the financial resources to seek out the ultimate burial places of most of their own dead.

By the 1990s the Vietnamese government was working to establish a bureaucracy and legal system which foreigner businesses could work with and trust. Unfortunately the country has continued to hold a reputation among businessman as one of the most difficult places to work in Southeast Asia.

Politically a new leadership team has also emerged over the last year. After a fairly significant struggle between the army and the party a compromise candidate Tran Duc Luong, a relatively minor figure from the politburo, was elected President. For the important position of Prime Minister, Vo Van Kiet was replaced by the former deputy prime minister Phan Van Khai late in 1997. Party leadership has also changed with the appointment of Le Kha Phieu, a military man and army political commissar, as the new Communist Party chief. As a group, Phieu is considered the most conservative of the three. This leadership change, which some have hailed as the dawn of a new generation, has important leadership challenges before it—not only the economic challenges brought on by the regional crises, but of social unrest closer to home.

More and more commonly the government has had to face peasant unrest aroused by excessive taxation and corrupt local officials. Given Hanoi's control of the media, the details are sometimes sketchy but the impression is that these disturbances have been relatively serious. Moreover, recent years have also seen significant criticism of the regime by former members of the communist leadership.

By the late 1990s it appeared that those who wished to see the pace of reforms slowed seemed to have gained important influence. This development is not terribly surprising given the general economic weakness which had enveloped so many of their neighbors since the onset of the Asian economic crisis began in 1997.

Foreign Relations

In July 1993, President Bill Clinton ended U.S. opposition to International Monetary Fund (IMF) loans to Vietnam. Somewhat later Clinton announced that American companies could bid on infrastructure projects funded by the international lending agencies.

The next year the 19-year U.S. trade embargo was finally ended. Full diplomatic relations were announced in July 1995 and more recently it has become even easier for American businessmen to invest and trade with Vietnam. Vietnam has even gone as far as paying back monies the former government of South Vietnam owed to the United States! There was even talk of developing some sort of "military relationship" between the two countries, an amazing development indeed for those who lived through the Vietnam War. And cooperation on a range of issues between the two wartime enemies became even more possible after U.S. Secretary of Defense Cohen's highly successful visit to Hanoi in early 2000.

Normalization of relations with the United States has clearly been a major element in Hanoi's efforts to strengthen their economy. Nevertheless, important matters still need to be resolved. Fortunately, real progress has been made. The two countries recently concluded a treaty on the protection of intellectual property—a very high priority for the United States in this era of an emerging global economy.

Vietnam has also finally been granted "most favored nation" (more correctly, normal trading status) by the Americans. This was important because it allows Vietnamese goods to enter the U.S. as cheaply as those from America's other trading partners.

The ties continue to grow. United States firms have become the 6th largest investor in Vietnam, though some like Nike, have come under considerable public criticism for the work conditions they established there. True, things have not always worked out as hoped. The Procter & Gamble Company's soap and shampoo making facility has been plagued by legal and supply problems and in March of 1998 it was temporarily shut down.

Still, the United States and Vietnam have yet to finalize an official trade treaty. It looked for a time last year like such an agreement would soon be signed but at the last moment Vietnam itself backed down. Why they did so is not clear though many were certainly willing to speculate. The only certainty is that a formal agreement is not yet in place.

Especially important as well has been Vietnam's integration with its Southeast Asian neighbors. Vietnam is now a member of ASEAN (Association of Southeast Asian Nations). Membership provides important economic and strategic benefits. For example being a member of ASEAN can provide Vietnam with support in its relations with China. An important example of this occurred when

the ASEAN states recently spoke out with one voice at the second ASEAN Regional (security) Forum in Brunei on the issue of conflicting claims in the South China Sea. China had insisted that these claims be addressed on a bilateral basis. Countries like Vietnam and the Philippines, who have had run-ins with the Chinese military in the sea, preferred the multilateral approach.

Fortunately, despite problems, relations with China, Vietnam's long term enemy, are also getting better. After more than eighteen years the border between them has opened for rail service. President Jiang Zemin of the People's Republic recently visited as well. These two still formally communist nations find they now have more in common in this era after the collapse of so many other socialist states than they once did.

And this warming of Sino-Vietnamese relations is certainly an improvement over their earlier relationship. The two fought one conflict in the late 70s, and have come to blows over conflicting claims in the South China Sea several times. As recently as 1994, relations worsened. A Vietnamese patrol boat seized three Chinese fishing boats off Bach Long Vi, an island claimed by Hanoi half way between Vietnam and Hainan island (Chinese territory). A Chinese boat opened fire the next day on another patrol, wounding two Vietnamese. More recently though progress has been made in resolving this important issue.

Vietnam also continued to talk with Cambodian officials about the treatment of ethnic Vietnamese located along the border just inside Cambodian territory. Relations, though, are not the best and they could deteriorate easily. In fact, there was considerable tension recently between the two as Cambodia claimed that Vietnam had actually moved the border

President Tran Duc Luong

Prime Minister Phan Van Khai

General Secretary Le Kha Phieu

Vietnam

Photo by Steven A. Leibo

markers between the two countries! Nor did the Cambodian government appreciate it when Hanoi, after some hesitation, followed their ASEAN colleague's lead and decided to temporarily halt Cambodia's entrance into ASEAN in the weeks after Hun Sen's coup.

Society and Culture

The Vietnamese have been influenced by the culture of the Chinese to a greater extent than all other nations of Southeast Asia, except Singapore, where there is a Chinese majority. Chinese characters were used to write the Vietnamese language until the French replaced them with quoc-ngu, a system based on the French alphabet. The Red River in North Vietnam is controlled with dikes of Chinese design. Religiously Vietnam includes large numbers of followers of *Mahayana* Buddhism, whose practices vary widely, and many Roman Catholics. Vietnamese Buddhism includes traditions ranging from animism and Taoism to Confucianism and Buddhism and is often simply called the Triple Religion or "Vietnamese Buddhism." Along with Korea and the Philippines, Vietnam has one of the highest percentages of Christians in Asia. There are also considerable numbers who follow minority traditions like the Cao Dai and Hoa Hao sects. Overall though society in recent years has become quite secular.

Most citizens are ethnically Vietnamese with a small percentage of Chinese and a block of some 60 different smaller groups that are sometimes collectively known as Montagnards. Unlike China which has committed itself to reducing the population growth, Vietnamese efforts have not been nearly as dedicated and few restrictions exist to limit the number of children a family might want.

Other controls though still remain strong. The government decides how much free speech, or press freedoms are allowed and outside sources of information ranging from telephones to e-mail and faxes are controlled. Still, change is coming fast to Vietnam. The Internet is increasingly available though still limited to a very few. Nevertheless, there have been enough improvements in recent years that many Vietnamese who earlier fled are returning home. That has been allowed though they are not permitted to take part in any public activities.

Most of the population remains poor and largely rural. The real economic changes made in recent years have been significant but they have as well added to the gap between the rich and poor. In fact, half of all Vietnamese still live under the World Bank's standard of poverty. And burdens have become even more demanding in recent years as people are now required to pay for their own health care, something that was available without expense earlier.

As mentioned in the background section of *East, Southeast Asia and the Western Pacific*, Southeast Asian women have historically enjoyed more rights than their sisters in other parts of Asia. In modern Vietnam, women often played important roles in the nationalist struggle, though the first female did not take her place in the party's all important politburo until the summer of 1996. Today women still represent only 21% of the managerial positions in business, and within the central committee of the Communist Party males still dominate with 89% of the seats. Women have made strides however. REE, the Refrigeration Electrical Engineering corporation, one of the more successful State companies, is run by a woman.

Economy

Vietnam had, for several years, appeared as if it were on the verge of becoming another "Asian Tiger." The term, referred to the rapidly growing economies of Asia: Singapore, Taiwan, South Korea and Hong Kong. In Ho Chi Minh City, fine restaurants, new high-rise buildings, television, and lots of new cars were increasingly plentiful. From 1987 to 1994, the country experienced a real boom. This was based on the Communist Party's policy of *doi moi*, or restructuring, which ushered in a series of market reforms. Many restrictions on the private sector were removed. One result is that Vietnam is currently the world's fourth largest exporter of rice, behind Thailand, the U.S., and India.

Excess labor from closed state enterprises was absorbed by almost five million new jobs in the private sector. However, in 1995,

. . . even as the Internet has arrived.

Photo by Steven A. Leibo

per capita income was still only about $270, or using figures adjusted for living standards, around $1,310. Foreign trade continued to expand with only a small deficit.

But there have been plenty of impediments to further integration in the world economy. One such issue has been the government's commitment to the state firms. Hanoi may be siphoning off resources needed by the private sector to help state enterprises. For example, textiles made in state concerns are given preference for export. These companies also benefit from better access to foreign currency loans. Foreign companies are even being forced to form joint ventures with local state owned businesses.

The state run companies are still a significant percentage of the GDP of the country. In contrast to China, which wants their importance diminished over time, Hanoi's leaders claim they hope to have these firms remain important.

Vietnam has yet to develop a stock market as China, its giant neighbor, did some years ago. But progress has been made. Arrangements were recently put in place to have experts from Taiwan set up such an exchange.

The government's goals are to join both the World Trade Organization and the Asian Pacific Economic Community. But the government's basic ambivalence about these changes continues to hamper its ability to reassure foreign investors. And of course the economic meltdown that hit so many of her neighbors over the last few years no doubt reinforced the influence of those that believed further economic opening might offer as many dangers as advantages.

For Vietnam itself which had already been slowing down before the economic crisis, it was clear that Vietnam's banking system was having problems similar to those that affected the rest of the region. The specifics though are difficult to learn given the controls—actually increasing—that the government holds over the local media.

There had been talk, even before the recent economic crises, of beginning a new era of further economic opening similar to that of the mid 1980s. Whether, given the general economic situation in the region, that opening is now more or less likely is less clear. Certainly there was plenty of ambivalence about the idea before the recent economic crisis; now one has to assume attitudes may be even stronger.

Still, there are clear bright spots in Vietnam's economic situation. Tourism is growing more and more important and Vietnam is even attracting significant numbers of Americans interested in learning more about the country that so transformed their own, now more than a quarter of a century ago.

The Future

The end of the U.S. embargo, full diplomatic relations, and the flood of foreign investment and personnel into the country will of course hasten the pace of change. Not all of this will be good. The environment will suffer and many individuals will not benefit from the initial stages of economic growth and development. Nevertheless, if the general trend continues a new middle class will emerge which will help improve people's lives generally and perhaps contribute one day to the creation of a more civil society—one less dependant on a single authoritarian political leadership.

But for now the Communist Party still runs the country, though Vietnam also has a new constitution and a National Assembly that has been given a greater voice in public affairs. There should be no misunderstanding that the party will try to hold on to power as long as possible. The principal issue for the future is how long the ambivalence will remain within the leadership regarding the changes occurring in the region and the world.

Hanoi understands that bringing Vietnam more into the global economy is important for improving the lives of its citizens and avoiding the sort of confrontations that have occurred elsewhere. Nevertheless, these changes bring with them potential challenges to the leadership's authority and offer no automatic guarantees of economic growth. For the moment, approaching the future with caution seems to be the order of the day.

Australia

Aberdeen Angus cattle on the Hunter River, New South Wales

Australian Information Service

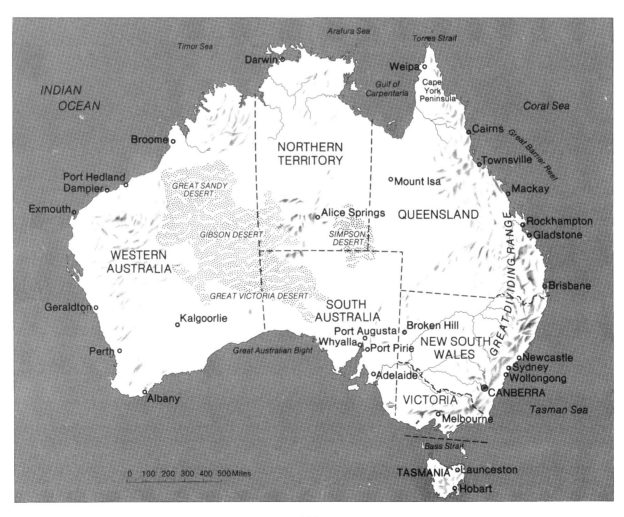

Area: 2,970,000 sq. mi. (7,692,300 sq. km.), slightly smaller than the continental U.S., the "lower 48" states.

Population: 19,001,000 (1998 estimate)

Capital City: Canberra (Pop. 265,000, estimated).

Climate: Tropical to subtropical in the north, temperate in the south; the interior is highly arid.

Neighboring Countries: Indonesia, Papua New Guinea lie to the north; New Zealand to the southeast.

Official Language: English.

Ethnic Background: British, other European, Asian, indigenous aborigines and aboriginal–European mixed ancestry.

Principal Religion: Christianity.

Main Exports: Coal, gold, wool, meat, iron ore and aluminum ore.

Main Imports: Automobiles, computers, petroleum and telecommunication equipment.

Currency: Australian Dollar.

Former Colonial Status: British dependency (1788–1900).

National Day: January 26 (anniversary of the first British settlement at Sydney in 1788).

Head of State: Her Majesty Queen Elizabeth II, represented by Sir William Deane, Governor General.

Head of Government: The Rt. Hon. John Howard, Prime Minister.

National Flag: A blue field with the Union Jack in the upper left quarter, a seven–pointed star in the lower left corner, and five stars at the right side.

Per Capita Annual GNP: $20,090 (1996 estimate)

The Rt. Hon. John Howard

The enormous island called Australia is so immense that it is classified as a continent—at 2.97 million square miles it is almost the size of the continental United States. Its 12,000 miles of coastline is relatively smooth with few harbors, but in the northeast the sandy coast is in the lee of the Great Barrier Reef, a 1,200 mile chain of coral reefs and islands extending north almost to Papua New Guinea. With its vivid coral and a profusion of other marine life, the reef is one of the world's natural wonders and a magnet for scientists and tourists.

Australia is one of the oldest of the continents and also one of the flattest and driest. Its few mountains have been worn with the passage of time and the highest peak today is Mt. Kosciusko at only 7,300 feet. The largest chain of mountains is found in the east and is called the Great Dividing Range; in the southeast they are known as the Australian Alps. They divide the narrow crescent of land along the coastline from the vast interior. It is in the fertile eastern coastal area that the great majority of Australians live and their largest cities are located.

To the west are large lowlands and plateaus which begin the vast interior region known to Australians as the Outback. This is the region containing the two–thirds of Australia classified as desert (fewer than 10 inches of rain annually) or semi–desert (fewer than 15 inches). The region's "rivers" often are chains of waterholes and flow only following infrequent rains. Most never reach the sea, but instead widen into areas called lakes which most of the time are actually mud flats encrusted with salt. By drilling to great depths it is possible in some parts of this region to locate limited amounts of ground water, making possible the raising of livestock. However, large areas are needed to support even small numbers of animals—some Outback cattle ranches in Australia are larger than the smaller European countries. Apart from mining settlements, population is scattered and averages fewer than two persons per square mile.

Australians many years ago introduced the Royal Flying Doctor Service, utilizing two–way radio and light aircraft to bring medical services to those living in this isolated environment. Outback children also use the radio system as students of the School of the Air, working through their daily lessons with a teacher in a studio–classroom in the nearest township hundreds of miles away. Large parts of the region are not inhabited at all. An occasional thunderstorm moistens the thirsty land, and grasses and wildflowers rapidly spring up, flower, wither and die, dropping their seeds to the ground to await the

many months before the next rainfall. To the southeast, in the regions of the Murray and Darling Rivers, the land becomes more moist, but the need for water is still so great that these rivers are dammed for irrigation.

Apart from its dry center, Australia has a widely varied climate. It covers more than 30 parallels of latitude and more than a third of the country is in the tropics. Normally snow falls only on the southeastern ranges during the winter as Australia's position surrounded by sea and the absence of marked physical features give a more temperate climate than other land in corresponding latitudes. Because of the low humidity in many places, the high summer temperatures are not as enervating. The North is subject to tropical cyclones (hurricanes), and the city of Darwin was almost completely destroyed by Cyclone Tracy in 1974.

Isolation from other countries by wide expanses of water has affected Australia in many ways from its plant and animal life to its contemporary culture. Australia has many wildflowers found nowhere else. The main native trees are 500 varieties of eucalyptus and 600 species of acacia (known to Australians as *wattle* and akin to the mimosa of North America). About half of Australia's native mammals are marsupials—animals which produce their young in embryo form which is a tiny fraction of the adult weight of the parent. The newborn offspring finds its way miraculously to the adult's pouch where it continues its development; the mammary glands on which it suckles are located within the pouch. Only when it is the equivalent of a three to five year old human does it leave the pouch, returning for nourishment as needed until even more mature. Marsupials include members of the kangaroo family, the koala, the wombat and possums. Australia is also the home of another of nature's oddities— the duck-billed platypus, a cross between bird and mammal. It lays eggs, but then nurses its young after they have hatched, yet its body is covered with fur and it lives in a water habitat. Australia's 800 bird species include the ostrich–like emu and many brightly colored parrots.

History

During the many centuries of development of the Western world, Australia was thinly populated by an estimated 300,000 Aborigines, a nomadic, tribal hunting and gathering society. (Strangely, they bear a striking resemblance to a similar people found in southern Africa.) About 160,000 Aborigines remain today, but many have embraced a largely Western life style; some later racially intermixed with the

Australia

This painting by Algernon Talmage shows the unfurling of the British flag at Sydney Cove. Captain Arthur Phillip and his men drink to the health of King George III.

Australian Information Service

European settlers. They now are a disadvantaged and increasingly assertive minority.

Ships of the Dutch East India Company touched on the Australian coastline in the early 17th century; the Dutch explorer Tasman circumnavigated the continent in 1642–43. The first real penetration was by the British, led by Captain James Cook, who claimed the eastern portion of the island in 1770 in the name of the British Crown.

The principal interest of Britain in Australia was initially as a penal colony where its criminals could be exiled or held in prison. The first settlers, numbering 270 soldiers and sailors and 760 convicts, landed on the present site of the city of Sydney in 1758 to establish the colony of New South Wales under the royally appointed Governor, Captain Arthur Phillip.

The Crown later permitted non–convict settlers to emigrate from the British Isles to Australia. Most of them became interested in sheep raising, to which the island was ideally suited. A close social organization quickly emerged among these free settlers; they dominated the New South Wales Corps, which was a special military police force. They became very influential and struggled with a succession of royal governors, sometimes gaining the right to use the services of convict labor at a low wage, and to expand their sheep raising activities. They also sought control over internal and external trade.

The notorious Captain Bligh, the former commander of HMS *Bounty*, struggled with the New South Wales Corps when he was governor in 1805 and lost. The next governor, Macquarie, was much more respected and successful. He curbed the power of the police force, set limits on land grants and organized and permitted rapid economic development. No more convicts were sent to Australia after 1868.

The discovery of gold in 1851 gave a great boost to the Australian economy and was accompanied by disorders in the mining camps, similar to those in the American West during the same period. In the succeeding decades, additional immigration of free settlers, exploration of the eastern and later the western parts of the continent, and with general economic development, took place at a steadily accelerating rate.

Six British crown colonies were successfully established in Australia from 1788 through the first half of the 19th century. All had been granted self–governing independence by the end of that century. In 1901, the colonies became the six States of an Australian Federation under the title Commonwealth of Australia. This status continues today.

Although an independent, self–governing nation, Australia, along with other countries of the British Commonwealth, recognizes the British sovereign as the head of state, symbolizing historical links with Britain. The Queen (or King) is represented in Australia by a Governor–General. Australia's chief executive is a Prime Minister elected by members of the majority party in the Federal Parliament. The Parliament consists of a Senate and a House of Representatives functioning under a written constitution which borrows from both British and American experience. There is no elected President. Cabinet officers must also be members of Parliament.

Australia sent volunteer units that fought bravely on the Allied side in the Middle East and on the Western Front during World War I. The demands of the British war effort benefited the Australian economy. During the period between the two World Wars, it continued to experience growth, as well as the emergence of a powerful labor movement pressing for benefits for workers. It was gripped by the worldwide depression, with a sharp drop in trade in 1931 and the following years.

Prior to World War II, the foreign policy of Australia was one of comparative isolation from the community of nations. In spite of this, Australia responded to the outbreak of World War II by coming to the aid of the British in the European War in 1939, and after 1941 joined the Allied war effort in the Pacific. For Australia, the war was made much more complicated and dangerous because of the closeness of Japan.

Japanese troops quickly conquered most of Southeast Asia by mid–1942. Australia became the base for the headquarters of General Douglas MacArthur after the fall of the Philippines. The main concern of the Australians was that they also might be invaded next. Darwin, the northern seaport, suffered heavy Japanese bombing raids. However, Allied victories in the Pacific and fighting by Australian troops in New Guinea prevented a Japanese invasion.

The *Labor Party*, led by Prime Minister John Curtin, had come to power in late 1941 and was responsible for major changes in Australian international thinking during World War II. After such close cooperation with the United States in achieving ultimate victory, Australian strategic thinking turned towards the United States after the war.

The end of World War II brought another period of growth and prosperity. Substantial immigration, encouraged by the government, resulted in a larger population, primarily Caucasian. Until 1966 Australian immigration policies discriminated against non–Europeans and in earlier years this had been known as the "white Australia" policy. Since 1966 successive governments have removed discriminatory restrictions. However, the overall rate of immigration was reduced during the 1970's. Today, one in every three Australians was born overseas or is the son or daughter of an immigrant. The influx of newcomers has brought marked changes in Australian society, lifestyle and culture.

The country was governed by a coalition of the *Liberal Party* and the *Country Party* between 1949 and 1972, for 17 years under its leader, the colorful Sir Robert Menzies, then Harold Holt, John Gorton and William McMahan. All maintained steady support for U.S. policies and efforts in Southeast Asia. Australian troops took part in the war in Korea, the campaign against communist terrorists in Malaya (1948–1960) and the Vietnam war.

Elections in 1972 returned the *Labor Party* to power. The new Prime Minister, E. Gough Whitlam, a man of strong personality and intellect, recognized the People's Republic of China and established diplomatic relations with North Vietnam, North Korea and East Germany. He also withdrew the remaining Australian troops from South Vietnam and moved to establish closer economic relations with Japan. He then abolished the draft, lowered the defense budget, began fairer treatment of the Aborigines and introduced ambitious domestic social programs.

The world oil crisis of the early seventies though affected Australia as it did other communities. Both inflation and unemployment went up. Faced with these problems, Whitlam called an election in April 1974 that reduced his majority in the House of Representatives but did enable him to continue in office.

By late 1975, the continuously poor state of the economy and controversy over various *Labor Party* programs prompted the *Liberal* and *National Country* parties (the latter previously known as the *Country Party)* opposition to press for new elections. When Whitlam refused, the opposition took the unprecedented action of using its Senate majority to block the government's budget appropriation bills, leaving it without authority to pay its creditors, including Federal employees and recipients of social security and other benefits. As the government's reserves of money ran out, the constitutional crisis intensified. It is at this point that one of the more peculiar features of Australia's government became apparent.

The Governor–General, the representative of the British Crown, stepped in, dismissed the sitting Prime Minister and asked J. Malcolm Fraser to form a new *Liberal* government. The party, in a coalition with the *National Party,* won the next election. Thus, a representative of a foreign nation was able substantially to interfere in Australia's domestic political process!

Politics and Government

Australia is a parliamentary democracy whose political institutions and practices follow the Western democratic model, reflecting both the British and American experience. The Australian federation has a three–tier system of government: the national government consists of Parliament (House of Representatives with 148 seats and the Senate with 76 seats) and the Government—the party or parties with a majority in the lower house constitute the government, controlling all ministries); six state governments, the Capital Territory and Northern Territory (similar to states); and some 900 local governmental bodies at the city, town, municipal and shire level. Senators in the Federal Parliament serve six year terms (Senators for the two territories serve three year terms), and Representatives serve for three years.

Australia has a written constitution which came into force on January 1, 1901, when the colonies federated to form the Commonwealth of Australia. The constitution can be amended if a majority of voters in a majority of states plus an over-

Kangaroos cavort on a reserve near Melbourne Australian Information Service

Australia

Barbecued chicken on Christmas Day at Sydney Harbor   Australian Information Service

all majority approve the change. Proposed changes must be passed by an absolute majority in both houses of Parliament. If an amendment is passed twice by one house but fails in the other, the Governor–General may submit the amendment to the electorate.

Australia pioneered the secret ballot in parliamentary elections and has used the system since 1879. Voting is compulsory at the national level. The franchise extends to everyone over 18 years of age except criminals and the mentally incompetent. The Australian system of law resembles the British system from which it was taken. Australian law places great importance on the rights of the individual. The law provides for *habeas corpus* (which prevents arbitrary arrest or imprisonment without a court hearing), bail, trial by judge and jury, the presumption of innocence until proven guilty, and prevention from double jeopardy.

The High Court resembles the American Supreme court and deals with federal and state matters. It has original jurisdiction in important areas, including interpretation of the Constitution, determination of legal disputes between the federal government and state governments, suits between state governments, and suits between citizens of different states. The Court has a Chief Justice and six other justices. The Federal Court is a specialized court dealing with matters such as copyrights, industrial law, trade practices, bankruptcy, and administrative law, appeals from territory supreme courts and tribunals administering federal laws. The other specialized court is the Family Court which deals with divorce, custody of children, and associated matrimonial property disputes.

All states and territories have supreme courts and magistrates' courts, and several have intermediate district or county courts which deal mainly with state laws, federal criminal offenses and federal income tax. The supreme courts have the same role at the state level as the High Court does federally. Magistrates' courts deal summarily with most ordinary offenses and preliminary hearings to determine whether sufficient grounds exist in more serious offenses to be tried before a judge and jury. The capital territory and external territories of Norfolk Island, Christmas Island and the Cocos islands have court systems similar in general to the states. Australia has independent federal, state and territory police.

Political Issues

Today the two major political parties are the Australian *Labor Party* (ALP), and the conservative *Liberal Party*. The *ALP*, under the leadership of Prime Minister Robert Hawke controlled the government from 1983 to 1991 when Paul Keating from the Labor Party replaced him as head of the Labor Party and Prime Minister. In recent years though the government has been directed by John Howard of the conservatives.

In addition to the two major parties, other parties often represented in the parliament are the *National Party*, the *Australian Democrats*, the *Northern Territories Country Liberal Party*, and the *Western Australia Greens*. A new party, the *One Nation Party*, appeared on the scene in 1997 and for a time gathered significant support.

Nationally, the conservative *Liberal Party* has been experiencing a resurgence. John Howard was selected as the new party leader and in March 2, 1996, the conservative *Liberal-National* coalition won a landslide victory in national elections which gave the new government a 40 seat margin in the lower house of Parliament. Two years later Howard called for elections again with a platform advocating tax code changes and was reelected. The new coalition government which was formed after the October 1998 election included both Howard's Liberal Party and the National Party. Together, the two parties won 49% of the vote.

The reelection of the *Liberal Party* continued the country's move away from the more leftist *Labor Party* which had directed Australia for the previous generation and indicated the strength of the moderate right in Australian politics. But the swing to the right which had begun in 1996 has at times gone beyond the move toward the conservatives in the country's political life.

In September 1996, a newly elected political independent, a former operator of a fish and chips shop named Pauline Hansen, rose to give her maiden speech in parliament. Once standing she proceeded to attack the Australian Asian and Aboriginal community with considerable vehemence. Hansen claimed that Asian immigration was swamping Australia. Her attacks on Australia's non-white community were nothing new. Indeed, for much of Australian history a largely "whites only" policy had been the norm. But this was in late 1996 and after years of official attempts by the government and business community to improve their relationship with Asia. The storm of controversy she began has not yet let up. Indeed, early political polls showed that 10% of the population supported her racist comments and many showed support for the new political movement, the *One Nation* party, which she launched during the spring of 1997.

Though pushed to do so for months, not until March of 1997 did the conservative Prime Minister, John Howard, launch an official effort to discredit the racism of her message. Given her new party's poll numbers, that may have been more of a political than a moral decision. Nevertheless, the momentum of her movement seemed to slow down over time. In fact, by late 1999 Hansen herself had lost her parliamentary seat and considerable internal dissension had broken out within her own *One Nation Party*. Nevertheless, the issues Hansen had raised still attracted 8% of the vote in the national elections of October 1998.

The most recent drama of Australian politics was the referendum which took place over the question of replacing the Governor-General, the representative of Great Britain's monarch, with a president chosen by the Australian parliament. It was a struggle which revolved both around questions of Australia's continuing ties to Great Britain and whether a president chosen by the parliament rather than at large by the population was a good idea. In the end the referendum went down to defeat when only 45% of the population voted to support it while 55% opposed the idea.

Foreign Relations

As is often the case, Australian's foreign relations have revolved around its relationships with its geographic neighbors, the Asian states of the region and the Western countries whose cultures are more similar to those of Australia. Historically, Australia tended to orient itself more toward the Western communities of North America and Europe but in recent years the emphasis has been more on its regional relationships. That movement was begun by the former Australian governments led by the Labor Party.

In early 1996, however, there were indications that the new more conservative government intended to orient the country's foreign affairs position once again to emphasize Australia's relationships with

the West. There were even some tensions with China during Howard's early months in office especially when he seemed to associate himself with those Americans who were talking of "containing" China.

Indeed the new government seemed to be backing away from trends toward integrating Australia more closely into Asia but that change never really developed into anything significant. By April 1997 Howard had led an influential group to Beijing and then later received the soon to be Chinese Prime Minister Zhu Rongji as his guest. More recently China's President Jiang himself visited Australia.

And it was not merely the early conservative government's policies that caused strains with Asia at times. The overt racism of the *One Nation* party and its leader Pauline Hansen caused problems. Certainly such developments have reinforced those in the Asian community who have not welcomed Australia's recent attempts to associate itself more closely with Asia.

But it was relations with Indonesia that especially complicated Australia's inter-

national position over the last year. Reversing themselves after a generation of supporting Indonesia's control over East Timor, the Australians began supporting East Timorese independence aspirations. And even more dramatically they ended up leading the United Nations international intervention force, which included 5000 Australians, into East Timor in the late summer of 1999. Realistically the government had little choice.

Although a generation of Australia's leaders had understandably believed that Canberra's relationship with the entire country of Indonesia was more important that the East Timorese plight, the wave of violence that occurred after Jakarta agreed to the referendum in East Timor aroused the ire and sympathy of the Australian population. And it was more than the Australian population that was incensed over the East Timorese crisis. Within Indonesia there was an outpouring of popular Indonesian anger over the loss of East Timor which was often directed against the Australians. Clearly it will take time for the wounds to heal from that tragedy.

Aerial view of Canberra with Lake Burley Griffin in the background Australian Information Service

Australia

Society and Culture

In the years after Europeans first began settling in Australia it quickly became a society largely dominated by Westerners whose culture resembled that of North America and England. The original aboriginal peoples, like Native Americans, increasingly lost their land to the aggressive Westerners and immigration laws strongly discriminated against Asians. This "Whites Only" attitude of Australia was a feature of Australian society until fairly recently. Within those parameters, Australians built a society similar to many other Western societies.

Education is free and compulsory through the secondary school level. There are no tuition fees at the 18 government-funded universities and many colleges offering diplomas, degrees and post-graduate studies.

Because of the climate, outdoor sports such as swimming, surfing, several types of football and tennis are very popular, and Australia has produced many Olympic champions. Horse racing is widely enjoyed, and betting on the horses is a consuming topic of interest among many.

Though it has vast spaces and relatively few people, Australia is highly urbanized, perhaps because most population growth and development has taken place only over the past 75 years. More than 80% of the population lives in urban centers and more than 60% are concentrated in five major state capitals.

Two cities dominate urban life. Sydney faces the southeast coast and has a population of more than 3.5 million; Melbourne (2.8 million) faces the southern Bass Strait. All of the cultural entertainment and events common to Europe and America are abundant in both. Perth, with a population of 850,000 and lying on the southwestern coast, is caressed by a gentle climate similar to that found in the Mediterranean and Caribbean resorts of the western world.

Australia's Federal Capital is Canberra, the basic plan for which was conceived by Chicago architect Walter Burley Griffin shortly before World War I. Today, it is a garden city of more than 265,000 people-with over 8 million trees planted in the last half century—and it occupies the site of a former sheep station (ranch) in the foothills of the Australian Alps.

The world of white Australia has usually not been shared equally with that of the aboriginal community whose lot is decidedly less attractive. Aboriginal Australians can expect to live twenty years less than whites and a quarter of them are unemployed.

Of late new controversies have entered the public arena that have aroused even more tensions between the two communities. On one hand there is growing sentiment against the social welfare programs the government supplies for the aboriginal community but on the other, great anxiety about a number of recent court decisions that have authorized greater aboriginal rights to millions of acres of land now being used by Australian ranchers.

From the perspective of some aboriginal leaders, these new rights should allow their people to wean themselves from government welfare programs, something whites should theoretically welcome. But since aboriginal economic empowerment is, in the case of the land, tied to competing white claims the problems are not likely to be resolved soon.

More recently as well, Australia has been facing up to other realities of their historical treatment of aborigines. Over the last few years a greater sensitivity has developed about aboriginal history. This growing consciousness had taken the form of rewriting Australian history to include aboriginal perspectives and heroes as well as recognizing culturally "genocidal" policies like those that had seen generations of lighter skinned aborigines taken from their families to be raised in the white world.

Economy

Australia's economy has changed much in the last fifty years from one which relied heavily on primary production to a mature, diverse one with nearly two-thirds of production in the service sector. World War II and post-war immigration spurred rapid expansion of secondary industry, diversification and overall economic growth. Large investments were made in mining and energy projects. Although the agricultural and mining sectors account for a small part of the country's production, they account for a large per cent of total exports. Australia leads the world in wool production and is a major supplier of wheat, meat and sugar. Australia is also a leading exporter of coal and a major supplier of coal, iron ore, gold, bauxite, and alumina.

The export base was diversified in the 1980s, with the fastest growth in manufactured products and in services. Tourism has been strong though there is some concern of late that the new racial tensions make the country less attractive to Asian tourists. The country has had strong economic and employment growth over the past twenty years.

Overall, Australia entered the new century with a particularly strong economy, in fact better than it had had for generations. And unlike some of its neighbors, it was not merely recovering from the regional economic downturn of previous years. Australia had not really been much affected by the Asian economic crises which enveloped so many of its neighbors. Even at the height of the crisis in 1998 Australia had kept its economy in the black with its GNP registering a respectable 3% growth rate. And now as the entire region begins to grow again, Australia should be able to look forward optimistically toward the future economically.

The Future

Australia faces no immediate external threats. Her growing involvement with the countries of Asia, particularly the ASEAN states of Southeast Asia, can only help to improve her regional position. But they will require a sophisticated handling of the recent resurgence of some white Australian racist sentiments and tensions associated with her role during the East Timor crisis.

Growing trade with Japan, China, and Vietnam will also provide a boost to her economy. Increasing tensions in the ASEAN region over the South China Sea and arms build-ups may require a greater military presence by Australia in the region, especially if the United States becomes less visible over the next few years. Australia has the resources and location to be a vital full partner with the countries of East Asia.

Koala kindergarten

New Zealand

Cosmopolitan Wellington at dusk

Area: 103,000 sq. mi. (268,276 sq. km., the land surface somewhat smaller than Colorado).

Population: 3.6 million.

Capital City: Wellington (Pop. 365,000, estimated).

Climate: Temperate, with ample rainfall; subtropical conditions at the northern tip of the North Island, with colder temperatures in the South Island.

Neighboring Countries: Australia, about 1,200 miles to the northwest.

Official Language: English.

Ethnic Background: European, mostly British (over 80%), Maori (estimates range from 8.9% to 15%)

Principal Religion: Protestant Christianity (82%).

Main Exports (to Australia, U.K., Japan, U.S.): Meat and dairy products, fish, wool.

Main Imports (same trading partners): Petroleum, cars, trucks, iron and steel.

Currency: New Zealand Dollar.

Former Colonial Status: British Colony (1839–1907).

National Day: February 6 is Waitangi Day, anniversary of the signing of the Treaty of Waitangi in 1840 between the British and the Maoris.

Chief of State: Her Majesty Queen Elizabeth II, represented by Governor General Dame Catherine Tizard (since December 1987).

Head of Government: Rt. Hon. Helen Clark, Prime Minister (since December 1999).

National Flag: A purple field with the Union Jack in the upper left corner and four 5–pointed stars in the right half of the field.

Per Capita GNP Income: U.S. $15,720.

The remote islands of New Zealand are about 1,200 miles from their nearest neighbor, Australia. Prior to the advent of air transportation New Zealand was one of the world's most isolated nations. The North Island is the more habitable of the two, and, though smaller than the South Island, it has more than half the country's population.

In the North Island there are volcanic and thermal areas dominated by three volcanic peaks, Ruapehu, Ngauruhoe and Tongariro. All of them are active and given to occasional eruptions of steam and ash. In the central plateau area there is activity caused by the thermal pressure from deep within the earth in the form of geysers, hot springs, steam vents and foul–smelling deposits of sulphur. The average annual rainfall for the whole country is about 60 inches, which allows for quick growth of rich vegetation to feed the millions of sheep that abound in New Zealand.

The South Island is much more rugged and contains the Southern Alps which equal their European namesake in beauty and wildness. In this mountainous region the climate can sometimes be subarctic. In contrast to the abundant growth of the North Island, the grasses of the South Island are more suited to rearing Merino sheep which have a fine coat to protect them from the chilly air. Most of the sheep of the North Island are crossbreeds, designed to produce both meat and wool.

In terms of the Northern Hemisphere, New Zealand occupies a position in the

Southern Hemisphere which would run from the mild climate of southern California northward to the much cooler central part of British Columbia. The reversal of warm and cold zones and of summer and winter in the Southern Hemisphere make northern New Zealand the warm, subtropical area and the southern region the colder one.

History

Though it is known that the Maori, the original peoples of New Zealand initially came from Eastern Polynesia the dating of this event varies widely. Their arrival has been dated from as early as the third century of the common era to as late as the 13th. An extraordinary people, they were the heirs of one of the most impressive seagoing communities the world has ever seen. Even today the descendants of those great sea voyagers live throughout much of the Pacific.

Establishing themselves in their new home must have been especially demanding given that their society had originated in the warmer climates to the north. Upon arrival the most important food was the flightless birds, the moa, which they initially found in large numbers. Unfortunately over time these animals were apparently hunted to extinction. Other foodstuffs, from marine life to small scale farming, also contributed to the diet of these early peoples.

The Maori were not a united community. Rather, they were divided by both tribal ties and the different locations of their settlements. Once the Europeans arrived in the 17th century, access to advanced Western weapons became available thus making intra-tribal warfare even more deadly. Other factors also lowered the local population as well. As was common throughout the colonized world the Maori

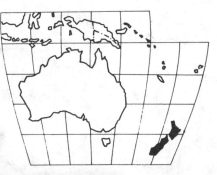

lacked the anti-bodies necessary to resist Western diseases which also depleted their numbers.

The first well documented European visit is that of Abel Janszoon Tasman, a Dutch sailor who apparently visited the islands around 1642. An account still remains of the first encounter which saw several Maori row out to the Dutch ship attempting to communicate. Unfortunately, that effort turned ugly and only a short time later, Tasman lost three of his sailors in a clash with Maori from the southern Island. Hardly encouraged by that first encounter the Dutch sailed away leaving only their naming of the place, initially Nieuw Zeeland, as a contribution.

More than a century after Tasman left, the famous Captain James Cook arrived for an extended visit which included charting of the islands and a much more sophisticated contact with the Maori, whom Cook described as quite intelligent in his well known work *A Voyage Towards the South Pole and Round the World* (1777). Unfortunately though for the Maori, Cook also wrote of the suitability of the islands for colonization. Over the next decades visits by various Europeans would become common.

The growth of the whaling industry in the early nineteenth century also affected the islands as it attracted increasing European interest as whalers, especially those from Australia, created bases in New Zealand. The Maori were also drawn into the whaling economy as they supplied the Europeans with provisions and themselves received rum and weapons from the outsiders. One Maori leader not only traveled to Australia and England but bought weapons abroad which he later used to attack rival Maori tribes. Predictably, these bloody struggles disturbed local life enough to make settlement easier for the arriving Europeans.

Along with whalers and escaped convicts, religion also came to New Zealand via Australia. Missionaries settled in 1814 and quickly began the task of converting the Maoris to Christianity. Despite the Maori reputation for aggressiveness and cannibalism some early missionaries were convinced that the Maori would be good candidates for conversion. Several branches of Western Christianity were active among Maori with denominations ranging from Anglicans to Catholics and Methodists. Eventually most Maori came to embrace some form of Christianity

Over time the islands became increasingly integrated with other British holdings in the South Pacific. Initially considered part of their Australian holdings it soon became a separate crown colony. In 1840, with the signing of the Treaty of Waitangi, Britain assumed direct control

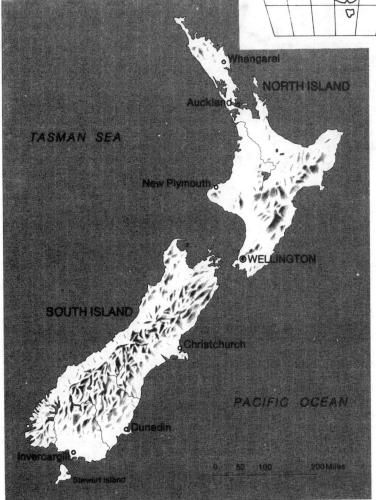

New Zealand

Late afternoon at Lake Hayes, South Island

and per the terms of the treaty was obligated not only to protect the Maori but ensure their land holdings. Not surprisingly, those promises were not upheld and by mid century the English found themselves often in open warfare with the Maori community. As was the case elsewhere the indigenous community was not able to successfully resist the powerful Europeans and over time the Maori not only lost lands but saw their own numbers dwindle significantly. As time passed the Maori population also underwent a gradual transformation as many of them adopted western dress, and began to practice agriculture and animal husbandry in the manner of the English.

Even for the European settlers, the economy of the islands allowed only a very difficult existence until the turn of the 20th century, when faster ships and re-frigeration boosted the export of New Zealand's agricultural products.

Among the settlers the main political issues during the nineteenth century were demands for greater representative government for the colony. By the mid 1850s, with the establishment of the New Zealand Constitution Act, the settler community gained more authority over domestic matters. Nevertheless, the British governors remained powerful and their clashes with elected local assemblies over their respective authority not infrequent.

New Zealand was granted dominion status within the British Commonwealth in 1907 as a result of a new vigor imparted to the country's politics and administration by energetic Liberal leader Richard John Seddon, Prime Minister from 1893 to 1906. For all practical purposes New Zealand was independent from that time on. Nevertheless, it would not become officially independent until 1947.

As it entered World War I, New Zealand was governed by the Reform Party, and later by a coalition government. New Zealand fought on the allied side especially in battles such as Gallipoli and though their soldiers won admiration for their fighting skills the losses were enormous. Later, New Zealand took part as an independent state in the peace settlement at Versailles. It also joined the League of Nations and was awarded a mandate over the islands of Western Samoa which had been captured from the Germans.

Adverse economic conditions during the 1920–1940 period created an increase in labor organization and unrest. By the late 1930's, however, aided by an ambitious program of public works and social security under a succession of *Labour Party* governments, prosperity began to return.

New Zealand took an active part in World War II. After the Pacific War began in 1941 its troops were engaged in battle not only in Europe but against imperial Japan. During the war years, both parties, *Labour* and *National* worked together in a coalition. But once the war was over *Labor's* political domination continued through the late 1940s when the more conservative *National Party* returned to power.

Despite New Zealand's ties to Great Britain, it was understood that its war time defense depended more on the Americans than on the British. Thus after the war, New Zealand, recognizing the declining influence of Great Britain and the rise of U.S. as an Asian power, joined the ANZUS treaty (Australia, New Zealand and the U.S.) to provide security. It also joined the American led Southeast Asian Treaty Organization (SEATO) to meet the threat posed by the growth of communism in the region. During the 1960s New Zealand supplied troops for the American supported struggle in South Vietnam.

In 1972 *The Labour Party* came to power once again on a platform of more welfare benefits. The move to the left was reversed by late 1975 when the *Labour Party* was defeated by a reinvigorated *National Party* which returned to power. Over the next few years, as so often in previous decades, the two parties rotated in power as New Zealand, buffeted by the loss of its British markets due to the growth of the European Common Market suffered financially.

During the mid 1980s ties to the United States were strained when the Labor Party run government announced that no nuclear-armed U.S. naval vessels would be allowed to call at New Zealand's ports. Since the U.S. refused on principle to say whether or not any particular vessel was nuclear-armed, this meant that no U.S. naval vessel could dock in New Zealand. As the U.S. began to apply counter-pressures, including the withholding of some intelligence information and threats to cut back on imports from New Zealand, the ANZUS alliance came under serious strain.

Finally, in June 1986, at a meeting in Manila between Prime Minister Lange and the U.S. Secretary of State George Shultz, the chain broke—at least temporarily. Good naturedly, Shultz admitted to the press that, "We part company on security matters as friends, but we part." Lange was equally gracious, but stood by his government's policy. Eventually the U.S. suspended its security arrangements with New Zealand until "adequate correc-

tive measures" were taken. Thus ended New Zealand's military alliance with the United States.

New Zealand does maintain defense ties with Australia though. The Lange government also proposed in early 1987 a buildup of New Zealand's defensive forces. His stand was quite popular and contributed to *Labour's* reelection.

In August 1987 the Labor Party won reelection with a 15-seat majority in the 97-member parliament. In sharp contrast to previous *Labour* government policies Lange's administration now worked for economic liberalization and privatization which eventually weakened its support.

In 1990 the *National Party*, under the leadership of Jim Bolger again returned to power, though on votes that appeared to be more tied to domestic concerns over the state of the economy than the continuing controversy with the United States over its nuclear weapons.

Politics and Government

New Zealand is a member of the British Commonwealth with a parliamentary form of government. Differences with the British model include a unicameral House of Representatives with 99 seats, and a three year term for the Prime Minister. The political system is multi-party in nature with the major parties being the *National Party, Labour Party, Alliance,* and *New Zealand First.* The Queen of England is represented by a Governor General. Recently the electoral law was changed to a mixed-member proportional representation system. Proportional representation, which awards seats in a district based on the percentage of votes won by a party, tends to help smaller parties and encourage a multi-party system. Six seats in parliament are specifically reserved for Maoris.

Until quite recently, the *National Party*, which had come to power in November of 1990, led the country. Their last elective victory was in 1996. Nevertheless, the last few years have been one of realignment among the country's political parties. The *National Party* under the leadership of then Prime Minister Jim Bolger maintained control but its majority eroded and a coalition with minor parties was required to remain in office. Particularly significant in recent years was the growing strength of the *New Zealand First Party*. Led by Winston Peters, a Maori lawyer, it has lashed out against Asian immigration which its supporters claimed had swamped the country with people who lacked a commitment to New Zealand. As we have seen in Australia, the anti-immigration campaign has attracted not only considerable attention and controversy but political support as well.

Thus, it is not surprising that Win-

New Zealand

ston Peters of the New Zealand First Party ended up in a coalition government again headed by the *National Party's* Jim Bolger. Peters took the post of deputy and treasurer. But that relationship, controversial in itself, did not work well. Over time tensions between Peters and his political colleagues fell to such an all time low that they caused Bolger himself to lose his position as both head of the Nationalists and Prime Minister!

In November of 1997 Jenny Shipley, the transport minister, successfully challenged Bolger—taking over the party leadership and becoming the prime minister. If she had acted to strengthen the conservatives, it was too late, for polls had been showing that the *National Party* was losing support to New Zealand's *Labour Party* led by Helen Clark.

By the fall of 1999 the *Labour Party* had returned to power along side the smaller Alliance party. For Clark herself, a university lecturer in political science, it must have been a gratifying moment indeed. Clark had led the *Labour Party* since the early 1990s and had, twice before, almost become prime minister.

While the shifting political landscape attracted the most attention, there were other issues of importance as well. Race relations between the indigenous Maoris and the British-descended New Zealanders have been especially complicated in recent years. The problems date back to the 1840 Treaty of Waitangi which first saw the British officially establish themselves in New Zealand and, of course, the loss of so much Maori land to the new Anglo immigrants.

Today, the Maori constitute somewhere between 9% and 15% of the population (estimates vary), but they have shared little in the development of modern New Zealand. After public demonstrations in early 1995, both sides agreed to a multimillion dollar settlement involving both money and the return of some Maori lands. The May 1995 deal also included an official apology for land which was confiscated as a result of conflict in the 1860s. By 1997 the government had agreed to the return of an equivalent of $450 million and some expected the eventual total to reach $750 million. More symbolic but nevertheless important, the country's highest peak has now been renamed from its previous name, Mount Cook (named after the explorer) to Aoraki which means Cloud-Piercer in Maori. All these changes, like those going on in Australia or for that matter, the United States, have been part and parcel of an attempt to make peace with the injustices of the past while not totally transforming the present.

Most New Zealanders hoped these settlements would mark the beginning of improved relations. But realistically, these are no more than partial payments on past debts and much more will have to occur before a society emerges where the Maori share equally with the more recent New Zealanders the fruits of their society.

Foreign Policy

Over the last few years there has been more contact between New Zealand's leaders and those of the United States. In March 1995, a significant step was taken to put New Zealand-U.S. relations back on track when Prime Minister Bolger headed for Washington for a meeting with President Bill Clinton. Leaders of the two countries had not met since former Prime Minister David Lange banned a U.S. ship suspected of carrying nuclear weapons from entering a New Zealand port. More recently Secretary Albright made the first visit by a U.S. Secretary of State since the Tripartite ANZUS pact ended. Though nothing dramatic was accomplished, relations have clearly improved somewhat in recent years.

New Zealand had also opposed French nuclear testing in the Pacific. In 1995 the government sent a ship with two members of parliament to Mururoa Atoll to observe. Military cooperation with France was suspended and the ambassador to France was briefly recalled.

Since the establishment of a free trade area with Australia the economies of those two nations have been closely intertwined though that has not always guaranteed that the two former British colonies would get along well. The two have differed, for example, on the details of the Bougainville settlement in Papua New Guinea's civil war. New Zealand, like Australia, has also attempted over the last generation to turn more toward Asia with its tremendous potential as an export market.

And like Australia, New Zealand too has been working to improve its relations with the People's Republic of China. She has finally concluded the first bi-lateral trade agreement with Beijing and reinforced its commitment to greater econom-

Prime Minister Helen Clark
Leader, *Labour Party*

Rt. Hon. Jenny Shipley
Leader, *National Party*

Rt. Hon. Winston Peters
Leader, *New Zealand First Party*

ic cooperation. And again like Australia, New Zealand found itself embroiled in regional politics as it too contributed to the international intervention in East Timor though its ability to actually support such an effort turned out to highlight significant deficits in the country's military equipment.

Society and Culture

Apart from the Maori community, life in New Zealand is predominantly British—more so than in any other nation of the British Commonwealth except for the British Isles. Isolated and relatively small, it has a reputation for being somewhat provincial and conservative, whereas British cultural values have rapidly changed since World War II. Thus, the old saying that New Zealanders are more British than the British has some validity today.

The accent of the great majority of the people is similar to that of the middle and upper class gentry of England, and in the southern highlands around Dunedin and Invercargill it is reminiscent of the Scottish speech of their forbearers.

The Maori community itself, though more politically active in recent years, nevertheless lags behind its non-Maori neighbors in the basic social indicators such as longevity and unemployment. Most of the Maori live in urban areas having lost the bulk of their lands to the whites during the nineteenth century. Today there is considerable intermarriage between the Maori and the non-Maori New Zealanders.

Nevertheless, as a group they are less represented in the professional classes. Unfortunately, they are over represented among prison populations and experience a far higher unemployment record than their neighbors. Compared to their non-Maori neighbors they are as well more likely to depend on the government for employment.

Economy

Agriculture, livestock raising and dairying predominate in the New Zealand economy. Mining and other industries have been added in the post World War II era which will continue gradual expansion. The economy is very dependent on foreign trade and this has caused some difficulty for unskilled workers. The government has taken the position, however, that this is the best course for the country in the long

Christchurch: Anglican Cathedral at night

Courtesy: New Zealand Information Service

term. Recent governments have undertaken significant privatization efforts. The past years have seen a restructuring of the economy which make it one of the least regulated in the world. Significant cuts in welfare have also been undertaken and there have been significant losses in jobs.

During the mid 1990s the economy grew at a healthy rate of around 6% but the economy has slowed considerably in the last few years. Tourism though, which has been much reduced by the Asian economic crisis, has begun to improve recently.

Efforts to enhance New Zealand's trading relationships picked up steam as well over the last year with progress made on establishing potential trading relation-

ships with Singapore, South Korea and possibly even Chile.

The Future

New Zealand compared to so many of its neighbors, has plenty to be grateful for. The economy has remained reasonably stable and some progress has been made in dealing with the injustices of the past through efforts at reconciliation with the Maori people. Tensions have also lessened a bit over relations with the immigrant Asian community as even the controversial Winston Peters has backed off on some of his more anti-Asian sentiments.

Smaller Nations of the Western and Southern Pacific

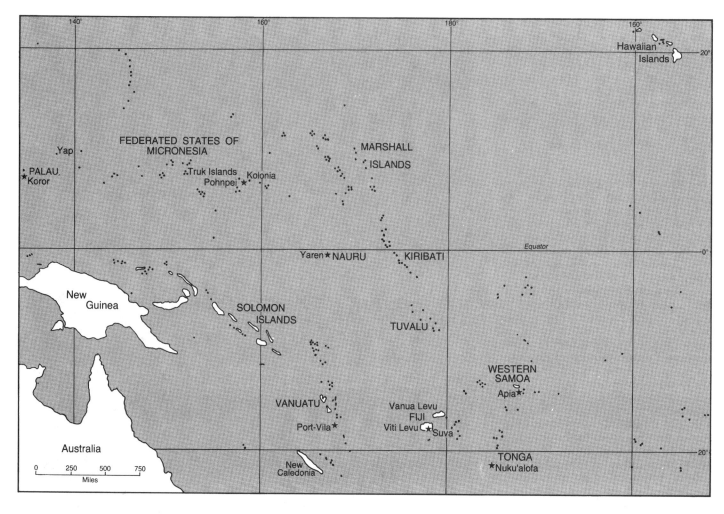

(From the preamble to the Constitution of the Federated States of Micronesia)

Scattered like brilliant pieces of jade across an area covering more than 3 million square miles of the Pacific Ocean lie a number of island states which have achieved independence or have become self-governing; they have been under British, German, French, U.S., Japanese, Australian or New Zealand administration either as colonies, protectorates, or UN trusteeships. They range in population from Fiji's 832,000 to Nauru's 12,000 inhabitants. Most islanders are ethnically Polynesian, Melanesian or Micronesian, although some Asian groups such as Indians, Chinese and Vietnamese have settled in the islands.

On the majority of the islands the terrain is generally low, sometimes only a few feet above sea level (of coral origin) or mountainous (of volcanic origin) covered by lush vegetation and bordered by legendary white beaches. Many, however, bear the scars and rusted armaments left to them by the savage engagements waged throughout the region during World War

II; gentle wavelets brush the bows of hulking battleships sunk during those years, while palm trees sway in the cooling breezes which moderate the tropical climate. World-renowned for their beauty, the islands are subject to fierce typhoons from June to December. Long before the era of Christianity, Asian peoples migrated into the area. Spanish explorers plumbed the region for gold and spread Christianity among the people, a belief which was often blended with their traditional deities. Spain laid claim to much of this area of scattered islands.

In the latter 1800s, as part of the German program to establish an overseas empire in competition with an already widespread and successful colonization by other European powers, German control was eventually imposed over most of the Spanish-claimed region. After World War I, Japan, which had joined the victorious Allies, was rewarded with possession of the former German-held islands north of New Guinea, but during World War II an island-by-island struggle by Allied troops wrested the area from the Japanese, and the islands came under control of the United States, Great Britain, France, Australia and New Zealand, with the Dutch reclaiming their

former colony of the Dutch East Indies—most of which now forms Indonesia. Over the years the islands achieved independence (see individual nation entries).

Following World War II, the United Nations established a trusteeship over three primary archipelagos north of the equator: the Carolines, the Marshalls, and the Marianas (except for Guam, a U.S. possession since the end of the Spanish-American War in 1898.) The U.S. was the trustor, and the Department of the Interior took jurisdiction over these islands from the Navy in 1951.

In 1975 the Northern Marianas (again, except for Guam) were given separate status as a commonwealth. The rest of the territory was divided into the Marshall Islands (in the East), the Federated States of Micronesia (in the South), and the Republic of Palau (in the Southwest).

In January 1986 the United States, having held the role of trustor for the UN's Trust Territory of the Pacific Islands, approved a Compact of Free Association for them; it consists of two agreements included in the same act of Congress—one between the U.S. and the Federated States of Micronesia and the other between the U.S. and the Marshall Islands. The Compact provides for extensive cooperation in numerous areas such as law enforcement, narcotics control, economic and technical assistance, resolution of nuclear-cleanup programs, health care, fishing rights, etc. With the enactment of the Compact, the Trust Territory of the Pacific Islands essentially ceased to exist. The FSM and the Marshall Islands are now independent republics and members of the United Nations.

Some exports of the islands are quite specific, as in the case of Nauru with its dependence on phosphate deposits, but others generally produce in varying quantities basic products of a tropical climate: coconut and palm oil, fish, copra, fruits and—in the case of Fiji—sugar and some gold. Timber is also an important export for both Fiji and the Solomon Islands. Another prime source of income which all are striving to develop is tourism. Most recently several of these island communities have cashed in on the emerging globalized Internet economy by selling their Internet country codes to those looking for easy and readable world wide web addresses!

The Solomon Islands, Tonga, and Vanuatu are members of the (British) Commonwealth of Nations. Nauru and Tuvalu are special members, i.e., they may participate in all functional Commonwealth meetings and activities, but do not have the right to attend meetings of the Commonwealth Heads of Government. The states of this region, including Australia and New Zealand, have formed an organization called the South Pacific Forum. In 1985 they signed a South Pacific Nuclear-Free Zone Treaty barring such weapons from the region's territories, but not banning transit of its waters by nuclear-armed or nuclear-powered ships. More recently, a new organization emerged called the Forum Economic Minister's Meeting (FEMM) which held its first meeting recently at Cairns, Australia. The new group, which has largely been sponsored by Australia, was partly a result of the latter's concern about the increasing economic weakness of its South Pacific island neighbors.

In recent years there has been talk of expanding cooperation between the nations of the region on global political and economic issues. Those talks came to fruition last year when the new South Pacific Free-trade Area was created. Such a move had been felt necessary in order to have a unified voice speak for these communities in negotiations with emerging trade blocks like the Northern American NAFTA and European Community.

With similar ideas in mind several of these island nations recently joined the United Nations in order to give more voice to their concerns within the forums of the United Nations. The perils of not having such a voice were especially obvious during the era of nuclear testing.

During the Cold War the Eniwetok and Bikini atolls in the Marshalls were the site of H-bomb tests in the 1950s and are still considered contaminated. Not surprisingly there has been considerable local discontent over the use of the region as a nuclear testing area. The most recent tensions rose considerably when, in 1995, the French announced plans to resume nuclear testing in the region. The decision resulted in an unsuccessful effort by New Zealand to use the International Court of Justice to pressure Paris not to start testing again as well as to arouse a world wide protest that included both governments, religious and anti-nuclear groups.

Finally in January of 1996, French President Jacques Chirac announced that having carried out six of the originally planned eight nuclear tests, the French would discontinue the program. Ending the French nuclear program played a role as well in finally facilitating an agreement signed in May of 1998 to move New Caledonia on the road to independence early in the next century.

Probably most significant to the region has been the end of the long-running civil war in Papua New Guinea which was resolved after agreement was reached between many of the states in the region to provide military units for peace-keeping on Bougainville.

Economically, the effect of the *El Niño* weather front proved to be a major disaster for much of the region as the anticipated rains did not come and local agriculture suffered greatly. An enormous amount of outside help was needed to try to alleviate suffering in the region. And even more recently devastating tidal waves hit Papua New Guinea which killed thousands of people further straining the region's resources.

One of the most interesting new challenges for the region will be to plan for the introduction of new technologies for mining the sea during the 21st century. At that point, some have speculated that the ocean floors surrounding these islands may be worth billions of dollars. Working out the legal and financial details now will make harvesting the advantages in the future easier.

On the positive side, the economies of most the Pacific Islands were not as hurt by the Asian economic crisis as some had foreseen. In fact, some even benefited as tourists changed their plans from potential visits to Southeast Asia to the Pacific Islands.

Typical island scene, this one in Micronesia　　Courtesy of Marianna H. Rowe

The Republic of FIJI

General Sitiveni Rabuka

Area: 7,055 sq. mi. (330 islands) of which about 97 are inhabited).

Population: 832,000 (1999 estimate)

Capital City: Suva (Pop. 151,000 estimated).

Languages: English (official), Fijian, Hindi.

Principal Religion: Christianity.

Main Exports: food stuffs, tobacco, textiles, chemicals

Currency: Fiji dollar.

GDP Per Capita (US$, 1996): $6,500.

Former Colonial Status: British Crown Colony.

Independence Date: October 10, 1970.

Chief of State: Ratu Sir Kamisese Mara, President.

Head of Government: Uncertain as of June 2000.

One of the best known of the many island nations of the South Pacific, Fiji attracts tourists from Australia, New Zealand and North America. Sadly, this former crown colony of the British has often experienced considerable ethnic tensions between the native Fijians who make up around 45% of the population and the many Fijians of South Asian and mixed heritage. The primary cause of the tensions has been the effort of the Fijian dominated government to maintain their political control over the other ethnic communities. This struggle caused considerable tensions in their relationship with India which were only recently improved.

Fiji is attempting to raise the level of its foreign relations with its neighbors. The country's central location, among the Pacific island states, places it in a geographically advantageous position. In 1994 a memorandum of understanding was completed on fisheries and handicrafts with

Tuvalu. Fiji is a member of the Pacific Forum but has thus far declined membership in other, more sub-regional groupings such as the Melanesian Spearhead Group. Fiji is broadening its horizons with a new "look North" policy which will focus more on Asia. The country already has well developed ties to the West with Australia and New Zealand.

Like many of its Southeast Asian neighbors, Fiji was forced early in 1998 to devalue its currency in hopes of spurring exports and tourism

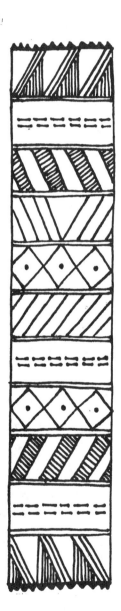

The Republic of KIRIBATI
(pronounced Kiri–baas)

Beretitenti **(President) Teburoro Tito**

Area: 338 sq. mi. (34 small islands).

Population: 84,000 (1998 estimate)

Capital City: Bairiki (on Tarawa).

Languages: English (official), Gilbertese.

Principal Religion: Roman Catholic (48%), Protestant (Congregational) 45%.

Main Exports: Fish, copra.

GDP Per Capita: $800 (1996 est.)

Currency: Australian dollar.

Former Colonial Status: British Colony as the Gilbert Islands.

Independence Date: July 12, 1979.

Chief of State: Teburoro Tito (pronounced See-Toe), President (since October 1994). Also, now serving as the leader of the Micronesian Leadership Council.

One of the least developed countries of the world, Kiribati is made up of 34 islands whose population is overwhelmingly Micronesian in origin. Most families live by growing produce such as bananas, breadfruit and taro. In recent years the leading export has been copra, the "meat" of a coconut which is used for its oil and as an animal feed. Among this small nation's leading resources is its control of fishing rights in its territories.

Politically, the Republic of Kiribati is governed by a unicameral parliament which nominates candidates for the presidency. Candidates for president are then voted upon in elections which allow for universal suffrage. A parliamentary vote of no confidence can bring down the government.

The Republic of the MARSHALL ISLANDS

President Imata Kabua

Area: 68 sq. mi. (31 small islands).
Population: 61,000 (1999 estimate)
Capital City: Majuro.
Language: English.
Principal Religion: Christianity, mostly Protestant.
Main Exports: Copra, copra oil, agricultural products, handicrafts.
GDP Per Capita (US$, 1997): $1,719
Currency: U.S. dollar.
Former Political Status: Part of the UN Trust Territory of the Pacific under U.S. administration.
Independence Date: October 21, 1986.
Chief of State: Amata Kabua, President.

The inhabitants of the Marshall Islands have been among the peoples most affected by the nuclear arms race; for once the United States assumed its control from Japan after World War II, they were chosen as nuclear test grounds. From 1946 to 1958 the islands of Bikini and Enewetak were used as test grounds for nuclear weapons - after their people were removed to other islands. After attempts to clean up the toxic effects of the bombing were carried out some former inhabitants of Bikini attempted to return home but by the late 1970s they had to leave again. The area was found to be still too contaminated. The Kwajalein atoll is still used by the United States as a missile testing ground. Economically the island nation is dependent on the United States for 90% of its income.

The Republic now has embassies in China, Fiji, Japan, the U.S., and the United Nations; with consulates in California and Hong Kong. The Chinese are using the Marshall Islands to circumvent the limit on the amount of garments that it can export to the United States. China

and the Marshall Islands agreed on a joint venture in December 1993 to build a garment factory. It will produce almost one million pieces a year and will employ Chinese workers initially. Marshallese will eventually take over all of the production jobs.

As with so many of their neighbors, the drought caused by the *El Niño* weather front has caused major problems in this island community. The United States has been especially involved in helping the Marshall Islands deal with these problems.

The Federated States of MICRONESIA

President Jacob Nena

Area: 271 sq. mi (about 600 islands, the largest of which are Pohnpei, Truk, Yap, and Kosrae).
Population: 140,000 (1999 estimate)
Capital City: Kolonia (on Pohnpei).
Language: English, although other indigenous languages are spoken.
Principal Religions: Mostly Roman Catholic and Protestant.
Main Export: Copra, fish, coconut oil
Currency: U.S. dollar.
GDP Per Capita: $2,560 (1997 est.)
Former Political Status: Part of the UN Trust Territory of the Pacific under U.S. administration.
Independence Date: November 3, 1986.
Chief of State: Jacob Nena, President (since May 1997).

Over the years the islands that became the Federated States of Micronesia have been ruled successively by Spain, Germany, Japan and the United States. Independent since 1986, Micronesia is still dependent on the United States for financial grants. Other sources of income include fees from foreign ships fishing in national waters. Most people live by subsistence farming and fishing.

Under the terms of its relationship with the United States the latter continues to provide for the country's security and defense as well as financial aid which is expected to total 1.3 billion during the period from 1986 to 2001.

The Republic of NAURU

President Bernard Dowiyogo

Area: 8.2 sq. mi.
Population: 12,000 (1999 estimate)
Capital City: There is no capital city as such, but most of the government offices are located in the Yaren District of the island.
Language: Nauruan (official); English is widely spoken and used in government and commerce.
Principal Religions: Protestant (65%), Roman Catholic (30%).
Main Export: Phosphates.
Currency: Australian dollar.
GNP Per Capita: $8,100 (1993)
Former Political Status: UN trusteeship under Australia, New Zealand, and the UK.
Independence Date: January 31, 1968.
Chief of State: Bernard Dowiyogo, President (since April 2000).

Unlike most of its Pacific neighbors whose nations are often made up of hundreds of islands, Nauru consists of only a single island. But that single island is richly endowed with phosphate, a mineral important in making fertilizer. Thus Nauru's small population enjoys one of the highest standards of living in the world. Education is free and there are two well-equipped hospitals.

Politically, things were quite complicated over the last year when three of the country's parliament members were dismissed for making derogatory comments about the parliament's leaders and then later returned to office by the electorate.

The Republic of PALAU

President Kuniwo Nakamura

Area: 364 sq. mi. of land on approximately 200 (mostly tiny) islands.
Population: 19,000 (1999 estimate)
Capital City: Koror (Pop. 10,501, estimated).
Language: Palauan (official), but English is widely used in government and commerce.
Principal Religion: Predominantly Roman Catholic and Protestant.
Currency: U.S. dollar.
GDP Per Capita: $8,800 (1997 est.)
Former Political Status: The last remaining entity in the UN Trust Territory of the Pacific, it was largely responsible for its domestic affairs. The U.S. remained the UN-designated trustee for Palau, responsible for its international relations, until the country declared its Independence.
Independence date: October 2, 1994.
Chief of State: Kuniwo Nakamura, President.

The background of the Palauans is a mixed heritage made up of peoples from Micronesia, Malaya, Polynesia and the Philippines. Historically the islands were held by a variety of colonial powers from the Spanish to the Germans. Eventually, Japan administered them and made Palau the center of its South Sea activities during the Second World War. After the war the United States assumed their administration which was formally terminated in 1994.

The main source of income is working for the government. Palau still receives 90% of its government revenue from the United States. People also support themselves through a combination of subsistence agriculture and fishing. Tourism also brings in important currency and the island's growing reputation as an especially good spot for diving may help in the future.

SAMOA (formally Western Samoa)

**His Highness
Sasuga Malietoa Tanumafili II**

Area: 1,097 sq. mi. (Two large islands—Savai'i and Upolu—and seven smaller ones).
Population: 184,000 (1999 estimate)
Capital City: Apia (Pop. 30,000 estimated) on Upolu.
Languages: Samoan, English.
Principal Religion: Christianity.
Main Exports: Coconut oil and cream, taro.
Currency: Tala.
GDP Per Capita: $2,100 (1996 est.)
Former Political Status: UN trusteeship administered by New Zealand.
Independence Date: January 1, 1962.
Head of State: His Highness Susuga Malietoa Tanumafili II.
Head of Government: Tuila'epa Sa'ilele Malielegaoi, Prime Minister (since November 1998).

A constitutional monarchy like Tonga, Samoa has in its turn been both a German colony and later a New Zealand League of Nations Mandate. Most recently it even changed its name dropping the "Western" from its official title. The vast majority of its people are farmers who produce a wide variety of crops ranging from coconuts and bananas to tropical fruits, nuts and yams. There have been efforts to expand the islands' industrial base with foreign aid. Tourism is also an important part of the local economy.

Most inhabitants are descended from Polynesians who arrived thousands of years ago. There are as well small communities of Europeans and Chinese.

SOLOMON ISLANDS

Bartholomew Ulufa' alu

Area: 10,640 sq. mi.
Population: 412,902 (July 1996 est.)
Capital City: Honiara (Pop. 25,000, estimated) on the island of Guadalcanal.
Languages: Over 100 indigenous tongues, with a Melanesian pidgin used for simplified communication. English is used in government and commerce.
Principal Religion: Nominally Christian, with many denominations and indigenous beliefs.
Main Exports: Fish, timber, copra, palm oil.
Currency: Solomon Islands dollar.
GDP Per Capita: $3,000 (1997 est.)
Former Political Status: British protectorate.
Independence Date: July 7, 1978.
Chief of State: Queen Elizabeth II.
Head of Government: Manasseh Sogavare, Prime Minister (since June 30, 2000).

The Solomons were named after an early Spanish explorer's belief that they were the source of the biblical King Solomon's gold mines. But despite that early European contact, the inhabitants' resistance to Western encroachment kept the islands outside of the colonial system until the late nineteenth century when the British established a protectorate.

Today, the vast majority of the population is involved in subsistence agriculture though there is considerable commercial economic activity as well ranging from a large lumbering establishment to fish processing.

On November 7, 1994, Solomon Mamaloni was elected Prime Minister. He defeated Sir Beddeley Devesi, 29 votes to 18 in a secret ballot election in the national Parliament. This is the third time for Mamaloni to be chosen Prime Minister. His government fell though after a general election in the fall of 1997 to

Bartholomew Ulufa'alu who ran a campaign against corruption.

The government faced a minor political crisis in March 1994 when Michael Miana, Minister of Tourism and Culture, was charged with 28 counts of misconduct. He was the first cabinet officer to face such charges. In March 1994, the PNG government paid the Solomon Islands $500,000 for damages incurred from an illegal border violation in 1992, which took the lives of three people.

The region's economic and environmental problems hit the Solomons as well. Not only did it have to contend with El Nino but Japan, its largest aid donor, itself caught in a weakening financial crunch announced it was going to cut its donations by 10%.

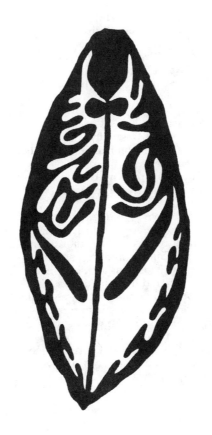

The Kingdom of TONGA

His Majesty the King of Tonga

Area: 283 sq. mi. (171 islands).
Population: 106,466 (July 1996 est.)
Capital City: Nuku'alofa (Pop. 32,000 estimated).
Languages: Tongan, English.
Principal Religion: Christianity.
Main Exports: Coconut oil, copra, bananas, other fruits and vegetables.
Currency: Pa'anga.
GDP Per Capita: $2,160 (1995 est.)
Former Political Status: British Protectorate.
Independence Date: June 4, 1970.
Chief of State: His Majesty King Taufa'ahau Tupou IV.
Head of Government: Baron Vaea - since August 1991.

Tonga's government, which today operates as a semi-constitutional monarchy, has existed since the 10th century. The current royal family though has only held the throne since the nineteenth century. The government includes a one house legislature that represents both commoners and nobles. Most recently tensions have arisen in the kingdom over the efforts to move the government toward a more open constitutional system. Meanwhile the royal family itself has been feuding internally over the island's potentially lucrative satellite communications system.

Most of its people, who speak a language derived from Samoan, live in villages and work in the production of cash crops ranging from coconuts and bananas to vanilla beans. Some manufacturing goes on mostly associated with food processing. Although tourism has begun to grow, unemployment is high and many people have left the country. Education and health care is free and Tonga has a high literacy rate.

TUVALU

Prime Minister Ionatana Ionatana

The Republic of VANUATU

Former President Jean–Marie Leye

Area: 10 sq. mi. (nine islands).
Population: 10,146 (July 1996 est.)
Capital City: Funafuti (Pop. 3,000, estimated).
Languages: Tuvaluan, English.
Principal Religion: Christianity, mostly Protestant.
Main Export: Copra.
Currency: Tuvaluan and/or Australian dollar.
Per Capita GDP Income: $800. (1995 estimate)
Former Political Status: British Protectorate as the Ellice Islands.
Independence Date: October 1, 1978.
Chief of State: Queen Elizabeth II.
Governor General: Sir Tomasi Puapua.
Head of Government: Ionatana Ionatana (since April 1999).

Part of the British Commonwealth, Tuvalu has few natural resources. The originally coral base of the islands makes them a poor base for agriculture. Even finding enough fresh water is at times difficult. Nevertheless, its people live largely on a subsistence farming and fishing economy. The sale of the country's postage stamps are an important source of outside revenue.

The vast majority of the population is of Polynesian origin. Formally known as the Ellice Islands, the small island community is economically poorer than many of its neighbors. The prime minister is chosen from a 12 person parliament. Councils also operate on the outer islands.

Area: 4,750 sq. mi. (82 islands).
Population: 177,504 (July 1996 est.)
Capital City: Port Vila (Pop. 21,000 estimated).
Languages: English and French.
Principal Religion: Christianity, especially Presbyterian, Anglican, Catholicism interlaced with indigenous beliefs.
Main Exports: Copra, cocoa.
GDP Per Capita: $1,117 (1997 est.)
Currency: Vatu.
Former Political Status: British Protectorate as the New Hebrides.
Independence Date: July 30, 1980.
Chief of State: John Bani, President (since April 1999).
Head of Government: Donald Kalpokas, Prime Minister (since March 1998)

Once known as the New Hebrides, Vanuatu's people are primarily Melanesian but there are also small minorities of Europeans, Chinese and Polynesians. Economically the islands are doing relatively well compared to many others in the region. Although many of the inhabitants practice subsistence agriculture the economy also includes large scale plantation farming of produce from cocoa to coffee for the export market. Tourism offers additional revenue as does a developing banking industry.

The Samoan coast

THE DEPENDENCIES

The active interest of the United States and European nations in ruling colonies in the countries of Asia was dramatically lessened by two elements of World War II: Japanese military conquest, and the economic drain of the war against Germany and Japan. Shortly after the end of the war two colonial wars erupted, the first against the French in Indochina and the second against the Dutch in Indonesia. The necessity for the West to yield to nationalistic pressures made it clear that the age of colonialism in Asia was over. Nevertheless, several communities have only recently gained their independence or still remain under the control of the Western powers.

French Dependencies

New Caledonia

Area: 8,550 square miles.
Population: 187,784 (July 1996 est.)
GDP per capita: $8,000 (1995 est.)

This island group is located east of Australia. Its economic importance is as a major exporter of nickel. It has a limited degree of self-government, but it is not yet scheduled to become independent.

The indigenous Kanakas (or Kanaks) who are Melanesians, are outnumbered by the combined European, Asian and Polynesian settlers. The majority wants a continuation of French rule, but a militant group of the Kanakas demands independence—which Paris fears might destabilize French Polynesia to the east—and has taken to violence. President Mitterrand visited the island in early 1985 in an atmosphere of crisis, and offered it limited independence in association with France. This proposal seemed to please neither side.

In elections held in September 1985, the Kanaks won majorities in three of the four regions, although pro-French elements (Europeans and Asians) won an overall majority in the territorial assembly.

The French government of then Premier Jacques Chirac in 1986 canceled the previous political concessions pending the outcome of elections. A referendum held in September 1987 was boycotted by most of the Kanaks, and accordingly the vote was 98% in favor of continued existence as a French territory (rather than as an independent state). Pro-independence demonstrations by Kanaks were then suppressed by French police.

In June 1988, a new French government worked out an agreement with both sides; following a year (1989) of direct French rule, there would be a period of limited self-government and accelerated economic development, followed by a referendum on independence in 1998. Although highly controversial, this agreement was approved in a referendum held in both France and New Caledonia. Real progress was finally made in May of 1998 when the French prime minister signed a document that will eventually lead to New Caledonia's independence.

French Polynesia

Area: 1,545 square miles.
Population: 224,911 (July 1996 est.)
GDP per capita: $8,000 (1995 est.)

Scattered over a wide area in the South Pacific, this group of islands includes the famous tourist attraction of Tahiti. The islands have limited self-government. The most controversial issue in recent years has been French nuclear tests which have been a cause of grave concern and charges of serious environmental contamination.

In the generation since the French established a military facility there many of the inhabitants have moved from work in a subsistence agricultural setting to jobs working for the military and of course for the famous tourist trade.

New Zealand Dependencies

Cook Islands

Sir Geoffrey Henry

Area: 90 square miles.
Population: 19,561 (July 1996 est.)
GDP per capita:$4,000 (1994 est.)
Prime Minister: Sir Geoffrey Henry.

These islands, located about 1,700 miles northeast of New Zealand, have a predominantly Polynesian population. They have had internal self-government since 1965, but New Zealand continues to control their defense and foreign relations. The northern islands are relatively poor; the southern islands are rather prosperous.

The Cook Islands is one of the world's smallest nations, with 18,500 people, spread over one of the largest sea areas in the world. The country is known as a tax haven and has a reputation for rough and tumble politics. Unfortunately, the country also has a foreign debt of approximately NZ$100 million.

United States Dependencies

Guam

Area: 212 square miles.
GDP Per Capita: $19,000 (1996 est.)
Population: 156,974 (July 1996 est.)

The United States acquired Guam, which is the southernmost of the Marianas, from Spain in 1898 as a result of the Spanish American War. The population is predominantly Micronesian and Catholic. Guam has self-government but is not yet a Territory or Commonwealth, like Puerto Rico. Its residents are U.S. citizens but do not vote in American national elections. Guam has been the site of a major U.S. air base since it was recaptured from the Japanese during World War II. Now that the U.S. has lost its naval base in the Philippines, it is considered as a possible alternative site.

Guam was much in the news during 1997 because of the crash of a Korean airliner. Although preliminary reports suggested part of the problem was caused by procedures among the airlines personnel, local rescue forces were particularly slow to respond to the emergency.

American Samoa

Area: 76 square miles.
Population: 59,566 (July 1996 est.)
GDP Per Capita:$2,600 (1995 est.)

The inhabitants of these seven islands, located just east of Samoa, are mostly Polynesian. They enjoy limited self-government under the jurisdiction of the Department of the Interior. The main occupations are farming and fishing.

The U.S. has recently launched a major effort to improve the economic well-being of the territory by stimulating private enterprise to take over government-administered enterprises ("privatization").

The lush jungle on Guam cannot erase the traces of World War II

Photo by Cdr. Thornton W. Wilt

Selected Bibliography of Key English Language Sources

General

Borrego, John, et al., eds. *Capital, the State, and Late Industrialization: Comparative Perspectives on the Pacific Rim.* Boulder, CO: Westview Press, 1996.

Bracken, Paul. *Fire in the East: the Rise of Asian Military Power and the Second Nuclear Age.* New York: HarperCollins Publishers, 1999.

Bundy, Barbara K., et al., eds. *The Future of the Pacific Rim: Scenarios for Regional Cooperation.* New York: Praeger, 1994.

Clifford, Mark L. and Peter Engardio. *Meltdown: Asia's Boom, Bust, and Beyond.* Old Tappan, NJ: Prentice-Hall Press, 1999.

Cotterell, Arthur. *East Asia: from Chinese Predominance to the Rise of the Pacific Rim.* New York: Oxford University Press, 1994.

Das, Dilip K., ed. *Emerging Growth Pole: the Asia-Pacific Economy.* Paramus, NJ: Prentice Hall, 1997.

Dutta, Manoranjan. *Economic Regionalization in the Asia-Pacific: Challenges to Economic Cooperation.* Northampton, MA: Edward Elgar Publishing, 1999.

Eccleston, Bernard and Michael Dawson, eds. *Asia Pacific Profile.* New York: Routledge, 1998.

Indorf, Hans H. and Patrick M. Mayerchak. *Linkage or Bondage: U.S. Economic Relations with the ASEAN Region.* Westport, CT: Greenwood Press, 1989.

Jones, Eric L. *Coming Full Circle: an Economic History of the Pacific Rim.* Boulder, CO: Westview Press, 1993.

Lasserre, Phillippe. *Strategies for Asia Pacific: Beyond the Crisis.* New York: New York University Press, 1999.

Liu, Ts-ui-jung, ed. *Asian Population History.* New York: Oxford University Press, 1999.

Moore, Larry F. and P. Devereaux Jennings, eds. *Human Resource Management on the Pacific Rim: Institutions, Practices, and Attitudes.* Hawthorne, NY: Walter De Gruyter, 1995.

Muhlhausler, Peter. *Linguistic Ecology: Language Change and Linguistic Imperialism in the Pacific Rim.* New York: Routledge, 1996.

Olds, Kris. *Globalisation and the Asia-Pacific: Contested Territories.* New York: Routledge, 1999.

Preston, Peter. *Pacific Asia in the Global System: an Introduction.* Malden, MA: Blackwell Publishers, 1998.

Seagrave, Sterling. *Lords of the Rim: the Invisible Empire of the Overseas Chinese.* New York: Putnam, 1995.

Simon, Denis F., ed. *Techno-Security in an Age of Globalization: Perspectives from the Pacific Rim.* Armonk, NY: M.E. Sharpe, 1997.

Simone, Vera and Anne T. Ferara. *The Asian Pacific: Political and Economic Development in a Global Context.* White Plains, NY: Longman Publishing Group, 1999.

Terry, Edith B. *The Rise and Fall of Asia's Miracle Economies: How Asia Got Rich, What Went Wrong, and How to Fix It.* Armonk, NY: M.E. Sharpe, 2000.

Thompson, Roger C. *The Pacific Basin since 1945: a History of the Foreign Relations of the Asian, Australasian, and American Rim States and the Pacific Islands.* White Plains, NY: Longman Publishing, 1994.

Weinbaum, Marvin G. and Chetan Kumar, eds. *South Asia Approaches the Millennium: Reexamining National Security.* Boulder, CO: Westview Press, 1995.

The Wilson Chronology of Asia and the Pacific. Bronx, NY: H.W. Wilson, 1999.

Yomamato, Yoshinobu, ed. *Globalism, Regionalism, and Nationalism: Asia in Search of Its Role in the 21st Century.* Malden, MA: Blackwell Publishers, 1999.

Yu, George T., ed. *Asia's New World Order.* New York: New York University Press, 1997.

East and Southeast Asia

Adams, F. Gerard and Shinichi Ichimura, eds. *East Asian Development: Will the East Asian Growth Miracle Survive?* Westport, CT: Greenwood Publishing Group, 1998.

Alagappa, Muthiah, ed. *Political Legitimacy in Southeast Asia: the Quest for Moral Authority.* Stanford, CA: Stanford University Press, 1995.

Ball, Desmond, ed. *The Transformation of Security of the Asia-Pacific Region.* London: Frank Cass & Company, 1996.

Bessho, Koro. *Identities and Security in East Asia.* New York: Oxford Universit Press, 1999.

Blomqvist, Hans C. *Economic Interdependence and Development in East Asia.* Westport, CT: Greenwood Publishing Group, 1997.

Borno, Silvio, et al. *Political Credibility and Economic Development.* New York: Saint Martin's Press, 1995.

Chowdhury, Anis. *Asia Pacific Economies: an Analytical Survey.* New York: Routledge, 1997.

Christie, Clive J. *A Modern History of Southeast Asia: Decolonization, Nationalism, and Separatism.* New York: Tauris Academic Studies, 1996.

Deng, Yong. *Promoting Asia-Pacific Economic Cooperation: Perspectives from East Asia.* New York: Saint Martin's Press, 1997.

Garnaut, Ross, ed. *East Asia in Crisis: from Being a Miracle to Needing One?* New York: Routledge, 1998.

Harland, Bryce. *Collision Course: America and East Asia in the Past and in the Future.* New York: Saint Martin's Press, 1996.

Heidhues, Mary Somers. *Southeast Asia: a Concise History.* New York: Thames & Hudson, 2000.

Huxley, Tim and Susan Willett. *Arming East Asia.* New York: Oxford University Press, 1999.

Ikeo, Aiko, ed. *Economic Development in Twentieth Century East Asia: the International Context.* New York: Routledge, 1997.

Keay, John. *Empire's End: a History of the Far East from High Colonialism to Hong Kong.* New York: Scribner, 1997.

Kelly, David and Anthony Reid, eds. *Asian Freedoms: the Idea of Freedom in East and Southeast Asia.* New York: Cambridge University Press, 1998.

Leifer, Michael, ed. *Dictionary of the Modern Politics of South-East Asia.* New York: Routledge, 1995.

Leipziger, Danny M., ed. *Lessons from East Asia.* Ann Arbor, MI: University of Michigan Press, 1997.

Levine, Alan J. *The United States and the Struggle for Southeast Asia, 1945–1975.* New York: Praeger, 1995.

MacIntyre, Andrew, ed. *Business and Government in Industrialising Asia.* Ithaca, NY: Cornell University Press, 1994.

McCloud, Donald G. *Southeast Asia: Tradition and Modernity in the Contemporary World.* Boulder, CO: Westview Press, 1995.

Morley, James W. *Driven by Growth: Political Change in the Asia-Pacific Region.* Armonk, NY: M.E. Sharpe, rev. ed. 1998.

Mulder, Niels. *Inside Southeast Asia: Religion, Everyday Life, Cultural Change.* Boston, MA: Charles E. Tuttle Company, 1997.

Murphey, Rhoads. *East Asia: a New History.* Reading, MA: Addison-Wesley Educational Publishers, 1997.

Neher, Clark D. *Southeast Asia in the New International Era.* Boulder, CO: Westview Press, 2nd ed. 1994.

Reid, Anthony. *Southeast Asia in the Age of Commerce, 1450–1680, Volume 1: the Lands below the Winds.* New Haven, CT: Yale University Press, 1990.

Reid, Anthony. *Southeast Asia in the Age of Commerce, 1450–1680, Volume 2: Expansion and Crisis.* New Haven, CT: Yale University Press, 1993.

Rodan, Garry, ed. *The Political Economy of Southeast Asia: an Introduction.* New York: Oxford University Press, 1998.

Rowen, Henry S. *Behind East Asian Growth: the Political and Social Foundations of Prosperity.* New York: Routledge, 1998.

Shaffer, Lynda N. *Maritime Southeast Asia to 1500*. Armonk, NY: M.E. Sharpe, 1996.

Sponsel, Leslie E., ed. *Endangered Peoples of Southeast and East Asia*. Westport, CT: Greenwood Publishing Group, 1999.

Tartling, Nicholas, ed. *The Cambridge History of Southeast Asia, Volume 1: from Early Times to c. 1800*. New York: Cambridge University Press, 1992.

Tartling, Nicholas, ed. *The Cambridge History of Southeast Asia, Volume 2: the Nineteenth and Twentieth Centuries*. New York: Cambridge University Press, 1992.

Tongzon, José L. *The Economies of Southeast Asia: the Growth and Development of ASEAN Economies*. Northampton, MA: Edward Elgar Publishing, 1998.

Trocki, Carl. *Gangsters, Democracy, and the State in Southeast Asia*. Ithaca, NY: Cornell University Press, 1998.

Viviano, Frank. *Dispatches from the Pacific Century*. Reading, MA: Addison-Wesley, 1993.

Wolters, Oliver W. *History, Culture, and Region in Southeast Asian Perspectives*. Ithaca, NY: Cornell University, Southeast Asia Program Publications, 1999.

Woo-Cumings, Meredith. *Development States in East Asia*. Ithaca, NY: Cornell University Press, 1999.

World Bank Staff. *East Asia: the Road to Economic Recovery*. Washington, DC: The World Bank, 1999.

Yamamoto, Tadashi, ed. *Emerging Civil Society in the Asia Pacific Community: Nongovernmental Underpinnings of the Emerging Asia Regional Community*. Seattle, WA: University of Washington Press, 1995.

Zhao, Suisheng. *The Dynamics of Power Competition in East Asia: from the Old Chinese World Order to the Post-Cold War Regional Multipolarity*. New York: Saint Martin's Press, 1997.

Australia

Adelman, Howard, et al., eds. *Immigration and Refugee Policy: Australia and Canada Compared*. Toronto: University of Toronto Press, 1994.

Andrews, E.M. *The Anzac Illusion: Anglo-Australian Relations during World War I*. New York: Cambridge University Press, 1993.

Argy, Fred. *Australia at the Crossroads: Radical Free Market or a Progressive Liberalism?* Concord, MA: Paul & Company Publishers Consortium, 1998.

The Australian Reference Dictionary. New York: Oxford University Press, 1992.

Baker, Richard W., ed. *The ANZUS States and Their Region: Regional Policies of Australia, New Zealand, and the United States*. New York: Praeger, 1994.

Bassett, Jan. *The Oxford Illustrated Dictionary of Australian History*. New York: Oxford University Press, 1996.

Beilharz, Peter. *Transforming Labor: Labour Tradition and the Labor Decade in Australia*. New York: Cambridge University Press, 1994.

Bennett, Tony, et al. *Accounting for Tastes: Australian Everyday Cultures*. New York: Cambridge University Press, 1999.

Brawley, Sean. *The White Peril: Foreign Relations and Asian Immigration to Australasia and North America, 1919–1978*. Sydney: University of New South Wales Press, 1995.

Brett, Judith, et al., eds. *Developments in Australian Politics*. South Melbourne: Macmillan Education Australia, 1994.

Broeze, Frank. *Mr. Brooks and the Australian Trade: Imperial Business in the Nineteenth Century*. Melbourne: Carlton University Press, 1993.

Butlin, N.G. *Forming a Colonial Economy, Australia 1810–1850*. New York: Cambridge University Press, 1994.

Castles, Stephen, et al. *Immigration and Australia*. Concord, MA: Paul & Company Publishers Consortium, 1998.

Davidson, Alastair. *From Subject to Citizen: Australian Citizenship in the Twentieth Century*. New York: Cambridge University Press, 1997.

Davidson, Alastair. *The Invisible State: the Formation of the Australian State, 1788–1901*. New York: Cambridge University Press, 1991.

Davidson, Graeme, et al., eds. *The Oxford Companion to Australian History*. New York: Oxford University Press, 1998.

Dean, Mitchell, ed. *Governing Australia: Studies in Contemporary Rationalities of Government*. New York: Cambridge University Press, 1998.

Docherty, James C. *Historical Dictionary of Australia*. Lanham, MD: Scarecrow Press, 2nd ed. 1999.

Emy, Hugh V., ed. *Australia and New Zealand*. Brookfield, VT: Ashgate Publishing Company, 1999.

Emy, Hugh V. *Remaking Australia: the State, the Market and Australia's Future*. St. Leonards, NSW: Allen & Unwin, 1993.

Hassam, Andrew. *Sailing to Australia: Shipboard Diaries by Nineteenth-Century British Emigrants*. New York: Manchester University Press, 1994.

Heathcote, R.L. *Australia*. London: Longman Scientific & Technical, 2nd ed. 1994.

Inglis, K.S. *Australian Colonists: an Exploration of Social History 1788–1870*. Carlton, Victoria: Melbourne University Press, 1993.

Jamrozik, Adam, et al. *Social Change and Cultural Transformation in Australia*. New York: Cambridge University Press, 1995.

Kenny, John. *Before the First Fleet: Europeans in Australia, 1606–1777*. Kenthurst, NSW: Kangaroo Press, 1995.

Lines, William J. *False Economy: Australia in the 20th Century*. Portland, OR: International Specialized Book Services, 1998.

Macintyre, Stuart. *A Concise History of Australia*. New York: Cambridge University Press, 2000.

McIntyre, W. David. *Background into the ANZUS Pact: Strategy and Diplomacy, 1945–55*. New York: Saint Martin's Press, 1995.

McMinn, W.G. *Nationalism and Federalism in Australia*. New York: Oxford University Press, 1994.

Mediansky, Fedor A., ed. *Australian Foreign Policy: into the Next Millennium*. Concord, MA: Paul & Company Publishers Consortium, 1998.

Meredith, David and Barrie Dyster. *Australia in the Global Economy: Continuity and Change*. New York: Cambridge University Press, 2000.

Murphy, Brian. *The Other Australia: Experiences of Migration*. New York: Cambridge University Press, 1993.

Painter, Martin. *Collaborative Federalism: Economic Reform in Australia in the 1990s*. New York: Cambridge University Press, 1998.

Paul, Erik. *Australia in Southeast Asia: Regionalism and Democracy*. Concord, MA: Paul & Company Consortium Publishers, 1998.

Reynolds, Henry. *Aboriginal Sovereignty: Reflections on Race, State and Nation*. New York: Paul & Company Publishers Consortium, 1997.

Scates, Bruce. *A New Australia: Citizenship, Radicalism and the First Republic*. New York: Cambridge University Press, 1997.

Simon, Julian L. *The Economic Consequences of Immigration*. Ann Arbor, MI: University of Michigan Press, rev. ed. 1999.

Singh, Anoop. *Australia: Benefiting from Economic Reform*. Washington, DC: International Monetary Fund, 1998.

Smith, Gary. *Australia in the World: an Introduction to Australian Foreign Policy*. New York: Oxford University Press, 1998.

Smyth, Paul and Bettina Cass, eds. *Contesting the Australian Way: States, Markets and Civil Society*. New York: Cambridge University Press, 1999.

Trainor, Luke. *British Imperialism and Australian Nationalism: Manipulation, Conflict and Compromise in the Late Nineteenth Century*. New York: Cambridge University Press, 1994.

Uhr, John. *Deliberative Democracy in Australia: the Changing Place of Parliament*. New York: Cambridge University Press, 1998.

Wiseman, John. *Global Nation? Australia and the Politics of Globalisation*. New York: Cambridge University Press, 1998.

Brunei *Darussalam*

Ranjit Singh, D.S. *Historical Dictionary of Brunei Darussalam*. Lanham, MD: Scarecrow Press, 1997.

Burma *(Myanmar)*

Becka, Jan. *Historical Dictionary of Myanmar*. Lanham, MD: Scarecrow Press, 1995.

Carey, Peter, ed. *Burma: the Challenge of Change in a Divided Society*. New York: Saint Martin's Press, 1997.

Herbert, Patricia M. *Burma*. Santa Barbara, CA: ABC-CLIO, 1991.

Lintner, Bertil. *Burma in Revolt: Opium and Insurgency since 1948*. Boulder, CO: Westview Press, 1994.

Rotberg, Robert I., ed. *Burma: Prospects for a Democratic Future*. Washington, DC: Brookings Institution Press, 1998.

Suu Kyi, Aung S., edited by Michael Aris, foreward by Vaclav Havel. *Freedom from Fear and Other Writings*. New York: Penguin, 1991.

Suu Kyi, Aung S. *Letters from Burma*. New York: Viking Penguin, 1998.

Cambodia

Chandler, David P. *A History of Cambodia*. Boulder, CO: Westview Press, 2nd ed. 1992.

Chandler, David P. *Facing the Cambodian Past: Selected Essays, 1971–1994*. Seattle, WA: University of Washington Press, 1998.

Curtis, Grant. *Cambodia Reborn? The Transition to Democracy and Development*. Washington, DC: Brookings Institution Press, 1998.

Dith, Pran and Kim DePaul, eds. *Children of Cambodia's Killing Fields: Memoirs of Survivors*. New Haven, CT: Yale University Press, 1997.

Ebihara, May M., et al., eds. *Cambodian Culture since 1975: Homeland and Exile*. Ithaca, NY: Cornell University Press, 1994.

Kamm, Henry. *Cambodia: Report from a Stricken Land*. New York: Arcade Publishing, 1998.

Kiernan, Ben, ed. *Genocide and Democracy in Cambodia: the Khmer Rouge, the United Nations and the International Community*. New Haven, CT: Yale University Southeast Asia Studies, 1993.

Kiernan, Ben. *The Pol Pot Regime: Race, Power, and Genocide in Cambodia under the Khmer Rouge, 1975–79*. New Haven, CT: Yale University Press, 1996.

Lizée, Pierre. *Peace, Power and Resistance in Cambodia: Global Governance and the Failure of International Conflict Resolution*. New York: Saint Martin's Press, 2000.

Mabbett, Ian and David Chandler. *The Khmers*. Malden, MA: Blackwell Publishers, 1995.

Marin, Marie Alexandrine. *Cambodia: a Shattered Society*. Berkeley, CA: University of California Press, 1994.

Morris, Stephen J. *Why Vietnam Invaded Cambodia: Political Culture and the Causes of War*. Stanford, CA: Stanford University Press, 1998.

Ross, Russell R., ed. *Cambodia, a Country Study*. Washington, DC: U.S. GPO, 3rd ed. 1990.

Welaratna, Usha. *Beyond the Killing Fields: Voices of the Cambodian Survivors in America*. Stanford, CA: Stanford University Press, 1993.

China

Barme, Geremie R. *In the Red: Contemporary Chinese Culture*. New York: Columbia University Press, 1999.

Blunden, Caroline and Mark Elvin. *Cultural Atlas of China*. New York: Facts on File, rev. ed., 1998.

Brook, Timothy. *Quelling the People: the Military Suppression of the Beijing Democracy Movement*. New York: Oxford University Press, 1992.

Burstein, Daniel and Arne J. De Keijzer. *Big Dragon: China's Future: What It Means for Business, the Economy, and the Global Order*. New York: Simon & Schuster, 1998.

Chang, Tony H., comp. *China during the Cultural Revolution, 1966–1976: a Selected Bibliography of English Language Works*. Westport, CT: Greenwood Publishing Group, 1999.

Cheng, Chu-Yuan. *Behind the Tiananmen Massacre*. Boulder, CO: Westview Press, 1990.

Clough, Ralph N. *Cooperation or Conflict in the Taiwan Strait?* Lanham, MD: Rowman & Littlefield Publishers, 1999.

Dreyer, June T. *China's Political System*. Reading, MA: Addison-Wesley Educational Publishers, 2000.

Dryer, Edward L. *China at War, 1901–1949*. White Plains, NY: Longman Publishing, 1995.

Faust, John R. and Judith F. Kornberg. *China in World Politics*. Boulder, CO: Lynne Rienner, 1995.

Fewsmith, Joseph. *Dilemmas of Reform in China: Political Conflict and Economic Debate*. Armonk, NY: M.E. Sharpe, 1994.

Finkelstein, David Michael. *Washington's Taiwan Dilemma, 1949–1950: from Abandonment to Salvation*. Fairfax, VA: George Mason University Press, 1993.

Fitzgerald, John. *Awakening China: Politics, Culture, and Class in the Nationalist Revolution*. Stanford, CA: Stanford University Press, 1996.

Foot, Rosemary. *The Practice of Power: US Relations with China since 1949*. New York: Oxford University Press, 1995.

Giquel, Prosper. Edited and translated by Steven A. Leibo. *A Journal of the Chinese Civil War, 1864*. Honolulu, HI: University of Hawaii Press, 1985.

Goldstein, Alice and Wang Feng, eds. *China: the Many Facets of Demographic Change*. Boulder, CO: Westview Press, 1996.

Grunfeld, Gregory E., ed. *The Making of Modern Tibet*. Armonk, NY: M.E. Sharpe, rev. ed 1996.

Guldin, Gregory E., ed. *Farewell to Peasant China: Rural Urbanization and Social Change in the Late Twentieth Century*. Armonk, NY: M.E. Sharpe, 1997.

Gurtov, Mel and Byong-Moo Hwang. *China's Security: the New Role of the Military*. Boulder, CO: Lynne Rienner Publishers, 1998.

Henderson, Callum. *China on the Brink: the Myths and Realities of the World's Largest Market*. New York: McGraw-Hill, 1999.

Hook, Brian and Dennis Twitchett. *The Cambridge Encyclopedia of China*. New York: Cambridge University Press, 2nd ed. 1991.

Huang, Ray. *Broadening the Horizons of Chinese History: Discourses, Syntheses, and Comparisons*. Armonk, NY: M.E. Sharpe, 1999.

Huot, Claire. *China's New Cultural Scene: a Handbook of Changes*. Durham, NC: Duke University Press, 1999.

Jiaqi, Yan and Gao Gao. Translated by D.W.K. Kwok. *Turbulent Decade: a History of the Cultural Revolution*. Honolulu, HI: University of Hawaii Press, 1996.

Joseph, William A., ed. *China Briefing: the Contradictions of Change*. Armonk, NY: M.E. Sharpe, 1997.

Ju, Yanan. *Understanding China: Center Stage of the Fourth Power*. Albany, NY: State University of New York Press, 1996.

Kennedy, Thomas L. *The Arms of Kiangnan: Modernization in the Chinese Ordnance Industry, 1860–1895*. Boulder, CO: Westview Press, 1978.

Ke-wen, Wang, ed. *Modern China: an Encyclopedia of History, Culture, and Nationalism*. New York: Garland Publishing, 1999.

Kluver, Alan R. *Legitimating the Chinese Economic Reforms: a Rhetoric of Myth and Orthodoxy*. Albany, NY: State University of New York Press, 1996.

Lampton, David M., et al., eds. *United States and China Relations at a Crossroads*. Lanham, MD: University Press of America, 1995.

Leibo, Steven A. *Transferring Technology to China: Prosper Giquel and the Self-Strengthening Movement*. Berkeley, CA: University of California Press, Institute of East Asian Studies, 1985.

Leung, Edwin Pak-Wah, ed. *Historical Dictionary of Revolutionary China, 1839–1976*. Westport, CT: Greenwood Press, 1992.

Levine, Marilyn Avra. *The Found Generation: Chinese Communists in Europe during the Twenties*. Seattle, WA: University of Washington Press, 1993.

Lieberthal, Kenneth. *Governing China*. New York: W.W. Norton, 1995.

Lin, Bih-Jaw and James T. Myers. *Contemporary China and the Changing Inter-*

national Community. Columbia, SC: University of South Carolina Press, 1994.

Lo, Dic. *Market and Institutional Regulation in Chinese Industrialization, 1978–94.* Saint Martin's Press, 1997.

MacFarquhar, Roderick, ed. *The Politics of China: the Eras of Mao and Deng.* New York: Cambridge University Press, 1997.

MacKerras, Colin and Donald H. McMillen, eds. *Dictionary of the Politics of the People's Republic of China.* New York: Routledge, 1998.

Malik, Hafeez, ed. *Roles of the United States, Russia and China in the New World.* New York: Saint Martin's Press, 1997.

Mathias, Jim, ed. *Computers, Language Reform, and Lexicography in China: a Report.* Pullman, WA: Washington State University Press, 1980.

Meisner, Maurice. *The Deng Xiaoping Era: an Inquiry into the Fate of Chinese Socialism, 1978–1994.* New York: Hill & Wang, 1996.

Miles, James A. *The Legacy of Tiananmen: China in Disarray.* Ann Arbor, MI: University of Michigan, 1995.

Mok, Ka-Ho. *Intellectuals and the State in Post-Mao China.* New York: Saint Martin's Press, 1998.

Murowchick, Robert E., ed. *China: Ancient Culture, Modern Land.* Norman, OK: University of Oklahoma Press, 1994.

Nathan, Andrew J. *The Great Wall and the Empty Fortress: China's Search for Security.* New York: W.W. Norton & Company, 1997.

Nie Zeng Jifen. Translated and annotated by Thomas L. Kennedy; edited by Thomas L. Kennedy and Micki Kennedy. *Testimony of a Confucian Woman: the Autobiography of Mrs. Nie Zeng Jifen, 1852–1942.* Athens, GA: University of Georgia Press, 1993.

Ogden, Suzanne. *China's Unresolved Issues: Politics, Development, and Culture.* Englewood Cliffs, NJ: Prentice-Hall, 3rd ed. 1995.

Overholt, William H. *The Rise of China: How Economic Reform is Creating a New Superpower.* New York: W.W. Norton, 1993.

Pearson, Margaret M. *China's New Business Elite: the Political Consequences of Economic Reform.* Berkeley, CA: University of California Press, 1997.

Perkins, Dorothy. *The Encyclopedia of China: the Essential Reference to China, Its History and Culture.* New York: Facts on File, 1998.

Schell, Orville. *Mandate of Heaven: a New Generation of Entrepreneurs, Dissidents, Bohemians, and Technocrats Lays Claim to China's Future.* New York: Simon & Schuster, 1994.

Segal, Gerald and Richard H. Yang, eds. *Chinese Economic Reform: the Impact on Security.* New York: Routledge, 1996.

Shambaugh, David. *Beautiful Imperialist: China Perceives America, 1972–1990.* Princeton, NJ: Princeton University Press, 1991.

Shambaugh, David, ed. *China's Military in Transition.* New York: Oxford University Press, 1998.

Shanor, Donald and Constance Shanor. *China Today.* New York: Saint Martin's Press, 1995.

Shih, Chih-yu. *China's Just World: the Morality of Chinese Foreign Policy.* Boulder, CO: Lynne Rienner Publishers, 1993.

Sullivan, Lawrence R., ed. *China since Tiananmen: Political, Economic, and Social Conflicts.* Armonk, NY: M.E. Sharpe, 1995.

Sun, Yan. *The Chinese Reassessment of Socialism, 1976–1992.* Princeton, NJ: Princeton University Press, 1995.

Sutter, Robert G. *Shaping China's Future in World Affairs: the Role of the United States.* Boulder, CO: Westview Press, 1996.

Tanner, Murray Scott. *The Politics of Lawmaking in Post-Mao China: Institutions, Processes, and Democratic Prospects.* New York: Oxford University Press, 1999.

Teiwes, Frederick C. and Warren Sun. *China's Road to Disaster: Mao, Central Politicians and Provincial Leaders in the Unfolding of the Great Leap Forward, 1955–1959.* Armonk, NY: M.E. Sharpe, 1998.

Vogel, Ezra F., ed. *Living with China: U.S.—China Relations in the Twenty-First Century.* New York: W.W. Norton & Company, 1997.

Wang, Gabe T. *China's Population: Problems, Thoughts, and Policies.* Brookfield, VT: Ashgate, 1999.

Wang, Hui. *The Gradual Revolution: China's Economic Reform Movement.* New Brunswick, NJ: Transaction Publishers, 1994.

Wang, Shaoguang and Angang Hu. *The Political Economy of Uneven Development: the Case of China.* Armonk, NY: M.E. Sharpe, 1999.

Wasserstrom, Jeffrey N. and Elizabeth J. Perry, eds. *Popular Protest and Political Culture in Modern China.* Boulder, CO: Westview Press, 1994.

Waters, Harry J. *China's Economic Development Strategies for the 21st Century.* Westport, CT: Greenwood Publishing Group, 1997.

Wei-ming, Tu, ed. *China in Transformation.* Cambridge, MA: Harvard University Press, 1994.

White, Gordon. *Riding the Tiger: the Politics of Economic Reform in Post-Mao China.* Stanford, CA: Stanford University Press, 1993.

Winckler, Edwin A., ed. *Transition from Communism in China: Institutional and Comparative Analysis.* Boulder, CO: Lynne Rienner Publishers, 1999.

Worden, Robert L., et al., eds. *China: a Country Study.* Washington, DC: U.S. GPO, 4th ed. 1988.

Wortzel, Larry M. *Dictionary of Contemporary Chinese Military History.* Westport, CT: Greenwood Publishing Group, 1999.

Wu, Yanrui. *China's Consumer Revolution: the Emerging Patterns of Wealth and Expenditure.* Edward Elgar Publishing, 1999.

Young, Susan. *Private Business and Economic Reform in China.* Armonk, NY: M.E. Sharpe, 1995.

Zhai, Qiang. *The Dragon, the Lion, and the Eagle: Chinese-British-American Relations, 1949–1958.* Kent, OH: Kent State University Press, 1994.

Hong Kong

Butenhoff, Linda. *Social Movements and Political Reform in Hong Kong.* Westport, CT: Greenwood Publishing Group, 1999.

Callick, Rowan. *Comrades and Capitalists: Hong Kong since the Takeover.* Portland, OR: International Specialized Book Services, 1998.

Chan, Ming K., ed. *Precarious Balance: Hong Kong between China and Britain.* Armonk, NY: M.E. Sharpe, 1994.

Cohen, Warren I., ed. *Hong Kong under Chinese Rule: the Economic and Political Implications of Reversion.* New York: Cambridge University Press, 1997.

Keay, John. *Empire's End: a History of the Far East from High Colonialism to Hong Kong.* New York: Scribner, 1997.

Ku, Agnes S. *Narratives, Politics, and the Public Sphere: Struggles over Political Reform in the Final Transitional Years in Hong Kong (1992–1994).* Brookfield, VT: Ashgate, 1999.

Patten, Christopher. *East and West: the Last Governor of Hong Kong on Power, Freedom and the Future.* New York: Times Books, 1998.

Postiglione, Gerald A. and James T. H. Tang, eds. *Hong Kong's Reunion with China: the Global Dimensions.* Armonk, NY: M.E. Sharpe, 1997.

Roberti, Mark. *The Fall of Hong Kong: Britain's Betrayal and China's Triumph.* New York: John Wiley & Sons, 1994.

Roberts, Elfed Vaughan, et al. *Historical Dictionary of Hong Kong and Macau.* Lanham, MD: Scarecrow Press, 1992.

Segal, Gerald. *The Fate of Hong Kong: the Coming of 1997 and What Lies Beyond.* New York: Saint Martin's Press, 1993.

Shipp, Steve. *Hong Kong, China: a Political History of the British Crown Colony's Transfer to Chinese Rule.* Jefferson, NC: McFarland & Company, 1995.

Thomas, Nicholas. *Democracy Denied: Identity, Civil, Society and Illiberal Democracy in Hong Kong.* Brookfield, VT: Ashgate Publishing Company, 1999.

Tsang, Steve. *Modern History of Hong Kong, 1841–1998.* London: I.B. Tauris & Company, 1998.

Van Kemendade, William. *China, Hong Kong, Taiwan, Incorporated.* New York: Alfred A. Knopf, 1997.

Indonesia

Anwar, Dewi Fortuna. *Indonesia in ASEAN: Foreign Policy and Regionalism.* New York: Saint Martin's Press, 1994.

Baker, Richard W. *Indonesia: the Challenge of Change.* New York: Saint Martin's Press, 1999.

Bresnan, John. *Managing Indonesia: the Modern Political Economy.* New York: Columbia University Press, 1993.

Cribb, Robert. *Historical Atlas of Indonesia.* Honolulu, HI: University of Hawaii Press, 1998.

Cribb, Robert. *Historical Dictionary of Indonesia.* Lanham, MD: Scarecrow Press, 1992.

Cribb, Robert, ed. *The Late Colonial State in Indonesia: Political and Economic Foundations of the Netherlands Indies, 1880–1942.* Leiden: KITLV Press, 1994.

Cribb, Robert and Colin Brown. *Modern Indonesia: a History since 1945.* New York: Longman, 1995.

Emmerson, Donald K., ed. *Indonesia beyond Suharto.* Armonk, NY: M.E. Sharpe, 1998.

Frederick, William H. and Robert L. Worden, eds. *Indonesia: a Country Study.* Washington, DC: U.S. GPO, 5th ed. 1993.

Gardner, Paul F. *Shared Hopes, Separate Fears: Fifty Years of U.S.—Indonesian Relations.* Westport, CT: Westview Press, 1997.

Hill, Hal, ed. *Indonesia's New Order: the Dynamics of Socio-Economic Transformation.* Honolulu, HI: University of Hawaii Press, 1994.

Kipp, Rita Smith. *Dissociated Identities: Ethnicity, Religion, and Class in an Indonesian Society.* Ann Arbor, MI: University of Michigan Press, 1993.

Krausse, Gerald H. and Sylvia C. Engelen Krausse. *Indonesia.* Santa Barbara, CA: ABC-CLIO, 1994.

Ramage, Douglas E. *Politics in Indonesia: Democracy, Islam, and the Ideology of Tolerance.* New York: Routledge, 1995.

Ricklefs, Merle Calvin. A *History of Modern Indonesia: c. 1300 to the Present.* Stanford, CA: Stanford University Press, 1993.

Schiller, Jim and Barbara Martin-Schiller, eds. *Imagining Indonesia: Cultural Politics and Political Culture.* Athens, OH: Ohio University Press, 1997.

Schwartz, Adam. *A Nation in Waiting: Indonesia in the 1990s.* Boulder, CO: Westview Press, 1994.

Uhlin, Anders. *Indonesia and the "Third Wave of Democratization": the Indonesian Pro-Democracy Movement in a Changing World.* New York: Saint Martin's Press, 1997.

Vatikiotis, Michael R.J. *Indonesian Politics under Suharto: the Rise and Fall of the New Order.* New York: Routledge, 1999.

Japan

Abe, Etsuo and Robert Fitzgerald, eds. *The Origins of Japanese Industrial Power: Strategy, Institutions and the Development of Organisational Capability.* London: Frank Cass & Company, 1995.

Abe, Hitoshi, et al. Translated by James W. White. *The Government and Politics of Japan.* Tokyo: University of Tokyo Press, 1994.

Alinson, Gary D. and Yasunori Sone, eds. *Political Dynamics in Contemporary Japan.* Ithaca, NY: Cornell University Press, 1993.

Banno, Junji. *The Establishment of the Japanese Constitutional System.* New York: Routledge, 1995.

Beasley, W.G. *The Japanese Experience: a Short History of Japan.* Berkeley, CA: University of California Press, 1999.

Browring, Richard and Peter Kornicki, eds. *The Cambridge Encyclopedia of Japan.* New York: Cambridge University Press, 1993.

Buckley, Roger. *Japan Today.* New York: Cambridge University Press, 1999.

Carlile, Lonny E. and Mark Tilton, eds. *Is Japan Really Changing Its Ways? Regulatory Reform and the Japanese Economy.* Washington, DC: Brookings Institution Press, 1998.

Cohen, Stephen D. *An Ocean Apart: Explaining Three Decades of U.S.-Japanese Trade Frictions.* Westport, CT: Greenwood Publishing Group, 1998.

Curtis, Gerald L., ed. *Japan's Foreign Policy after the Cold War: Coping with Change.* Armonk, NY: M.E. Sharpe, 1993.

Dolan, Ronald E. and Robert L. Worden. *Japan: a Country Study.* Washington, DC: U.S. GPO, 5th ed. 1992.

Dower, John. *Embracing Defeat: Japan in the Wake of World War II.* New York: W.W. Norton & Company, 1999.

Drysdale, Peter and Luke Gower. *The Japanese Economy.* New York: Routledge, 2000.

Edstrom, Bert. *Japan's Evolving Foreign Policy Doctrine: from Yoshida to Miyazawa.* New York: Saint Martin's Press, 1999.

Eisenstadt, Samuel N. *Japanese Civilization.* Chicago: University of Chicago Press, 1998.

Fukushima, Akiko. *Japanese Foreign Policy: the Emerging Logic of Multilateralism.* New York: Saint Martin's Press, 1999.

Funabashi, Yoichi, ed. *Japan's International Agenda.* New York: New York University Press, 1994.

Garby, Craig and Mary Brown Bullock, eds. *Japan: a New Kind of Superpower?* Baltimore, MD: Johns Hopkins University Press, 1994.

Garon, Sheldon. *Molding Japanese Minds: the State in Everyday Life.* Princeton, NJ: Princeton University Press, 1997.

Giffard, Sydney. *Japan among the Powers, 1880-1990.* New Haven, CT: Yale University Press, 1994.

Gordon, Andrew, ed. *Postwar Japan as History.* Berkeley, CA: University of California Press, 1993.

Green, Michael J. *Arming Japan: Defense Production, Alliance Politics, and the Postwar Search for Autonomy.* New York: Columbia University Press, 1995.

Hall, Ivan P. *Cartels of the Mind: Japan's Intellectual Closed Shop.* New York: W.W. Norton & Company, 1997.

Hall, Maximilian J. *Financial Reform in Japan: Causes and Consequences.* Northampton, MA: Edward Elgar Publishing, 1999.

Hayao, Kenji. *The Japanese Prime Minister and Public Policy.* Pittsburgh, PA: University of Pittsburgh Press, 1993.

Heneshall, Kenneth G. *A History of Japan: from Stone Age to Superpower.* New York: Saint Martin's Press, 1998.

Herbig, Paul A. *Innovation Japanese Style: a Cultural and Historical Perspective.* Westport, CT: Quorum Books, 1995.

Herzog, Peter J. *Japan's Pseudo-Democracy.* New York: New York University Press, 1993.

Holgerson, Karen M. *The Japan-U.S. Trade Friction Dilemma: the Role of Perception.* Brookfield, VT: Ashgate Publishing Company, 1998.

Hsu, Robert C. *The MIT Encyclopedia of the Japanese Economy.* Cambridge, MA: MIT Press, 1994.

Huber, Thomas M. *Strategic Economy in Japan.* Boulder, CO: Westview Press, 1994.

Huffman, James L. *Modern Japan: an Encyclopedia of History, Culture, and Nationalism.* New York: Garland Publishing, 1999.

Inoguchi, Takashi. *Japan's Foreign Policy in an Era of Global Change.* New York: Saint Martin's Press, 1993.

Iriye, Akira. *Japan and the Wider World: from the Mid-Nineteenth Century to Present.* New York: Longman, 1997.

Irokawa, Daikichi. Translated by John K. Urda. *The Age of Hirohito: in Search of Modern Japan.* New York: Free Press, 1995.

Itoh, Mayumi. *Globalization of Japan: U.S. Efforts to Open Japan from Commodore Matthew Perry to Defense Secretary William Perry.* New York: Saint Martin's Press, 1998.

Japan: an Illustrated Encyclopedia. 2 vols. New York: Kodansha America, 1994.

Johnson, Chalmers. *Japan: Who Governs?* New York: W.W. Norton, 1995.

Johnson-Freese, Joan. *Over the Pacific: Japanese Space Policy into the Twenty-First Century.* Dubuque, IA: Kendall/Hunt Publishing, 1993.

Koppel, Bruce M., ed. *Japan's Foreign Aid: Power and Policy in a New Era.* Boulder, CO: Westview Press, 1993.

Lincoln, Edward J. *Japan's New Global Role.* Washington, DC: Brookings Institution Press, 1993.

Luney, Percy R., Jr. and Kazuyuki Takahashi, eds. *Japanese Constitutional Law.* Tokyo: University of Tokyo Press, 1993.

Maher, John C. and Gaynor Macdonald, eds. *Diversity in Japanese Culture and*

Language. New York: Kegan Paul International, 1995.

McNeil, Frank. *Democracy in Japan: the Emerging Global Concern*. New York: Crown Publishing, 1994.

Murphy, R. Taggart. *The Weight of the Yen*. New York: W.W. Norton, 1996.

Nagatani, Keizo and David W. Edgington, eds. *Japan and the West: the Perception Gap*. Brookfield, VT: Ashgate Publishing Company, 1998.

Nester, William R. *American Power, the New World Order and the Japanese Challenge*. New York: Saint Martin's Press, 1993.

Ozawa, Ichiro. *Blueprint for a New Japan: the Rethinking of a Nation*. New York: Kodansha America, 1994.

Ramseyer, J. Mark and Frances McCall Rosenbluth. *Japan's Political Marketplace*. Cambridge, MA: Harvard University Press, 1993.

Reischauer, Edwin O. and Marius Jansen. *The Japanese Today*. Cambridge, MA: Harvard University Press, rev. ed. 1995.

Richardson, Bradley M. *Japanese Democracy: Power, Coordination, and Performance*. New Haven, CT: Yale University Press, 1997.

Sato, Kazuo, ed. *The Transformation of the Japanese Economy*. Armonk, NY: M.E. Sharpe, 1999.

Sato, Ryuzo. *The Chrysanthemum and the Eagle: the Future of U.S.-Japan Relations*. New York: New York University Press, 1994.

Schaller, Michael. *Altered States: the United States and Japan since Occupation*. New York: Oxford University Press, 1997.

Schoppa, Leonard J. *Bargaining with Japan: What American Pressure Can and Cannot Do*. New York: Columbia University Press, 1997.

Smith, Dennis B. *Japan since 1945: the Rise of an Economic Superpower*. New York: Saint Martin's Press, 1995.

Smith, Patrick. *Japan: a Reinterpretation*. New York: Pantheon, 1997.

Stockwin, J.A. *Governing Japan: Divided Politics in a Major Economy*. Malden, MA: Blackwell Publishers, 1998.

Sugimoto, Yoshio. *An Introduction to Japanese Society*. New York: Cambridge University Press, 1997.

Tachi, Ryuichiro. *The Contemporary Japanese Economy: an Overview*. Tokyo: University of Tokyo Press, 1993.

Unger, Daniel and Paul Blackburn, eds. *Japan's Emerging Global Role*. Boulder, CO: Lynne Rienner, 1993.

Uriu, Robert M. *Troubled Industries: Confronting Economic Change in Japan*. Ithaca, NY: Cornell University Press, 1996.

Vestal, James E. *Planning for Change: Industrial Policy and Japanese Economic Development, 1945–1990*. New York: Oxford University Press, 1993.

Weiner, Michael, ed. *Japan's Minorities: Illusion of Homogeneity*. New York: Routledge, 1997.

Woronoff, Jon. *The Japanese Economic Crisis*. New York: Saint Martin's Press, 1993.

Woronoff, Jon. *The Japanese Social Crisis*. New York: Saint Martin's Press, 1997.

Yasutomo, Dennis T. *The New Multilateralism in Japan's Foreign Policy*. New York: Saint Martin's Press, 1995.

Zhang, Wei-Bin and Ake E. Andersson. *Japan Versus China in the Industrial Race*. New York: Saint Martin's Press, 1998.

Korea

Alford, C. Fred. *Think No Evil: Korean Values in the Age of Globalization*. Ithaca, NY: Cornell University Press, 1999.

Bedeski, Robert E. *The Transformation of South Korea: Reform and Reconstitution in the Sixth Republic under Roh Tae Woo, 1987–1992*. New York: Routledge, 1994.

Cho, Sun. *The Dynamics of Korean Economic Development*. Washington, DC: Institute for International Economics, 1994.

Cumings, Bruce. *Korea's Place in the Sun: a Modern History*. New York: W.W. Norton, 1997.

Eberstadt, Nicholas. *Korea Approaches Reunification*. Armonk, NY: M.E. Sharpe, 1995.

Hamm, Taik-Young. *Arming the Two Koreas: State, Capital, and Military Power*. New York: Routledge, 1999.

Helgensen, Geir. *Democracy and Authority in Korea*. New York: Saint Martin's Press, 1998.

Hulbert, Homer B. *History of Korea*. Honolulu, HI: University of Hawaii Press, 1998.

Hunter, Helen-Louise. *Kim Il-Sung's North Korea*. Westport, CT: Greenwood Publishing Group, 1999.

Hwang, Eui-Gak. *The Korean Economies: a Comparison of North and South*. New York: Oxford University Press, 1993.

Jung, Walter and Xiao-Bing Li, eds. *Korea and Regional Geopolitics*. Lanham, MD: University Press of America, 1998.

Kihl, Young Whan. *Korea and the World: beyond the Cold War*. Boulder, CO: Westview Press, 1994.

Kim, Dae Jung. *Mass Participatory Economy: Korea's Road to World Economic Power*. Lanham, MD: University Press of America, 1996.

Kim, Eun M. *Big Business, Strong State: Collusion and Conflict in South Korean Development, 1960–1990*. Albany, NY: State University of New York Press, 1997.

Kim, Gye-Dong. *Foreign Intervention in Korea*. Brookfield, VT: Dartmouth Publishing Company, 1993.

Kim, Hakjoon. *Korea's Relations with Her Neighbors in a Changing World*. Elizabeth, NJ: Hollym International, 1993.

Koo, Hagen, ed. *State and Society in Contemporary Korea*. Ithaca, NY: Cornell University Press, 1993.

Kuznets, Paul W. *Korean Economic Development: an Interpretive Model*. New York: Praeger, 1994.

Kwack, Sung Yeung, ed. *The Korean Economy at a Crossroad: the Development Prospects, Liberalization, and South-North Economic Integration*. New York: Praeger, 1994.

Lancaster, Lewis R., et al. *Religion and Society in Contemporary Korea*. Berkeley, CA: Institute of East Asian Studies, 1998.

Lee, Chae-Jin. *China and Korea: Dynamic Relations*. Stanford, CA: Hoover Institution Press, 1996.

Lee, Hyung-Koo. *The Korean Economy: Perspectives for the Twenty-First Century*. Albany, NY: State University of New York Press, 1996.

Lee, Kenneth B. *Korea and East Asia: the Story of a Phoenix*. Westport, CT: Greenwood Publishing Group, 1997.

Lee, Peter H., ed. *Sourcebook of Korean Civilization, vol. 1: from Early Times to the Sixteenth Century*. New York: Columbia University Press, 1993.

Lee, Peter H., ed. *Sourcebook of Korean Civilization, vol. 2: from the Seventeenth Century to the Modern Period*. New York: Columbia University Press, 1996.

Lee, Yur-Bok and Wayne Patterson, eds. *Korean-American Relations, 1866–1997*. Albany, NY: State University of New York Press, 1998.

Lie, John. *The Political Economy of South Korea*. Stanford, CA: Stanford University Press, 1998.

Macdonald, Donald Stone. *The Koreans: Contemporary Politics and Society*. Boulder, CO: Westview Press, 3rd ed. 1996.

Mazarr, Michael J. *North Korea and the Bomb: a Case Study in Nonproliferation*. New York: Saint Martin's Press, 1995.

McNamara, Dennis L. *Trade and Transformation in Korea, 1876–1945*. Boulder, CO: Westview Press, 1996.

Nahm, Andrew C. *Historical Dictionary of the Republic of Korea*. Lanham, MD: Scarecrow Press, 1993.

Oberdorfer, Don. *The Two Koreas: a Contemporary History*. Reading, MA: Addison Wesley Longman, 1997.

Oh, John K. *Korean Politics: the Quest for Democratization and Economic Development*. Ithaca, NY: Cornell University Press, 1999.

Oliver, Robert T. *A History of the Korean People in Modern Times: 1800 to the Present*. Cranbury, NJ: University of Delaware Press, 1993.

SaKong, Il. *Korea in the World Economy*. Washington, DC: Institute for International Economics, 1993.

Savada, Andrea Matles, ed. *North Korea: a Country Study*. Washington, DC: U.S. GPO, 4th ed. 1994.

Savada, Andrea Matles and William R. Shaw, eds. *South Korea: a Country Study*. Washington, DC: U.S. GPO, 4th ed. 1992.

Sigal, Leon V. *Disarming Strangers: Nuclear Diplomacy with North Korea*. Princeton, NJ: Princeton University Press, 1998.

Simons, Geoff. *Korea: the Search for Sovereignty.* New York: Saint Martin's Press, 1995.

Suh, Dae-Sook, ed. *North Korea after Kim Il Sung.* Boulder, CO: Lynne Rienner Publishers, 1998.

Swartout, Robert R. *Mandarins, Gunboats, and Power Politics: Owen Nickerson and the International Rivalries in Korea.* Honolulu, HI: Asian Studies Program, University of Hawaii, 1980.

Laos

Castle, Timothy N. *At War in the Shadow of Vietnam: U.S. Military Aid to the Royal Lao Government, 1955–1975.* New York: Columbia University Press, 1993.

Cordell, Helen. *Laos.* Santa Barbara, CA: ABC-CLIO, 1991.

Savada, Andrea Matles. *Laos: a Country Study.* Washington, DC: U.S. GPO, 3rd ed. 1995.

Stuart-Fox, Martin. *A History of Laos.* New York: Cambridge University Press, 1997.

Stuart-Fox, Martin. *Historical Dictionary of Laos.* Lanham, MD: Scarecrow Press, 1992.

Than, Mya and Joseph L.H. Tan, eds. *Laos' Dilemmas and Options: the Challenge of Economic Transition in the 1990s.* New York: Saint Martin's Press, 1997.

Macau

Cheng, Christina M. *Macau: a Cultural Janus.* Hong Kong: Hong Kong University Press, 1999.

Porter, Jonathan. *Macau, the Imaginary City: Culture and Society, 1557 to the Present.* Boulder, CO: Westview Press, 1996.

Roberts, Elfed Vaughn, et al. *Historical Dictionary of Hong Kong and Macau.* Lanham, MD: Scarecrow Press, 1992.

Shipp, Steve. *Macau, China: a Political History of the Portuguese Colony's Transition to Chinese Rule.* Jefferson, NC: McFarland & Company, 1997.

Malaysia

Bruton, Henry J. *Sri Lanka and Malaysia.* New York: Oxford University Press, 1992.

Gomez, Edmund T. *Malaysia's Political Economy: Politics, Patronage and Profits.* New York: Cambridge University Press, 1997.

Jomo, K.S. *Industrialising Malaysia: Policy, Performance, Prospects.* New York: Routledge,1993.

Kaur, Amarjit. *Historical Dictionary of Malaysia.* Lanham, MD: Scarecrow Press, 1993.

Kaur, Amarjit. *The Shaping of Malaysia.* New York: Saint Martin's Press, 1999.

Lucas, Robert E. *Restructuring the Malaysian Economy: Development and Human Resources.* New York: Saint Martin's Press, 1999.

Milne, R.S. *Politics under Mahathir.* New York: Routledge, 1999.

Munro-Kua, Anne. *Authoritarian Populism in Malaysia.* New York: Saint Martin's Press, 1997.

Mongolia

Nordby, Judith. *Mongolia.* Santa Barbara, CA: ABC-CLIO, 1993.

Sanders, Alan J.K. *Historical Dictionary of Mongolia.* Lanham, MD: Scarecrow Press, 1996.

Worden, Robert L. and Andrea Matles Savada, eds. *Mongolia: a Country Study.* Washington, DC: U.S. GPO, 2nd ed. 1991.

New Zealand

Alves, Dora, ed. *The Maori and the Crown: an Indigenous People's Struggle for Self-Determination.* Westport, CT: Greenwood Publishing Group, 1999.

Baker, Richard W., ed. *The ANZUS States and Their Region: Regional Policies of Australia, New Zealand, and the United States.* New York: Praeger, 1994.

Barretta-Herman, Angela. *Welfare State to Welfare Society: Restructuring New Zealand Social Services.* New York: Garland Publishing, 1994.

Boston, Jonathan, et al., eds. *Redesigning the Welfare State in New Zealand: Problems, Policies, Prospects.* New York Oxford University Press, 1999.

Clements, Kevin P. *Breaking Nuclear Ties: New Zealand's Nuclear-Free Course.* Boulder, CO: Westview Press, 2000.

Emy, Hugh V., ed. *Australia and New Zealand.* Brookfield, VT: Ashgate Publishing Company, 1999.

Jackson, William K. and Alan McRobie. *Historical Dictionary of New Zealand.* Lanham, MD: Scarecrow Press, 1996.

McKinnon, Malcolm. *Independence and Foreign Policy: New Zealand in the World since 1935.* Auckland: Auckland University Press, 1993.

McLeay, Elizabeth. *The Cabinet and Political Power in New Zealand.* New York: Oxford University Press, 1995.

Rice, Geoffrey W., ed. *The Oxford History of New Zealand.* New York: Oxford University Press, 2nd ed. 1992.

Rudd, Chris, ed. *The Political Economy of New Zealand.* New York: Oxford University Press, 1997.

Sharp, Andrew, ed. *Leap into the Dark: the Changing Role of the State in New Zealand since 1984.* Auckland: Auckland University Press, 1994.

Sinclair, Keith, ed. *The Oxford Illustrated History of New Zealand.* New York: Oxford University Press, 2nd ed. 1996.

Papua New Guinea

Gewertz, Deborah B. and Frederick K. Errington. *Emerging Class in Papua New Guinea: the Telling of Difference.* New York: Cambridge University Press, 1999.

Rannells, Jackson. *PNG: a Fact Book on Modern Papua New Guinea.* New York: Oxford University Press, 2nd ed. 1995.

Turner, Ann. *Historical Dictionary of Papua New Guinea.* Lanham, MD: Scarecrow Press, 1994.

The Philippines

Broad, Robin. *Plundering Paradise: the Struggle for the Environment in the Philippines.* Berkeley, CA: University of California Press, 1993.

Corpuz, O.D. *An Economic History of the Philippines.* Honolulu, HI: University of Hawaii Press, 1999.

Cullather, Nick. *Illusions of Influence: the Political Economy of United States-Philippines Relations, 1942–1960.* Stanford, CA: Stanford University Press, 1994.

Dolan, Ronald E., ed. *Philippines: a Country Study.* Washington, DC: U.S. GPO, 4th ed. 1993.

Guillermo, Artemio R. *Historical Dictionary of the Philippines.* Lanham, MD: Scarecrowm Press, 1997.

Kwiatkowski, Lynn M. *Struggling with Development: the Politics of Hunger and Gender in the Philippines.* Westport, CT: Westview Press, 1998.

Reid, Robert H. and Eileen Guerrero. *Corazon Aquino and the Brushfire Revolution.* Baton Rouge, LA: Louisiana State University Press, 1995.

Singapore

Clammer, John. *Race and State in Independent Singapore: the Cultural Politics of Pluralism in a Multiethnic Society.* Brookfield, VT: Ashgate Publishing Company, 1998.

Gopinathan, S., et al., eds. *Language, Society and Education in Singapore: Issues and Trends.* Portland, OR: International Specialized Book Services, 1998.

Haas, Michael, ed. *The Singapore Puzzle.* Westport, CT: Greenwood Publishing Group, 1999.

Hill, Michael and Lian Kwen Fee. *The Politics of Nation Building and Citizenship in Singapore.* New York: Routledge, 1995.

Huff, W.G. *The Economic Growth of Singapore: Trade and Development in the Twentieth Century.* New York: Cambridge University Press, 1994.

Kong, Lily. *Singapore: a Developmental City State.* New York: John Wiley & Sons, 1997.

LePoer, Barbara Leitch, ed. *Singapore: a Country Study.* Washington, DC: U.S. GPO, 2nd ed. 1991.

Ling, Qui G. *The City and the State: Singapore's Built Environment Revisited.* New York: Oxford University Press, 1997.

Mulliner, K. and Lian The-Mulliner. *Historical Dictionary of Singapore.* Lanham, MD: Scarecrow Press, 1991.

Rodan, Garry, ed. *Singapore Changes Guard: Social, Political and Economic Directions in the 1990s*. New York: Saint Martin's Press, 1993.

Von Alten, Florian. *The Role of Government in the Singapore Economy*. New York: Peter Lang Publishing, 1995.

Taiwan

Bullard, Monte. *The Soldier and the Citizen: the Role of the Military in Taiwan's Development*. Armonk, NY: M.E. Sharpe, 1997.

Chao, Linda. *The First Chinese Democracy: Political Life in the Republic of China on Taiwan*. Baltimore, MD: Johns Hopkins University Press, 1997.

Clough, Ralph. *Cooperation or Conflict in the Taiwan Strait?* Lanham, MD: Rowman & Littlefield Publishers, 1999.

Copper, John F. *Historical Dictionary of Taiwan*. Lanham, MD: Scarecrow Press, 2nd ed. 2000.

Copper, John F. *Words across the Taiwan Strait: a Critique of Beijing's "White Paper" on China's Reunification*. Lanham, MD: University Press of America, 1995.

Finkelstein, David Michael. *Washington's Dilemma, 1949–1950: from Abandonment to Salvation*. Fairfax, VA: George Mason University Press, 1993.

Garver, John W. *The Sino-American Alliance: Nationalist China and American Cold War Strategy in Asia*. Armonk, NY: M.E. Sharpe, 1997.

Hickey, Dennis Van Vranken. *United States-Taiwan Security Ties: from Cold War to Beyond Containment*. New York: Praeger, 1994.

Hood, Steven J. *The Kuomintang and the Democratization of Taiwan*. Boulder, CO: Westview Press, 1997.

Hughes, Christopher. *Taiwan and Chinese Nationalism: National Identity and Status in International Society*. New York: Routledge, 1997.

Lasater, Martin L. *U.S. Interests in the New Taiwan*. Boulder, CO: Westview Press, 1993.

Maguire, Keith. *The Rise of Modern Taiwan*. Brookfield, VT: Ashgate Publishing Company, 1998.

McBeath, Gerald A. *Wealth and Freedom: Taiwan's New Political Economy*. Brookfield, VT: Ashgate Publishing Company, 1998.

Rubinstein, Murray A., ed. *Taiwan: a New History*. Armonk, NY: M.E. Sharpe, 1998.

Schive, Chi. *Taiwan's Economic Role in East Asia*. Washington, DC: Center for Strategic and International Studies, 1995.

Shambaugh, David, ed. *Contemporary Taiwan*. New York: Oxford University Press, 1998.

Skoggard, Ian A. *The Indigenous Dynamic in Taiwan's Postwar Development: the Religious and Historical Roots of Entrepreneurship*. Armonk, NY: M.E. Sharpe, 1996.

Sutter, Robert G. and William R. Johnson, eds. *Taiwan in World Affairs*. Boulder, CO: Westview Press, 1994.

Tsang, Steve and Hung-mao Tien. *Democratization in Taiwan: Implications for China*. New York: Saint Martin's Press, 1999.

Tsang, Steve, ed. *In the Shadow of China: Political Developments in Taiwan since 1949*. Honolulu, HI: University of Hawaii Press, 1993.

Wachman, Alan M. *Taiwan: National Identity and Democratization*. Armonk, NY: M.E. Sharpe, 1994.

Wu, Hsin-Hsing. *Bridging the Strait: Taiwan, China, and the Prospects for Reunification*. New York: Oxford University Press, 1994.

Wu, Jaushieh Joseph. *Taiwan's Democratization: Forces behind the New Momentum*. New York: Oxford University Press, 1995.

Zhao, Suisheng. *Power by Design: Constitution-Making in Nationalist China*. Honolulu, HI: University of Hawaii Press, 1996.

Thailand

Campbell, Burnham O., et al., eds. *The Economic Impact of Demographic Change in Thailand, 1980–2015*. Honolulu, HI: University of Hawaii Press, 1993.

Dixon, Chris. *The Thai Economy: Uneven Development and Internationalism*. New York: Routledge, 1999.

Hall, Denise. *Business Prospects in Thailand*. Paramus, NJ: Prentice Hall, 1997.

Jansen, Karel. *External Finance in Thailand's Development: an Interpretation of Thailand's Growth Boom*. New York: Saint Martin's Press, 1997.

Krongkaew, Medhi, ed. *Thailand's Industrialization and Its Consequences*. New York: Saint Martin's Press, 1995.

LePoer, Barbara Leitch, ed. *Thailand: a Country Study*. Washington, DC: U.S. GPO, 6th ed. 1989.

Mulder, Niels. *Inside Thai Society: an Interpretation of Everyday Life*. Boston, MA: Charles E. Tuttle, 1997.

Muscat, Robert J. *The Fifth Tiger: a Study of Thai Development Policy*. Armonk, NY: M.E. Sharpe, 1994.

Phongpaichit, Pasuk and Sungsidh Piriyarangsan. *Corruption and Democracy in Thailand*. Seattle, WA: University of Washington Press, 1998.

Skagner, Kerbo. *Modern Thailand*. New York: McGraw-Hill, 1999.

Warr, Peter G., ed. *The Thai Economy in Transition*. New York: Cambridge University Press, 1993.

Vietnam

Chapuis, Oscar M. *A History of Vietnam: from Hong Bang to Tu Duc*. Westport, CT: Greenwood Press, 1995.

Cima, Ronald J., ed. *Vietnam: a Country Study*. Washington, DC: U.S. GPO, 1989.

Clodfelter, Michael. *Vietnam in Military Statistics: a History of the Indochina Wars, 1772–1991*. Jefferson, NC: McFarland & Company, 1995.

Davidson, Phillip B. *Vietnam at War: the History, 1946–1975*. New York: Oxford University Press, 1991.

Duiker, William J. *Historical Dictionary of Vietnam*. Lanham, MD: Scarecrow Press, 1997.

Harvie, Charles and Tran Van Hoa. *Vietnam's Reforms and Economic Growth*. New York: Saint Martin's Press, 1997.

Hunt, Michael H. *Lyndon Johnson's War: America's Cold War Crusade in Vietnam, 1945–1968*. New York: Hill & Wang, 1996.

Jamieson, Neil L. *Understanding Vietnam*. Berkeley, CA: University of California Press, 1993.

Kamm, Henry. *Dragon Ascending: Vietnam and the Vietnamese*. New York: Arcade Publishing, 1996.

Kerkvliet, Benedict J. Tria and Doug J. Porter, eds. *Vietnam's Rural Transformation*. Boulder, CO: Westview Press, 1995.

Lomperis, Timothy J. *From People's War to People's Rule: Insurgency, Intervention, and the Lessons of Vietnam*. Chapel Hill, NC: University of North Carolina Press, 1996.

McNamara, Robert T. *Argument without End: in Search of Answers to the Vietnam Tragedy*. New York: Public Affairs, 1999.

Morley, James W. and Masashi Nishihara, eds. *Vietnam Joins the World*. Armonk, NY: M.E. Sharpe, 1997.

Moses, George D. *Vietnam, an American Ordeal*. Englewood Cliffs, NJ: Prentice-Hall, 1994.

Murray, Geoffrey. *Vietnam: Dawn of a New Market*. New York: Saint Martin's Press, 1997.

Rotter, Andrew J., ed. *Light at the End of the Tunnel: a Vietnam War Anthology*. Wilmington, DE: Scholarly Resources, 1999.

SarDesai, D.R. *Vietnam: Past and Present*. Boulder, CO: Westview Press, 1998.

Schulzinger, Robert D. *A Time for War: the United States and Vietnam, 1941–1975*. New York: Oxford University Press, 1997.

Stern, Lewis M. *Imprisoned or Missing in Vietnam: Policies of the Vietnamese Government Concerning Captured and Unaccounted for United States Soldiers, 1969–1994*. Jefferson, NC: McFarland & Company, 1995.

Tucker, Spencer C. *Vietnam*. Lexington, KY: University Press of Kentucky, 1999.

Vandemark, Brian. *Into the Quagmire: Lyndon Johnson and the Escalation of the Vietnam War*. New York: Oxford University Press, 1991.

Wolff, Peter. *Vietnam: the Complete Transformation*. London: Frank Cass Publishers, 1999.

Pacific Islands

Craig, Robert D., ed. *Historical Dictionary of Oceania.* Westport, CT: Greenwood Press, 1981.

Gorman, G.E. and J.J. Mills. *Fiji.* Santa Barbara, CA: ABC-CLIO, 1994.

Hanlon, David L. *Remaking Micronesia: Discourses over Development in a Pacific Territory.* Honolulu, HI: University of Hawaii Press, 1998.

Lal, Brij V. *Broken Waves: a History of the Fiji Islands in the Twentieth Century.* Honolulu, HI: University of Hawaii Press, 1992.

Leibowitz, Arnold H. *Embattled Island: Palau's Struggle for Independence.* New York: Praeger, 1996.

Levy, Neil M. *Micronesia Handbook.* Chico, CA: Moon Publications, 4th ed. 1997.

Sahlins, Marshall D. *Islands of History.* Chicago: University of Chicago Press, 1987.

Stanley, David. *South Pacific Handbook.* Chico, CA: Moon Publications, 6th ed. 1996.

Wuerch, William L. and Dirk Anthony Ballendorf. *Historical Dictionary of Guam and Micronesia.* Lanham, MD: Scarecrow Press, 1994.

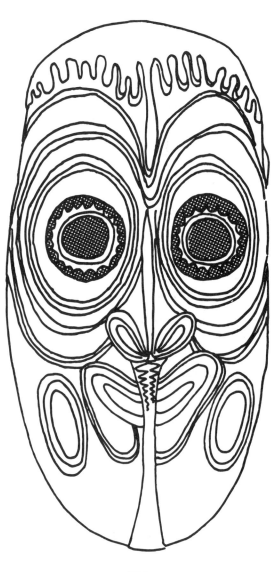